SUNSHINE STATE
ALMANAC
BOOK OF FLORIDA-RELATED STUFF

PHIL PHILCOX
BEVERLY BOE

PINEAPPLE PRESS, INC.
SARASOTA, FLORIDA

Inquiries should be addressed to:
Pineapple Press, Inc.
P.O. Box 3899
Sarasota, Florida 34230

Library of Congress Cataloging in Publication Data

Philcox, Phil.
        The Sunshine State almanac and book of Florida-related stuff / Phil Philcox. Beverly Boe. - 1st ed.
                    p.   cm.
        Includes bibliographical references.
        ISBN 1-56164-178-2 (alk. paper)
        1. Florida-Miscellanea. 2. Almanacs, American-Florida. I. Boe, Beverly. II. Title.
        F311.P49   1999
        975.9-dc21   98-42751
                                CIP

First Edition
10 9 8 7 6 5 4 3 2 1

Design by Osprey Design Systems
Printed and bound by Edwards Brothers, Lillington, North Carolina

DEDICATED TO THE MEMORY OF
GOVERNOR LAWTON CHILES
1930–1998

Table of Contents

*I*ntroduction

P utting together an almanac that covers a variety of Florida-related subjects is best done with contributors who have varied interests and areas of expertise and are willing to share their knowledge with others. To that end, weather experts told us what makes Florida's weather so unique and what we can expect in the future. Farmers who raise ostriches, alligators, and catfish explained the art of animal farming and of cooking the crop. Event planners in every corner of the state provided information on who's doing what, where, and when. Some of the top seafood chefs revealed the dishes that earned them their gourmet rating in the kitchen.

In this—the ultimate guide to lots of assorted stuff about Florida—you'll find out how to avoid seasickness, how to attract butterflies to your garden, what kind of sunglasses to buy, how to build a backyard pond, where to vacation around the state, how to buy a Florida home with no money down, and where the famous plastic pink flamingo lawn ornament came from. If you're interested in canoeing, hunting lobster, or buying an exotic pet, you've come to the right place.

History prevails, but names, addressees, telephone numbers, and statistics change, so enjoy this book with the understanding that it was current as of press time. Any changes will be included in future issues.

If you have something to contribute to the next Sunshine Almanac, we welcome your participation. Anything goes . . . as long as it has that Florida connection. You can fax any ideas, comments, and suggestions to 850-233-9724 or e-mail us at pphilcox@aol.com. If we use your idea, we'll list you as a contributor (You'll be famous!). Include the basic idea as well as your name, phone number, and e-mail address (if you have one). We'll get back to you if we need more information.

The many contributors to this book are listed in the Contributors' Section.

The
Sunshine State
Almanac
& Book of
Florida-
Related
Stuff

ANIMALS

*F*loridians find alligators everywhere. They're seen in lakes and canals in residential areas, creeping around in sewers and water pipes, in garages and under decks, alongside the highway, in the middle of the highway, behind refrigerators and washing machines, and even in swimming pools. Alligators have been seen in downtown areas, escaping the hot sun by sprawling under parked automobiles right there on Main Street. Attacks aren't very common, but they can happen. In the last 40 years, there have been more than 200 documented alligator attacks and 10 reported fatalities. Alligators are suspected of killing several hundred dogs and other pets each year, but nobody knows for sure, since one day the pet is running around, and the next day it's missing.

There are now more than a million alligators in Florida, up considerably from 1966, when they were considered an endangered species. Each year, the alligator population increases, and if you run into an alligator looking for a love partner (usually around April and May)—look out!

The alligator is an amazing reptile, having survived almost unchanged since the time of the dinosaurs. After being hunted almost to the brink of extinction, this reptile has made an amazing comeback in recent years, inhabiting almost every body of water in Florida.

The relationship between alligators and man dates back thousands of years. The first human residents of Florida hunted the alligator for its hide and meat. The teeth of an alligator were believed to provide magical protection against snakebite, as alligators were thought to be immune to the venom of poisonous snakes. Natives used the hide to make many items, even musical instruments such as drums.

When the Spaniards arrived in Florida, they were amazed at this large reptile and called it *el lagarto*, or "the lizard." The word "alligator" is derived from this early Spanish term. An alligator can grow to an extremely large size—wild alligators 13 feet long have been captured. Fortunately, alligators in the wild exhibit a natural fear of man. If left alone, an alligator would much rather stay away from humans than attack them. In Florida it is illegal to feed a wild alligator, as doing so tends to make the animal associate humans with food and it loses its natural fear of man.

Attacks on humans do occur, and there have been several fatal alligator attacks in Florida. There are certain times of the year when alligators are mating and don't like to be disturbed. But most attacks can be attributed to human error—people getting too close to the alligator or harassing it. Should you see an alligator in the wild, leave it alone. Alligators should be respected rather than feared. Their jaws have a crushing power of three thousand pounds per square inch. Despite their appearance, alligators are extremely quick and agile. They are capable of amazingly fast bursts of speed, if only for a short distance. It has been said that an alligator can outrun a horse for a distance of 30 feet.

Alligators are protected by both state and federal regulations. It is illegal to hunt or trap a wild alligator without a permit. The Florida Game and Fresh Water Fish Commission over-

It is said that an alligator can outrun a horse for a distance of 30 feet.

sees several management programs for the alligator. One is the nuisance alligator program, where alligators deemed to be dangerous to man or domestic animals are removed by private trappers. Should you have any questions or complaints about alligators in your area, consult your local office of the State Game and Fresh Water Fish Commission.

The American Alligator (*Alligator mississippiensis*) is just one type of large reptile belonging to the family Crocodylidae. Crocodilians date back to the Triassic period, some 230 million years ago. Alligators and their kin are modern dinosaurs, having existed virtually unchanged for the past 65 million years. The crocodilians can be broken into four main groups: alligators, caimans, crocodiles, and gharials.

The alligator is found only in the southeastern United States, from the Carolinas down to Florida and over to Texas, and in China. The rare Chinese Alligator (*Alligator sinensis*) can be found only in the Yangtze River Basin in China.

Alligators inhabit primarily areas of fresh or brackish water. They occasionally can be found in salt water, but since they lack the salt-extracting glands of crocodiles, they are unable to survive in salt water for extended periods of time. Alligators are regularly seen at Anhinga Trail and Shark Valley in the Everglades. The highest populations of alligators are found in Florida, Louisiana, and southern Georgia. In Florida, alligators can be found in almost every single body of water, with the highest concentrations in central and south Florida. Examples of prime alligator habitats are large, shallow lakes, marshes, ponds, swamps, rivers, creeks, and drainage canals.

Alligators are carnivorous reptiles whose primary feeding time is at night. Small alligators will eat snails, frogs, insects, and small fish. Larger gators will eat fish, turtles, snakes, waterfowl, small mammals, and even smaller alligators. Examinations of alligators' stomachs have even found such objects as stones, sticks, cans, and fishing lures.

Alligators swallow their food whole. Alligator teeth are conical and are made for grabbing and holding, not for cutting. When dealing with larger prey, an alligator may shake its head or spin its body to tear off a piece small enough to swallow. Gators also have been known to hold food in their mouths until it deteriorates to the point where they can swallow it.

Alligators have a specialized valve in their throat called a glottis that enables them to capture prey underwater. However, an alligator must lift its head out of the water to swallow its food.

Sex and the Single Alligator

The sexual maturity of the alligator depends more on the size of the animal than its age. An alligator is considered sexually mature when it reaches a length of six feet or more. Depending on environmental factors, a wild alligator may attain this length in about 10 to 12 years. In a controlled captive environment, sexual maturity may occur in a much shorter time span. The alligator breeding season begins in April, during which time the courtship rituals begin. These rituals are quite complex and involve touching, rubbing, blowing bubbles, and vocalizing. The actual mating takes place in open water and involves a coitus method similar to that of most animals. Alligators are not monogamous—one male may service more than ten females in his territory. Male alligators are territorial animals during the breeding season and will defend their area against other male intruders.

After mating, the female alligator moves into the marshy areas and shoreline, where she will begin to construct a nest. Using her back feet, the female will scratch together a mound of sticks, mud, and vegetation into which she will deposit her eggs. The breakdown of the nesting material keeps the eggs warm. Female alligators begin to lay their eggs in late June and early July. Alligators tend to lay about 40 to 45 eggs; however, the rate of fertility varies with the age of the female.

The eggs incubate for 65 days. During this time the female alligator guards her nest against intruders such as raccoons, which are notorious nest raiders and have been known to destroy a nest. The eggs begin to hatch from August through September, during which time the baby alligators make high-pitched grunting noises to alert the mother gator. The female alligator then uncovers the nest, releasing the babies. Some females have even been known to carry their young to the water. Young alligators, known as hatchlings, are about six to eight inches long at birth. The hatchlings form groups called pods and may stay in the same vicinity of their nesting site for several years. Until the next breeding season begins, the female alligator will remain near her brood, defending them against predators.

The first few years of a hatchling's life are the most dangerous, as anything that can eat a small alligator will. Snakes, wading birds, osprey, raccoons, otters, large bass, garfish, even larger alligators will feed upon the young alligator. But once an alligator reaches about four feet in length, its only real predator is man.

The Big One

In late 1997, an alligator measuring 14 feet, five-eighths of an inch long and weighing more than 800 pounds was pulled from Lake Monroe in central Florida and killed as a nuisance alligator. A trapper was called after a homeowner reported the alligator was cruising the area, probably looking for a meal. The hunters baited the alligator early in the morning, catching him on a large hook. The line was secured to a dock and the alligator was allowed to thrash around until he wore himself out. After a few hours, the hunters slipped a noose around the alligator's mouth and taped it shut. Then they killed him.

The previous record in Florida was an alligator just a quarter of an inch over 14 feet and weighing 750 pounds, killed at the Apalachicola River in 1989.

ALLIGATOR ATTACKS

Florida alligators are dangerous. There are an estimated one million alligators in Florida. Since the state began keeping records, there have been more than 200 reported alligator attacks. Between 1973 and 1997, the Florida Game and Fresh Water Fish Commission logged nine confirmed deaths by alligators:

August 16, 1973—Oscar Scherer
    State Park in Sarasota County
September 28, 1977—Peace River
    Canal in Charlotte Country
September 10, 1978—Martin County
August 6, 1984—St. Lucie County
June 13, 1987—Wakulla River in
    Wakulla County
June 4, 1988—Hidden Lake in
    Charlotte County
June 1993—Loxahatchee River in
    Martin County
October 5, 1993—Lake Serenity in
    Sumter County
March 1997—New Smyrna Beach in
    Martin County

Alligators and Turtles in the Everglades

A visit to Everglades National Park would not be complete without seeing an alligator. This large reptile is indeed the symbol of the Everglades. However, 50 other species of reptiles are found in the park, including 27 kinds of snakes and 16 species of turtles in terrestrial, freshwater, and saltwater habitats.

The park's other amphibians are more often heard than seen. They range from the rare Florida Mud Turtle (*Kinosternon subrubrum*), which can also be found in the Florida Keys and Big Cypress National Preserve, a buffer zone for the Everglades, to the uncommon Stinkpot, or Musk, Turtle (*Sternotherus ordoratus*), which lives in freshwater marshes and water holes.

The Florida Snapping Turtle (*Chelydra serpentine*) is uncommon in freshwater marshes and dry prairies. Sightings are scarce, perhaps because of the turtle's nocturnal habits. Large specimens are rare.

The Striped Mud Turtle (*Kinosternon baurii*) is common in freshwater marshes, sloughs, ponds, and water holes. Occasionally, they're seen in hardwood hammocks. They are common at Royal Palm in Everglades National Park.

The Florida Box Turtle (*Terrapene carolina*) is common in pinelands and hardwood hammocks and is occasionally seen in freshwater marshes. Fire-scarred and three-legged specimens are not uncommon.

The Diamondback Terrapin (*Malaclemys terrapin*) is common in estuarine areas of mangroves. It can be seen basking on Ten Thousand Islands and Cape Sable and is common on some Florida keys.

The Florida Redbelly Turtle (*Pseudemys nelsoni*) is common in freshwater marshes, ponds, and solution holes.

The Florida Chicken Turtle (*Deirochelys reticularia*) is uncommon

in freshwater marshes and ponds, and infrequently seen at Anhinga Trail and Shark Valley.

The Gopher Tortoise (*Gopherus polyphemus*) is locally common on Middle and East Cape Sable. Specimens are occasionally found on Long Pine Key.

The Atlantic Leatherback (*Dermochelys coriacea*) is an endangered species.

The Green Turtle (*Chelonia mydas*) is an endangered species.

The Peninsula Cooter (*Pseudemys floridana*) is found in the same habitat as the Florida Redbelly, although it is less common. It is often seen at Shark Valley.

Alligator Farming

The alligator is a vital part of the state's wildlife heritage and plays an extremely important part in Florida's ecosystem. During the dry season, alligators create "gator holes," which may be the only source of water around. These holes provide sustenance for the wildlife of the area as well as the alligator. Alligators feed on trash fish like gars, which are natural predators of young game fish such as bass. The alligator is now considered to be a renewable resource. Although it is protected by state and federal laws, it is important to Florida's growing aquaculture industry.

The alligator is prized for its hide and meat. The hide is considered a fine and durable leather, used for boots, wallets, purses, shoes, briefcases, and other leather items. The meat is considered a gourmet delicacy, low in fat and high in protein. Not just the tail but all of the meat of the alligator is edible and is sold in restaurants throughout Florida.

Records show that the alligator was first used commercially in the late 1800s in Florida. During the early to mid 1900s the harvesting of alligators was unregulated, leading to depletion of alligator populations. Concern over this decline led to establishment of a four-foot minimum size limit in 1943. Despite this regulation, the decline continued, and in 1954 a statewide six-foot minimum size limit was imposed. This regulation also did little to stop the decimation, however, and in 1962 the legal harvesting of alligators ended.

The alligator population continued to decrease in the 1960s. Poaching was widespread, and because of a loophole in state laws, authorities were unable to shut down the interstate network of illegal hide dealers. Finally, in 1967, the American Alligator was placed on the first Endangered Species List. In 1970, federal regulations were imposed that effectively ended the illegal alligator market, and the populations of alligators began to rebound. It has been speculated that perhaps the alligator population was never as low as originally thought, but that the alligator had just become more adept at eluding humans.

In 1977, the alligator was reclassified from an endangered to a threatened species. This change in status allowed the alligator to once again be available for commercial use. During the 1980s, the alligator became to be viewed as a renewable resource, and several alligator management programs were instituted by the state of Florida. These programs allowed for controlled hunting of the alligator by private individuals and the collection of eggs and hatchlings by licensed alligator farms.

Alligator farming is

The alligator is now considered to be a renewable resource.

now a thriving business in Florida, with an estimated 30-plus alligator farms in the state. This multimillion-dollar industry generates approximately 300,000 pounds of meat and more than 15,000 skins a year. Alligator meat averages five to seven dollars a pound wholesale. While skin prices vary from year to year, the average price is around 25 dollars per foot

Long before the fashion industry took a fancy to alligator skins, gator meat was very popular in regions with large crocodilian populations. The hunting of alligators for their skins so depleted the population that broad marketing of the meat was not possible. Now, with a growing network of farms and ranches raising alligators, the populations have been replenished and this delicious meat is available worldwide.

Alligator meat is low in calories and fat. A one-hundred-gram piece of alligator meat contains 29 percent of the recommended daily allowance for protein, only 3 percent fat, 65 milligrams of cholesterol, and a scant 140 calories.

Everglades Alligator Farm

Everglades Alligator Farm is a working ranch-cum-safari park at the edge of the Everglades in Homestead. The local alligator population was in decline when the owners cleared 70 acres of rusting trucks to create the farm. Over time, the farm was responsible for hatching and releasing up to one million alligators and crocodiles back into their natural habitats. Once the census of wild reptiles was stable, the farmers could then do what farmers do—raise and harvest their crop.

Being cold-blooded, all reptiles are very sensitive to changes in temperature. An alligator's life begins in March or April, when the swamp begins to warm from its winter chill and the gators are roused from their long hours of sleep. They have one thing on their minds, and engage in it at every opportunity. The females then build nests and produce up to 50 eggs each. In the wild, only two of these eggs become adults. Alligator eggs are tasty morsels to many of the animals who themselves become tasty morsels to grown alligators.

Mother gators in the swamp do their best to nurture their hatchlings, and the few who survive remain with her until they're about three years old. At the farm, the gator eggs are collected by two-person teams who scour the hammock looking for eggs. One looks for eggs while the other watches for irate mothers. The eggs go to a hatchery on the farm, and every effort is made to control the gender of the alligators that hatch. Cooler temperatures produce females; warmer temperatures, males. The hatch rate is almost 100 percent.

Newborn alligators stay warm and wet in a series of "growout" pens similar to those used by fish hatcheries. Visitors to the farm can watch alligators and crocodiles in various stages of growth.

The Everglades Farm offers educational shows and 45-minute airboat tours in the gator- and snake-infested waters. At the alligator show, the demonstrator drags, coaxes, and nudges the alligators and crocodiles into performing for the audience. This includes wrestling matches with full-grown alligators. Because alligators have a brain half the size of a human thumbnail and are basically untamable, this can be a dangerous occupation. Snakes are included in the show as well. Four types of poisonous snakes—corals, cottonmouths, water moccasins, and rattlers—are residents of the farm.

The Everglades Alligator Farm is located in Homestead at Southwest 192 Avenue (305-247-2628).

The Alligator vs. the Crocodile

While alligators and crocodiles do look alike, they have their differences. Alligators have a short, blunt, and rounded snout. Adults tend to have grayish-black backs with pale undersides, while the young are more colorful, with yellow or white highlights on a black body. The American Crocodile (*Crocodylus acutus*) is a rare and endangered species, occasionally seen in mangrove swamps and creeks of Florida Bay. Caiman (*Caiman crocodilus*) is an introduced species from tropical America and has been spotted at Anhinga Trail.

The crocodile's snout is sharp and pointy; a fourth tooth on the lower jaw is exposed when the mouth is closed. Young crocodiles have dark bands on their backs and tails; adults are gray-green across the back with a pale underside. Crocodiles are generally found in estuarine areas along coastal mangrove swamps in southern Mexico, Central America, south of Ecuador, Venezuela, the Caribbean, and extreme southern regions of Florida. Like alligators, crocodiles can grow to 13 feet in length.

ALLIGATOR MYTHS AND FACTS

Myth: Alligators live for hundreds of years.

Fact: Alligators in the wild are believed to live 35 to 50 years. In captivity their life span may be significantly longer, perhaps 60 to 80 years.

Myth: Alligators can grow to enormous proportions, more than 20 feet in length and weighing a ton or more.

Fact: The longest recorded length for an alligator captured in the United States is 19 feet, 2 inches. This animal was trapped in the early 1900s in Louisiana. Most wild alligators do not grow longer than 13 feet, but they could weigh 600 pounds or more.

Myth: Crocodiles and alligators open their jaws differently. The jaws of the crocodile are hinged to open the top jaw, while alligators open their bottom jaw.

Fact: Alligator and crocodile jaws are hinged the same. The jaws of both animals are hinged on the bottom—the top jaw is simply an extension of the skull.

Myth: Alligators are immune to the bite of poisonous snakes.

Fact: Alligators are not immune to snake poison. However, they do have extremely tough skin and an armored back protected by bony plates. It is possible that this protection may prevent a snake's fangs from penetrating the skin.

Myth: Only the tail of the alligator is edible.

Fact: Although the tail of the alligator is considered the prime cut, all the meat of the alligator is edible.

Contrary to common belief, alligators are not immune to snake poison.

BAT BASICS

Blood-sucking vampire bats make for dramatic literature, but in real life, bats are highly sophisticated creatures that are beneficial to humans. The Lubee Foundation near Gainesville, Florida, is devoted to the research and preservation of bats in all their fascinating variety. According to the staff, bats have quite a bit to offer humans, as they spread seeds from which new plants grow, which subsequently nourish other animals.

Old World fruit bats, for example, help to pollinate rainforests, deserts, and other areas by eating their meals in flight and dropping the seeds in barren areas. According to a study by Bat Conservation International, more than 450 commercial products in Southeast Asia depend on bat propagation.

The Lubee Foundation, believed to be the only one of its kind, houses seven species of bats, including two endangered species: the Little Golden Mantled Flying Fox, indigenous to the Philippines, and the Rodrigues Fruit Bat, native to Mauritius, an island off the coast of Africa.

Vampire bats have a wingspan of about a foot and weigh less than two ounces. Their main diet is blood from animals like horses and cows. A vampire bat usually lives longer in captivity (up to 18 years) than in the wild (less than 10 years). Because they dine on blood rather than hard food, vampire bats have fewer teeth than other bats. They don't have any sucking ability but make an incision with their razor-sharp teeth and lap up the blood.

Bat Facts

A bat will eat up to 600 mosquitoes per hour and is a natural alternative to pesticides. The most common species in Florida is the brown bat, which has a body about four inches long and a wingspan of about a foot. Besides being ugly, bats are feared because they can carry rabies, but experts are trying to reassure the public by stressing bats' benefits. For example, a vampire bat's saliva contains an anticoagulant that is many times stronger than any anti-clotting agent known to science.

SHARK ETIQUETTE

If you leave sharks alone, they'll probably leave you alone—probably. Last year there were fewer than 80 shark attacks reported worldwide. An average of ten people a year die from encounters with sharks. Actually, you're 30 times more likely to die from getting hit by a lightning bolt than being attacked by a shark, especially in Florida.

Shark victims are usually diving, swimming somewhere off an open beach, or surfing. Sharks in Florida are usually smaller than sharks elsewhere in the world and are generally less aggressive because of the abundance of fish. As long as they're swimming around on a full stomach, your chances of getting bitten are slim. But it always pays to be careful. Keep an eye out when swimming in open waters, and avoid murky waters which limit a shark's vision. Never swim if you're bleeding. It's best not to swim at night. Before you enter the water, remove any jewelry that can act as a lure. If you see a shark in the water, roll over on your back, keep your legs from dangling, avoid sudden movements, and slowly back-paddle toward shore. If you're bitten by a shark, stop the bleeding and seek medical help immediately.

Here's a breakdown of reported shark attacks worldwide from 1990 to 1996. It's estimated that for every reported attack, there are 10 to 20 unreported attacks.

1990	39 attacks	3 deaths
1991	34 attacks	3 deaths
1992	50 attacks	5 deaths
1993	52 attacks	13 deaths
1994	61 attacks	7 deaths
1995	72 attacks	11 deaths
1996	36 attacks	2 deaths

Between 1990 and 1996, there were 344 unprovoked shark attacks reported which resulted in 44 known deaths. According to records, the last fatal Florida attack was in 1988 in northwestern Florida's Panhandle.

MOTHER TURTLES AND LITTLE TURTLES

Sometime between May and September, the female sea turtle crawls onto the upper beaches and deposits more than a hundred eggs into a hole she digs with her hind flippers. This process may be repeated several times during the nesting season. Despite the numerous eggs laid, only one turtle per nest is likely to survive to adulthood.

Over the years, the sea turtle's reproductive habits have adjusted to allow for losses to natural predators like raccoons, which eat the eggs, or birds and fish, which feed on the hatchlings. Additional hazards include humans. Poachers take turtle eggs. Newly hatched turtles, confused by artificial lights, have been known to wander inland and starve or try to cross highways and get crushed by cars. The building of bulkheads and increasing development on beaches threaten not only the turtles but the environment as well.

THE WATER BUFFALO BURGER

There are only a couple of thousand water buffaloes in the United States, and several hundred of them live in Florida. In the town of Chiefland, outside Ocala, a veterinarian keeps ten water buffalo as breeders and pets and wouldn't think of serving them up on a plate or a bun. But just outside of Gainesville, there's a water buffalo ranch where the buffalo are being raised as a substitute for beef.

Water buffalo meat is reported to be leaner than regular beef but is more expensive—about 50 percent higher in cost. Water buffalo can supply milk and cream for cheese and yogurt. The cheese—similar in taste to mozzarella—sells for about 20 dollars a pound at gourmet shops around the state. There isn't enough buffalo meat to go around, so chances are you won't find it at the meat counter in your supermarket. If you want some, you'll have to go right to the source. And don't underestimate the public's desire for water buffalo meat.

A few years ago, the ranch at Gainesville tested the market at a local supermarket and sold more than fifteen hundred pounds in a day and a half. Supermarket officials were so impressed, they decided this must be the ground meat of the future. "How much can you provide the store every week?" they asked. When they found out it was a mere one or two water buffalo a month, they declined. Obviously, you can't make any real money in retailing water buffalo meat unless you deal in volume.

FLORIDA PANTHERS

Florida panthers are among the most endangered animals in the world. Researchers believe fewer than 50 panthers still roam in the wild, nearly all of them in the Big Cypress National Preserve, Fakahatchee Strand State Preserve, Everglades National Park, and nearby private lands. Panthers once ranged throughout the southeastern United States. The Florida panther measures about 6 feet from nose to tail and weighs anywhere from 80–125 pounds. Its diet is mainly small animals like rabbits and raccoons.

Before Columbus came to America, panthers roamed throughout the southeastern portion of the North American continent, ranging from what is now Arkansas to South Carolina, south to the tip of Florida. From the 1600s to 1900s, the panther's range became more restricted and fragmented as European settlements expanded. Panthers were persecuted as perceived threats to humans, livestock, and game animals. Around 1887, the state of Florida authorized a five-dollar bounty for panther scalps and the population was further reduced.

In 1950, panthers were given partial protection when the Florida Game and Fresh Water Fish Commission listed it as a game animal to be taken only during deer season or as a nuisance. In 1958, the commission closed the season on Florida panthers, and in 1967, the U.S. Department of Interior listed the Florida panther as endangered. After that, in 1972, the first field surveys for panther were con-

Researchers believe fewer than fifty panthers still roam in the wild.

ducted in southern Florida. Panthers were verified in the Fisheating Creek area of Glades County.

In 1973, Congress passed the Endangered Species Act and in 1974 approved the purchase of 570,000 acres of swamps and uplands in southwest Florida to form the Big Cypress National Preserve. Fakahatchee Strand State Preserve was purchased by the state of Florida, conserving another 75,000 acres of panther territory. The Florida Panther Record Clearinghouse was established in 1976.

In 1981, the Florida Panther Recovery Plan was established, outlining actions to prevent the extinction of the big cat. Field research was expanded by the Florida Game and Fresh Water Fish Commission. The primary mission was to capture panthers and outfit them with radio transmitters for study. A year later, the panther was adopted as Florida's state mammal. A year after that, the Florida Legislature passed the Florida Panther bill establishing the Panther Trust Fund.

Around 1986, the Florida Panther Interagency Committee was formed to better coordinate activities and information exchange among the agencies involved in recovery efforts, namely the Florida Game and Fresh Water Fish Commission, Florida Department of Natural Resources, U.S. Fish and Wildlife Service, and National Park Service. To evaluate the area's potential as panther habitat, Texas mountain lions were released in northern Florida in 1988 and a year later, 24,000 acres of habitat were put under protection as a Florida Panther National Wildlife Refuge. In 1994, the U.S. Fish and Wildlife Service approved the Florida Panther Interagency Committee's plans to restore gene flow between Florida panthers and other cougar populations by releasing nonnative cougars in southern Florida. The Florida Game and Fresh Water Fish Commission proposed strategic habitat conservation areas in southwest Florida and the potential reintroduction of the panther elsewhere in the state.

While the panther, mountain lion, and cougar all belong to the species *Felis concolor*, the panther is in the subspecies *Coryi* and is physically distinguished from its mountain lion and cougar cousins by a more exaggerated rise of the nasal arch, smaller paws, and slightly longer legs. The panther also has a more crooked tail and shorter hair, along with a whorl of hair in the middle of its back.

These differences are contributed by regional separation. Before the panther's isolation from the other big cats, it was common for different subspecies to interbreed, keeping genetic diversity high.

In 1995, two female Texas cougars were released in the Florida wild, and six more shortly thereafter. Some feel that the survival of the panther in Florida depends on the success of this program. It is hoped that the cats will establish territories and mate, and that with each new generation, the genetic variability will improve the panther's health and allow it to survive in the wild.

For more information on the Florida panther, contact the Florida Panther Society, Box 1895, White Springs 32096, 904-397-2945.

THE KEY DEER

Earliest mention of the Key deer is found in the memoirs of Escalante Fontaneda (1575), a Spaniard who was held captive by Indians. Later references suggest that the small deer were abundant in the Keys as far south as Key West and were used as food by residents and by crews of passing ships. Published records provide little reliable information on the population levels and distribution of these deer in the lower Keys, but most say we can presume that where there was mature forest land, there were deer.

With the growth of the human population in the mid to late 1800s and the increase in farming activities and harvesting of wooded areas, deer were forced to live and forage closer to humans. Key deer were treated as pests and were hunted for food, and by the late 1800s and early 1900s, the deer population had been nearly wiped out. A lack of enforcement made the Florida Legislature's ban on deer hunting in 1939 ineffective. Hunting continued, and by the 1950s, the deer population was at an all-time low. Official action started to be taken around 1950, when an effort was made to introduce legislation to establish a Key Deer National Wildlife Refuge.

In 1957, a 5,930-acre Key deer refuge was established which included parcels of land on islands

between Cudjoe and Little Pine Keys. The Key deer was placed on the federal list of endangered species on March 11, 1967.

In 1974 there were an estimated 200–250 deer on Big Pine Key and evidence of 100–150 deer on twenty-two other islands. At last count, the Key deer population numbered around 250–300 animals.

COYOTES

Coyotes have been known to move into well-populated areas in Florida and live among people. People with pets that roam outside are not too happy about that. In suburban areas, coyotes raid garbage cans and kill domestic pets.

After having pups, the female coyote begins prowling the area looking for food—and small pets are always a target. The howl of a coyote is only one call in an extensive repertoire. A coyote starts a howl with a series of high-pitched yelps before launching into a prolonged sirenlike wail.

FLORIDA BLACK BEARS

At one time there were more than 12,000 black bears in Florida and parts of southern Georgia and Alabama. Florida's bears were found in every part of the state, including the Florida Keys. Today, there are fewer than 1,500 bears remaining in scattered and isolated populations, less than 20 percent of the bear's historic range. The state of Florida considers this unique subspecies (*Ursus americanus floridanus*) threatened with extinction.

Florida's bears prefer certain forest habitats such as sand-pine scrub, oak scrub, upland hardwood forests, and a variety of forested wetlands, especially riverine swamps. They are omnivores and eat a wide variety of foods, including berries, acorns, the tender parts of saw palmettos, and the hearts of the sabal palm. They also eat insects like carpenter ants, termites, and walking sticks, as well as armadillos, wild pigs, and deer.

Maintaining a healthy bear population is an important way to conserve the diversity of Florida's native species. Protecting the habitat of the wide-ranging black bear benefits many other species that depend on the same habitat type, such as the threatened scrub jay and the eastern indigo snake. For this reason, bears are often referred to as an "umbrella species." Scientists also consider the bear to be an indicator species. In other words, the health of the bear populations can be used as a measurement of the well-being of other species present in the same ecosystem.

The animal-protection group Defenders of Wildlife in Washington, DC, estimates that only about 1,500 black bears remain in Florida from a population that once numbered in the tens of thousands. The 1995 study concluded that isolated bear populations need a minimum of 500,000 to 1,000,000 to ensure their long-term survival. Only in the Apalachicola region of the state is there this much bear habitat in public ownership, and even there, not all the protected areas are adjacent to one another. Currently, the five major black bear populations are found in the Ocala, Apalachicola, and Osceola National Forests in northern and central Florida, at the Eglin Air Force Base and Blackwater State Forest complex in the Panhandle, and in the Big Cypress Swamp area in south Florida. Unfortunately, many of these private and public lands are fragmented by roads, and current conservation areas in Florida do not adequately protect the habitat base needed for the long-term survival of the state's black bear population.

Roads are considered the leading cause of Florida bear mortality. According to the Florida Department of Transportation (FDOT), the state's high-speed paved roads have increased at the rate of 4.5 miles per day over the last fifty years. At least 463 bears are documented to have been killed by vehicles since 1976. In 1995, 34 of 50 bears recorded killed

statewide were reported in the Ocala/Wekiva River Basin. This bear population is considered one of the most threatened in the state. In 1996, a total of 53 bears were killed statewide in collisions with vehicles. Moreover, the bear continues to be threatened by road-widening projects that destroy its habitat. Road-widening projects increase the danger of vehicle-caused mortality and the possibility of extinction by reducing population size and isolating individuals from food, shelter, and mates.

The black bear subspecies is perhaps the strongest symbol for Florida's diverse wildlife. A wide-ranging omnivore, the bear shares habitat with many of Florida's other native species. By protecting the bear and its habitat, conservationists also support many other animals and plants.

Development, habitat fragmentation from road construction, and vehicle-caused mortality all threaten the long-term survival of this unique subspecies. To help save the Florida black bear and the many other species that depend on the same habitat, Defenders of Wildlife and the Florida Chapter of the Sierra Club launched the Habitat for Bears Campaign in 1973. The campaign has gained credibility with state agency officials and developed a statewide network of over seven hundred citizen activists. Tens of thousands of Floridians have seen the slide show "The Imperiled Bears of Florida," and nearly 100,000 viewed a special exhibit and video presentation the campaign sponsored at various locations around the state. To join the fight against black bear extinction in Florida or to get further information, call 352-735-6906 or 813-821-9585 or write: The Habitat for Bears Campaign, Defenders of Wildlife, 1101 14th Street Northwest/1400, Washington, DC 20005.

GREYHOUNDS

Greyhounds are one of the oldest breeds of dogs. In ancient Egypt, the greyhound was a companion of Cleopatra. Centuries ago, greyhounds were bred to be hunting companions to noblemen. Only the fastest, healthiest, and most amiable were chosen to breed. Greyhounds were originally brought to America by western farmers to stem crop devastation by jackrabbits and other pests. Neighborly competition among farmers was the forerunner of modern parimutuel racing.

Greyhounds are members of the hound family. They vary in size and are usually between 25 and 29 inches tall at the shoulder and weigh between 50 and 90 pounds. Female dogs are generally smaller than males. Greyhounds are red, fawn, black and white, or blue (gray). They can also have several shades of brindles or a combination of these colors. Their coats are short-haired and very smooth.

Greyhounds are quiet, gentle, good-natured, friendly dogs who get along well with children and other dogs. Many also get along with cats. These intelligent dogs are easily trainable with positive and rewarding methods. Their activity level is low and sometimes they're called "couch potatoes," but they can run at speeds of up to 40 miles an hour for short distances.

Greyhounds Provide Model for E. Coli in Humans

In racing greyhounds, it's called Alabama Rot; in people, E. coli food poisoning or hemolytic uremic syndrome. Both can cause acute renal failure, sometimes death, and both are believed caused by the E. coli bacteria. The greyhound disease was first recognized at a greyhound race track in Alabama, although now it occurs nationwide. Some veterinarians believe the similarity of the diseases in greyhounds and humans will prove useful in researching the diseases caused by the deadly bacteria Escherichia coli, commonly known as E. coli. The bacteria is common to the environment and can be found in undercooked or raw ground meat. Racing greyhounds are fed raw ground meat, which makes them prime candidates for E. coli exposure. E. coli food poisoning in humans is caused by eating poorly cooked meat.

Hemolytic uremic syndrome is a life-threatening disease and the most common cause of acute kidney failure in infants and children.

Adults, adolescents, and newborns also can be affected.

The disease in greyhounds appears to be the best model of the human disease. Using dogs as a model, researchers are able to gain a better understanding of the underlying disease process, innovative approaches to treatment, and possible ways to prevent hemolytic uremic syndrome.

In research on Alabama Rot in greyhounds, veterinarians found a striking similarity between the changes in the kidneys of infected greyhounds and of humans with hemolytic uremic syndrome. In dogs, because the blood supply to the skin also is affected, the disease usually starts with ulcers on the skin. Like humans, some of the dogs also have kidney failure due to blockage of the blood supply to part of the kidney. Humans don't get the skin form, but when the disease advances to the kidney fail-ure stage in both humans and dogs, it is almost identical.

The problem with *E. coli* infection is that there is no cure or specific therapy. The toxins produced by the bacteria attack the cell lining of the blood vessels. Only the symptoms, such as diarrhea and dehydration, can be treated. That's why the discovery of an animal model is so important. Supportive care can involve intravenous fluids, transfusions, and dialysis, the same treatment provided to children with hemolytic uremic syndrome.

Fifteen Places to Bet on the Hounds

Ebro County Kennel Club
558 Dog Track Road in Ebro
850-234-3943

Flagler Greyhound Track
401 Northwest 38th Court in Miami
305-649-3000

Hollywood Greyhound
Park
831 North Federal
Highway in
Hallandale
954-454-9400

Jacksonville Kennel
Club
1440 North McDuff
Avenue in
Jacksonville
904-646-0205

Jeffferson County
Kennel Club
U.S. 19 North in
Monticello
850-997-2561

Melbourne Greyhound
Park
1100 North
Wickham Road in
Melbourne
407-259-9800

Orange Park Kennel
Park
455 Park Avenue in
Orange Park
904-646-0001

Palm Beach Kennel
Club
1111 North Congress
Avenue in West Palm
Beach
561-683-2222

Pensacola Greyhound
Track
951 Dogtrack Road
in Pensacola
850-455-8595

Sanford-Orlando
Kennel Club
301 Dogtrack Road
in Longwood
407-831-1600

Sarasota Kennel Club
5400 Bradenton
Road in Sarasota
941-355-7744

Seminole Greyhound
Park
2000 Seminole
Boulevard in
Casselberry
407-699-4510

St. Johns Greyhound
Park
24901 Phillips
Highway in
Jacksonville
904-646-0420

St. Petersburg Kennel
Club
10490 Gandy
Boulevard in St.
Petersburg
813-576-1361

Tampa Bay Track
8300 North
Nebraska in Tampa
813-932-4313

Adopting a Greyhound

There's a place in Jacksonville where you can adopt a greyhound that has been spayed or neutered, tested for heartworm, and given all the necessary shots. As a bonus, they throw in a six-month supply of heartworm medicine and a list of recommended veterinarians in Florida who have experience treating greyhounds.

Currently, the fee is $125. The agency has a 24-hour answering service at 904-389-2940. Leave your name and number and they'll call you back and answer any questions you may have. Once an application is completed, returned, and approved, you'll be contacted for an appointment to visit your new pet. Additional information is available from Greyhound Pets of Northeast Florida, Box 54249, Jacksonville FL 32245. Regional offices can also supply information on the adoption program.

*Adopt a Florida
Greyhound*
489 Southwest
College Park Road in
Port St. Lucie
561-336-3752

*Adopt a Greyhound of
Central Florida*
Brian Smith
1135 Utah Boulevard
in Orlando
407-897-3283

*Brandywine Downs
Greyhound
Rescue*
Joan
Schernekau
1200
Northwest
73rd Terrace
in Ocala
352-873-2727

*Ebro Greyhounds as
Pets*
Tammy Hess
6558 Dog Track
Road in Ebro
850-234-3943

Friends of Greyhounds
Mark Hess
6558 Greyhound
Road in Ebro
800-811-1588 (fax)

**Greyhound Adoptions
of Florida**
Gainesville Chapter
Sherry Scruggs
13875 Southwest
Archer Lane in
Archer
352-495-2933

Gainesville Chapter
Danielle Mauragis
2720 Southeast 39th
Place in Gainesville
352-375-0761

Largo Chapter
12286 Mallory Drive
in Largo
727-395-7852

Largo Chapter
Arlene Jackson
610 12th Street
Northwest in Largo
727-559-0243

Lutz Chapter
Niki Rysdale
19017 Cedar Lane in
Lutz
813-949-8380

*St. Petersburg
(Florida/Tampa Bay
Chapter)*
8851 15th Way
North in St.
Petersburg
727-577-3387

Tom Smith in
Casselberry
407-366-0006

**Greyhound Pets of
America**
*Central Florida
Chapter*
Sarah and Edward
Jones in Sharpes
407-632-0832

Cocoa Chapter
Monique Moore
4215 Havana Drive
407-639-8883

*Daytona Beach
Chapter*
Sandy Snyman
2201
International
Speedway
*904-239-
3647*

*Delray
Beach Chapter*
Donald and
Diantha Grant
5188 Tennis Lane
561-495-9215

Fort Pierce Chapter
Pam Stephenson
4062 Greenwood
Drive
561-465-8399

Melbourne Chapter
Dennis Tyler
407-242-9010

North Palm Beach Chapter
Marg and Pat Stanhope
2058 South Palm Circle
561-775-9244

Orlando Chapter
Lisa Nolet
407-332-9209

Port St. Lucie Chapter
Doug and Pam Reinhart
237 Southwest Inwood Avenue
561-878-1940

Southeast Coast Chapter
Wally and Emily Griffin
3808 Gulfstream Road in Lake Worth
561-965-9581

Greyhound Rescue and Adoption of Tampa
Kimberly and Adam Wyler
813-971-4732

Greyhound Rescue of Tallahassee
Katherine Crawford
850-878-1204

Greyhounds as Pets of Northeast Florida
Shirley Kane
904-389-2934

Hollydogs Greyhound Adoption
Silvana Rizzi
1600 South Dixie Highway in Hollywood
954-925-7758

Humane Society of North Pinellas
Roy Faulkner, DVM
3040 State Road 590 in Clearwater
727-797-7722

Humane Society of Seminole County
Betty Munoz
2800 County Home Road in Sanford
407-323-8685

Lake Whippet and Greyhound Rescue
Mary Beth Lake
570 Myrtle Street in Sanford
407-321-5893

The National Greyhound Foundation
Beverly Sebastian in Homosassa
352-628-2281

Second Chances for Greyhounds
Helen Banks
10826 Dean Street in Bonita Springs
941-947-2365

Greyhounds and Children

Greyhounds are patient and sensitive with children, but, of course, they don't want to be abused by anyone. Special care should be taken to avoid accidental injury to either dog or child when very young children are in the home. Greyhounds live with other dogs during their racing careers and usually adapt well to other pet dogs. Cars are unknown to greyhounds, so new owners will need to familiarize them with the vehicles. A little extra time and care will make a happy home for all.

THE WEST INDIAN MANATEE

Florida's West Indian manatee is a large, gray-brown aquatic mammal with a body that tapers to a flat, paddle-shaped tail. It has two flippers with three to four nails on each flipper, and the head and face are wrinkled with whiskers on the snout. Although a manatee looks similar to a walrus or seal, its closest relatives are actually the elephant and the hyrax, a small furry animal that resembles a rodent. The average adult manatee is about 10 feet long and weighs about 1,000 pounds.

Manatees are a migratory species and can be found in shallow, slow-moving rivers, estuaries, saltwater bays, canals, and coastal areas. Within the United States, West Indian manatees are concentrated in Florida in the winter, but can be found in summer months as far west as Louisiana and as far north as Virginia and the Carolinas. West Indian manatees can also be found in the coastal and inland waterways of Central America and along the northern coast of South America, although distribution in these areas may be spotty.

Manatees are gentle and slow-moving animals. They can swim up to 20 miles an hour in short bursts but usually swim only about 3 to 5 miles an hour. Most of their time is spent eating, resting, and traveling. Manatees are herbivores (plant-eaters), and they can consume 10 to 15 percent of their body weight in vegetation daily. They graze for food along water bottoms and on the surface. They may rest submerged at the bottom or just below the surface, coming up to breathe about every three to five minutes. When manatees are using a great deal of energy, they may surface to breathe as often as every 30 seconds.

Because manatees have no natural enemies, it's believed they can live 60 years or more. Many manatee deaths are human-related, and most of these are from collisions with watercraft. Other causes of human-related manatee deaths include being crushed or drowned in canal locks and flood control structures; ingesting fish hooks, litter, and monofilament line; and becoming entangled in crab trap lines. Ultimately, however, loss of habitat is the most serious threat facing manatees today. There are approximately 2,600 West Indian manatees left in the United States.

The reproductive rate for manatees is slow. Female manatees are not sexually mature until five years old, and males are mature at approximately nine years of age. It is believed that one calf is born every two to five years. Twins are rare. The gestation period is approximately 13 months. Mothers nurse their young for a long period, and a calf may remain dependent on its mother for up to two years.

Protecting Manatees

West Indian manatees in the United States are protected under federal law by the Marine Mammal Protection Act of 1972 and the Endangered Species Act of 1973, which make it illegal to harass, hunt, capture, or kill any marine mammal. West Indian manatees are also protected by the Florida Manatee Sanctuary Act of 1978. Anyone convicted of violating Florida's state law faces a possible maximum fine of $1,000 or imprisonment for up to 60 days or both. Conviction on the federal level is punishable by a fine of up to $100,000 or one year in prison or both.

Even sharks and alligators leave manatees alone.

The Manatee Recovery Plan was developed as a result of the Endangered Species Act. The recovery plan is coordinated by the U.S. Fish and Wildlife Service and sets forth a list of tasks geared toward recovering manatees from their current endangered status. In October 1989, Florida's governor and cabinet directed the Florida Department of Environmental Protection to work with thirteen manatee counties in Florida to reduce injuries and deaths. These counties include Duval, Volusia, Citrus, Brevard, Indian River, St. Lucie, Martin, Palm Beach, Broward, Dade, Collier, Lee, and Sarasota. More than 80 percent of manatee deaths have occurred in these counties. The first task of these county governments is to develop, working with the state, site-specific boat speed zones to reduce watercraft collisions. The second task is to develop comprehensive manatee protection plans at the local level.

Other conservation measures deemed important to saving manatees include conducting research covering the biology, mortality, population and distribution, behavior, and habitat of manatees; implementing management plans; posting regulatory speed signs and levying fines for excess speeds in designated areas; instituting manatee education and public awareness programs; and acquiring critical habitat and creating sanctuaries.

Manatees have no natural predators. Even sharks and alligators leave them alone. People are more of a threat than any animal. Florida's Save the Manatee Club, a nonprofit organization advocating conservation efforts to help save endangered manatees, says we should all err on the side of caution and leave them alone. Swimming with manatees tends to alter their behavior and affects their natural migration. The Adopt-A-Manatee program is the primary source of funding for Save the Manatee Club, established in 1981 by U.S. Senator Bob Graham and singer Jimmy Buffett. Funds from the program go toward education and public awareness programs, manatee research and rescue and rehabilitation efforts, and lobbying to help protect manatees and their habitat.

For more information on manatees or the Adopt-A-Manatee program, or for free manatee protection tips for boaters, write the Save the Manatee Club at 500 North

Maitland Avenue, Maitland 32751, or call 1-800-432-JOIN (5646).

Crystal River is Manatee Country

Images of two manatees adorn City Hall, and residents can bowl at Manatee Lanes or look over the cars at Manatee Motors. In a still largely rural region that depends on tourism (with 152,000 acres of wildlife preserve), manatees are a godsend, bringing hordes of visitors from as far away as Japan and Germany to interact with this rarest of marine mammals. Citrus County is the only Florida county to adopt a Manatee Protection Plan that, among other things, mandates idle boat speeds and no wakes in all coastal areas that manatees are known to frequent. Manatees might prefer to be left alone, but in an imperfect world, hordes of loving tourists are probably not the worst problem to have.

Manatees are attracted to the warm water in the Crystal River spring, which maintains a 72-degree temperature most of the year. They can die when the water temperature drops below 68 degrees.

Swimming with Manatees

People love to swim with manatees, but is too much familiarity dangerous? Most people who have encountered manatees in the water say that once you've met one, you're hooked. They're blubbery and lovable, big and friendly. Because they are so peaceful, are almost as cute as dol-phins, and are unique to Florida waters, swimming with the manatees has become a big ecotourism business, particularly in west coast Florida's Citrus County, which hosts the biggest winter manatee population (in the shallow Crystal River). But swimming with manatees tends to alter their behavior and affects their natural migration, so if you really love these gentle giants, the best thing you can do for them is to leave them alone.

Watching Manatees

Here are some places the Save the Manatee Club recommends visiting if you're interested in seeing manatees up close.

Blue Spring State Park in Orange City (904-775-3663). Located 30 miles north of Orlando, Blue Spring State Park is the home of twenty-two of the manatees in the Save the Manatee Club's Adopt-A-Manatee program. During the winter, usually November through March, manatees leave the St. Johns River for the warm waters of Blue Spring, which maintains a constant 72-degree temperature year-round. A boardwalk and nature trail along the spring run provides good views of the manatees. During the winter months, the park also features an interpretive program about manatees. Open year-round. Entry fee.

Florida Power and Light Company Manatee Observation Center in Riviera Beach (800-552-8440). This plant is one of the warm-water gathering areas of manatees on Florida's east coast.

An outdoor observation area is available to see manatees taking refuge in the warm water outflow from the plant. An indoor education center features a video and information. Open seasonally from January 2 through February 28. No entry fee.

Tampa Electric Manatee Viewing Center in Tampa (813-228-4289). The Manatee Viewing Center has an environmental education building with exhibits and a film about manatees. The outdoor observation areas offer the opportunity to observe manatees in their natural habitat. Open seasonally, usually December through March, from 10 A.M. to 5 P.M. No entry fee.

Lee County Manatee Park in Fort Myers (941-694-3537). Manatees can be viewed at the Lee County Manatee Park in the winter, usually November through March. The park, located on the southwest coast of Florida, features a sidewalk area for viewing manatees and a kiosk featuring manatee information. Free guided walks are available. Open year-round. Parking fee.

Homosassa Springs State Wildlife Park, located 75 miles north of Tampa (352-628-5343). This park serves as a rehabilitation center and refuge for manatees who have been orphaned or injured. Five manatees in the Save the Manatee Club's Adopt-A-Manatee program call the park their home. Manatees can be observed along the nature walks or from a special underwater viewing room. A manatee interpretive center is located at the park, and a manatee education program is offered daily. Open year-round.

The Lowry Park Zoo in Tampa (813-935-8552). This park has a manatee exhibit and is licensed by the U.S. Fish and Wildlife Service to rescue and medically treat manatees. A self-guided program is available year-round. Guided tours are also available at group rates. Entry fee.

Sea World of Florida in Orlando (407-351-3600). Sea World has a two-level manatee exhibit and is licensed by the U.S. Fish and Wildlife Service to rescue and medically treat manatees. They also conduct an Animal Lover's tour. Entry fee.

Epcot Center's Living Seas in Orlando (407-560-6365). The Living Seas at Epcot Center features a two-level manatee exhibit where manatees can be observed year-round. Guests can speak with animal care staff members about the plight of the manatee. Entry fee.

The Miami Seaquarium in Miami (305-361-5705). The Seaquarium has a manatee exhibit and interpretive program year-round. Entry fee.

Manatee Facts

The name manatee comes from the Haitian word *manati*, which also means manatee. The scientific genus name *Trichechus* is Latin for "hair."

Adult manatees have been known to exceed lengths of 13 feet

and weigh more than 3,500 pounds.

Manatees prefer waters that are three to seven feet deep. They are found in both salt and fresh water. Along the coast, manatees tend to travel in water that is 10 to 16 feet deep, and they are rarely seen in areas over 20 feet deep.

In the winter, usually November through March, manatees are concentrated primarily in Florida. Manatees are susceptible to cold-related disease, so they gather near warm water sources such as natural springs or warm water effluents of power plants. Water temperatures below 68 degrees usually cause manatees to move into these warm water refuge areas. Individual manatees often return to the same wintering areas year after year.

Manatee fossils have been found all over the world and go back as far as 60 million years. Modern manatees evolved from four-footed land mammals. Manatee fossils found in Florida's springs date back about 45 million years.

Manatees are herbivores, feeding on a large variety of submerged, emergent, and floating plants. Seagrass beds are important feeding sites for manatees. Some favorite foods of manatees are manatee grass, turtle grass, shoal grass, and widgeon grass in salt water; and hydrilla, eelgrass, water hyacinth, and water lettuce in fresh water.

OSTRICHES AND OSTRICH FARMS

Raising ostriches has become a new agricultural industry, and there are ostrich farms right here in Florida. Although markets are small (not too many people have shown an interest in ostrich meat yet), there are still 18,000 functioning ostrich farms around the country.

Once sought primarily for their plumage and hide, ostriches are now providing chefs with a source of exotic and healthy red meat. Ostriches and their cousins, emus—both members of the ratite family of flightless birds—have become increasingly popular with American livestock breeders.

Ostriches were first commercially domesticated in the mid nineteenth century in South Africa, where all farming and research information related to the birds was closely guarded from the rest of the world. In recent years, the red meat of the ostrich and emu has emerged on the international culinary scene, offering chefs a unique combination of flavor, versatility, and texture as well as low fat content. The most common response is that the meat tastes like beef, and chefs find it has a great ability to accept spices and recipes. Lower in fat than skinless chicken, ostrich or emu meat is also higher in protein than poultry.

The ostrich (*Struthio camelus*) is considered the largest living bird and, at 120 million years old, is one of the oldest living species. When fully grown, ostriches have one of the most advanced immune systems known to mankind. They are the second-fastest animal in the world: They can run 40 miles an hour and maintain this speed for at least 30 minutes. Contrary to rumor, ostriches do not bury their heads in the sand.

Ostriches have been known to grow to 10 feet tall and weigh over 300 pounds. They're generally friendly, but if cornered or threatened, they kick out with their giant feet outfitted with two-clawed toes and can cause considerable damage. The body is covered with plumelike white feathers, but under those feathers, males are generally black while females are gray-brown. In the wild, they feed on plants, fruits, leaves, and an occasional bird or mouse. They usually live in small flocks of several hundred, and a typical family is one male and two to three females. All females lay their eggs in a nest, and both the male and female sit on the eggs. She works the day shift, he the late shift. A female can lay as many as 30 eggs, each measuring as much as 5 to 6 inches in width. The babies hatch in about a month and a half and can leap out of the egg and run immediately. It takes about six months before ostriches reach their full size.

HEADS IN THE SAND

Two female ostriches were chatting under a tree in south Florida. Two male ostriches approached. One female said to the other, "They're coming our way. What are we going to do?" The other female said, "Do what I do!" and buried her head in the sand. The two males stopped under the tree, looked around, and one said, "Where did they go?"

Ostrich—the Meat Factor

With 40 percent less fat than beef, a quarter-pound burger of ostrich meat contains less than three grams of fat. Ostrich and emu meats are low in cholesterol and calories and high in iron, and contain less than two grams of fat per four-ounce serving.

Because of its low fat content, the meat cooks faster than other higher-fat meat products. It cooks in half the time of beef, so when you pop it in the oven, be careful not to overcook, as it becomes tough and changes flavor. When cooking roasts, use low temperatures (190° to 225° Fahrenheit.)

The uncooked meat is slightly dark red to slightly cherry red in color, with some variation from one muscle group to another. If you are able to purchase ostrich/emu meat, remember it is a 100 percent yield: there is no gristle or fat to trim.

Information on ostrich and emu meat, where to get it, and how to cook it is available from:

The American Ostrich Association
3950 Fossil Creek Boulevard
Fort Worth, Texas 76137
817-232-1200

Florida Chapter of the
* American Ostrich Association*
410 Bunkers Cove Road
Panama City, Florida 32401
904-913-0908

American Emu Association
Box 8174
Dallas, Texas 75205
214-559-AEA1

For some interesting and tasty ostrich and emu recipes, see Chapter 9.

LIVE AND LET LIVE—SNAKES

Contrary to popular belief, the water moccasin, commonly known as the cottonmouth, is the only poisonous water-loving snake in the United States. It is a large, very thick-bodied snake with a chunky head and a short tail that tapers very abruptly from the body. The inside of its mouth is noticeably white and the moccasin, when surprised, has a habit of rearing its head back, opening the mouth wide, and beating its short tail back and forth in a vigorous steady rhythm. It looks as mean and dangerous as it really is.

The cottonmouth, an excellent swimmer, inhabits swampy areas, bayous, and rivers along the Atlantic Coast and the Gulf of Mexico. It's generally found on muddy banks of ponds, swamps, or sluggish streams, on partly submerged logs, or on low limbs of bushes and trees overhanging such water areas. Its diet generally consists of fishes, frogs, toads, and crayfish, although some of the smaller snakes also eat earthworms and slugs. Anglers believe that they destroy game fish and pan fish, but usually they capture only the slower, less desirable "rough" fish or those that are diseased.

Like most snakes, a cottonmouth will not attack if it can escape. Cottonmouths have been known to drop off overhead branches into the water as canoeists paddle by, then swim away under the water to shelter.

The Florida cottonmouth can grow to more than five feet long. Its scales are keeled and rough. Its color may be dull olive, sooty brown, or almost black, with indistinct dark bands which disappear in older snakes that become four or five feet long. A dark band that reaches from each eye to the rear of the jaw is also an identifying feature.

The cottonmouth, like the rattlesnake and its close relative, the copperhead, is a pit viper. It has a deep pit, apparently a sense organ, between each eye and the corresponding nostril. It also has two long hollow fangs at the front of the upper jaw, like hypodermic needles, for stabbing its prey and injecting its venom. The young, from 7 to 12 in number, are born alive and are bright brown and brilliantly marked with sulfur-yellow tails.

Garter Snakes

Most large brown snakes in Florida are garter snakes. Their color can vary from brown to gray or yellowish with a lighter stripe or row of spots along the side. A few can be found that are all black. The striped pattern on garter snakes looks like the pattern on garters once worn by men to hold up their socks.

They are common near pond and lake shores, as well as woodlands, rocky roadsides, farmlands, gravel pits, and abandoned buildings. Daytime is their active period. You may see the same snake on sunny days basking in a warm spot. Garters are excellent swimmers, moving over the surface of the water with an undulating motion. Some people call them water snakes. They eat a variety of small animals, such as salamanders, fishes, frogs, worms, and mice.

The babies are born alive in late summer, from 6 to 40 in a family. Baby garter snakes are greenish-gray, with no visible markings. They look like smooth gray worms with eyeballs. Garter snakes have teeth (but no fangs or poison), and do tend to bite you when first picked up. The bite is more surprising than it is painful—just a small puncture. They also produce a smelly fluid intended to make you let them go.

Copperheads

Florida is the southernmost range for the copperhead, a snake with pinkish tan skin and reddish brown cross-bands. The bands are wide along the sides and narrow along the back, forming something of an hourglass shape. A grown copperhead is about 30 inches long and could be mistaken for a cottonmouth snake. Look for copperheads in leafy and underbrush areas.

Coral Snakes

Coral snakes like to burrow under dead vegetation, then strike at their target as it passes by. Bands of black, yellow, and red distinguish this snake, though the harmless king snake has the same color bands but in a different order. Just remember: "Red touch yellow, kill a fellow; red touch black, good for jack." Also, the coral snake has a black nose; the king snake does not. Coral snake fangs are smaller than those of other poisonous snakes. Once bitten, the victim of a coral snake bite suffers from labored breathing, nausea, and vomiting.

Rattlesnakes

Considered Florida's most dangerous snake, the rattlesnake, with its diamond-shaped markings, can grow to seven feet long. The rattler's bite produces a hot, needlelike pain. If venom is injected—which occurs about 80 percent of the time—the victim suffers faintness, sweating, numbness or tingling, swelling, and muscle twitching.

RATS AND MICE

Gnawing mammals like the mouse and rat have been annoying Florida home and garden owners for as long as most people can remember. In addition to causing damage, they pose a threat to human health. Rats and mice can climb, swim, and jump great distances to gain entrance into homes and buildings. Entrance to a building is often made by enlarging existing holes or cracks in an effort to find food and shelter.

Evidence of rodent activity includes bite marks on wooden structures, pipes, clothing, and food, or the presence of fecal droppings. Rodents will eat almost anything and prefer dark hiding places. They're very smart and may be difficult to control once a population is established. Set a trap and it could sit there forever if a rat or mouse decides it's suspicious.

Rat and mouse presence can be detected by seeing the rodent or its fecal droppings, by spotting the chewing damage, or by hearing the noise. Rodents will chew or gnaw on almost anything, particularly at night. They will also chew to gain entrance to a dwelling. Many unexplained fires have been caused by rodents chewing on electrical wiring. Food supplies can become contaminated when rodents deposit urine and feces on them. The fecal droppings of mice are 1/4 of an inch long and pointy, while rat droppings are 3/4 of an inch long and oblong. Flea-infested rodents can introduce fleas to a pet or dwelling as well.

Since rats and mice reproduce quickly in large numbers, it is important to protect your home and health by denying them access. Search for potential entrances and take steps to avoid rodent infestation. Repair all openings with a strong material (cement, metal, etc.) to prevent rodent entry. Avoid leaving hiding places and concealed runways for rodents. Remove any vegetation close to the house and keep grass short to limit hiding places. Continuous monitoring is a must.

Sanitary measures also aid in control. Do not leave food in containers or packages which rodents can chew through—store it in heavy plastic or glass containers. Keep doors to pantries or other food storage areas closed and rodent-proof. Look around the house for other conditions which might attract rodents. Traps can be used to control rodent populations, but they require monitoring and follow-up.

Use gloves. Rodents have a very good sense of smell, so they'll know if you've been in the area or if a trap has been handled by humans. Gloves will also provide protection from disease.

The main types of traps include snap, multicatch, and glue board. Since rodents follow familiar paths again and again, these traps should be placed at right angles to the wall where activity has been spotted. Place traps two to three feet apart. Bait can be used to lure rodents to these traps. Some effective baits are peanut butter, bread, dried fruit, or cheese.

If biological and physical control measures are not effective, use a pesticide which will have a minimal impact on you, your pets, and the environment. Anticoagulant baits are the least hazardous to humans and animals. Once the bait has been consumed, the rodent will experience internal bleeding and then die. The disadvantage of this method is that it may take some time for rodents to die after consuming the bait. As a result, they may die in a concealed place and produce a strong, offensive smell before being found.

The oldest and most common control of rodents has been the cat. People have adopted cats as pets solely for this purpose for centuries. However, some cats may be afraid of large rats, and they may also catch fleas from the rodents.

The common house mouse, which ranges in color from brown to gray, is small, measuring four to six inches in length. Mice have large ears, a pointed nose, sharp, flat teeth, and a long tail which is usually darker in color than the body. At the age of two to three months, a mouse can begin reproducing. During an average life span of 18 months, a mouse can produce approximately 12 litters of 5 or 6 young. The first litter is usually born three weeks after mating.

All species of rats have sharp teeth and poor eyesight. Rats can measure up to 12 to 18 inches long, including the tail. They have blunt noses, small, close-set ears, and long tails. Some rats nest in walls, attics, and trees while others nest in burrows. Rats also have a life span of up to 18 months, although many die before reaching this age. Rats will reproduce approximately nine times, with a litter of 6 to 14 young being born 3 to 4 weeks after mating.

RACCOONS

Raccoons are common in Florida. They can be found anywhere in the state and as far south as South America. Raccoons don't like heights or dry areas, so you'll never see a raccoon in a desert or on mountain tops higher than 10,000 feet. They rarely come out during the day unless they're hungry, preferring the night life. Raccoons will eat almost anything—bugs, snakes, birds and eggs, fish, and even vegetables.

Corner a raccoon and you might run into trouble. Last year, almost five thousand people nationwide acquired rabies from raccoon bites, so be careful if you encounter one. What do you do if you're bitten by a raccoon (or any wild animal, for that matter)? Wash the wound thoroughly with soap and warm water and seek medical help immediately. If you can catch the animal, it can be tested for rabies.

*The
Sunshine State
Almanac
& Book of
Florida-
Related
Stuff*

PEOPLE

THE BEACH LADY

O n American Beach on South Amelia Island, Florida, lives MaVynee Betsch, known by locals as "The Beach Lady." Betsch has made it her full-time mission since 1975 to preserve and protect American Beach from development and destruction.

Betsch is trying to convince the state of Florida to purchase part of the two hundred acres of American Beach and turn it into a nature preserve. The local county government has designated six acres of the beach as a park, including the island's tallest sand dune and the dwarf oaks sculpted by the northeast winds. But Betsch wants more, including protection for the loggerhead turtles and endangered right whales that live offshore.

She says there used to be hundreds of monarch butterflies in the area, but they lost their habitat when residents mowed wildflower patches and the county sprayed pesticides to control mosquitoes. She has convinced the local mosquito control board to install bat houses to help control the insects and has talked many residents into letting their lawns grow wild. "I'm trying to show people that there is a natural way to solve their problems," she says. "We can have mosquito control and butterflies, too."

To date, she has given her life savings—$750,000—to some 60 environmental organizations and causes, most of them involving animals. When Betsch isn't out on the beach picking up trash or giving weekend tours of the island and park, she is writing letters to politicians and newspaper editors or corresponding with others as a member of the advisory board of the Legal Environmental Assistance Foundation (LEAF).

THE OX WOMAN

S outh Dade County had a full complement of odd characters in its early days. Preacher Tems lived in a tree and had no visible means of monetary support. He preached and answered all questions in rhyme. John Wingate brought a huge hogshead to the area by wagon and lived in it while he worked his claim. When a hurricane blew it off his land, he calmly rolled it back after the storm. J. R. Walker was an unordained Methodist minister who preached at the Silver Palm School and always sang religious songs at the top of his voice as he walked the roads. He could be heard at least a quarter of a mile away.

But far and away the most celebrated character in the early 1900s was the "Ox Woman." The Widow McLain—or Aunt Sarah, as she was known to children—arrived in Dade County around 1907 driving her team of oxen and a two-wheeled cart from Georgia with her dogs and her shotgun for company. She camped for a while near the John Murray home and would sit on their porch and sing "Barbara Allen" and other sad songs. Sometimes she read the Bible and argued that the Seminoles were one of the lost tribes of Israel. She was 6 feet, 4 inches tall, weighed about 190 pounds, and was as strong as an ox (hence the name).

The Ox Woman eventually settled at Long Key, now in the Everglades National Park. She built herself a shack and farmed the prairie land, selling her surplus vegetables. She occasionally bought a side of beef and sold the cut-up sections at depots in the area. The beef was covered with fresh pine branches which kept it from spoiling. The Ox Woman charged the same price for all cuts—a neck cost the same as a flank.

On her selling trips up and down South Dade County, Sarah McLain stayed with anyone who had animals and would be able to feed her oxen or horse and dogs. She usually took a bath at each place she stopped and seemed happy to spend the night in a good bed. Once Fred Kosel took a male friend hunting near the widow's camp. The man looked around and thought it would be just the place to spend the winter, so he moved in with the Ox Woman. Twenty-four hours later he turned up at the Kosel home, complaining. He said when he got up in the morning he had to chop wood before he could have coffee, and before she would give him lunch, he had to swim across a slough and retrieve some sheet iron the Ox Woman had hauled in and dumped. That and the constant mosquito invasion were just too much, so he moved out.

Many settlers, seeing the feats of strength performed by the Ox Woman, declared that she was a man. Not so, answered Mrs. Clara Vihlen, whose home was a favorite stopover for the widow. Mrs. Vihlen always fixed a hot bath in the washtub in the kitchen for her friend, and said her skin was soft and white under her garments and her figure obviously that of a woman. The Ox Woman had blue eyes and wore her hair in a bun at the back of her neck as did many women at that time. She was always polite and well-spoken, behaved as a lady, and was grateful for anything that was done for her. There is no record of her ever having misused her great strength to injure anyone or do harm.

In 1908, Flora Caldwell reported seeing the Ox Woman during a visit to her father's home. The Ox Woman was driving a swaybacked horse and a covered wagon because Indians had stolen her oxen. The Ox Woman continued to live in the Everglades until she heard that her sister, Hannah Smith, known as Big Six, had been killed at a plantation in the Ten Thousand Islands, where she had been hired to chop firewood for a syrup mill. After burying her sister, the Ox Woman turned up at Chokoloskee and eventually moved to Immokalee, where she settled on an Indian mound of about ten aces. She built a palm-thatched shack and farmed for the next four years. In 1919, she suffered a stroke and died shortly thereafter. She was buried in Fort Denaud in an unmarked grave.

Hannah and Sarah were the only members of the family to become part of Florida legend. A poet, Annie Mayhew Fitzpatrick, once wrote:

> Yes, I be the Widow McLain.
> My man by a posse was slain.
> Neither witty nor pretty
> I'm asking no pity
> I'm off to my homestead again.
> I'm off to my home on Long Key
> My pigs and my cow avail me.
> In the open I cook, wash my clothes
>   in a brook
> I'm the Widow McLain, yes I be.

FLORIDA'S SEMINOLES— THE EARLY YEARS

The term "Seminole" is a derivative of "cimarron," which means "wild men" in Spanish. The original Seminoles were given this name because they were Indians who had escaped from slavery in the British-controlled Northern colonies. When they came to Florida, they were called Creeks—Indians of Muskogee derivation. The Muskogean tribes were part of the Mississipian culture of temple-mound builders. Among the Muskogean tribes were the Creeks, Hitichis, and Yamasees of Georgia; the Apalachees of Florida; the Alabamas and Mobiles of Alabama; and the Choctaws, Chickasaws, and Houmas of Mississippi.

The original Seminoles came to Florida because it was controlled by the Spanish, who had no interest in returning slaves to the British. They were mostly Lower Creeks who spoke the Miccosukee language, but other Indians—including Yuchis, Yamasees, and Choctaws who had confronted Ponce de León and Hernando DeSoto—also joined the tribe in the trek to northern Florida from Georgia during the early 1700s.

Seminole historians report that by this time, many of the tribes in Florida, including the Tequestas, Calusas, Apalachees, and Timucans, had been decimated by the Spanish presence, either in battle or by diseases such as smallpox. By the mid 1700s, the Indian population had dropped from an estimated 100,000 during the 1500s to fewer than 50.

In 1767, Upper Creeks from Alabama, who spoke the Muskogee language, settled in the Tampa area. The first recorded use of the name "Seminole" to denote an actual tribe was recorded in 1771. In 1778, the Seminoles were joined by more Lower Creeks and a few Apalachees.

Together with the Choctaws, Chickasaws, Creeks, and Cherokees, the Seminoles were called "The Five Civilized Tribes." The name was coined because these tribes in particular adopted many ways of the white civilization. They lived in cabins or houses, wore clothes similar to those of the white man, and often became Christians.

Although many of the other tribes acquired the institution of slavery from the whites and actually owned African slaves, the Seminoles never did. Indeed, many Africans escaping slavery in the Carolinas and Georgia came to Florida and built settlements near the Seminoles. They formed a strong union with the Seminoles—based on their mutual fear of slavery—which survived attempts by the U.S. government to break them apart. Intermarriages and friendships were common. In fact, they were so closely allied that the Africans became known as Black Seminoles.

PONCE DE LEÓN

Juan Ponce de León was a Spanish soldier and *adelantado* (colonial governor) best remembered as the European explorer who discovered Florida in 1513 and attempted to set up the first colony in 1521. Son of an aristocrat from the province of León in northwest Spain, he sailed on the second voyage of Christopher Columbus.

Landing on the Atlantic Coast of Florida, probably near Melbourne Beach, he named the area *La Florida* in honor of the Easter season known as *Pascua Florida*. Sailing around the Florida Keys, he mapped the coastline as far north as Charlotte Harbor. In 1521, he returned to Charlotte Harbor to build a colony and encountered the hostile Calusa Indians, who attacked his search party and seriously wounded him. He was taken to Cuba, where he died from his wounds and was buried in the cathedral in San Juan.

HENRY FLAGLER— THE RAILROAD KING

Born in Hopewell, New York, on January 2, 1830, Flagler was a grain merchant in Ohio in 1850 when he first met John D. Rockefeller. The two men would later start an oil business in Cleveland that in 1908 became the giant Standard Oil corporation, with Flagler as vice president.

Coming to St. Augustine with

his ailing wife, Mary, in 1883, Flagler decided to extend the Jacksonville, St. Augustine, and Halifax Railroad into town. Several people convinced Flagler to invest further in Florida, and he built the Ponce de Leon Hotel (which later became Flagler College) and two other luxury palaces in St. Augustine. He later extended his East Coast Railroad south to Palm Beach, where he built Whitehall for his new wife, Ida Alice. In 1896, his railroad reached Miami. Town after town along the Florida Atlantic Coast boomed because of the new transportation to the North. In 1901, Flagler divorced Ida Alice and married his mistress, Mary Kenan. In 1912, Flagler's railroad reached Key West and opened up a whole new section of the state. Flagler died on May 20, 1913.

*The
Sunshine State
Almanac
& Book of
Florida-
Related
Stuff*

BIRDS

FLORIDA AUDUBON SOCIETY

*T*he Florida Audubon Society has 46 chapters around the state with a membership of 32,000. The Society operates a variety of programs, including environmental education, scientific research, and wildlife rehabilitation. The Adopt-A-Bird program is a unique way to participate in the conservation of birds of prey. An annual adoption helps pay for the care of permanently injured birds in the program and makes it possible for the Society's Center for Birds of Prey to continue its important work. For more information, call 800-874-BIRD.

CENTER FOR BIRDS OF PREY

The Center for Birds of Prey is dedicated to rehabilitating injured and orphaned birds of prey—hawks, owls, eagles, falcons, and kites—and telling the public about the need to preserve Florida's native wildlife. The residents of the Center play a big role as hunters and scavengers in maintaining nature's balance. Major declines in their populations  signal serious ecological damage to marine and terrestrial environments.

Located in Maitland, the Center is the foremost raptor rehabilitation facility in the Southeast, treating nearly 600 injured raptors every year. The

Center's main goal is to rehabilitate an injured bird to the point where it can be released back into its natural habitat. Since opening in 1979, the Center has released more than 2,000 birds back into the wild, including more than 160 bald eagles.

The Audubon Aviary provides a lifetime haven to nonreleasable eagles, hawks, owls, and falcons. The lakeside aviary is open to the public and offers an opportunity to raise awareness of Florida's birds of prey through guided tours.

Adopting Stray Birds

The Adopt-A-Bird program is an opportunity for everyone to participate in the conservation of birds of prey. There are several levels of adoption. You can become a Caretaker at $145, $185, or $250; a Steward at $65, $85, or $115; or a Parent at $25, $35, or $45. A Bird Buddy program is available for kids under age 16 at $20, $25, or $30. The Grandparent program is designed for senior citizens at $20, $25, or $30.

For information on the adoption program, call 800-874-BIRD or write:

Florida Audubon Society
Birds of Prey Center
1101 Audubon Way
Maitland, Florida 32751

BIRDS AND CATS— THEY DON'T MIX

Researchers estimate that house cats and feral cats are responsible for killing approximately 78 million small mammals and birds annually. Millions of backyard birds and other animals are killed by cats each year. Cats are a serious threat to fledglings, birds roosting at night, and birds on the nest, at the feeder, or in a birdbath.

If you are unwilling to restrain free-roaming cats, do not attract birds to your yard by putting out feeders, nest boxes, and baths. Responsible pet owners keep their cats indoors. Most local jurisdictions have enforceable leash laws for cats and dogs, so report any violators.

LOST AT SEA

The U. S. Coast Guard has spent $146,000 to train rescue pigeons to locate people lost at sea. The pigeons would fly overhead in Coast Guard aircraft, looking out the windows. When they spotted survivors in the water, they would flick a switch with their bills and receive a reward. During trials, pigeons out-rescued Coast Guard crews 90 to 38.

During World War II, sea gulls were used off the Atlantic Coast to detect German U-boats. As most people know, sea gulls hang around trash dumps looking for food. To train the gulls to locate submerged vessels, submarines would head offshore and dump garbage while submerged. As the garbage floated to the surface, the birds would congregate over the submarine. Eventually, the gulls would congregate when they saw a long, dark shadow under the water's surface.

THE MOURNING DOVE

These large birds are easy to recognize, as they show the typical dovelike features—small head on a plump body supported by very short legs. They're usually brown or gray with a medium-long, thin beak and are similar in size to a blue jay. In flight, the body appears streamlined and the wings taper to a point—features that also suggest a merlin. They can be distinguished from other members of this family by their overall light brown color and long, wedge-shaped tail. Closer inspection will reveal that every mourning dove sports a small black beauty spot on each side of its face. Males and females look almost identical, but in late winter, if you look carefully, you may notice that some birds develop a light pink wash over their chests. The pink wash is part of the breeding plumage of the male mourning dove and is the best way to tell the difference between the two sexes.

Late March is the time to start to listen for the soft, drawn-out cooing of the mourning dove. Once you hear their sad-sounding song, you will know why they were named mourning doves. Sometimes people mistake the cooing call of the mourning dove for the hooting of an owl. The barred owl is well known for its daytime hooting, but the cooing of the dove is soft, while the hooting of the owl tends to be much more robust. Another mourning dove sound to listen for is a distinctive high-pitched whistling produced by their rapid and powerful wingbeats while taking off from the ground.

When mourning doves first visit a new yard, they are rather skittish and tend to fly away easily, but a well-stocked bird feeder can draw them back. Approximately 98 percent of the mourning dove's diet is composed of seeds. They are great birds to have around, as they eat enormous amounts of weed seeds.

HUMMINGBIRDS

You don't see too many hummingbirds in Florida—nothing like the situation up North where it is common to see eight to ten birds hovering together around a feeder. But there are hummingbirds in Florida, and you can attract them to your yard with a little determination, the right equipment, and some knowledge about what hummingbirds like.

Hummingbird nectar can be made from ordinary table sugar and water with a four-to-one ratio. Boil a cup of water and add about 1/4 cup of sugar, then stir. That's it. You could add a little red food coloring, but it really isn't necessary. Hummingbird feeders are available at any pet store. Once the birds locate your feeder, they'll be back.

Hummingbirds get all of their protein from eating insects. The nectar will last only a few days in the sun, so change it frequently—at least twice a week. Hang the feeder from a tree branch in the shade. Use a small feeder if you see only a few hummingbirds. A two-ounce feeder is fine for the number of hummingbirds you're likely to encounter in Florida.

WOODPECKERS—
FRIEND OR FOE?

Each year thousands of home-owners put out suet feeders to attract woodpeckers. These handsome birds reward us by consuming millions of noxious insects, including carpenter ants and carpenter bees. While it's rare, an occasional woodpecker may single out a house for drumming, or worse, for a nest or dining site. Each spring, when males set up territories and attract mates, they make their presence known by drumming. Normally they pick a resonant dead tree trunk, but as more and more homeowners remove dead trees, woodpeckers may turn to metal gutters, house siding, and television antennas.

You can eliminate the drumming noise by filling the hollow spaces with caulk to deaden the resonant area. Then distract the bird from the drumming site by using scare techniques like balloons; a child's pinwheel; flash tape; strings of shiny, noisy tin can lids; wind chimes; or pulsating water sprinklers. If these don't work, create a physical barrier by screening the drumming site with hardware cloth, sheet metal, or nylon bird netting. You might encourage the birds to leave altogether by creating an alternative drumming site nearby.

If you have dead trees in your yard, you might think removing them will solve the woodpecker problem. The opposite might be true. Cutting down dead and decaying trees deprives these birds of nesting, drumming, and food sites, and they may be forced into choosing your home instead. Sometimes, you just can't win.

BIRDS AND WINDOW
COLLISIONS

Homes in Florida often have wide expanses of glass, and commercial buildings sometimes use insulated and reflective glass instead of solid walls. While these windows may be aesthetically pleasing to the human eye and functional in areas where the weather is good year-round, they are often lethal to birds. Many birds cannot distinguish the difference between the real sky and a reflection of the sky in a window.

In the United States alone, it is estimated that each year during migration, millions of birds fly full tilt into windows and are seriously injured or killed. If this is a problem in your area, you can minimize these collisions by breaking up the reflection on the outside of the window with a window screen, flash tape, and bird netting. Life-size, animate "scares" (like plastic falcons, owls, and balloons) and falcon or owl silhouettes attached to windows with suction cups usually are not effective deterrents. Planting trees and installing window awnings to prevent the sun from hitting the window may eliminate some reflection.

Migration isn't the only time homeowners have trouble with bird–window collisions. Birds may hit your windows during breeding season. Male cardinals, woodpeckers, and mockingbirds may actually fight their own reflections in windows and often in car mirrors as well. You can discourage them from doing this with screens and other barrier techniques.

Regardless of the season, birds can fly into windows when they're frightened during a visit to a feeding station. Either move the feeders a considerable distance away from the window or immediately adjacent to the window (which prevents them from getting up to flight speed before hitting the window).

INJURED AND ORPHANED BIRDS

Thud. A bird hits the window. You look out and see some feathers sticking to the corner of the pane. You rush outside and find a tiny yellow bird, still alive, lying under the window. It's not moving. What's the right thing to do? Get a towel and fold it into a box. Gently put the bird in the box or a large paper bag. Put the bird in a warm, quiet place. Get the bird to a veterinarian or a local wildlife agency (listed in the white pages of your telephone directory).

Do not offer first aid—without proper training, you're likely to do more harm than good. Do not offer food or water.

If you feed birds, sooner or later you'll come across a baby bird. You'll have to decide whether you should rescue it or leave it to fend for itself. In most cases, it is best to let nature take its course and not interfere.

If the bird is fully feathered, chances are it doesn't need your help. Each spring, baby birds leave the nest to learn to be adults. Their parents are usually nearby and are best equipped to take care of the babies. You can help fledglings by keeping your dogs and cats in the house.

However, if the bird is unfeathered, try to return it to the nest. If that's not possible, put it in a shoe box, cover it, and take it to a licensed wildlife rehabilitator. Do not attempt to take care of it yourself. No matter what the "first aid for baby birds" books at the library say, you can kill baby birds by not knowing what to feed them and offering them a diet of human baby food, meat, fish, bird seed, or milk.

BIRD FEEDING

Bird feeding is a popular American pastime, and in Florida, there are birds to be fed everywhere. Provide them with food, water, and shelter and they'll flock to your backyard. Add the basic bird-watching tools—a bird identification book, a pair of binoculars, and a diary to log what kind of birds you've seen and when and where—and you're an official bird feeder and watcher.

Winter is a great time to feed birds. Days are shorter so they have less light to find food, and food is more difficult to find than in the warmer months. Once you start providing food for wild birds, you should continue to do so. But don't feel guilty if you can't:

the birds won't starve; they'll simply find a new place to feed.

Different birds like different foods. Some like seeds, others nuts, fruits, insects, and even small mammals. The chart on the following pages explains which birds like which foods. The most common bird food is the black oil sunflower seed—almost all birds like it. Sunflower seed can be used to attract more wild birds than any other seed available. It's cheap—you can buy a 25-pound bag for under $10 in most parts of the state.

Put your feeders in a sheltered area that offers the birds some protection from birds of prey flying overhead. Shelter them from the wind and rain. If there are shrubs nearby, the birds have a place to go if they're attacked by house cats, who love to stalk wild birds. Clean the feeders periodically to prevent diseases and to keep rats and mice away.

You can take some pine cones, tie a wire or string around them, smear them with peanut butter and bird seed or cranberries, then hang them from windows or trees. They make nice Christmas decorations and birds love them! Check the peanut butter occasionally. It could get rancid.

WHICH BIRDS EAT WHAT?

American goldfinch—oil (black), black-striped, and hulled sunflower seeds

Blue jay—peanut kernels and all sunflower seeds

Brown-headed cowbird—white and red proso millet, German (golden) millet, canary seed

Brown thrasher—hulled and black-striped sunflower seeds

Cardinal—all sunflower seeds

Chickadees—peanut kernels, black-striped and oil (black) sunflower seeds

Chipping sparrow—white and red proso millet

Common grackle—black-striped and hulled sunflower seeds, cracked corn

Dark-eyed junco—white and red proso millet, canary seed, fine cracked corn

English sparrow—white and red proso millet, German (golden) millet, canary seed

Evening grosbeak—all sunflower seeds

Field sparrow—white and red proso millet

House finch—oil (black), black-striped, and hulled niger sunflower seeds

Mourning dove—oil (black) sunflower seeds, white and red proso millet, German golden millet, pine siskin, all sunflower seeds

Purple finch—all sunflower seeds

Red-breasted nuthatch—black-striped and oil (black) sunflower seeds

Red-winged blackbird—white and red proso, German (golden) millet

Scrub jay—peanut kernels, black-striped sunflower seeds

Song sparrow—white and red proso millet

Starling—peanut hearts, hulled oats, cracked corn

Tree sparrow—white and red proso millet

Tufted titmouse—peanut kernels, black-striped and oil (black) sunflower seeds

White-breasted nuthatch—black-striped sunflower seeds

White-crowned sparrow—oil (black) and hulled sunflower seeds, white and red proso millet, peanut kernels and hearts

White-throated sparrow—oil (black), black-striped and hulled sunflower seeds, white and red proso millet, peanut kernels

BIRDS, BIRDS, BIRDS—EVERYWHERE!

When there are too many birds, or they have become annoying, what do you do? Any bird, no matter how cute, can become a problem. A mockingbird's midnight song may be music to some but an annoyance to others. The flicker might be welcome to the feeder but not to the cedar siding on your house. You might be tempted to feed geese as they pass through the area, but some carry disease and their droppings are usually not welcome on lawns. Birds can eat your cherries, drill holes in your birch trees, and even eat fish out of your backyard pond. Birds roosting by the hundreds are a health hazard, and birds setting up house in your hanging basket or, worse, your clothes dryer vents are a real annoyance.

What's the solution? You can't shoot them, poison them, or trap them and move them out of the neighborhood. All wild birds in Florida except pigeons, English sparrows, and starlings are protected by law. You can't trap, kill, or possess protected species without federal and state permits. The protection extends to nests and eggs as well.

The first step in solving your wild bird problem is to identify the birds and determine what's attracting them. If you remove what seems to attracts the birds, or build a barrier between the birds and what they find so attractive, they might go away. Before you take any action, consider: Could the solution hurt people, pets, and other wildlife? Is it worth the trouble or the cost? You can get good advice by calling the local office of the Fish and Wildlife Service, your state wildlife officer or the Department of Agriculture County Cooperative Extension agent.

Most bird problems do not have a simple solution. What eliminates a bird problem in one case may fail in another. Some solutions work for only a short time as the birds find alternatives. The secret to solving bird problems is to use several tactics and to vary them so birds don't become complacent.

HAWKS AND OWLS

The presence of hawks and owls may cause problems for people who have bird feeders or allow their small household pets to roam at night. Federal and state laws prohibit the capture, killing, or possession of hawks and owls. The best solution to most raptor problems is prevention. Keep your pets indoors.

If you feed wild birds, expect a visit from a hungry hawk or owl now and then. Raptors at a bird-feeding station are a problem only when they perch nearby, watching the other birds feed. When they're around, you won't see too many birds at your feeders. Stop filling your feeders for a couple of days and hopefully the raptors will look for dinner elsewhere.

NESTING BIRDS

Birds often pick what seem to be the strangest places to nest. They set up housekeeping in your house gutters, in clothes dryer fan vents, over a door, in a bucket in your garage, in hanging baskets, in a pile of twigs on your window sill, and in the shrubs around your house.

The most effective way to eliminate nesting problems is to discourage the bird before the nest is built by offering an alternative artificial nest nearby (but out of your way). If that doesn't work, contact a federal or state agent for advice. Resist the temptation to destroy the nest or harass the adults.

If you want to encourage nesting, you can build a nesting box and attach it to the side of a tree or fence.

Problems at the Nesting Box

Many homeowners invite birds to visit and nest in their yards by putting up nesting boxes. Almost two dozen bird species in Florida will consider a human-made nest. To make sure you get the right animal in the right box, first learn all you can about what the birds want and how to attract them to your area. Monitor any nesting boxes and evict any intruders.

Bugs are always a problem in nesting boxes. The safest solution to insect infestations is physical removal and soaping of the inside top of the box. If insects infest the box during nesting, apply a light dusting of rotenone or pyrethrin, two natural insecticides that have low-toxicity. Never use chemical sprays.

If snakes, squirrels, or climbing mammals are a problem, use physical barriers to deter them. Try a

PVC pipe over your metal bird nest pole, or metal sheeting on a tree or wood pole. Smear the PVC or metal with Vaseline laced with hot (cayenne) pepper. Avoid automotive grease—it can be lethal to wildlife.

Put a predator guard over the nest entrance hole. If you find other birds attacking the adults, eggs, or nestlings, what you can do depends on the perpetrators. All birds except house sparrows, pigeons, and starlings are protected by state and federal laws.

PLASTIC MILK JUG BIRD FEEDER

You can make a simple (and cheap) bird feeder using a plastic milk jug, a couple of small-diameter sticks or twigs about 18 inches long, and a few feet of cord. Draw four circles about one and a half inches in diameter on each side of the jug, about two inches from the bottom. Punch a half dozen small holes into the bottom of the jug. They'll act as a drain if water gets inside.

About one half inch under each hole, cut a small hole slightly smaller than the diameter of the sticks you're going to use. Insert a stick into each hole so it protrudes from both sides. The sticks cross inside the jar. Remove the cap and pour in bird seed. To secure the feeder to a tree limb, punch a small

hole in the center of the cap. Insert a piece of cord and tie a large knot on the inside of the cap. Replace the cap and tie the feeder to a tree limb. By keeping the amount of bird seed to a minimum and reducing the overall weight of the feeder, the cap and string should be able to support the feeder.

ROOSTING BIRDS

You don't have to park your car under a tree to discover why people have no patience with roosting birds. Everyone knows bird droppings pile up under a roost. An occasional bird perching on a tree limb, gutter, or fence may not be a serious concern. But problems arise when pigeons perch on your balcony railing, sparrows select your carport rafter, and gulls bask on your boat dock piling.

When starlings, grackles, blackbirds, and crows roost by the thousands in trees, they create a serious health hazard. Physical barriers may be the most effective way to control birds roosting on buildings. To eliminate birds on ledges, string wire or stretch a Slinky™ toy along the ledge, or string rows of monofilament one or two inches above each other about two feet apart. Sheet metal or hardware cloth placed at an angle on ledges may also make roosting more difficult. Pruning may eliminate birds roosting in trees. Removing some cover may be enough to make the roost site less attractive. Scare tactics may provide only temporary relief; you might have to start all over again if they return.

BIRDS ON ELECTRIC WIRES

Why don't birds get electrocuted when they perch on live electrical wires? For birds to get electrocuted from power lines, three conditions must exist. There must be sufficient potential and electric current to overcome the body resistance of the bird, there must be little or no insulation on the wire, and the bird must simultaneously contact the bare wire and a conductor providing a path to ground or another conductor with a different electric potential (a second phase of AC current, for example). Since most high electrical wires are sufficiently separated to prevent this from happening, it's unlikely a bird will get toasted. But there are exceptions; once in a while all of the above conditions exist.

KEEPING SQUIRRELS AWAY FROM YOUR BIRD FEEDER

To keep squirrels away from your bird feeders, you need some kind of baffle that squirrels can't jump on or around. Since squirrels can jump as far ten feet across and four to five feet up from the ground, you can see the problems. A baffle shaped like an umbrella is the best design to keep squirrels from climbing up a pole.

For hanging feeders in trees, choose a spot at least eight to ten feet from the tree trunk or branches and away from any spots the squirrels can use to launch themselves toward the feeder. Hang the feeder from a branch and install an umbrella baffle on the hang line to keep them away.

BIRD WATCHING

No one knows the sights and sounds of nature quite like a bird-watcher. By taking a half-second look at a small darting assemblage of brown, yellow, and white feathers, and listening to a call note that sounds something like "chip," a "birder" can tell you that the bird not only was one of forty-two different types of warblers, but that it specifically was a yellow-rumped warbler.

Florida has the third greatest number of bird species of any state.

To distinguish among the 780 species of birds found in North America, including those found in Florida, birders must quickly process information on color patterns, call notes, and even the shapes of bills. They have to know what to key in on when they see a strange bird and note its overall size, how it moves through a bush or tree, and the shape of the wings. Such sensory workouts help birders develop great visual and hearing acuity. In fact, birders are generally much more observant than the average person.

To the beginning bird-watcher, trying to identify even common species can be extremely frustrating, and many people give up quickly. A small gray bird flashes up to the top of a bush. Quick, grab your binoculars! Start flipping through your field guide. Take another look at the bird. Flip back a page or two. Suddenly the bird is gone, but there is a different one lower in the bush. The page riffling and binocular lifting begins anew.

Some say birding is simply too much fun to be missed. Sometimes frustrating (but always rewarding), it can take months to grasp the techniques. You need patience to become one of the truly tuned-in nature watchers.

Birds are highly visual creatures, and some species sport breathtaking combinations of yellows, blues, reds, blacks, and greens to make themselves more obvious. They also come in a wide variety of shapes and forms, which adds considerably to the pleasures of bird watching.

Birding will also make you more familiar with the natural beauty of Florida and perhaps will lead you to appreciate how quickly that beauty is being lost. Florida has the third greatest number of bird species of any state in the nation, but the continued existence of many of these species is threatened by the thousands of new residents who move to Florida each year. Many birds simply cannot tolerate the urban landscapes created by humans.

*The
Sunshine State
Almanac
& Book of
Florida-
Related
Stuff*

MISC.

I Told You I Was Sick!

Key West's historic 1847 Cemetery is located in the "dead" center of Old Town, bounded by streets and roads named Angela, Margaret, Frances, Olivia, and (appropriately) Passover Lane. The whitewashed, above-ground tombs and statues were moved to higher ground after the 1847 hurricane disinterred bodies from the first burial ground near the southernmost point in town. They are an interesting introduction to Key West's history. A stroll through this historic graveyard can tell as much about the town's quirky character as any history lesson.

The main entry gates open at the corner of Margaret and Angela Streets. Walk straight ahead to the first corner of Palm and Magnolia, where you'll see the USS *Maine* plot surrounded by an ornate wrought-iron fence painted silver. This scrolled grillwork encircles a solitary bronze sailor, dedicated on March 15, 1900, to commemorate the victims of the 1898 sinking of the battleship USS *Maine* in Havana Harbor.

Turn right along First Avenue to the beautifully carved winged angel, a reminder of a young child's early death. Notice the twin red-barked gumbo limbo trees that flank an unusual brick monument to the Mitchell family. Continue past the plot of General Abraham Lincoln Sawyer, a 40-inch-tall midget whose final wish was to be buried in a man-sized tomb. Next is the decorated gray marble shaft that marks the resting place of William Curry, supposedly Florida's first millionaire. Behind the monument is a fallen obelisk etched with Ellen Mallory's name. She was the mother of Stephen Mallory, U.S. Senator and Confederate Navy Secretary.

Pass by the purple hedge of bougainvillea to where Duncan Cameron, supervisor of lighthouse construction in 1847, was laid to rest in 1855. Next along the path is a tiny arched stone that commemorates 22-year-old Reverend J. Van Duzen, the first missionary to Cuba. Along 4th Avenue, you'll see the life-sized statue of Earl Saunders Johnson. Those are his own shoes enclosed in plaster. Captain Francis Watlington, a mariner and Confederate blockade runner who lived from 1804 to 1887, owned the "Oldest House," and Johnson was its last family heir.

Walk a bit further to see the decaying ornate fence surrounding the four-generation Porter clan. Joseph Yates Porter was the founder of public health in Florida. To the right are two classic angels posed at the Navarro family plot. Still further on 4th Avenue you'll see the white marble stone marking the grave of Thomas Romer, a black Bahamian, privateer, and "good" citizen for 65 of his 108 years, according to the tombstone. It's signed by Gallagher, a nineteenth-century stone cutter. Turn right on Violet Street and look for the tomb of Sloppy Joe Russell, hidden behind the crypt marked by a hand-painted "eternal flame."

As you walk along 7th Avenue, look for the black archway with the letters "B'nai Zion" marking the Jewish Cemetery entrance. To the immediate left is a large white crypt with a facing tablet inscribed "I Told You I Was Sick." Cross the cemetery toward Angela Street along Laurel and note the uplifted marble casket of a tiny Cuban woman whose grandfather penned the national anthem of Cuba. An expansive bricked lot to the left features pink granite gravestones for three Yorkshire terriers and Elfina, a pet deer, along with members of the prominent Otto family. Dr. Otto was a Prussian-born medical officer at Fort Jefferson who fought the yellow fever epidemic. On the right is the Catholic Cemetery, founded in 1868. The large gray mausoleum marks the burial place of the Toppino family, the producers of Keys' concrete and builders of the Overseas Highway bridges. Look for the inscription "devoted fan of Julio Iglesias" near here.

Walk back toward the entrance along Palm Avenue and look towards Angela Street. You may spot the unusual carved statue of a naked bound woman at the 1966 tomb of Archibald Yates. A metal archway along Palm, bearing the inscription A Los Martires de Cuba ("To the Cuban Martyrs"), denotes a symbolic 1892 memorial to heroes of the 1868 Cuban revolution, and the tomb of Cuban Consul Antonio Diaz Carrasco, buried here in 1915. Look to your left for the "God Was Good to Me" epitaph, carved in wood and mounted on an aboveground crypt.

If navigating all those lanes and streets sounds just too spooky to do alone, call Sharon Wells at 305-294-8380 and sign up for her one-hour guided cemetery tour.

THE HISTORY OF THE PINK PLASTIC FLAMINGO

Y ou see them everywhere—on front lawns in California, in windows of homes in Texas, and on the sand beaches in France. According to legend, Don Featherstone designed the first pink plastic flamingo around 1957. A designer with a company called Union Products in Leominster, Massachusetts (he's now the president), he was looking for something to do one day and came up with the idea of a lawn ornament in the shape of a flamingo.

Union Products was designing flat ornaments when the idea of a three-dimensional ornament came to Don's mind. The first project was a duck Don designed after studying a duck's anatomy for months. Today, the company sells as many ducks as it does flamingos, but not too many people know that. The company sells an average of a quarter of a million pink flamingos a year.

Winners of the recent "what to do with a plastic flamingo" contest include a woman in Georgia who painted her flamingos with black spots and posed them with her Dalmatian dogs, and a Florida woman who placed a sheet of glass over four flamingos planted in pots for a flamingo coffee table. Despite inflation, you can still buy a pair of plastic flamingos for about $15 (the original price was $12). Plastic flamingos are usually sold only in pairs, so you may not be able to buy just one. If you can't find the genuine article, call Celebration Fantastic at 800-235-3272 to place an order or to get a free catalog.

FLORIDA'S GRAND OPERA

T he Florida Grand Opera was created as the Southeast's first regional opera company on May 31, 1994, by founding companies The Greater Miami Opera and the Opera Guild, Inc., of Fort Lauderdale.

The Greater Miami Opera, begun in 1941, is the seventh-oldest opera company in the country. The Opera Guild, Inc., was founded 4 years later, and for nearly 50 years the two companies worked together to present Greater Miami Opera productions in Broward County.

With an annual budget of $7.2 million, the Florida Grand Opera is recognized as the twelfth largest opera company in the nation. The company produces masterpieces of the standard repertoire and lesser-known operas by the great composers in addition to its commissions and productions of the works of living composers. Premieres have included the world premiere of Robert Ward's *Minutes Till Midnight* and the American premieres of Gioachino Rossini's *Bianca e Falliero* and the final revised version of Alberto Franchetti's *Cristoforo Columbo*.

The Opera's Young Artist and Technical Apprentice Program, begun in 1984, provides a training ground for talented young performers and technicians pursuing careers in opera. This program provides a valuable bridge for young artists making the difficult transition from education to the professional world. Many former Young Artists have moved on to successful careers singing with opera companies throughout the world as well as returning to sing with the Florida Grand Opera in Miami.

FLORIDA AIRPORTS

Southeast

West Palm Beach
　Palm Beach International Airport
　561-471-7400
　Three miles west of West Palm Beach

Stuart
　Witham Field
　561-287-6636
　One mile southeast of Stuart

Miami
　Miami International
　305-876-7077
　Five miles northwest of Miami

Marathon
　Marathon Airport
　305-743-2155
　In Marathon at Mile Marker 52

Key West
　Key West International Airport
　305-296-7223
　Southeast corner of the island

East Central

Daytona Beach
　Daytona Beach International Airport
　904-248-8030
　In Daytona Beach

Melbourne
　Melbourne International Airport
　407-723-6227
　In Melbourne

St. Lucie
　St. Lucie International Airport
　561-468-1732
　Three miles northwest of Fort Pierce

Vero Beach
Vero Beach Municipal Airport
561-567-4526
One mile northwest of Vero
Beach

Northeast

Gainesville
Gainesville Municipal Airport
352-373-0249
Four miles northeast of
Gainesville

Jacksonville
Jacksonville International Airport
904-741-2000
Ten miles north of Jacksonville

Southwest

Punta Gorda
Charlotte County Airport
941-639-1101
Three miles southeast of Punta
Gorda

Naples
Naples Municipal Airport
941-643-6785
Two miles northeast of Naples

Fort Myers
Southwest Florida International
Airport
941-768-1000
Ten miles southeast of Fort
Myers

West Central

Brooksville
Hernando County Airport

352-799-7275
Forty miles north of Tampa

Tampa
Tampa International Airport
813-870-8700
Five miles west of downtown
Tampa

St. Petersburg-Clearwater
St. Petersburg-Clearwater
International Airport
727-531-1451
Seven miles southeast of
Clearwater

Sarasota
Sarasota-Bradenton International
Airport
941-359-5200
Three miles north of Sarasota

Venice
Municipal Airport
941-485-9293
Half-mile south of Venice

The Panhandle

Destin
Okaloosa County Air Terminal
850-651-7160
One mile east of Destin

Panama City
Panama City-Bay County
International Airport
850-763-6751
Four miles northwest of Panama
City

Pensacola
Pensacola Regional Airport
850-435-1746
Three miles northeast of
Pensacola

Tallahassee
Tallahassee Regional Airport
850-891-7800
Five miles southwest of
Tallahassee

Williston
Williston Regional Airport
352-528-4900
One mile southwest of Williston

Central

Orlando
Orlando International Airport
407-825-2001
Seven miles south of Orlando

Orlando-Sanford
Orlando-Sanford Airport
407-322-7771
Two miles east of Sanford

Sebring
Sebring Regional Airport
941-655-6444
Seven miles southeast of Sebring

Airport Codes

Here's a list of major Florida airports and their codes.
Naples Municipal (APF)

Daytona Beach International
(DAB)

Key West International (EYW)

Fort Lauderdale Executive (FXE)

Fort Lauderdale-Hollywood
International (FLL)

Fort Myers-Page Field (FMY)

Fort Myers-Southwest Florida
International (RSW)

Fort Walton Beach (VSP)

Gainesville Regional (GNV)

Jacksonville International (JAX)

Marathon (MTH)

Miami International (MIA)

Miami-Kendall Executive (TMB)

Melbourne International (MLB)

Orlando Executive (ORL)

Orlando International (MCO)

Pensacola Regional (PNS)

St. Petersburg-Clearwater
International (PIE)

Sarasota-Bradenton International
(SRQ)

Tallahassee Regional (TLH)

Tampa International (TPA)

Vero Beach (VRB)

West Palm Beach International
(PBI)

Scanning the Airways
Scanning is a popular Florida pastime. Kids do it, retirees do it, and anyone can do it. With a programmable scanner, you can dial in the frequencies used by police, fire departments, airports, city services, and others, and listen in on what's going on. It's completely legal; all you need is the equipment and the information on what frequencies to scan. Here are

the latest frequencies used at Florida's major airports by aircraft taking off and landing, control towers, and ground crews. You'll hear a lot of roger's and out's if you listen to these frequencies. ATIS is the terminal information frequency, and UNICOM is the universal communications frequency.

Craig Municipal
  Airport (Jacksonville)
UNICOM: 122.95
ATIS: 125.4
Ground: 121.8
Tower: 132.1, 242.7
Approach: 120.75
Departure: 118.0,
120.75

Fort Lauderdale-
  Hollywood
  International Airport
UNICOM: 122.95
ATIS: 135.0
Ground: 121.4, 121.7
Tower: 119.3, 257.8,
120.2
Approach: 118.1,
128.6, 133.775
Fort Lauderdale
Approach: 119.3,
120.2
Miami Departure:
119.7, 126.05, 128.6
Clearance Delivery:
128.4, 119.3, 119.7,
120.2, 128.6,
133.775, 128.4

Fort Lauderdale
Executive Airport
UNICOM: 122.95
ATIS: 119.85
Ground: 121.75
Tower: 120.9, 239.3
Miami Approach:
119.7
Miami Departure:
119.7
Clearance Delivery:
127.95

Jacksonville
International Airport
UNICOM: 122.95
ATIS: 125.85
Ground: 121.9, 348.6
Tower: 118.3, 317.7
Approach: 118.0,
118.6, 119.0, 120.75,
121.3, 123.8, 124.4,
124.9, 127.0, 284.8,
319.9, 322.4, 335.6,
347.8, 351.8, 379.9
Departure: 118.0,
118.6, 119.0, 120.75,
121.3, 123.8, 124.4,
124.9, 127.0, 284.8,
319.9, 322.4, 335.6,
347.8, 351.8, 379.9
Pre-Taxi Clearance:
118.0, 118.6, 119.0,
120.75, 121.3, 123.8,
124.4, 124.9, 127.0,
284.8, 319.9, 322.4,
335.6, 347.8, 351.8,
379.9
Emergency: 121.5,

243.0

Key West International
Airport
UNICOM: 122.95
Ground: 121.9
[0700-2100]
Tower: 118.2, 257.8
Key West Navy Base
Approach: 124.45
Key West Navy Base
Departure: 124.45
Clearance: 121.9,
121.5, 243.0

Miami International
Airport
UNICOM 123.0
ATIS: 119.15
Ground: 121.8,
127.5, 348.6
Tower: 118.3, 123.9,
256.9
Approach: 120.5,
124.85, 322.3, 379.9,
125.75, 319.9
Miami Departure:
119.45, 120.5,
124.85, 125.5, 301.5,
354.1, 379.9

Miami Heliport
  UNICOM: 123.05

Naples Municipal
Airport
UNICOM: 123.0
ATIS: 134.225
Ground: 121.6
Tower: 128.5
Fort Myers
Approach: 119.75
Fort Myers
Departure: 119.75

Clearance: 118.0,
121.6

*St. Petersburg-
Clearwater Airport*
UNICOM: 122.95
ATIS: 134.5
Ground: 121.9, 348.6
Tower: 118.3, 257.8,
128.4
Tampa Approach:
125.3
Tampa Delivery:
125.3
Clearance Delivery:
120.6, 350.2

*Orlando International
Airport*
UNICOM: 122.95
ATIS: 121.25
Ground: 121.8
Tower Approach:
275.8, 118.45, 124.3,
253.5, 288.15,
118.45, 288.15,
119.4, 120.15, 121.1,
124.8, 135.3, 259.1,

284.7, 307.0, 351.9,
397.85, 123.85,
125.55, 134.05,
338.2, 339.8, 385.65
Departure: 119.4,
120.15, 121.1, 124.8,
135.3, 259.1, 284.7,
307.0, 351.9, 397.85,
Clearance: 134.7,
341.7, 120.15, 121.1,
135.3, 259.1, 284.7,
351.9, 397.850
Emergency: 121.5,
243.0, 124.8, 307.0

*Pensacola International
Airport*
UNICOM: 122.95
ATIS: 121.25
Ground: 121.9, 348.6
Tower: 119.9, 257.8
Approach: 118.6,
119.0 120.0, 286.0,
343.65, 398.95
Departure: 118.6,
119.0, 120.05, 286.0,
343.65, 398.95, 251-
339

Clearance: 121.9,
348.6, 118.6, 120.05,
343.65, 398.95,
119.0, 286.0, 121.5,
243.0, 121.9, 348.6
*Tampa International
Airport*
UNICOM: 122.95
ATIS: 126.45,
128.475
Ground: 121.7,
269.4, 121.35
Tower: 119.5, 269.4,
119.05
Approach: 118.15,
118.8, 119.65, 269.1,
319.8, 362.3,
Departure: 118.15,
118.8, 119.65, 269.1,
319.8, 362.3
Clearance Delivery:
133.6, 119.65, 19.9,
125.3, 290.3, 362.3,
363.8
Emergency: 121.5,
243.0
Final: 118.5

Emergency Landings
If you're flying around lost, looking for some place to touch down, here are some locations that will take anyone in an emergency. Some are rural airports; others, just grassy fields. Call them from the cockpit on your cellular phone, and watch out for trees and cows.

Prior to filing a flight plan, pilots in Florida should call 800-WX-BRIEF to get information on weather conditions around the country.

Southeast Florida
  Key Largo: The Ocean Reef Club 305-367-3690
  Key West: Sugar Loaf Shores 305-745-2217
  Palm Beach: Garden PGA National Heliport 561-627-2800

East Central Florida
  Daytona Beach: Spruce Creek 904-760 5884 or 756-6125

Fort Pierce: Treasure Coast Airpark 561-466 3536
Geneva: Sutherland Strip 407-349-5814
New Port Richey: Hidden Lake 813-842-6805
Scottsmoor: Tradewinds Aerodrome 407-258-9515
Sebastian: Fulton Springs 561-723-5699
Vero Beach: Marsh Airstrip 561-562-9176

Northeast Florida
Gainesville: Capra Farms Blue Diamond Ranch 352-332 9700
Hastings: Airpark 904-692-5951
Hastings: Hutson Airfield 904-694-2224
Jacksonville: Heliport 904-393-25l7
Micanopy: Paines Prairie Heliport 352-793-7190
Oak Hill: Dalphonse Ranch 904-761-3231
Orange Park: Doctors Lake Springs 904-264-0102
St. Augustine: Sunshine Farms 904-824-0238

Southwest Florida
Fort Myers: Morning Star South 941-283-8470
Immokalee: Big Cypress Airfield 941-983-7677
Labelle: Southwest Citrus 941-615-4005
Miles City: Calusa Ranch 305-443-5162
Naples: Wing South Airpark 941-775-3693

West Central Florida
Port Charlotte: Lake Suey Estates 941-629-5007
St. Petersburg: Bay Medical Center Heliport 727-893-6010

Florida's Panhandle
Altha: Cattle Creek Ranch 904-762-3334
Baker: Sky Ranch 904-537-5000
Blountstown: Airpark 850-674-5127
Bonifay 850-547-2344
Branford: Flints Flying Ranch 904-935-3846
Greenville: Ranch 904-948-4999
Jay: Douglas Flying Service 904-675-3188
Lake City: Cannon Creek 904-752-1957
Lake City: Delta 904-752 0428
Lee: Flying G Ranch 904-971-5031
Live Oak: Florida Sheriffs Boys Ranch 904-842-5501
Madison: Rockyford 904-973-2156
Mayor O Ranch 904-294-1471
McAlpin: Lime River 904-963-4545
McAlpin: Buckner 904-935-2711

Milton: JZZ Ranch 850-994-7053
Monticello: Jefferson Landings 850-997-3063
Munson: Black Water Airfield 904-9574201
Panama City: Coastal Helicopter Charter 850-769-6117
Panama City: Coastal Helicopters (East) Heliport 850-769-6117

Central Florida
Belleview: Jordan Airport 352-288-6060
DeLand: Bradshaw Farm 904-357 4413
Fruitland Park: Flying Palomino Ranch 352-787 9225
Groveland: Klinger Aero 352-429-2250
Groveland: Seminole Lake Gliderport 352-394 5450
Haines City: Oak Harbor 941-956-1341
Kissimmee: 407-331-5155
Kissimmee: Cole's Springs 407-846-6831
Lake Placid: Kings Port 941-465-2067
Lake Placid: Lakes 941-465 0424
Ocala: Eagles Nest Inc. Heliport 352-237-6730
Ocala: Leeward Air Ranch 352-245 7007
Okeechobee: River Oak Acres 941-763-0044
Okeechobee: Sunniland Ranch 941-467-7777
Okeechobee: Mulgrew Ranch 941-763-2478
Oklawaha: Woods and Lakes Airpark 352-625-3202
Orlando: Y-Bolt Ranch 407-568-2257
Orlando: Yelvington 407-423-7625
Prairie Lake: Mooring Facility 407-331-5655
Sanford: Springs 407-321-3909
Tavares: Lake Eustis Springs 352-742 7729
Umatilla: Fly'n R Ranch 904-821-2855
Wellborn: 904-755-5596
Wimauma: Air Park 813-633-1118
Zellwood: Spotter 407-889-2071

FLORIDA BEACHES

Weather permitting, hanging out on the beach is America's number one outdoor recreational activity in every area of the United States except Alaska and the Rocky Mountain states. A recent study by the Laboratory for Coastal Research at the University of Maryland cited Hawaii and Florida as having the best beaches in the United States, so if you're Florida-bound or fortunate enough to live in Florida, you're in luck.

With 1,600 miles of coastline bordering the Atlantic Ocean and the Gulf of Mexico, Florida has more named beaches than any other state. From Fernandina Beach near Jacksonville south to Miami, then west to Naples and north to the Panhandle, you can follow the coastline and beach-hop your way around the state.

A beach study by the University of Maryland several years ago concluded that the north-west Panhandle had the most pristine beaches in the country and, though battered slightly by recent hurricanes, they still rate high on the list.

Because tourism is big business in Florida and different people require different things from beaches, the atmosphere ranges from tranquil and low-key (Sanibel and Captiva) to crowded and alive with action (Daytona Beach and Panama City Beach). You can bask in the sun or splash in the surf or hop aboard a roller coaster and go for a ride.

Along the Gulf Coast, the flattest and lowest coastline in the United States, the beaches are some of the best in the country because of the white sand and warm, clean Gulf waters. All of the top ten–rated Florida beaches in the University of Maryland study stretch from Panama

City Beach to Pensacola. The beaches on Panama City Beach are wide, backed by high-rise hotels that stretch from one end of the beach to the other. Despite the development, the beaches remain pristine. This area is where Hilton hotels get their supply of sand for ashtrays in their hotel lobbies.

Just west of Panama City Beach, Gulf Islands Seashore on Santa Rosa Island offers some of the clearest swimming waters in the state. At Fort Walton Beach and Destin, shell searching is popular. Even when beaches have been swept bare by violent weather, you can still find cockles, clams, and striped cowries. A bit farther out, a reef of limestone captures thousands of beach-bound seashells, some up to 20 inches in length, including horse conchs.

Some argue that the best beaches are in areas maintained by the state— areas that restrict growth and commercialism. This may be true, but most visitors to Florida require more than just bare-bones beaches. The majority of beaches of interest to vacationers offer accommodations, an assortment of dining-out spots, and entertainment. These facilities can be a block or two away or right on the water's edge.

Traveling east and then south from the Panhandle, the beaching opportunities are sparse until you reach Clearwater and St. Petersburg. The Pinellas Suncoast includes 28 miles of beaches along the Gulf of Mexico in an area encompassing a group of vacationing communities like Clearwater Beach, Dunedin, Indian Rocks Beach, Madeira Beach, St. Petersburg Beach, Indian Rocks Beach, and other lesser-known beaches. The weather in this area of the state provides for year-round boating and fishing, but swimming in the winter might be reserved only for the brave.

South of St. Petersburg and Clearwater is the Sarasota area, laced with public beaches surrounding islands accessible by bridges. Here you'll find Lido Key, Siesta Key, Longboat Key, and Casey Key, all stretched out along a 35-mile stretch in Sarasota County. At the far north end of Lido Beach is a half mile of white sand surrounded by towering Australian

pines. During the week, the area is pleasantly uncrowded. Lifeguards are on duty during the peak season. The widest and most popular beach in the area is Siesta Public Beach, a 40-acre facility. The University of Maryland study chose this beach as having the whitest and most powdery sand in the world, beating 29 other entries, including the Bahamas and Grand Cayman. Crescent Beach, famous for its pristine quartz sand and Point of Rocks area, is popular with snorkelers. The most popular getaway in the area is Palmer Point on the south end of Siesta Key, with 24 acres of sloping beach and unspoiled waterfront near the former Midnight Pass.

The Lee Island coast in the southwest is made up of Sanibel and Captiva Islands, Fort Myers Beach on Estero Island, and the beaches on Gasparilla Island. Beachcombing visitors usually head for the barrier islands of Captiva and Sanibel. The beaches here are a sheller's paradise, with a steady input of shells and marine life from the constantly shifting tides. Each year, the community holds a Shell

Fair that draws serious shellers from around the world. Some of the more popular public beaches in this area are at the Sanibel Lighthouse area on Bowman's Beach and at Blind Pass, where Sanibel and Captiva meet. The tourist-oriented activity in this area is low-key. The main features are beach-side accommodations and good restaurants and shops.

If you round the bend of southwest Florida, then head east and south past the Everglades, you'll reach the Florida Keys. Surprisingly, the beaches here are limited to those at state parks and a few short stretches between Key Largo and Key West. In the 1950s, when the Keys were going through a rapid growth period, many of the beaches were man-made. One man-made beach at Key Colony Beach is the result of tons of sand reclaimed from the open waters. The best beach in the Keys is at Bahia Honda State Park in the mid Keys just south of Marathon. Further south in Key West, the best beaches are behind some of the more luxurious hotels and at Smathers Beach.

North of the Keys along the southeast coastline is Miami Beach, the state's most well-known beach. It's the engineering product of a 1970s' restoration program that dumped more than ten million cubic yards of sand along an eight-mile coastline, creating an artificial beach that lured vacationers to the southeastern corner of the state. Nearby Miami boasts thousands of hotels, resorts, and restaurants. The hotels and restaurants along Miami Beach's streets bordering the beach are in an Art Deco restoration program that is bringing life to an area that once was given up for dead. Overall, the area is still one of the most popular destinations in Florida.

Further north, Fort Lauderdale Beach vies with Miami Beach for "most popular" beach. The sands stretch along a two-mile strip bordering Highway A1A. The birthplace of Florida's Spring Break mania, it's slowly being edged out by Daytona Beach and Panama City Beach as the places to go when school is out. Every Fourth of July, visitors build elaborate sand castles along Fort Lauderdale's beach. The area—along with Hollywood and Hallandale—is in a constant state of beach restoration, with 100 to 250 feet of beach being added at a cost of $9.4 million to date.

In the Greater Fort Lauderdale area, Hollywood's six miles of beaches are dotted with quaint motels and an eclectic collection of shops and restaurants. Dania Beach is not the largest in Broward County, but it's very popular with visitors. Frequently mentioned as one of the state's best southern beaches, the 244-acre area offers diversions both on and off the sand.

Further north, the Palm Beach area is made up of a 47-mile stretch of shoreline from Jupiter to Boca Raton. Here you'll find Highland Beach, Delray Beach, Palm Beach, Juno Beach, and other beaches that stretch along the Atlantic Ocean off Highway A1A. Cocoa Beach in Brevard County has been called the Small Wave Surfing Capital of the World, as

well as one of the best surfing locations on the east coast. An annual surfing contest is held at Canaveral Pier, drawing surfers from around the
world. Public beaches stretch for 12 miles.

In 1959, the hot rods that roared across the beaches of Daytona Beach
and Ormond Beach to the north moved to the Daytona International
Speedway—and beachside residents sighed with relief. Today, the beach is
open to vehicular traffic and while we're not aware of any sunbathers being
run over, the possibility exists, even though the parking lot line is well back
from the water line.

North of Daytona Beach, the beaches
around Jacksonville (located 12 miles from
the downtown area) include Jacksonville,
Atlantic, Neptune, and Ponte Vedra Beaches.
They all stretch along Highway A1A, also
known as the Buccaneer Trail. Kathryn
Abbey Hanna Park is one of the more
remote beaches in the area, 60 acres with
nary an attraction in sight and a mile and a
half of sand running along the Atlantic.
Fernandina Beach, just north of
Jacksonville, is a 300-year-old Florida town
listed on the National Register of Historic
Places. A half hour south of Jacksonville is
St. Augustine Beach. Just outside St.
Augustine, America's oldest city, there are 43
miles of beaches in St. Johns County,
including Ponte Vedra, Vilano, St. Augustine,
Butler, and Crescent Beaches.

SAND SOUNDS

Dry sand produces a kind
of dull, crunchy sound
while wet sand has a
crisper, louder sound. The
reason? Dry sand moves laterally while wet sand tends to
stick together. When someone
steps on wet sand, the grains
are so tightly packed together that they squeak as they're
separated by the weight of a
foot. That friction accounts
for the sound.

No matter where you go in Florida, you're no more than 65 miles from
the Gulf or the Atlantic, so explore, and when you find the beach that fits
your leisure style, put it at the top of your list.

HOW TO GET UNSTUCK FROM THE SAND

There are Florida beaches where you can drive your car right up to
the water's edge and (pick one) picnic, get your tires wet, or watch
the boats and the world go by. But sand is soft, cars are heavy, and
rarely do the two of them mix. If you get stuck, try these tips. If they don't
work before the tide starts coming in, abandon ship and call a tow truck.

Put the car in drive and slowly move forward, then shift into reverse,
alternating until the car is rocking back and forth. Keep your wheels
straight ahead. If you can increase the rocking back and forth, you should
roll right out of the sand. If people are standing around watching your
plight, ask them to help you rock the car. You can let some air out of the
tires to increase the traction. If you can find some wood or hard debris to

put under the tires, you can increase traction and maybe roll right out of the sand.

EARLY FLORIDA CEMETERIES

During the mid 1880s, slaves in rural areas were usually buried on the plantations and farms where they worked. Generally, slave burials took place in segregated graveyards near the family graveyards of the white owners. Markers placed at the graves of slaves were generally ephemeral in nature, such as field stones, wooden stakes or crosses, or grave goods which have long since deteriorated or been scattered and lost. Today, rectangular grave-shaped depressions in the earth are the only remaining evidence of slave graveyards at most former plantation sites.

In urban areas, slaves and free people of color were commonly buried in segregated sections of public burying grounds or in cemeteries separate from those for white burials. This practice reflected the social structure of the time. In contrast, the burying grounds of the Spanish colonial towns of Pensacola and St. Augustine were probably not sharply segregated until after U.S. acquisition of the Florida Territory from Spain in 1821, because Spanish authorities allowed free people of color some degree of equality.

After Emancipation in 1865, through the Reconstruction period, and well into the twentieth century, most African Americans living in rural areas were buried in church-yards or in family or otherwise privately owned graveyards. In urban areas, they continued to be buried in segregated cemeteries.

In Tallahassee, a plan to establish a separate cemetery exclusively for African American burials was apparently initiated in 1936. In September of that year, City Ordinance 272 established an official cemetery and public burying ground, Evergreen Cemetery, for African Americans of the city of Tallahassee. Members of Tallahassee's African American community registered opposition to the site. At a city commission meeting in October 1936, a delegation of African-American citizens objected to the establishment of Evergreen Cemetery. The Commission took the objections of the delegation under advisement. Two weeks later, commission members said they had talked to those who had objected and said all but one of the Committee were in favor of the Evergreen Cemetery going ahead as planned. The single objector was J.R.D. Laster, an African-American undertaker.

Political Cemeteries

Cemeteries have always been fascinating places to some people. Not everything about cemeteries is morbid. A cemetery is an open-air reference library, a statuary park, a gallery of architectural styles, a carefully constructed model landscape, a repository of community memory, and a complex cultural artifact. Cemeteries may change or even be uprooted, but they are usually much more stable than their surroundings and can serve as a historic window to the past. Every cemetery or graveyard is different, the differences reflecting varieties of landscape, the history of the people in the area, politics, economics, transportation, climate, and attitudes toward nature—and death.

Old elite cemeteries often are the most interesting to visit. Considering the power and resources of those who organized and maintained the burial ground over the years, you'll find the best materials, the gaudiest ornaments, the most extensive and successful landscape design, and the fanciest mausoleums. Usually, they're relatively well-preserved. If they're not preserved, important historic and community resources are lost to

neglect and vandalism.

If you are interested in doing research on a specific cemetery, the best place is at the cemetery's own office. Here you'll find the source of most records. If there isn't an office located at the cemetery grounds, it may be located elsewhere in town. The state may have interesting records of the original incorporation and annual reports. You can also check old U.S. Geological Survey maps and aerial photos, Sanborn insurance maps, local libraries, and historical societies. In many places, records and inscriptions were recorded and typed for local libraries, deeds, and land records. This information might be available at county courthouses, local funeral homes, and monument companies. Don't forget to check microfilmed newspapers published around the dates of death on interesting headstones for

obituaries.

Almost every state has some kind of biographical compilation of its major elected officials, including members of the state legislature. Ask at the reference desk of the state library or at the state historical society. It is also typical for state legislatures to pass memorial resolutions to observe the death of a former member, and these can contain valuable information.

If you have a computer with an Internet connection, you can go online to discover what's going on politically and historically at Florida cemeteries. For a geographical index to cemeteries around the state, listed by county, and information on who in Florida politics is buried where, go to http://www.pot/fos.com/tpg/geo/fl/kmindex.html.

When visiting the cemeteries of Florida, you can usually get an up-close introduction to and reminder of who lived here, who had money and who didn't (judging by the size of the tombstone), who suffered tragedies such as losing children, and who made contributions to local society. Cemeteries are peaceful places, parklike and green year-round. Looking for the oldest gravestone is an interesting excuse to stop alongside the road and get some exercise.

Gravestone Rubbings

When you find an interesting stone, try gravestone rubbing. All you need is a sheet of paper (tissue paper, paper from an artist's pad, blank newsprint paper, or any thin paper) and a crayon. Place the paper over the area you want to imprint. Remove the paper wrapping from a crayon and, holding the crayon lengthwise, rub lightly over the paper. You'll get an imprint of the engraving on the stone.

Planning Ahead

If you're shopping around in advance for your final resting place, there's a company in Florida that can give you information on purchasing new and used plots, mausoleum and ground crypts, cremation niches, caskets, vaults, urns, and other funeral-related paraphernalia. The International Burial Exchange maintains a database of people who want to sell their plots or crypts and acts as an international burial exchange to put owners and buyers in touch with each other. The listings are by location. For further information, contact The International Burial Exchange (1617 South Lakeview Terrace, Sebring 33870) or go to http://www.burielexchange.com.

BUYING A HOME—THE NO-MONEY-DOWN SOLUTION

Thinking of moving to Florida? There are tens of thousands of homes for sale, ranging from one-bedroom/one-bath cottages to homes with six bedrooms, six baths, an indoor swimming pool, and a boat dock. Most home buyers today buy a home with an average of 10 percent down, while 10 years ago, most home buyers put 20 percent down. Buyers who can't come up with a large down payment look for alternatives—and the ultimate alternative is no money down. How do you buy a house with no money down?

If the seller owns the home, the seller can offer owner financing with little or no money down. This is common in Florida when the seller doesn't want to pay a real estate commission and is more interested in a monthly income than in-hand cash. Sales like this usually include some kind of one-time balloon payment of the balance five or ten years later. By that time, the buyer should have enough equity in the home to borrow against it and pay off the balloon payment.

Trading for the down payment isn't common, but it is done. Say you have a car worth $6,000 or a boat worth $10,000 or an empty lot worth $15,000 in an area the seller is interested in. You offer to give the seller the car, boat, or lot (or all three) as the down payment, and have the seller or a bank carry the rest of the mortgage.

You can take over the payments on an existing mortgage. Many sellers have little or no equity in their home and are trying to get out of the debt. Defaulting would ruin their credit rating, so they're looking for someone to take on the debt. If they have little or no equity in the home, no cash changes hands.

You can borrow money from relatives for a down payment and if they want collateral, you can offer them a percentage of the home. Example: you borrow $10,000 from your parents for the down payment of a $100,000 home, so they own 10 percent. If you sell the home later, they get their money back and if there's a profit, they also get 10 percent of that profit. Put everything in writing. Once you've made a few years of payments, you can refinance, pay the money back, and the home is 100 percent yours.

If you have a steady income and a good credit rating, check with the Federal Housing Authority (FHA) or the Veterans Administration (VA) or Fannie Mae. Some offer no-money-down deals if you qualify.

There are also lease-to-buy arrangements. You move in, pay rent for a specific period of time, and the seller agrees to put a percentage of the rent paid toward the down payment. If a seller is really desperate to sell, that

INCOME FACTS

According to the Florida Department of Labor's 1996 statistics, the average personal income statewide is about $21,300, compared with the U.S. average of $26,900. The median household income is $32,264, down a few thousand dollars from five years ago but near the U.S. average. Average teachers' salaries in Florida are $32,500, compared to $36,800 nationwide. Fourteen percent of Florida residents live below the poverty level.

percentage of the rent could be as much as 100 percent. If you make any improvements, they should be credited toward the purchase price.

HOW TO WRITE AND SELL A BOOK ABOUT FLORIDA

If you've ever thought of becoming a Florida writer, here are simple steps to take. First, come up with an idea with Florida as the subject. Then write a one-page letter and send it to publishers who specialize in Florida subjects. The ultimate writer's guide to publishers is Writer's Market, published by F&W Publications, 1507 Dana Avenue, Cincinnati, Ohio 45207. It's available as a book or on CD-ROM. Check your local library.

Explain why there's a need for such a book and why you're qualified to write it. If publishers are interested, they'll get back to you for more information. While you're waiting for a positive reply, work on improving your presentation. If they request more information, send them a table of contents and one or two sample chapters.

In most cases, you don't have to write the entire book until you find someone interested. If they like your idea, you'll get a contract and you're on your way to becoming a published author. You'll receive a royalty (usually five to ten percent of net sales) on each copy sold.

WATCH YOUR STEP!

The Florida Department of Labor and Employment Security reports that the two major causes of injury to workers in Florida are being struck by objects and falling. More than half of the more than 180,000 nonfatal injuries in Florida during the last reporting period were due to those causes. Overexertion, primarily from lifting objects, leads all other injury categories. Sprains and strains are the leading cause of lost work hours, accounting for almost 30 percent of all reported cases.

Field workers, mainly in the sugar industry, ranked first in the rate of injuries due to being struck by an object. Motion picture theaters led all other businesses in the rate of injuries due to workers falling.

As you grow older, you're more likely to be more seriously injured on the job. Workers between the ages of 16 and 35 averaged 5 lost work days compared to 11 days for those 55 years and older.

MOTOR VEHICLE ACCIDENTS

Last year, more than 20 million automobile accidents were reported to the National Safety Council. So what do you do if you're involved in an automobile accident? Here are some tips:

Try to remain calm. Pull completely off the road and stop. Turn on your flashers. If you're blocking a street and have flares or reflective signs, place them in front and to the rear of the vehicle. Call the police, even if there are no injuries and only minor damages. While you have the police on the phone, let them know if medical assistance is required or if any of the vehicles might require towing.

Don't discuss the accident with the other person. Do not agree to any settlement at the scene. Just provide them with your driver's license number, information on the car, and your insurance company's name and the policy number. Give them your telephone number. Get the same information from them.

See if you can find any witnesses. Get their names and telephone numbers. Remember how the accident happened. Write down the time, date, and road conditions, and if possible draw a map showing street identifications, directions, etc. Write down the damage to the cars and passengers. Then contact your insurance company.

GET A JOB!

L ooking for a good government job? Working for state and local governments and government agencies has its advantages. You get health benefits, you probably won't be relocated out of state, and you get to know almost everybody in town. Unless you're the tax collector, you can probably retire some years later with a good reputation. If you're interested, call any of these offices and ask them how you go about applying for a job. If the city you're looking for is not listed here, consult a telephone directory or call directory assistance and ask for the main number of the local county, city, or town government office.

City and County Agencies

Brevard County Government in Titusville	407-633-2032
City of Altamonte Springs	407-263-3747
City of Apopka	407-889-1721
City of Casselberry	407-263-3998
City of Daytona Beach	904-258-3167
City of Longwood	407-260-3474
City of Maitland	407-539-6263
City of Melbourne	407-729-9675
City of Orlando	407-246-2178
City of Oviedo	407-977-6007
City of Sanford	407-330-5676
Lake County Government in Mount Dora	904-343-5627
Oceola County Government in Kissimmee	407-847-1444
Orange County Government in Orlando	407-836-5660
Orange County Sheriff in Orlando	407-836-4071
Orlando Police Department in Orlando	407-246-2473
Seminole County Government in Sanford	407-330-9540
Seminole County Sheriff in Sanford	407-330-6687
Volusia County Government in Deland	904-736-5921

State Agencies

Florida Department of Labor and Employment Security
  in Tallahassee   904-488-5627
Florida Department of Agriculture and Consumer Services
  in Tallahassee   904-487-2474
Florida Department of Business Regulation
  in Tallahassee   904-488-4874
Florida Department of Commerce
  in Tallahassee   904-488-0869
Florida Department of Corrections Orlando Region
  in Orlando   407-245-0064
Florida Department of Education
  in Tallahassee   904-487-2367
Florida Department of Environmental Protection
  in Tallahassee   904-487-0436
Florida Department of Game and Fresh Water Fish
  in Tallahassee   904-488-5805
Florida Department of Highway Safety and Motor Vehicles
  in Tallahassee   904-487-3669
Florida Department of Insurance
  in Tallahassee   904-487-2644
Florida Department of Law Enforcement
  in Tallahassee   904-488-0797
Florida Department of State
  in Tallahassee   904-488-1179
Florida Lottery   904-487-7731

Go to http://www.homefair.com/homefair/cmr/salcalc.html on the Internet for a salary comparison for different cities and states around the country. Just select the origin and destination cities to find out the salary you would need in different cities to maintain your current standard of living. The answers are based on cost-of-living indexes for hundreds of Florida, United States, and international cities.

HOW TO BECOME A BOAT CAPTAIN

There are about 11,654 titles for jobs you can have in Florida. They range from grocery bagger in a supermarket to bank president. Somewhere in the middle is boat captain, cruising the open waters of the Gulf of Mexico and Atlantic Ocean in a charter boat.

To become a boat captain for hire, you need either an operator's license (for six or fewer passengers) or a master's license (to operate inspected vessels with more than six passengers—vessels like ferries and other large boats). Most people settle for the less-demanding operator's license.

To get a license, you must file an application with the Coast Guard

Regional Exam Center (51 Southwest First Avenue, Miami, 305-536-6548). You must have at least 360 days of experience operating boats and be at least 18 years old for an operator's license or 19 years old for the master's license. You must pass a physical exam and an eye exam that includes testing for color blindness to make sure you can see the difference between colored markers. You must pass a drug test and a written test, be fingerprinted, and have a current first aid and CPR certificate.

Before you can take the written test, you must file an application along with the results of the physical and drug tests. Once you're approved, they send you a letter or card telling you where to call to schedule your test.

The test is in four sections: rules, deck general and safety, general navigation, and chart navigation. The test is usually an all-day affair, with the rules, deck, and general navigation taking half the time and the chart navigation the rest. About 25 percent of applicants who are self-taught pass on their first try. If you fail one portion of the test, you can take that test again during the next 90 days without having to take the entire test again. If you do not pass within 90 days or 3 attempts, you must take the entire test again. There are several schools around the state that prepare you for the exam. The local Coast Guard office should be able to point you in the right direction.

THE FLORIDA LAND BOOM

During the early land boom, John Martin, three-time mayor of Jacksonville, was elected to serve as governor on a platform of expansive construction and development. The Florida Legislature in 1924 passed laws prohibiting state income and inheritance taxes, moves designed to convince wealthy visitors to make Florida their permanent residence. Rural politicians were even willing to concede economic power to big cities like Miami and St. Petersburg to promote tourist development.

Florida was the place for high-stakes speculation, but not all projects gained support. Cornelius Vanderbilt Jr., son of the railroad tycoon, discovered Floridians weren't interested in a railroad from Miami to Fort Myers. People preferred land closer to the ocean. To attract investors, the rural, conservative Florida Legislature liberalized rules for the development of horse and dog racing, providing for the rural counties to get a disproportionate share. That was hardly a concern to booming Miami, whose vices included illegal casinos and drinking parlors.

If the Vanderbilts and the railroad barons dominated the pre-1920 years, the land developers dominated the 1920s' land boom. They didn't just design developments: they created entire cities. The architects and engineers did more than build houses: They created a way of life that became known throughout the world as "the Florida lifestyle."

The architectural style tended to be Mediterranean Revival, since Florida was quickly replacing places like for Southern California and the European Riviera as a desirable place to live. Architects incorporated Florida's climate and outdoor living into their home designs.

On Davis Island in Tampa Bay, in Temple Terrace outside of Tampa (one of the first golf vacation communities), and on Snell Island in St. Petersburg, access to urban commuting resulted in new housing developments. Further down Florida's west coast, one of the first retirement communities was laid out in Venice, and Barron Collier started Naples and Marco Island as winter resorts. The most spectacular developments occurred in southeast Florida, where Henry Flagler's railroad provided direct access to New York City. Carl Fisher, founder of the Indianapolis Speedway, teamed with developer John Collins to build a causeway to a mangrove island off Miami: They turned Miami Beach into the world's most famous resort address by 1950.

In areas lacking a waterfront, developer Merrick designed Venetian Pool, the largest swimming pool in the nation. He hired William Jennings Bryant to give Biblical lessons to the Midwestern farmers and recruited major sports celebrities to work out in his outdoor facilities. Merrick even started the one thing booming Miami couldn't get from Tallahassee: a college. He started the largest private university in the South, the University of Miami.

A Californian named Joseph W. Young selected an ugly ocean plat north of Miami and turned it into wide-avenued Hollywood, Florida, larger today than Young's original hometown. Less successful but more praised for his activities was architect Addison Mizner. He designed the Boca Raton Hotel (Cloister Hotel) and the town that soon surrounded it. These were just some of the developers who made the name Florida synonymous with palm trees and beaches, wide avenues and golf courses. Southernmost Florida became known as the American Riviera. Writers from around the world made pilgrimages to this fascinating new mecca. Florida was a place to vacation, a place to have fun, a place to make money.

But there was plenty of evidence that the Florida land boom was on swampy ground. *Forbes* magazine warned that Florida land prices were based solely on the expectation of finding a customer, not on any reality of land value. New York bankers, losing money on Florida investments, attacked the entire invest-in-Florida operation as one great sham. By 1925, there were other signs that things were getting bad. Companies were laying off construction and other blue-collar workers while the numbers of realtors and auto mechanics were still increasing. Jacksonville, the state's main entrance from the north, outgrew its facilities but became leery of financing services for people heading further southward.

Yet on the surface, the land boom seemed on track. In 1924, enough lumber arrived in Florida to encircle the equator with an eight-foot boardwalk. But careful city managers were wondering if their towns had overextended their credit to construct roads and sewers for people who would never settle there.

Florida tourism had changed forever from its pre–land boom days, and few groups had a greater impact than "tin-can" tourists, who arrived by automobiles and trucks loaded with tents and food supplies. They were named for the heavy metal cans they carried for extra gasoline and water. Sometimes as many as three families shared an automobile. While they, too, hoped to buy some Florida real estate, their trip to Florida was a vacation. They could not afford the fancy hotels and restaurants built for the Victorian tourist. They didn't play golf or tennis. They wanted to play in the sunshine on the beaches.

As early as 1919, Tampa had a tin-canners club. As the automobile grew in popularity, these clubs became more important to local tourist economies. Towns began to build tourist camps with recreational facilities. Owners along the major highways built small cabins for these tourists. Soon, mobile homes replaced most of the tents.

The influx of motorized tourism convinced Florida's leaders that new roads were needed. The most amazing highway project was the development of a highway across the once impregnable Everglades. Surveyors discovered that the "River of Grass" was no deeper than six feet. In 1915, realtor Captain J. F. Jaudon gained financing for a road—called the

Tamiami Trail—from Miami to Tampa.

Construction crews began to erect gangways of cypress logs to roll the heavy dredges over the swamps. Engineers waded through alligator-infested waters to locate the best roadbed. Sleeping in elevated cabins kept out the snakes and gators but did not protect workers from the terrible heat and bugs. The Seminoles were both amused and angered by this intrusion into their home, despite promises that canoe trails would be bridged.

In 1923, the project was delayed due to lack of funding. Ora E. Chapin, a Fort Myers resident and proponent of the road, led a caravan of Model-T Fords, tractors, and wagons— "Tamiami Trail Blazers"—across the incomplete roadway to convince the public that the project was both feasible and desirable. It took ten laborious days. In April 1928, 13 years after its inception, the 283-mile road was completed. It cost $7 million, a meager sum by today's costs. South Florida's two coasts were connected.

The influx of people prompted an increase in farming, particularly large-scale agriculture along Lake Okeechobee, often called "the Muck Bowl" for its marshy terrain. In the 1920s, canals and dikes were built across the region, diverting much-needed water from the Everglades. This development hurt Florida's Panhandle farmers, already suffering from rising inflation, by lowering farm prices.

Despite the general prosperity of the 1920s for middle-class Americans, the rapid social and economic changes of the decade helped foster rising racism and nativism. The anti-immigration movement fostered the rise of the Ku Klux Klan in Florida. Individual racial incidents led to white mobs attacking African Americans and burning their homes in Perry, Rosewood, and Oconee.

Florida migrant workers came from both the Deep South and the Caribbean. Working for 9 to 15 dollars per week in the tropical sun, they lived in crude company towns, often just a few miles from the glamour of the coastal resorts. Many migrant areas lacked schools and health facilities. They usually did not lack a "jook joint," or tavern and frontier dance hall where music poured out of a coin-operated phonograph. Jooks were usually the only recreational refuge for the migrant worker. It was ironic to drive through the silent blackness of south Florida to discover a noisy, neon shack blaring music that at least temporarily lessened the agony of daily life.

The small farmers of Florida did not benefit from the Florida land boom of the 1920s. Neither did most towns in north Florida unless they were on a major highway. The migration of many young Floridians to urban areas crippled Florida's small towns. In 1925, the inevitable began to occur in the real estate industry. Land prices had reached such a zenith that new customers failed to arrive and old customers began to sell their land. Suddenly, there were only sellers for Florida land.

The larger cities felt the impact first. They had borrowed heavily to finance new road and public service construction and had used sales taxes and land fees to pay their debts. Now the Yankee dollars were vanishing. Caught without customers, many real estate agents folded up business. One clever Pinellas realtor found a way to send his binder boys (couriers who delivered paperwork from client to agent) back up North without personal cost. He contracted with a funeral company that by law had to escort the bodies of deceased retirees to Northern cemeteries. The realtor and funeral director cashed in the two-way tickets for one-way tickets and placed binder boys on the trains as escorts instead of funeral employees.

THE FLOOD AND HURRICANE OF '26

By 1926, Florida's main slogan wasn't "buy land"—it was "don't buy land." The market was so depressed it was crippling the tourist industry. Despite the continued boom in the stock market, people no longer trusted Florida's real estate industry. Land was overpriced, and promised improvements were not made.

As if the land collapse wasn't bad enough, a hurricane hit south Florida in September with winds in excess of 125 miles per hour. Traveling parallel to the Atlantic Ocean, the storm turned west across Palm Beach County into the heart of the muck lands. The migrant workers and small farmers of Lake Okeechobee were asleep. Few had radios. They had no automobiles for a quick escape. As the winds of the hurricane moved counterclockwise across the lake, the south end of the lake dried up. When the storm passed by, a huge tidal wave crashed down on the people of Belle Glade and Moore Haven.

The tidal wave drowned 300 people, and the storm killed another 115 people in Miami. The news of victims drowning in a huge wave 30 miles from the Atlantic Ocean amazed people across the world. The nameless migrants were piled up and cremated to prevent the spread of disease. The hurricane was an unwelcome coup de grâce to the Florida land boom. More than 13,000 homes were destroyed. Major developments were in ruins, many of them unable to recover.

It would take years to rebuild the confidence and spirit of the Florida land boom. When the Great Depression hit Florida, it had a limited impact since many Floridians were already in a weak financial state.

CAN YOU WIN THE LOTTERY THIS WAY?

There are 13,983,816 possible combinations of 6 numbers selected from the pool of 1 through 49. There has never been a

The storm was an unwelcome coup de grâce to the Florida land boom.

Florida Lotto drawing in which all 13.9 million Florida Lotto combinations have been played, but people have thought about it. The closest the Florida Lottery has ever come to having complete coverage of the combinations was in September 1990, when the jackpot was estimated at $100 million. With ticket sales of more than $109 million, there was a 99.59 percent coverage of combinations sold for that drawing, which still left 57,001 combinations of numbers not played.

What if someone bought all the Florida Lotto combinations? To demonstrate the monumental undertaking this would involve, we have compiled a few statistics.

First, the player fills out play slips with all 13.9 million combinations—no small task. It would take one on-line terminal more than 62 weeks to print all combinations—and that's printing 1 ticket every 2 seconds and running the machine from 6 A.M. until midnight. This doesn't take into consideration changing the ticket stock or ribbons.

If you laid these tickets end-to-end, they would span 45,447,402 inches, or 3,787,283.50 feet, or 717.29 miles, a distance stretching from Pensacola to Jacksonville and back again. Then the player would have to check all 13.9 million tickets within the 180 days allowed to claim a prize. One person working 12 hours a day would have to check 10.7 tickets per minute to meet the deadline. If the player were able to sort through the tickets within the 180-day time frame, he or she would have:

* 258 tickets matching five of six winning numbers
* 13,544 tickets matching four of six winning numbers
* 246,802 tickets matching three of six winning numbers

The Florida Lottery—Where Does the Money Go?

When you buy a one dollar Florida Lottery ticket, 50 cents goes to paying prizes, 38 cents goes to the Educational Enhancement Trust Fund, 5 cents goes to the ticket sellers, 4 cents goes to the people who run the Lottery, and 3 cents goes to on-line and instant ticket vendors.

Lottery drawings are held every Saturday at about 11 P.M. You can buy a ticket up to ten minutes before the drawing. If there is no jackpot winner, 67 percent of that drawing's total winning prize pool is rolled over and allocated for the next jackpot prize. Every Sunday, the Lottery announces an estimated jackpot based on the actual cash carried over from the previous drawing plus the cash the Lottery estimates will be generated by sales. The odds of winning the big jackpot are estimated to be 13,983,816 to 1. In the first two years of operation, the Florida Lottery earned about $2.2 billion.

In December 1977, the lottery reached $60 million. If you had the winning ticket, you'd have paid $840,000 in federal income tax and received $2,160,000 a year or $41,538.46 every week for 20 years. If you win the jackpot, your name and the city where you bought the winning ticket are released to the news media. Most lottery experts suggest changing your name and moving out of town.

Astrology, Numerology, and Winning the Jackpot

From the dawn of time, mankind has looked with wonder to the heavens for some sign that there are things out there that can influence our lives, our futures, and our finances.

Many of the major decisions rulers made in the past thousand years were based on the position of the stars and planets. Although many people believe that astrology is just mumbo-jumbo devised by charlatans for the gullible, there are those who sincerely believe that one's destiny, choices, and fate are written in the position of the stars and planets at the time of birth.

In the past 20 years, astrology has made a comeback and picked up many new followers. In the mid 1980s, Wall Street brokers were calling prominent astrologers on the sly to get their predictions on the rise and fall of the stock market. First Ladies Nancy Reagan and Hillary Clinton have consulted astrologers on family, health, and even national matters.

Many serious Lottery players believe that choosing the winning numbers is a combination of birth reference, astrological references, numerology, and pure luck. If you believe, then you can play the numbers that line up with your astrological and numerology destinies and see what happens. If you're a nonbeliever, what have you got to lose by following a system?

For the uninitiated, your astrological horoscope is determined by the position of all of the planets at the moment of your birth or any specific date. Each planet is said to have some effect on events associated with specific dates. If that date is the drawing of the lottery, we have the beginnings of our basic winning predictions. If we also assume that numbers chosen by an astrological and/or numerological system are as good as or better than any numbers chosen at random, then we can say that we have as good a chance of winning with our system as with numbers chosen at random or from some other connection (birth date, children's ages, home address, etc.).

Your Lucky Numbers

The science of numerology has had many believers over the years, and you might want to try your luck. Using the chart below, you can determine your lucky number. Take the letters in your first name or the first name of someone you love and add them together using this table:

1	2	3	4	5	6	7	8	9
A	B	C	D	E	F	G	H	I
J	K	L	M	N	O	P	Q	R
S	T	U	V	W	X	Y	Z	

If your name is Beverly, your numbers are 2+5+4+5+9+3+7=35. Add 3+5 and your lucky number is 8.

Here are some lucky numbers based on your birth date.

Aries	4, 7, 10, 14, 16, 23, 25, 29, 32, 35
Taurus	11, 14, 18, 22, 23, 24, 26, 30, 33, 38
Gemini	2, 5, 8, 16, 22, 24, 31, 38, 39, 45
Cancer	6, 8, 12, 13, 14, 22, 24, 38, 44, 46
Leo	11, 14, 16, 28, 30, 33, 34, 38, 40, 42
Virgo	3, 5, 7, 9, 13, 15, 18, 19, 22, 40
Libra	11, 14, 18, 22, 28, 29, 32, 34, 40, 44
Scorpio	2, 4, 9, 14, 18, 22, 29, 34, 35, 38
Sagittarius	22, 26, 29, 33, 35, 38, 39, 40, 44, 48
Capricorn	12, 16, 18, 19, 20, 23, 26, 27, 29, 30
Aquarius	8, 11, 13, 16, 18, 22, 27, 29, 33, 38
Pisces	9, 24, 27, 29, 30, 31, 33, 35, 40, 42

According to some people, lucky numbers also dictate your personality and values. If your lucky number is:

1—You are focused, with an unswerving drive toward achievement. You are self-reliant and obstinate, and you have few close friends and little interest in friendship. Number One-ers look after themselves and rarely follow other people's advice.

2—You are sweet-natured and tactful with a conciliatory nature. You're happy to play second fiddle, following rather than leading. You tend to be shy and self-conscious, and can irritate others by changing your mind all the time. You may have a dark and sinister private side.

3—You are imaginative, witty, brilliant, versatile, energetic, charming, and lively. You've got everything going for you! You take things lightly and may often appear to succeed without trying, but you need approval from others to give you confidence.

4—You are down-to-earth, calm, steady, industrious, and respectable. You enjoy hard work, and a routine in your life makes you feel safe. Many consider you a pillar of society. You do not like those who appear to be different, and you are prone to outbursts of anger.

5—You are clever, restless, impatient, and fascinated by the unusual and the bizarre. Responsibility is low on your list of needs and being trapped in a rut is an anathema. You like lots of variety in your life and are constantly seeking change.

6—You like harmony and domesticity. You are kindly, even-tempered, affectionate, and idealistic. You make friends easily and keep them for life. You are convivial and love a gossip. No one would call you brainy. You are capable at what you do, but you do not have a flair for business. Because you are happy with your life, some find you smug and self-satisfied.

7—You are the scholar and the great thinker. You have little interest in money or physical comfort. Your powerful intellect makes you appear dreamy, even mystical. Sarcasm is often your tool to put down fools.

8—You are interested in power, money, and materialism. You either succeed or fail, but you do it to extremes. Strong and practical, you are usually a high achiever in business and politics. In an effort to achieve, you can seem cold, selfish, tyrannical, and unscrupulous.

9—High mental and spiritual achievement is your main concern. Essentially, you are a great visionary and idealist with a desire to help others. You can be easily imposed upon, yet you are strong-willed and determined. You have a dread of ugliness and old age and, being a romantic, you are always in and out of love.

FLORIDA WEDDINGS

To be legally married in Florida you need (among other things) a Florida marriage license from any county courthouse in the state. You may need to provide photo identification. Both parties must be 18 years or older, or 16 with parental consent. If you are divorced or widowed, you'll need the date and/or the certificate of death or divorce if requested. There is no waiting period, and no blood test is required.

Looking for a special place to hold that wedding? Chapel by the Sea offers weddings in an island setting in historic Harborwalk in Key West's Old Town. A variety of wedding programs are available, including the Champagne Sunset Sailing Cruise, which includes a two-hour champagne/sunset cruise aboard one of the local catamarans; a wedding ceremony performed onboard; champagne, beer, and wine; tropical flowers for two; and photography service that includes color photos during the trip. For a few dollars more, they'll fly overhead with a plane trailing a banner that reads "I love you!"

If price is no object, investigate the Chapel Romantics Package, which includes the ceremony and press release, tropical flowers, a champagne toast with souvenir glasses, a gourmet tray of snacks (including shrimp), a private charter out into open waters, a wedding cake decorated with fresh flowers, limo service to your favorite restaurant, and an armful of professional photos.

When the ceremony is over, the staff can advise you on the most romantic hotels in town. Similar affairs are available for groups of 100 people. For information, write to Chapel by the Sea Wedding Service, 205 Elizabeth Street, Key West 33040, or call 305-292-5177.

If you want to do your own hotel shopping, call:

I Love Key West	800-733-5397
Key West Motel and Guesthouse Information	888-222-5090
Truman Annex Rentals	888-884-7368
AA Accommodations Resort Condos	800-732-2006

FLORIDA AND THE MOVIES

In 1910, Jacksonville was the first motion picture capital of the United States. The picture industry fled the winters of New Jersey and New York, and movie producers like Kalem, Gaumont, Klutho, and Edison all made films in Duval County. Actors like Oliver Hardy and Lionel Barrymore began their careers in Jacksonville.

But the conservative citizens of the town opposed the sexual themes and the reckless use of public property for automobile chases in the films. Eventually, this restrictiveness chased the film industry to Hollywood.

Although Hollywood, California, is now considered the film-making capital of the United States, Florida's climate and environmental diversity make the state one of the top film-producing locations. Major films and television programs are shot all over the state.

Some films made in and about Florida have become classics (*The Yearling*), but many more (*Honky Tonk Freeway*) have been panned by the critics. Here are the best of the best and the worst of the worst in chronological order.

So-so—*Hell Harbor* (UA, 1930): This was the first major studio film made in Florida. It was the story of Morgan the Pirate and was filmed in Tampa at the Rocky Point area.

Excellent—*The Yearling* (MGM, 1946): Based on the story by Florida's Marjory Kinnan Rawlings and shot in the areas where Rawlings lived—Cross Creek, Hawthorne, and Micanopy—it captures rural life in Florida. The film was nominated for Best Picture and for Best Actor (Gregory Peck) and Best Actress (Jane Wyman).

Excellent—*Twelve O'Clock High* (Fox, 1949): Filmed at Eglin Air Force Base outside Fort Walton Beach and nominated for Best Picture, this is one of the best war films ever made. Dean Jagger won a Best Supporting Actor award, but Gregory Peck was the star of this biography of Major General Frank Armstrong. A majority of Army Air Corps officers were trained in this area of Florida during World War II.

Very good—*Easy To Love* (MGM, 1953): This is the best of Esther Williams' Florida swim films. Producers say it convinced Floridians to buy an inground pool, practice synchronized swimming, and take a trip to Cypress Gardens.

Corny, but good—*Creature from the Black Lagoon* (Universal, 1954): The black lagoon here was Wakulla Springs. This is considered one of the all-time campy horror films of the drive-in theater days.

Excellent—*The Greatest Show on Earth* (Paramount, 1957): Filmed in Sarasota at the then-winter headquarters of the Ringling circus, this film beat out *High Noon* as Best Picture of the Year. Cecil B. DeMille produced a spectacular show that reflected the life of circus people. It starred Betty Hutton, Charlton Heston, and Jimmy Stewart, who actually did some of the circus stunts.

So-so—*Where The Boys Are* (MGM, 1960): This film caused a stampede to Fort Lauderdale during spring break and has been forever ingrained in the minds of a generation of college students. It doesn't matter that Dolores Hart became a nun. Some critics think it was Palm Beach native George Hamilton's only decent film.

Bad—*Follow That Dream* (UA, 1962): Elvis Presley cranked out several bad B-movies in the Sunshine State, but none as insulting as this no-brainer about homesteaders in Yankeetown. Not only did the movie fail to capture the atmosphere of that delightful hamlet, but Elvis' movie family ignored the nearby scenic Withlachoochee River, electing instead to build a cabin on the off-ramp of Bird Creek Bridge. Even the songs drew blanks.

Excellent—*Flipper* (MGM, 1963): Director Ivan Tors made America aware of Florida's tropical environment. Filmed around Miami, the movie convinced thousands of kids they wanted to move to Florida and work in the Everglades.

Excellent—*Goldfinger* (MGM, 1964): Many James Bond films had Florida locations. This one boasted the glories of Miami Beach and the Fountainebleu Hotel at the zenith of their popularity. People are still requesting the hotel room where Shirley Eaton became gilded gold.

The second worst—*Two Thousand Maniacs* (BSO, 1964): The ghosts of Confederate soldiers attack vacationing Northerners in the town of St. Cloud. Very bad for tourism.

The worst—*Fat Spy* (Magna, 1966): Can you imagine Phyllis Diller, Jayne Mansfield, and Brian Donlevy looking for the Fountain of Youth in Coral Gables? Neither can anyone else.

So-so—*Semi-Tough* (UA, 1977): No Floridian has tried harder to promote Florida as a film location than Jupiter's Burt Reynolds. Unfortunately, most of his Florida flicks have been disasters. This is one of his best, with Burt playing a football star in Miami's Orange Bowl.

Silly, but OK—*The Norseman* (American International, 1978): Lee Majors and Mel Ferrer are eleventh-century Vikings landing in Tampa Bay. Wouldn't you think people from Scandinavia would land on Florida's east coast rather than the Gulf Coast? And why is the Big Bend Electric Plant smokestack in the background of every Viking ship shot?

Really, really bad—*Honky Tonk Freeway* (EMI, 1981): This is considered by critics to be the worst film ever made in Florida. Producers spent more than $26 million on what is essentially an automobile chase movie that earned only $500,000 during its entire run. It was filmed around Mount Dora, which was called Toclaw in the movie. Supposedly, chambers of commerce in four surrounding counties shudder when you mention their connection with the film.

Excellent—*Cross Creek* (EMI, 1983): This biography of Marjory Kinnan Rawlings, filmed at Cross Creek and starring Mary Steenburgen as the author, is a classic about rural Florida. Rip Torn was nominated for Best Actor and Alfree Woodard for Best Supporting Actress. Rawlings' surviving husband, Norton Baskin, had a cameo.

Good, but . . . —*Jaws 3* (Universal, 1983): A good cast and a big budget couldn't convince people that a 35-foot great white shark swam to Sea World in Orlando when the town is more than 60 miles from the nearest body of salt water.

Bad—*Where The Boys Are* (ITC, 1984): Rumor has it the original cast ran away when invited to do a sequel to this film. After this flick, the college crowd moved to Daytona and started a spring break party that lasted for years. To male viewers, the film's high point was Lisa Hartman in a bathing suit.

Very good—*Cocoon* (Fox, 1985): This film, directed by Ron Howard, turned St. Petersburg's senior citizens into real people with real concerns other than sitting around on park benches and playing shuffleboard. Don Ameche breakdanced into the Best Supporting Actor award and introduced the public to St. Petersburg's Coliseum, a showplace of the 1920s.

Silly and bad—*Brenda Star* (Tomorrow Entertainment, 1986): Sheik Abdul Aziz Al-Ibrahim financed this big budget bore to feature his favorite actress, Brooke Shields. It took four years to locate a film distributor. The producer angered the local chamber of commerce from the start by proudly announcing that he selected Jacksonville because it reminded him of New York City in the 1940s.

The most profitable Florida film ever made may be the adult film *Deep Throat*, starring Linda

Lovelace. It was filmed in Fort Lauderdale on a budget of $24,000 and earned more than $300 million worldwide.

CRIME FACTS

Unfortunately, the Florida Department of Law Enforcement reports that Florida ranks first in the nation in violent crimes, with 1,244 crimes per 100,000 people compared with 732 crimes per 100,000 people nationwide. Currently, 45 out of every 10,000 Florida residents are in a federal or state prison.

FLORIDA DAILY NEWSPAPERS

Boca Raton News
33 Southeast Third
Street
Boca Raton 33432
561-395-8300

Bradenton Herald
Box 921
Bradenton 34206
941-748-0411

Cape Coral Daily
Breeze
2510 Del Prado
Boulevard
Cape Coral 33904
941-574-1110

Citrus County
Chronicle
1624 North
Meadowcrest
Boulevard
Crystal River 32629
352-563-6363

Clay Today
Box 1209
Orange Park 32073
904-264-3200

Daily Commercial
Box 490007
Leesburg 34749-0007
352-787-4515

Daytona Beach News-
Journal
Box 2831
Daytona Beach
32120
904-252-1511

Desoto Sun Herald
Arcadia 33821
941-494-7600

Diario Las Americas
2900 Northwest 39th
St.
Miami 33142
305-633-3341

Florida Times-Union
Box 1949
Jacksonville 32231
904-359-4111

Florida Today
Box 419000
Melbourne 32941
407-242-3500

Gainesville Sun
Box 147147
Gainesville 32614
352-374-5000

Jackson County
Floridian
Box 520
Marianna 32447
850-526-3614

Key West Citizen
Box 1800
Key West 33041
305-294-6641

Lake City Reporter
Box 1709
Lake City 32055
904-752-1293

Ledger
Box 408
Lakeland 33802
941-687-7000

Miami Herald
1 Herald Plaza
Miami 33132
305-350-2111

Naples Daily News
Box 7009
Naples 33940
941-262-3161

News Chief and Daily
Highlander
Box 1440
Winter Haven 33882
941-294-7731

News Herald
Box 1940
Panama City 32402
850-763-7621

News-Press
Box 10
Fort Myers 33902
941-335-0200

New Volusion
Box 1119
De Land 32721
904-734-3661

Northwest Florida
Daily News
Drawer 2949
Fort Walton Beach
32549
850-863-1111

Observer
Box 10
New Smyrna Beach
32170
904-428-2441

Okeechobee News
Box 639
Okeechobee 34973
941-763-3134

Orlando Sentinel
Box 2833
Orlando 32802
407-420-5000

Palatka Daily News
Box 777
Palatka 32178-0777
904-328-2721

Palm Beach Daily
News
265 Royal Poinciana
Way
Palm Beach 33480
561-655-5755

Palm Beach Post
2751 South Dixie
Highway
West Palm Beach
33405
561-820-4100

Pasco Times, Citrus
Times, and
Hernando Times
Box 879
Port Richey 34673
813-862-7644

Pensacola News
Journal
101 East Romana
Pensacola 32501
850-435-8500

St. Augustine Record
Box 1630
St. Augustine 32085
904-829-6562

St. Petersburg Times
Box 1121
St. Petersburg 33731
813-893-8111

Sanford Herald
Box 1667
Sanford 32772
407-322-2611

Sarasota Herald-
Tribune
Box 1719
Sarasota 34230
941-953-7755

Star-Banner
Box 490
Ocala 34478
352-867-4010

Stuart News
Box 9009
Stuart 34995
407-287-1550

Sun-Herald
Box 2390
Port Charlotte 33949
941-629-2855

Sun-Sentinel
200 E. Las Olas
Boulevard
Fort Lauderdale
33301
954-356-4000

Tallahassee Democrat
Box 990
Tallahassee 32302
904-599-2100

Tampa Tribune	Tribune	Vero Beach Press-
Box 191	Box 69	Journal
Tampa 33601	Fort Pierce 34954	Box 1268
813-259-7600	561-461-2050	Vero Beach 32961
		561-562-2315

FLORIDA RESIDENTS USE THEIR LIBRARIES

Floridians value their libraries highly. According to the Florida state government's Internet site, more than 52 million people walked through public library doors in the state in the last year. If libraries were open 365 days a year, that would be 142,000 people every day. And that doesn't include the tens of thousands of Floridians who visit libraries via a computer hookup and fax machine.

At last count, more than 6.5 million Floridians had active library cards, and they checked out more than 70 million books, videos, and magazines. Library staff answered more than 25 million questions posed by Floridians last year, and 2.5 million residents attended programs conducted by their libraries.

FLORIDA STATE ARCHIVES PHOTOGRAPHIC COLLECTION

The Florida State Archives photographic collection in Tallahassee has entered the computer age and is on-line. From your computer via the Internet, you can search through thousands of images dating back to the 1800s, then select collections by general subject or a specific subject. Once the thumbnail images are on screen, click for a larger version. Copies of any photograph in the collection are available for a nominal copying fee. For on-line access, go to the following Internet address:
http://www.dos.state.fl.us/dlis/barm/archives.html.
Here's a sample of what's available:

Mosaic—650 images of Jewish life in Florida between the 1880s and 1960s
Forrest Granger—1,650 images of Tallahassee and surrounding areas from
the 1940s and 1950s
Harper—2,000 images of Tallahasseans and the Tallahassee area between
1884 and 1911
Peithmann—573 images of Florida Seminole Indians from the 1950s
LaCoe—410 glass lantern slides of Florida industries and cities between
1910 and the 1930s
The Postcard Collection—5,000 picture postcards of Florida attractions,
cities, and people from 1900 through the 1970s
Newberry—78 images of Newberry and rural Alachua County
Madison—486 photographs of Madison County area people, industries,

and agriculture

General (unprinted)—a growing collection of approximately 6,000 images from unprinted reference files

HOW MUCH DOES THAT LETTER WEIGH?

You can make an instant postage scale using a pencil, 5 quarters, and a 12-inch ruler. Lay the pencil on a flat surface and place the ruler across the pencil with the six-inch mark directly over the pencil. Place the five quarters on the three-inch mark and your letter on the nine-inch mark. If the quarters outweigh the letter, you'll need one first-class stamp. If the letter outweighs the quarters, one stamp isn't going to do it.

HOW TO MAKE A KEY WEST COCKTAIL

Mix one and a half ounces of white tequila with a half ounce of Triple Sec, a half ounce of Rose's lime juice, four ounces of sweet and sour mix, and crushed ice. Pour the ingredients into a blender and blend at high speed until smooth. Rub the rim of a tall, exotic-looking glass with a lime wedge and dip the rim in a saucer of salt. Pour the mix into the glass, garnish with a lime wedge and a drink umbrella, and serve. This drink sells at Key West nightclubs for $4.50.

FLORIDA'S MOST EXPENSIVE RESTAURANTS

Florida's most expensive restaurants are located where the tourists are: Miami, Naples, Key West, and around Disney World. In Florida, an expensive restaurant is any eatery that charges between $30 and $50 per person for entrees. Move up to "very expensive" and it will cost more than $50 per

person. Two of the state's very expensive restaurants are the Victoria at Disney's Grand Floridian Beach Resort in Lake Buena Vista and the Grill at the Ritz-Carlton in Naples.

*Most Expensive Restaurants
in the Florida Keys*
Atlantic's Edge
Cafe des Artistes
Cafe Marquesa
Little Palm Island
Louie's Backyard
Pier House
Square One
Yo Sake

*Most Expensive Restaurants
in Palm Beach County*
Arturo's Ristorante
Auberge le Grillon
Bice Ristorante
Cafe Chardonnay
Cafe du Parc
Cafe Floresta
Cafe L'Europe
Casablanca Cafe Americain
Chef Reto's Restaurant
Citrus of Boca

Continental
Damiano's at the Tarrimore House
Florentine and Circle Dining Room
Gazebo Cafe
Jo's Restaurant of Palm Beach
La Finestra
La Vieille Maison
La Villetta
Marcellos' La Sirena
Maxaluna Tuscan Grill
Maxwell's Chophouse
Mon Petit Chou
Nick's Italian Fishery
Rabelais
Renato's Restaurant
Restaurant at the Four Seasons
Ruth's Chris Steak House
Ta Boo Restaurant
Vittorio

*Most Expensive Restaurants
in Miami and Dade Counties*
Aragon Cafe in Miami Beach
Blue Door in Miami Beach
Caffe Abbracci
Caffe C.J.
Chef Allen's 4
Christie's
Colony Bistro
Dominique's
The Fish Market
Follia Restaurant
The Forge
Giacosa
Giovanna's Place
The Grand Cafe
Il Ristorante
Il Tulipano
Joe's Stone Crab
La Bussola
Le Festival

Le Pavillion
Mark's Place
Max's South Beach
The Mayfair Grill
Mimosa
Nick's Miami Beach
Norman's New World Cuisine
Osteria del Teatro
Pacific Time
Palm Restaurant
Renato's
Ruth's Chris Steak House
Shula's Steak House
Veranda at Turnberry
Yuca

*Most Expensive Restaurants
in the Fort Lauderdale Area*
Brooks
Burt and Jack's
Cafe Arugula
Chameleon
The Down Under
Il Tartufo
La Cucina Toscana
La Ferme
La Reserve
Le Dome
The Left Bank
Mark's
Plum Room
Primavera
Rainbow Place
Ruth's Chris Steak House
San Angel

*Most Expensive Restaurants
in the Orlando Area and
Central Gulf Coast*
Armani's
Arthur's 27
Atlantis
Beach Bistro
Bern's Steak House

The Black Swan
Cafe L'Europe
Carmichael's
Christini's Restaurant Italiano
The Colony Restaurant
Del Frisco's Steakhouse
Donatello
Euphemia Haye
Grand Cru
La Coquina
Lafite
Maison et Jardin
Manuels
Maritana Grille
Michael's on East
Palio
Peter Scott's
Phoenix
Ruth's Chris Steak House
Shula's Steak House
Sign of the Vine
Sum Chow's
Tuscany
Yachtsman Steakhouse

*Most Expensive Restaurants
in Central and Mid-Florida*
Chalet Suzanne
Vinton's New Orleans

POTPOURRI

To many people, potpourri just smells good. Others sneeze and get clogged noses when they're around potpourri. If you're a potpourri fan, you can make your own with a mixture of fragrant materials derived from flowers, leaves, roots, barks, woods, resins, and gums, many of which are available right here in Florida.

A properly blended potpourri will last for months, and its uses are unlimited. Use your imagination. Perfume the air with its continual fragrances, scent drawers and closets, make sweet-smelling stationery, add a final touch to room decorations with attractive baskets and bowls filled with your favorite mixture, or create personal gifts to share with friends.

Fragrance and beauty are not the only uses for a potpourri. Some blends of potpourri repel moths and other insects, while other potpourri mixtures protect woolens in storage (where they stay most of the time in Florida—buy cotton sweaters!).

There are two ways to prepare potpourris: the dry method and the moist, or wet, method. The moist method uses scented, fresh materials which ferment and mature in a crock container for several weeks. Wet potpourris retain their fragrance for a longer period of time but are not visually appealing. Dry potpourris consist of dried, scented, crisp materials concocted for beauty as well as fragrance.

Practice in fragrance blending will help you learn to adapt potpourri formulas, so you can create other scented products such as cologne, bath salts, or incense. The base blend system makes it easy to learn by experimenting and eventually leads to the creation of your own distinctive formulas.

So grab a handful of this herb and some of that bark and toss it together with a little seed and some flower petals and see what happens. Don't forget to write down your secret formula. If you invent something you like, you'll want to make more.

DEPARTMENT OF HIGHWAY SAFETY AND MOTOR VEHICLES DATA

The Department of Highway Safety and Motor Vehicles (DHSMV) maintains the Florida driver's license and motor vehicle databases, as a well as several smaller, secondary databases. These databases are queried and updated as residents of the state are issued licenses. They're available 24 hours a day for retrieval of driver- and vehicle-related data by law enforcement officers, insurance companies, and businesses. During peak business hours, the computer will process more than 76,000 inquiries and updates.

Florida public records law provides mail-in and electronic access to records within the DHSMV databases. Information from the various DHSMV databases is currently available online through CompuServe (800-848-8199), TML Information Services (800-743-7891), and Data Base Technologies (800-279-7710).

Data, including information on motor vehicles registered and titled in the state of Florida, can be accessed by using one of the following—the tag number, decal number, title number, or vehicle identification number (VIN). Provide the DHSMV with this information, and they can give you the owner's name and address, date of birth, sex, vehicle make, dates of issue, etc. Questions concerning motor vehicle data should be directed to:

Division of Motor Vehicles
Neil Kirkman Building, Room A122
2900 Apalachee Parkway
Tallahassee 32399
850-488-2454

GETTING YOUR BUSINESS LICENSED IN FLORIDA

If you're thinking of starting a business in Florida, you're probably going to need a license. Local occupational licenses are required for most businesses and are issued by counties and cities, so check with your local city clerk and county tax collector. Many businesses and professions also are licensed by the state. To find out if a state license is required, call the Florida Business Line at 800-342-0771. Will you be required to collect sales tax? Call Taxpayer Services at 800-352-3671 to find out.

If you decide to name your unincorporated business something unique and different, any fictitious name (as opposed to your own name, for example) must be registered with the state. The fictitious name also must be advertised once in a newspaper in the county where the business will be based. For more information on that requirement, write the Fictitious Name Registration Office, Florida Department of State, Box 1300, Tallahassee 32302.

SHOWER FACTS

When you climb into the shower and close the shower curtain, the air on either side of the curtain is equal, so the curtain drapes up and down. When you turn on the water, the hot water warms the air inside the shower, causing the air to expand and rise, resulting in lower pressure inside the shower stall and cooler air on the outside. The cooler air on the outside of the curtain pushes against it, forcing it inward.

RETIRING IN FLORIDA

Considering retiring in Florida? Here are some retirement facts you might find helpful. Florida has 26,000 physicians, 7,896 dentists, 672 nursing homes, and 309 hospitals. Overall, medical costs are comparable to those in other states.

The new home construction business is booming in Florida, so there are many homes on the market. Prices vary, but homes in Florida are a bargain. The American Association of Retired Persons (AARP) queried members who relocated from their home states to California, Texas, and Florida. The new Floridians reported that average home prices in the Sunshine State were 15-20 percent lower than in the state from which they moved. (Medical costs, by the way, were comparable to other states.) So if you're in the market for a house, local newspaper classified sections are a good place to start to comparison shop. Elsewhere in this chapter you'll find a list of daily newspapers you can contact. In addition, many communities have apartment finding and rental services. Long-distance directory assistance can furnish the number of services within a local community, and local tourist offices can also supply lists.

Although condominiums are a popular Florida housing option, they are not for everyone. Condo living entails developing close social relationships with other owners, adhering to rules and restrictions, and putting the community first. If this lifestyle fits into your plans, by all means consider a condo, apartment, or townhouse.

Retirement communities can offer totally independent living, varying levels of assisted living, or a combination of the two. Florida has 2,020 assisted living facilities and adult family care homes. Continuing Care Retirement Facilities (CCRCs) offer life care arrangements with accommodations for independent housing, assisted living, and skilled nursing on site.

Blue Cross/Blue Shield of Florida, the state's Medicare carrier, publishes a directory containing the names and addresses for all physicians and suppliers who filed participation agreements with Medicare. You can get a free copy of the MEDPARD directory by calling Blue Cross/Blue Shield at 904-355-3680. For a listing of CCRCs licensed in Florida, contact the Florida Department of Insurance, Office of Specialty Insurers, The Capitol, Tallahassee 32399, 904-922-3144, extension 2478.

Elderly Services

The Elder Helpline Information and Referral Service in each Florida county can tell you what legal assistance is available to older people in that area. There is also a legal issues counseling and referral service available by telephone to older Floridians:

Legal Hotline for Older Floridians
800-252-5997 (in Florida)
305-576-5997 (outside of Florida)

The Department of Elder Affairs is the Florida state agency responsible for the planning, development, and coordination of long-term care initiatives. Three primary objectives of the department's long-term care plan are to help older people remain in their homes and in the community, to promote wellness in elders, and to act as advocates on behalf of older people concerning aging issues.

Through a very competitive process, Florida was one of five states awarded a State Initiatives in Long-Term Care Planning grant from the Robert Wood Johnson Foundation. The department has proposed a demonstration project which will enable the state to contract with health plans to provide primary, acute, and long-term care services to Medicare and Medicaid recipients.

Abuse, Neglect, and Exploitation Protective Services

Elderly people are sometimes neglected, hurt, abused, exploited, or threatened by others—even by those responsible for their physical and emotional health and well-being. In some instances, elders may harm themselves through self-neglect due to mental impairment. Florida law requires that abuse of an elderly or disabled person be reported by calling 800-96-ABUSE (800-962-2873)

The State Long-Term Care Ombudsman Council uses trained volunteers to inspect long-term care and assisted living facilities and to be a voice for older residents.

Information regarding aging services available in a local community can be obtained by calling the Elder Helpline Information and Referral Service. The eligibility requirements and availability of services vary from county to county. One way to learn more about aging in Florida is to subscribe to Elder Update, the Department of Elder Affairs' monthly publication.

More Retiring Facts

Florida's senior population (people 60 years of age and older) has grown to more than 20 percent of the state's total population. The counties with the highest percentages of seniors are Charlotte (35%), Highlands (33%), Hernando (33%), Pasco (32%), and Sarasota (32%).

Retired life in Florida varies according to individual preferences and budgets. If you're considering retiring to Florida, experts suggest you travel around the state. If you find a place you like, rent for a few months—or, time permitting, a full year—to see if the community fits your needs. If it doesn't, you can always pick up and move.

As the southernmost state on the U.S. mainland, Florida has a climate that ranges from temperate in the north to subtropical in the south. Winter temperatures range from an average of 51°F in the north to 70°F along the southern Atlantic coast. Average summer temperatures are remarkably uniform throughout the state, ranging from the low- to mid-80s. Precipitation averages about 50 inches annually, with most of the rain occurring during the summer months. The year-round, semitropical climate, moderate rainfall, abundant sunshine, fresh and sea water, and freedom from the North's heavy frost, snow, and ice all combine to make Florida an appealing place to live. And if you think you'll miss the North's four seasons, consider moving to the northwest part of Florida.

According to the Governor's Office of Planning and Bud-geting, prices are generally higher in the southern half of the state than in the northern half. Other-wise, living costs are comparable to those of other states.

There is no state income tax in Florida. To alleviate the property tax burden, Florida grants homeowners relief under a homestead exemption provision. This exemption is available to any person who holds legal title to real property in Florida and uses the property as his or her permanent residence.

Working Full-Time or Part-Time as a Senior

The Florida Department of Labor and Employment Security (DLES) operates more than 90 employment offices in the state. These offices promote and encourage the fullest use of the skills, abilities, and experiences of Florida's older citizens. Identified as Jobs and Benefits Centers, DLES offices are located in all major metropolitan areas, medium-sized cities, and many of the rural areas of the state and are listed in community telephone directories. These offices have a staff member designated to assist older people whose age may be a barrier to employment. Services to job seekers include job placement, employment counseling, job development, referral to training, and support services.

DLES maintains an Older Worker Skills Bank—a listing of older people seeking employment—and makes it available to employers through local Jobs and Benefits Centers. This information is also available to the Department of Commerce and its economic development, international trade, and tourism programs to assist in creating jobs by educating potential employers to the availability of Florida's older workers and the benefits of hiring them. Individuals may register their names and skills at any Florida Jobs and Benefits Center.

You can take many steps to find a job before moving to Florida. The Job Service of Florida is linked to a national network of state-operated job services known as America's Job Bank System. It provides quick information about job openings in any state or region of the nation and may be accessed from any Jobs and Benefits Center. Consult the local telephone directory for the address of the state employment service office nearest you.

FLORIDA MARINE PATROL

The Florida Marine Patrol (FMP) is the law enforcement arm of the Department of Environmental Protection. Marine Patrol officers are charged with protection of marine resources of the state. They have legal authority to issue citations and to make arrests for violations of state and federal laws—even on land! The FMP can be reached toll-free from anywhere in the state by dialing 800-DIAL-FMP (800-342-5367). The FMP can also be reached on cellular phones by dialing *FMP. FMP headquarters is in the Marjory Stoneman Douglas Building, 3900 Commonwealth Boulevard, Tallahassee, 904-488-5757. The FMP also has offices in the following cities:

Carrabelle	850-697-3741
Fort Myers	941-332-6971
Homosassa Springs	352-382-5058
Jacksonville Beach	904-359-6580
Jupiter	561-624-6935
Marathon	305-289-2320
Miami	305-325-3346
Panama City Beach	850-233-5150
Pensacola	850-444-8978
Tampa	813-272-2516
Titusville	407-383-2740

Reporting Spills

Florida Law requires the reporting of all oil and hazardous substance spills. The state hotline is available 24 hours a day at 904-413-9911. The Florida Marine Patrol Hotline is manned 24 hours a day at 800-342-5367. The Department of Environmental Protection Response Offices are open from 8 A.M. to 5 P.M. and are located throughout the state.

Fort Lauderdale Office
407-467-5966
Fort Myers Office
941-332-6975
Jacksonville Office
904-448-4320
Orlando Office
407-894-7555
Panama City Office
850-872-7650
Pensacola Office
850-444-8320
Tallahassee Office
904-488-2974
Tampa Office
813-272-2456

SINKHOLES

Florida and Texas are areas where sinkholes are a common geologic hazard. Soil sitting on top of porous limestone or underground water tends to sink as the limestone erodes or as the water can no longer support the surface soil.

Sinkholes cause damage to houses, foundations, roads, and farmers' fields. Some sinkholes are large enough to severely reduce the fields' productivity. They are also direct conduits of rain water to ground water. In the past, many sinkholes were used for dumping trash, vehicles, and other wastes. This contributed directly to pollution of ground water and is no longer allowed. When sinkholes are found today, they are filled with soil or cement to protect the ground water.

SILLY SONGS

Here's a Quarter, Call Someone Who Cares by Travis Tritt
She's Acting Single and I'm Drinking Doubles by Gary Stewart
You're the Reason Our Kids Are Ugly by Conway Twitty
Everytime You Throw Dirt on Her, You're Losing Ground by George Strait
I'm Going to Hire a Wino to Decorate Our Home by David Frizzell
Did I Shave My Legs for This? by Deana Carter
Daddy Was a Preacher, Momma Was a Go-Go Girl by Joanna Neel

HISTORIC FLORIDA SHIPWRECKS—THE SS *TARPON*

The twin-screwed steamer SS *Tarpon* was built in 1887 at Wilmington, Delaware, by the renowned shipbuilders Pusey and Jones. The new ship, delivered to the Naugatuck Valley Steamboat Company of Derby, Connecticut, measured 130 feet in length, 26 feet in beam, and 8 feet deep in the hold. The superstructure and passenger areas were made of wood and the hull of iron. Competition with local railroads caused hard times for the steamship company, and within two years the ship was sold to Henry B. Plant, whose railroad empire terminated at Tampa, Florida.

The steamer was put into service in the local Tampa area. In 1891, she was sent back to her builders, who lengthened her hull by 30 feet and added several staterooms. The *Tarpon* returned to Florida and may have been one of the dozens of ships used to transport troops and supplies to and from Cuba during the Spanish-American War.

On August 30, 1937, five weeks short of her fiftieth birthday, the *Tarpon* was loaded at Mobile, Alabama, for her next journey east. The captain loaded as much cargo as he could fit on the steamer, a common practice. As she left Mobile, she held more than 200 tons of flour, sugar, canned goods, and beer. The ship made port in Pensacola and departed for Panama City the evening of August 31. She had taken on a quantity of iron for the paper mills. Almost 200 barrels of fuel oil were in her tanks, as well as 15 tons of fresh water in the hull. As *Tarpon* rounded the sea buoy and made for St. Andrews Bay, her freeboard was less than five inches.

At 2 A.M. on September 1, the engineer was awakened and told that the pumps were having difficulty keeping water pumped from the bilges due to a leak in the bow that was steadily increasing in rough seas. The ship began to list to port as the men worked the pumps. Several barrels of flour were jettisoned and the steamer returned to an even keel. Just before dawn, the winds reached gale force and the pounding seas began to pour through the ship's wooden bulkheads, causing her to list to starboard. The first mate turned *Tarpon* toward shore, intending to beach her before she sank. The captain ordered more cargo overboard, but *Tarpon* sank, taking 18 of her 31 crewmen with her.

The remains of *Tarpon* lie on a sand and rock bottom in 90 feet of water almost 8 nautical miles offshore. Her bow is on a bearing of 290°. The hard bottom has prevented the wreck from sinking into the sand. Water clarity generally is good at the wreck site, compared to other offshore shipwrecks that lie to the east.

STATE STUFF

The official state seal was adopted by the 1868 state legislature. The state flag is white with the state seal in the center and red bars extending from the seal to each corner of the flag.

The state's nickname is the Sunshine State.

The official state song is Old Folks At Home (Suwannee River) by Stephen Foster.

The state motto is In God We Trust.

The state tree is the sabal palm.

The state flower is the orange blossom.

The state beverage is (what else?) orange juice.

The state stone is agatized coral.

The state gem is the moonstone.

The state bird is the mockingbird.

The state freshwater mammal is the manatee.

The state saltwater mammal is the dolphin.

The state freshwater fish in the largemouth bass.

The state saltwater fish in the Atlantic sailfish.

The state reptile is the alligator.

The state insect is the zebra longwing butterfly.

The state shell is the horse conch.

The state soil (believe it or not) is Myakka sand.

Florida State Freshwater and Saltwater Fish

In 1975, the state legislature designated the largemouth bass as the state freshwater fish and the sailfish as the state saltwater fish. Florida is the only state to have two fish as state symbols, but Florida is not the only state to have the largemouth bass in its lakes and streams: The fish is native to or stocked in every state.

The largemouth bass is probably the most popular American freshwater game fish. It will eat almost anything put in front of it, making it a reasonably easy catch. The bass has a quick, smashing strike and is known for surface feeding sprees. It has been used in recent years for transplants and cross-breeding and can grow to up to 20 pounds. During the past 50 years, the scientific name of the largemouth bass has changed several times. It has been classified in the genus *Huro,* but currently is considered to be in the same genus as the smallmouth bass.

Florida State Insect

The state insect is the zebra longwing butterfly (*Heliconius charitonius*), designated on April 26, 1996. In 1972, the Senate had passed a bill to make the preying mantis the state insect, but the measure failed in the House. Twenty-four years later, everyone agreed on the butterfly.

The zebra longwing has elongated, black wings with yellow stripes, a thin abdomen, and long antennae. The butterfly's brilliant colors warn predators of its nauseating taste if it's eaten. The diet of the longwing larvae consists entirely of passion flowers. Studies show that longwings seem to be the most intelligent of all butterflies and have a structured social life. They sleep in groups and return to the same roost every night. The oldest butterflies seem to have first choice of sleeping perches. At dawn, the butterfly that wakes up first wakes the others by gently touching them.

Florida State Shell

Pleuroploca gigantea, the horse conch, also known as the giant band shell, has been Florida's official state shell since 1969. The shell is native to the marine waters around Florida, can grow to a length of two feet, and is the external skeleton of the soft-bodied animal that inhabits it.

At least 535 million years ago, mollusks acquired the habit of secreting a carbonate of lime solution that immediately forms a protective shell with the consistency of marble. The word conch comes from the Greek word meaning "shell" and is pronounced "konk."

FLORIDA FLEA MARKETS

If you're looking for an antique lamp, a used tire, or a television set without a remote, you might be able to find it at a flea market. Florida is a flea-market kind of place and has its share of indoor and outdoor markets, many operating year-round due to the moderate weather. Admission is always free, and the markets range in size from a few tables alongside the road to sprawling venues like the famous Fort Lauderdale Swap Shop. Here you'll find 800 outside booths, 100,000 square feet of indoor shops, and hundreds of vendors offering everything from rusty tools to gold watches. The Swap Shop operates daily from 7:30 A.M. to 6:30 P.M. and occasionally schedules music concerts.

At a flea market, you can be a buyer or a seller. The cost of renting a booth varies based on the reputation of the market and the buyer traffic, but you can usually find something for around $15 a weekend.

Flea marketing isn't an exact science, so some markets are here today, gone tomorrow. As a result, scheduling information is sketchy. Many are open only on weekends. Some dealers arrive long before the market opens, so if you're looking for a bargain, plan to arrive early to beat the crowds. At press time, the following flea markets were in full operation.

49er Flea Market
    10525 49th Street North in
    Clearwater
    813-573-3367

Florilnd Flea and Farmers Market
9309 North Florida Avenue in
Tampa
813-932-4310
Open Saturdays and Sundays
800 booths

Fort Lauderdale Swap Shop
3291 West Sunrise Boulevard in
Fort Lauderdale
954-791-7927

Frontenac Flea Market
5605 North Highway One in
Cocoa
407-631-0241
Open weekly
300 dealers/1000 booths

Fleamasters Fleamarket
4135 Dr. Martin Luther King Jr.
Boulevard in Fort Myers
941-334-7001
Open Fridays, Saturdays, and
Sundays

Frost Park Flea Market
300 Northeast 2nd Street in
Dania
954-921-8700
Open weekends
90 dealers/booths

Flea World
Highway 17 and 92 in Sanford
407-330-1792
Open Fridays, Saturdays, and
Sundays

Howard's Flea Market
Highway 19 in Homosassa
352-628-FLEA
Open Fridays, Saturdays, and
Sundays
100 dealers/100 booths

Florida Farmer's Market
4603 West Colonial Drive in
Orlando
407-296-3868
Open Saturdays and Sundays
125 dealers

Indoor Flea Market
3621 Highway 19 in New Port
Richey
813-842-3665
Open Fridays, Saturdays, and
Sundays
100 dealers/booths

International Market World
  1052 Highway 92 West in
  Auburndale
  941-665-0062
  Open three days a week
  1,000 dealers/booths

Jacksonville Market Place
  614 Pecan Park Road in
  Jacksonville
  No phone number available
  Open Saturdays and Sundays
  750 dealers/booths

The Market Place
  3600 Highway 441 South in
  Okeechobee
  941-467-6639
  Open weekends
  740 dealers/booths

Old Shrimp Road Flea Market
  5550 Fifth Avenue in Key West
  305-296-1784
  Open Saturdays and Sundays

Oldsmar Flea Market
  180 Race Track Road in Oldsmar
  813-855-5306
  75 dealers

Osceola Flea and Farmer's Market
  2801 E. Irlo Bronson Highway in
  Kissimmee
  407-846-2811
  Open Fridays, Saturdays, and
  Sundays

Pea Ridge Flea Market
  Highway 90 in Pace
  904-994-8056
  Open Fridays, Saturdays, and
  Sundays
  50 dealers/65 booths

Ramona Boulevard Flea Market
  7059 Ramona Boulevard in
  Jacksonville
  904-786-3532
  Open weekends
  585 dealers/700 booths

Renninger's Florida Twin Markets
  20651 U.S. Highway 441 in
  Mount Dora
  352-383-8393
  Open Saturdays and Sundays

Showtown Flea Market
  12200 34th Street North in St.
  Petersburg
  813-572-9966
  100 dealers/100 booths

Super Flea and Farmers Market
  4835 West Eau Gallie Boulevard
  in Melbourne
  407-242-9124
  Open Fridays, Saturdays, and
  Sundays
  900 booths

Trash-to-Treasures
  Stewart Street in Milton
  850-994-8056
  Open Fridays, Saturdays, and
  Sundays
  50 dealers/75 booths

Wagon Wheel Flea Market
  7801 74th Avenue North in
  Pinellas Park
  813-544-5319
  65 dealers

Webster Flea Market
  Highway 471 in Webster
  352-793-3551
  Open Mondays only

Zephyrhills Flea Market
  39336 Chancey Road in
  Zephyrhills
  813 782-1483
  Open Fridays, Saturdays, and
  Sundays
  100 dealers/300 booths

Tips for the Flea Market Shopper

If you're into serious flea market shopping, bring a cart or wagon, especially if you have to park a long distance from the vendors. Your kids' wagon will do fine, and they can ride around in it if they get bored. Better still, leave the kids behind.

Wear comfortable shoes and clothing. Remember, it's usually cooler in the morning and the temperature usually rises as the day progresses, so dress in layers.

Vendors will usually bargain, so offer a price 30 percent lower than the asking price to start. If you really want the item and they accept the offer, snatch it up. If you really want the item and they reject the offer, try 20 percent lower, then 10 percent. Not everyone is willing to bargain. You can try walking away and if the vendor doesn't call you back, you can walk back later and pay whatever he or she asks.

SLIPPING THROUGH THE CRACKS OF JUSTICE

Helen Grady was arrested in south Florida for shoplifting at a Fort Lauderdale department store. She slipped a blouse, two cartons of cigarettes, a six-pack of ballpoint pens, and three videotapes into a shopping bag and walked out the door. Caught by a store clerk, she was taken into the store office, and the police were called. When they added up her loot, it amounted to $106.85, making her eligible for the grand prize charge—felony retail theft for stealing more than $100, punishable by up to 10 years behind bars.

"No way," said her public defender. "The tapes and the blouse were both on sale that day, marked down 25 percent, reducing the overall value from just over $100 to well under $100—$87.45 to be exact." That amount qualified her for only a misdemeanor retail theft charge, punishable by, at most, six months. The judge gave her 90 days.

*The
Sunshine State
Almanac
& Book of
Florida-
Related
Stuff*

BUGS

*L*ightning bugs glow in the dark as part of a communication system they use to find mates. The females wait and flash at flying males. The males flash back and try to find the right species of female.

Lightning bugs glow by using two chemicals called luciferin and luciferase. Luciferase is an enzyme, a protein catalyst which is not consumed in its reaction with luciferin. Luciferin changes chemically and gives off light. Whenever an electron drops an energy level (a quantum leap) in a molecule, it gives off a photon of light.

LOVE BUGS

The first wave of love bugs came to the United States in the 1920s by way of Central America. They buzzed around the Southwest and Southeast for awhile, reaching Florida in the early 1970s. When the weather is warm and the love bug season rolls around—usually twice a year in April/May and August/September—they're everywhere. They fly around, hooked together at the tail and mating. The female is the larger one, the male, the smaller. The female lives only about three days, and the male, up to five days. Love bugs are attracted to car exhaust and the heat from cars sitting in the sun.

Surprisingly, birds, frogs, lizards, and other insect-feeders don't like love bugs, so the bugs either die a natural death or are killed when they fly into oncoming cars. Neither the larvae nor the adults are notably affected by diseases like fungus, bacteria, or viruses. Unfortunately, love bugs are just something Floridians have to live with at certain times of the year.

When the bugs are squashed on a car, they exude an acid that can damage the car's paint. There have been reports of love bugs completely blocking a car's radiator, causing the vehicle to overheat. To remove love bugs from a car, use hot, soapy water and rub briskly. Do this as soon as possible after the bugs land on the car. Some people like to coat the front of their cars with petroleum jelly or cooking spray, but this could damage the car's paint too.

THE MEDITERRANEAN FRUIT FLY—
WHAT FLORIDIANS NEED TO KNOW

The Mediterranean fruit fly, or medfly, is one of the most destructive insect pests in the world. This foreign pest attacks many fruits, nuts, and vegetables commonly grown by Florida homeowners and farmers. The adult fly cannot fly more than a few miles, so it is usually introduced into new areas by people carrying infested fruit. If it were established in the continental U.S., the medfly would ravage commercial agriculture and make it difficult and expensive for you to grow fruits, nuts, and vegetables in your backyard.

State and federal agricultural officials work to keep the Mediterranean fruit fly out of this country. One female medfly usually lays about three hundred eggs in her lifetime, but could lay as many as eight hundred.

Medflies attack tomatoes, peppers, eggplants, avocados, mangos, persimmons, guavas, pears, peaches, apples, figs, and many other fruits and vegetables. Countries with established medfly populations have typical crop losses of 25–50 percent. Total losses can occur. In most Florida counties, agribusiness is a major contributor of revenues to the local economy. For example, more than 90 percent of Hillsborough County's agricultural products are sold outside the county, bringing new cash into the local economy. Agriculture and related businesses employ fifty thousand people in transportation, farm supplies and services, packaging and marketing industries, real estate, banking and legal services, and they generate $4.8 billion a year.

Florida crops protected by the Medfly Eradication Program bring $10 billion a year to the state. If that revenue were lost, every citizen would have to pay an extra $700 in taxes to maintain our quality of life.

People cause medfly infestations when they bring or mail uninspected fruits, nuts, vegetables, or plants from foreign or domestic quarantine areas to uninfected areas of the United States. If you live in or travel through a medfly quarantine area, don't give away, mail, or accept home-grown fruits and vegetables like citrus, tomato, pepper, eggplant, fig, grape, mango, avocado, loquat, guava, papaya, and Surinam cherry. Canned, baked, frozen, or preserved foods are safe.

How the Medfly Invades Florida

Because Mediterranean fruit flies are not strong fliers, they spread through the movement of larval-infested fruit from one place to another. The major threats come from travelers, particularly airline passengers carrying infested fruit. The growing volume of international traffic increases the opportunity for infestations. With Florida's many ports of entry, especially the port of Miami and Miami International Airport, the state is particularly vulnerable.

Private shipments of fruit, particularly by mail among family members and friends, is another major infestation. Open-air produce stands have attracted illegal imports of exotic fruits that have not been treated to prevent the spread of pests. The problem has increased as Florida's ethnic diversity and changing tastes have created additional demand for exotic produce.

Stopping potential infestations at the point of entry is far cheaper than combating infestation outbreaks in communities. For example, California spent more than $100 million to eradicate the medfly in the early 1980s. Eradication efforts in Florida would cost a minimum of $1 million.

Several steps have been taken to put a halt to new infestations. State and federal officials are working with postal authorities to develop ways to inspect packages suspected of carrying contraband fruit. In addition, public education efforts have increased.

How to Spot a Medfly

Adults are black with yellow abdomens and yellow marks on their thoraxes. Their wings are banded with yellow. They reach a quarter of an inch in length. Eggs are white and deposited in holes in fruit rind. Larvae (maggots) are white, legless, and approximately one quarter of an inch long. They are found in fruit where they hatch and feed. Pupae are found in the soil. After they become adults, they are free-flying and can be found on plants, fruit trees, coffee plants, grapevines, shrubs, and other trees and plants.

FLORIDA COCKROACHES

Cockroaches have been around longer than the state of Florida—at least a couple of million years. The most common Florida cockroach is the German cockroach, smaller than regular cockroaches but more aggressive and annoying. Measuring about a half an inch in length, the German cockroach is light brown with dark stripes across its back. Provide cockroaches with food, water, and shelter, and they'll move in without an invitation. They'd rather live inside your house than outside because it's usually more damp in bathrooms, basements, and kitchens and around water pipes.

Just because you have roaches doesn't mean you're a slob. They may have arrived when you moved in, come from your neighbor's house or apartment, arrived in groceries (especially potatoes), or even sneaked in inside furniture crates.

Roaches avoid us as much as possible because we like the light and they don't. Turn on the lights and away they go, at least temporarily. Turn off the lights, leave the room, and out they come.

A contaminated roach could walk across your countertop and food and leave behind the bacteria that could cause salmonella, dysentery, and other diseases. The best defense against cockroaches is cleanliness. Don't leave uncovered food lying around, clean off your countertops after cooking, and keep bottles and other containers well sealed. Keep your bread and other yeast products in the refrigerator. Check potato sacks when you come back from the grocery store. All of this is no guarantee that roaches won't show up, but if you're clean, they'll probably go elsewhere.

Researchers have synthesized the pheromone emitted by cockroaches to attract mates and believe using these scents can lure cockroaches to their death. Once released into the air, these pheromones—which are already available commercially—can do a better job than toxic bug killers, scientists believe.

Cockroach Facts

Cockroaches will nibble on just about anything, from book bindings to film to starched linen to leather. They even love that sticky glue used to install paneling. German cockroaches can survive a whole month without food but last less than two weeks without water.

Under optimum conditions, one female cockroach can produce two million offspring in a year. An average breeding season produces 35,000 offspring. Two cockroaches beginning on New Year's Day will have 575,000 offspring by December 31. Mathematically it goes like this: 30 eggs per egg capsule, 30 days for each capsule to hatch, and 60 days to maturity when the new cockroaches can begin to breed.

A HOMEMADE COCKROACH TRAP

You can make your own cockroach traps by putting sticky tape in a small jar along with a small piece of bread. The roaches will spot the bread, climb inside the jar, and get their feet stuck on the tape. Replace the lid and toss them outside.

Discorides Pedanius, a Greek who doctored the Roman army during Nero's reign (A.D. 54–68), believed that cockroach entrails mixed with oil and stuffed into the ear could cure earaches.

WHERE DID THOSE TERMITES COME FROM?

Rumor has it that PT boat engines, shipped to New Orleans during World War II, contained Formosan termites that infested Navy bases in Louisiana, Texas, and South Carolina. A few years later, a termite-infested wooden pleasure boat docked at a pier outside a Broward County condominium and the first Formosan termites landed on Florida's shores.

Today, they're found in areas stretching from Pensacola in the Panhandle to Fort Lauderdale in the southeast.

Termites have caused over $200 million in damages a year in New Orleans alone, and have moved into the southeastern areas of Dade and Broward Counties. The infestations is so bad, homeowners say, that few termite companies provide any guarantees after treatment. Every year, termites do more than $750 million worth of damage, and most of the damage is done in Florida. They cause more damage in Florida annually than fires, storms, and earthquakes combined. Queens of some species of termites are reported to live for 50 years, although the life spans generally are closer to 15. A nesting colony can cover an area 300 feet wide. They'll eat not only wood but anything in their path, including concrete.

Originally from China, the Formosan termite differs from other termites in its aggressiveness and large colonies. Formosan termites feed on live oak trees as well as boards used in construction. During the evening hours they swarm toward any light source. The usual protection against termites— building a chemical barrier (a poison) between the ground and your home—is usually ineffective against Formosan termites, who can find their way around any barriers.

It's easy to confuse an ant with a termite. They're both about the same size and have winged stages. Ants are about 1/8 or 1/2 inch long and colored black, red, yellow, brown, or light tan. Their hind wings are smaller than their front wings and they have a pinched waist. Termites are about 1/8 to 3/16 of an inch long with a wider waist and both wings equal in size.

MOSQUITOES

There are roughly 2,700 species of mosquitoes in the world, and a lot of them live in Florida because they like the weather. Mosquitoes can be found at altitudes ranging from sea level to over 10,000 feet. Your average mosquito weighs roughly two to two and a half milligrams and can suck up around five-millionths of a liter of blood.

Male mosquitoes never suck blood.

Mosquitoes fly at an estimated velocity of one mile an hour, so they can be easily outrun. Some mosquitoes, especially salt-marsh mosquitoes, can migrate as far as 75–100 miles. Mosquitoes live for roughly 15 to 65 days and can detect a host from 25 to 30 meters away. (A meter is 39 inches.)

Mosquitoes locate their prey by vision and by detecting infrared radiation, carbon dioxide, and lactic acid emitted by hosts. Mosquito saliva contains anticoagulants to prevent the host's blood from clotting. These foreign proteins cause the itching associated with mosquito bites. Some people are more attractive to mosquitoes than others, but no one knows why. Male mosquitoes never suck blood. Females feed on blood only to obtain protein for egg production. Males and nonreproductive females feed on plant nectar. Mosquito eggs can remain dormant for more than a year and will hatch if flooded with water. More than 50 species of mosquitoes are known to be resistant to at least one insecticide.

Mosquitoes and AIDS

When a mosquito bites someone, it injects an anticoagulant to keep the blood flowing. But although certain mosquitoes are vectors—organisms that transmit diseases such as yellow fever, dengue, encephalitis, and malaria—most scientists agree a mosquito's bite cannot pass on the HIV virus, which is thought to cause Acquired Immune Deficiency Syndrome, or AIDS. A study in Africa by the World Health Organization in 1996 indicated that some isolated tribes living in remote corners of the country caught AIDS from tribes living nearby, but to date, there is no evidence this was transmitted by mosquitoes, although some say it's a possibility.

How Ticks Operate

Ticks love pets and will jump aboard every chance they get. They mate, grow up, then jump off the pet and lay anywhere from 1,000 to more than 5,000 eggs, usually in wooded areas, grass, and along baseboards in the home. The eggs hatch into seed ticks who start looking for a pet to climb aboard and feed on for up to six days. The seed ticks fall off the pet, molt for about two weeks, and become tick nymphs. The nymphs start looking for another host pet, start feeding, then fall off again. They molt and emerge as a new adult tick capable of reproducing. They mate and, unfortunately, the cycle starts all over again.

Fleas, Spiders, and Scorpions

History shows the flea has killed more people than all the wars men have fought in the last thousand years. Those pests that drive dogs and cats crazy spread the bubonic plague back in the fourteenth century that killed one-fourth of Europe's population. In fact, fleas are known to transmit 15 major disease-causing organisms. They also spread hundreds of other organisms which can make animal and human life miserable.

Fleas are amazing bugs. They've been around for millions of years, can jump 30,000 times without stopping, and can leap 150 times their own height. They feed upon external body surfaces much like their relatives: ticks, lice, bedbugs, chiggers, mites, flies, and mosquitoes.

The temperate climate that makes Florida living so attractive to humans is also welcome to fleas. These wingless ectoparasites/bloodsuckers thrive throughout the state, making life miserable for everybody, including dogs, cats, wild animals, and humans. What's the solution?

First, understand they'll always be around, so whatever you do is basically just temporary. Let the cat out of the house, take the dog for a walk, or hike in the woods, and the fleas are just waiting to jump aboard.

There are more than 2,000 species of fleas, and a lot of them live in Florida. They measure about 1/8 to 1/16 of an inch in length and can jump 100 times that distance. Most fleas are dark reddish-brown in color and are hard-bodied with three sets of legs. They survive by sucking the blood of their hosts. Although they prefer animals, humans will do in a pinch. Most fleas are female, and an active female can produce up to 18 eggs a day. There are four stages of life for fleas—egg, larval, pupa, and adult. As the female lays each egg, it sticks to the fur (or hair) of the host until it dies, then falls to the ground. The eggs themselves are smooth and transparent and hatch into their larvae stage in one to six days.

The larvae look like little worms (ugh!) and can actually move a few inches from where they hatch to avoid light. They feed primarily on dry fecal material produced by fleas on the host. The larval stage lasts from one to five weeks, at which time the larvae weave cocoons for their pupal stage. Flea pupae attach themselves to carpet and other fibers. Their cocoons

The first step in dealing with fleas is to perform a thorough

make them resistant to chemicals and therefore most difficult to control. The pupal stage generally lasts from seven to ten days, but if there is no host around, the adult flea can survive dormant in the cocoon for up to six months.

The first step in dealing with fleas is to perform a thorough cleaning in any place where fleas might be found. All carpets, rugs, and upholstered furniture must be vacuumed carefully. Wood and tile floors need to be swept and scrubbed, particularly along baseboards.

Concrete floors on patios, porches, and in the garage should be swept and washed if pets spend time there. A thorough vacuuming and scrubbing removes dirt and debris which can combine with an insecticide (if you use one) and keep it from coming in contact with the fleas. Vacuuming also removes some of the flea eggs and adult fleas. When done, dispose of the vacuum cleaner bags. Next, wash all pet bedding in hot water. You might also want to wash your children's bedclothes if they tend to sneak your pet into bed for a slumber party.

One area you need to concentrate on is under the beds, particularly if the pet sleeps or rests there. Vacuum carefully and even scrub the bed frame if you really want to do the job right. Finally, you may need to move some furniture and items from the floors of closets and the like to open up areas for pesticide use.

Finances permitting, you can have any pets treated by your veterinarian at the same time you're dealing with the home process. If both pet and home are not treated simultaneously, either could cause reinfestation. Insect growth regulators (IGRs) are effective against fleas and have no side effects on pets. When fleas bite an IGR-treated pet, they are rendered sterile—the eggs they lay cannot hatch. Additionally, because flea larvae feed on adult byproducts, they, too, are affected. Most IGRs come in spray form, but several flea collars, dips, and shampoos are on the market. Just recently, a monthly product for dogs and cats has become available and is proving very effective. Consult your veterinarian to determine the best treatment for your pet.

Don't forget to spray the pet carrier. Imagine how frustrated your pet would be if it goes through the hassles of dipping and pill-swallowing only to have fleas jumping back before even getting home. Now you can spray your home and the surrounding areas, using an insecticide that contains IGR. Because of the IGR's long residual life, the protection will last for months. Determine if your yard needs to be treated. In Florida, it's a good idea to treat the yard to prevent reinfestation, but rarely does the entire yard need to be sprayed. Since fleas hate sunlight, outdoor treatments can

cleaning in any place where fleas might be found.

be limited to areas where pets like to rest, such as decks and under trees and shrubs.

The most common reason that flea treatments fail is lack of planning. If it all sounds like too much trouble, pack up the family (including the pet) and take a weekend vacation while professionals do the job.

Spiders are another Florida annoyance. Most spiders bite, but the black widow's sting is said to be 15 times more deadly than the bite of a rattlesnake. On the underside of the black widow is a perfectly formed red hourglass mark. Another spider to watch out for is the brown recluse, which has a violin-shaped pattern on its thorax. It likes undisturbed areas like the backs of closets.

Scorpions are eight-legged relatives of spiders and attack by whipping their tails forward. Scorpions are active at night and hide during the day, often in shoes, piles of clothing, bedding, and furniture. There are more cases of scorpion stings than snakebite in the United States. The resulting symptoms are like those of strychnine poisoning: vomiting, sweating, shivering, and speech difficulties.

HOW TO OUTSMART BUGS

The Florida Pest Control Association suggests taking the following steps to protect your family, friends, and pets from pesky pests:

* Inspect your home regularly.
* Repair all holes in walls, floors, and foundations, and seal breaks around pipes and wires.
* Keep garbage in metal or plastic cans with tight lids.
* Empty household garbage daily.
* Fix damaged screens and doors.
* Put screens on vents and windows.
* Raise woodpiles off the ground.
* Keep firewood away from buildings.
* Vacuum carpeting, furniture, and your pet's favorite areas daily.
* Remove and dispose of the vacuum bag immediately.
* Store food in airtight containers and wipe up food spills immediately.

The Sunshine State Almanac & Book of Florida-Related Stuff

YOUR
HEALTH

Those Dangerous Ultraviolet Rays

ℰnergy from the sun sustains all life on earth. But some forms of sun energy can be harmful to people who overexpose themselves. The problem is the sun's burning, or ultraviolet, rays—the rays that cause sunburn and skin cancer. You can't see ultraviolet, or UV, rays because they are invisible forms of energy.

There are three types of UV rays: A, B, and C. A is the weakest form, but it can cause skin aging and wrinkles in humans and damage to plants and inanimate objects. B is stronger than A and is the most harmful to sun worshipers: B rays cause skin cancer and cataracts, a permanent clouding of the eye which reduces vision. B also reduces the growth of plants and may affect the health of animals. C is even stronger than B, but fortunately for us, it never reaches the earth's surface because it's filtered out by the atmosphere. In fact, most B rays are screened out by the ozone layer, a thin veil of gas high in the atmosphere. But the ozone layer is getting thinner, so more and more rays are reaching the earth's surface.

A thick, heavy layer of clouds can block some of the sun's rays, but you can get just as burned on a cloudy day as you can on a sunny day. You also receive more UV rays near snow, sand, water, and concrete, because these surfaces reflect the sun's rays back onto your skin, just like a mirror. The brighter the surface, the more UV rays that are reflected—fresh snow and dry sand reflect the most rays. We don't have to worry about snow here in Florida, but that white sand can really cause a burn.

You can still enjoy the great outdoors in Florida. Just remember to take a few simple precautions when you work or play outside, especially at the beach. Try to spend less time in the sun, or at least try to avoid being out in the sun around midday, when the sun's rays are hottest and most powerful. Wear clothes that cover your skin, such as hats, shoes, long pants, and long-sleeve shirts. Wear sunscreen on uncovered skin, especially if you're light-skinned. Reapply sunscreen every two hours or right after swimming or exercising. Sunscreen should block both UVA and UVB rays and have a sun protection factor (SPF) of at least 15. Finally, protect your eyes with sunglasses that are UV-rated.

Practicing Safe Sun

All the labels on bottles and tubes of sun care products may confuse you. But if you know the lingo, you can choose the product that's right for you. Just remember: A tan means that you have burned your skin, and it's in the process of healing.

A sunblock is stronger than a sunscreen. A sunblock contains chemicals that block the sun's rays by reflecting and scattering them. In other words, a sunblock acts as a physical barrier against the sun's rays. Previously, only titanium dioxide was used as a sunblock. You probably recognized it by all those white noses at the beach. Now, manufacturers distribute smaller particles of titanium dioxide throughout a sunblock so it doesn't create a "white shield," or they use other ingredients that also effectively block the sun's rays. These new sunblocks may also contain sunscreen chemicals; that's why they list SPF numbers.

The chemicals in sunscreens protect the skin by absorbing UV rays, thereby preventing them from penetrating the skin. Broad-spectrum sunscreens are recommended because they protect against both UVA and UVB rays. Protection from these rays is important as they can disrupt skin cells' genetic material and cause skin cancer.

The most important characteristic of a sunscreen is its SPF. A product's SPF tells you how many times longer you can stay in the sun without burning than if you had no sunscreen on at all. For example, if you burn in 20 minutes without sunscreen, a product with an SPF of 15 would allow you to stay in the sun for 5 hours (20 x 15 = 300 minutes) without burning.

SPFs range from 4 to 50. However, as you increase the SPF between 30 and 50, the amount of protection does not increase as much as it does between 15 and 30. A sunscreen with an SPF of 50 blocks only 1 to 2 percent more rays than one with an SPF of 30. In fact, the FDA is deciding whether to limit all sunscreens to an SPF of 30.

Protecting Your Children from the Sun

In Florida, it's never too early for parents to begin protecting their children from the sun. Most children are outside three times more than most adults, especially when they're on vacation in an area known for its sunshine and sandy beaches. Up to 80 percent of a person's lifetime exposure to the sun occurs before he or she reaches the age of 18. It can take 10 to 20 years for skin damage caused by childhood suntans and sunburns to result in skin cancer or premature aging.

If children regularly use a sunscreen before age 18, they can reduce their risk of getting some forms of skin cancer later in life by almost 50 percent. Here are some tips for protecting your children from the sun.

Use a sunscreen with an SPF of at least 15, and apply it 15 to 20 minutes before the kids head outside. Reapply sunscreen every 2 hours or after swimming or sweating. The sun's energy is strongest between 10 A.M. and 2 P.M., so avoid long periods of exposure during that time. Keep children under the age of 6 months out of the sun completely.

SUNGLASSES

Sunlight contains ultraviolet (sunburn rays) and infrared rays (heat rays), all dangerous to the human eye. Eyes exposed for any length of time can suffer damage ranging from itching and burning to actual blindness. In Florida, it's a good idea to take sunglasses with you when you go outdoors. Any sunglasses will work and provide protection, but there are specialized glasses with gradient-density coatings polarized to eliminate glare you normally find around water and white sand. Photochromatic lenses can change from dark to light and back again depending on the surrounding levels of light. When you spend a lot of money on sunglasses, you're usually paying for the frames, not the lenses, so if you don't need a prescription glass, you can survive nicely with a pair of drugstore glasses selling for under ten dollars.

GOT A BAD SUNBURN?

Hop into a tub filled with cool—not cold—water. Just sit there. Don't use soap or any bath oils, and don't scrub your skin. Moisten a soft towel, and pat your skin dry when you get out of the tub. To avoid chafing, use a moisturizer and product containing aloe, which soothes burns. If your skin blisters or you feel nauseous, see a doctor.

ACUPUNCTURE

Acupuncture is a form of medical therapy that involves sticking thin, solid needles into selective sites on the body. It's been part of Chinese medicine since ancient times, and there are practitioners across Florida.

The theory is that there is vital life energy flowing through a series of pathways or meridians, twelve of which are on each side of the body. Meridians are said to course through the deep tissues of the body, surfacing occasionally. The areas where the meridians touch the surface are considered useful treatment points for diseases, which are thought to be caused by imbalances in the energy flow.

Inserting a needle into certain points could increase energy flow. The needles are also used to drain away excessive pressure or to break down blocks or dams in energy flow. Meridians are related to all internal organs. The flow of energy in each meridian is read by taking the pulse associated with it at the wrist. Therapy is aimed at restoring normal energy flow so that perfect equilibrium exists throughout the body.

The use of acupuncture for controlling surgical pain is a recent development in China, and it does not strictly reflect the ancient medical philosophy. Classical Chinese medicine concerned itself with restoring normal function as opposed to creating abnormal conditions, such as total pain suppression. To control surgical pain in contemporary China, needles are inserted into various parts of the body, and the patient is stimulated by electrical current delivered through the needles or by the more traditional manual twirling of the needles. Practitioners may also inject various solutions at these body sites or use ultrasonic probes instead of needles. After about twenty minutes of stimulation, the surgery can begin. If the acupuncture treatment has been effective, the patient will be wide awake, alert, and aware of all the major surgical procedures but will experience little or no pain.

The mechanisms by which patients are able to tolerate surgery during acupuncture stimulation are still unknown. Some scientists speculate that large sensory fibers are activated, which inhibit transmission impulses from the small fibers carrying the sensory input of pain. Other scientists speculate that naturally produced morphinelike substances—endorphins and enkephalins—may be released within the brain in response to acupuncture. When these substances bind to opiate receptor cells, a pain-inhibition system is activated. More research is needed before mechanisms of acupuncture pain control can be specified. Almost certainly, psychological factors will be shown to play a crucial role.

Acupuncture pain control for surgery may well be more a scientific curiosity than a practical innovation in the West. It cannot compete with conventional anesthesia and nerve-block anesthesia because these procedures are safe, fast, and virtually 100 percent reliable. Acupuncture is time-consuming and significantly less reliable, although Chinese researchers assert that besides reducing pain, it also reduces the possibility of shock and infection. It holds some promise for treating such problems as backaches, headaches, and abdominal pain. Acupuncture is highly effective in giving short-term relief to patients suffering from such pain, but it is less impressive in terms of a long-term cure. Nevertheless, it offers hope to many patients who, having explored all conventional alternatives, have no place to turn. A small percentage of American physicians are adding acupuncture to their therapeutic methods because it is safe, it works well for

Acupuncture holds some promise for treating backaches, headaches, and abdominal pain.

certain problems, and it is an alternative to medications that have undesirable side effects.

For further information on acupuncture, visit the Website http://www.acupuncture.com or contact:

The American Academy of Medical
    Acupuncture
    800-521-2262
The American Association of
    Oriental Medicine
    610-266-1433
The National Acupuncture and
    Oriental Medicine Alliance
    253-851-6896

REALLY ALTERNATIVE MEDICINE

True believers say that bananas are the ultimate fruit. They're nice to look at, are high in potassium, taste good, and can be eaten raw with cereal or ice cream, baked, or slapped between two slices of bread and served with everything from mayonnaise to peanut butter. You can use them to make bread, muffins, pancakes, cookies, waffles, milkshakes, and pudding. But they're possibly best known among alternative medicine believers as a cure for a headache.

When you feel a headache coming on, peel a banana, throw the banana away (or eat it!), and place half of the skin on your forehead and the other half on the back of your head. Use Scotch™ tape, duct tape, or even rubber bands to hold everything in place. Scientists say that eating the banana supplements your potassium level, which could

reduce the chances of getting a headache in the first place. With the banana peels firmly in place, sit back in a chair and take it easy. If this really works, you should experience some relief in 10 to 15 minutes, and the headache should be completely gone within 30 minutes.

HANGOVERS

Floridians like to celebrate, but sometimes we celebrate too much. If you don't understand the curse of a hangover, just ask some of the "spring breakers" who flock to Florida every year when school is out. Chances are if you drink alcohol, at some point in your life you're going to drink too much and get a hangover. No one has come up with a common cure that works every time, but there are some things you can do to minimize the pain and get rid of those pink elephants.

If you know in advance that it's going to be one of those nights, take a gram or more of Vitamin C every day for a few days prior to the event. This may help your body clear the alcohol more quickly when it gets into your system. If you know that you'll be drinking in a few hours, make sure that you've got something in your stomach. Breads and pasta slow the absorption of alcohol, so sit down and eat a plate of spaghetti or a pizza.

If all of this advice is too late and you're hung over as you read this book, you need more instant relief. Some people recover in a couple of hours by just sitting it out. Others take all day sitting in a dark room. The instant-cure attempt starts with drinking lots of water, then taking Vitamin C and B-complex pills and some aspirin or other non-prescription analgesic. Eat simple foods like toast with honey and fruit and not-so-simple foods such as sauerkraut juice (honest!). Stay in a darkened room with a cool compress or moist washcloth on your forehead. Things will probably get better. If nothing else, you should recover within a day or two, so just be patient.

SEASICKNESS

Florida is surrounded by water—and when you have water, you have boats. If you're a visitor enjoying the boating opportunities in Florida or a resident who is fortunate enough to own a boat, the chances of your getting seasick are ten to two: studies show two out of every ten people who climb aboard a boat will get seasick, regardless of water conditions. Seasickness comes from the control center of the brain when it detects motion. Signals are sent to the eyes, ears, and other sensors. The fluid in your inner ear that affects your balance tells the brain one thing while the eyes tell it another. That conflict can cause your body to be out of balance, and the digestive system doesn't like that. Add the heat from the sun, fumes from the boat's engine, and other factors, and the end result is seasickness.

Avoid getting seasick by staying on deck and avoiding areas below where engine fumes might be present. Breathe lots of fresh air. Don't look backwards or sideways. Keep your eyes straight ahead and focus on the horizon. If you feel you're getting sick, stand up and breathe deeply. Don't lie down or even sit down.

If you're planning a cruise and spending all that money to have a good time, the last thing you want to do is get seasick. Sometimes the cheap cabins are the best for people who tend to get seasick. They're located lower in the ship, so there's less movement. Because there's little or no view, you won't get disoriented looking out a porthole. Avoid cabins forward or aft or off-center if you're prone to motion sickness. The middle of the boat is the best spot. So remember: low, middle, center and you'll probably have a nice trip.

Before you climb aboard a boat, avoid coffee but drink lots of water, and don't skip eating. You need something in your stomach just to keep your stomach acids occupied, but avoid greasy or acidic foods for at least six hours before boating—they take a long time to digest.

Dramamine, Meclizine, and Bonine are drugs available at any pharmacy. Just follow the instructions on the label. Some people say ginger works for them. It soothes the stomach and has no side effects. You can buy it almost anywhere in powder, tablet, or pill form. A good dose is one to four grams per day. Take it about 12 hours before you board. Ginger is also available in ginger ale and gingersnap cookies.

Other people swear by acupressure wrist bands, which apply pressure to a specific point on the wrist. This may have some effect on the body's balance points.

HANDICAP STICKERS

When a physician fills out a Physician's Statement of Certification for a Florida driver applying for a handicap sticker, it means one or more of the following:

1) the driver cannot walk two hundred feet without stopping to rest;
2) the driver cannot walk without the use of some apparatus such as a leg brace, cane, crutch, prosthetic device, or without the assistance of another person. If the assisting device significantly restores the person's ability to walk without severe limitation, the person is not eligible for the permit;
3) the driver permanently uses a wheelchair;
4) the driver is restricted by lung disease to the extent that the forced (respiratory) expired volume for one second, when measured by a spirometry, is less than one liter, or the arterial oxygen is less than 60 mm/hg at rest;
5) the driver uses portable oxygen;
6) the driver is restricted by a cardiac condition to the extent that the person's functional limitations are classified in severity as Class III or Class IV according to standards set up by the American Heart Association;
7) the driver has severe limitations in his or her ability to walk due to an arthritic, neurological, or orthopedic condition.

HICCUPS

Hiccups occur because nerves in the lower part of the esophagus and upper part of the stomach have been stimulated. If you eat too fast, you take in too much air. Under ideal conditions, that air would come out in the form of a burp. But sometimes air gets trapped between layers of food, and a couple of good hiccups can get that air out of your system. This happens so that we don't ingest any food or drink while we're hiccuping. Nature figures you'll get so uncomfortable and embarrassed about your hiccuping that you'll stop eating long enough to let the air escape.

To help your system get rid of that trapped air, tilt your head back so you're looking toward the sky and take deep breaths. Drink lots of water slowly. Eating sugar will stimulate digestion and could help. The old remedies like drinking from a cup backwards often work because the actions affect the sympathetic nervous system.

If you're a chronic hiccupper, you can help yourself by eating more slowly, not eating too much, and avoiding carbonated beverages and foods like hot peppers that stimulate the digestive system.

THE COMMON COLD

Coming down with a cold? Don't waste your money on doctor visits. If it's the ordinary common cold, there is no cure, and it will probably go away within seven to ten days. But there are things you can do to make yourself more comfortable while you're waiting for it to go away. Drink lots of fluids, get plenty of rest, and take over-the-counter medication like painkillers, decongestants, and antihistamines. Ask your pharmacist for some suggestions.

If you get a sore throat, gargle with salt water or use an anesthetic like viscous lidocaine. Antibiotics are needed only if the sore throat is caused by a Type A streptococcus. For coughs, take a cough suppressant. For sinus blockage, put on hot facial compresses or inhale steam (taking a long, hot shower helps). Sinusitis has symptoms similar to those of a cold: a runny nose, stuffy head, and aches and pains. If you have a fever of over 101 degrees that lasts for more than 24 hours, see your doctor.

You could also be coming down with the flu. How can you tell the difference? A cold rarely causes a fever or gives you a headache or causes severe aches and pains—the flu does.

YOU ARE WHAT YOU EAT—AND DRINK

If you're into healthy living, you probably know that eating the right foods is necessary for good health, and somewhere on the list of "right foods" is citrus fruit. Studies have shown that the nutrients in citrus fruits can reduce the risk of heart disease and cancer when combined with a healthy, low-fat diet rich in other fruits and vegetables. Citrus fruits, including tangelos and tangerines, have many nutritional benefits.

The Florida orange and grapefruit are the most popular citrus fruits in the country. An 8-ounce glass of Florida orange juice can supply 100 percent or more of the daily requirements for Vitamin C. Vitamin C helps maintain collagen, the body's component that helps repair body tissue. Scientists believe many of the antioxidants in citrus juice may help counteract free radicals—the cause of many diseases. Orange juice also contains folate, a B vitamin also found in green leafy vegetables, helpful in reducing the risk of certain type of birth defects.

Citrus juices like orange juice are natural sources of potassium. All citrus fruits are fat-, sodium-, and cholesterol-free. Research shows that regular exercise and a balanced diet high in fruit and vegetables and low in fat can help maintain a healthy weight. Fresh Florida oranges and grapefruit contain dietary fiber, including soluble fiber, which aids in digestion and elimination. Recent studies have reported a direct link between the nutrients found in citrus fruit and reduced cancer risk. Researchers at the National Cancer Institute have long maintained that a low-fat diet high in vitamin C-rich foods may help reduce the risk of some types of cancer. The Food and Drug Administration has concluded that a low-fat diet rich in fruits and vegetables may help fight against heart disease as well.

Research shows that women of childbearing age who eat plenty of fresh fruits and vegetables containing folate may decrease their risk of having children with birth defects. About 2,500 cases of neural tube defects, such as spina bifida and anencephaly, occur every year in the United States. Babies born with spina bifida have backbones that do not fully form around the nerves of the spinal column, while babies with anencephaly are born without most of the brain and cannot survive.

According to the Food and Drug Administration, women of childbearing age can dramatically reduce the risk of having a child with these birth defects by consuming plenty of fruits and vegetables to maintain adequate levels of folate (the most frequently consumed dietary source of folate is orange juice). Since most neural tube birth defects occur in the first six to eight weeks after conception, it is important that women of childbearing age consume adequate daily levels of folate before and soon after they become pregnant.

The old adage "You are what you eat" makes a lot of sense. Add to that the new adage: "You are what you drink." Down a glass of Florida orange or grapefruit juice on a regular basis and live a healthy life.

LIVING FOREVER

Scientists say the reason almost everything on Earth dies is because if everything lived forever, there would be no procreation, hence no evolution. All living things would eventually become too old to reproduce, and everything would become dried-up and stagnant. Eventually, there would be no people, no animals, no plants—nothing. Everything dies because it reaches a point where it can no longer properly function and conduct the activities required to sustain life, such as eating and digesting food and replacing worn-out parts.

HYPOTHERMIA

Exposure to cold causes loss of body heat, which is called hypothermia. To avoid hypothermia, avoid exposure to cold. If you fall into cold water, never discard your clothing unless it's pulling you below the surface. Then, discard only enough to keep you from going under. Clothing will help trap heat and also can be used as a flotation device if filled with air. Avoid moving as much as possible. A life jacket helps reduce the need to move around and helps insulate against heat loss. If several people are in the water, huddling together can conserve heat.

WHY DO I ITCH?

Skin specialists say an itch is a warning your skin sends out that something is wrong. You itch for many reasons: There may be pollen in the air; you might have the beginnings of a boil or cold sore; a wound or scar can trigger an itch; or your skin might be too dry from the Florida sun. Itching can be a sign of a serious disease like diabetes, so take the warning seriously. Generally speaking, though, everybody itches at one time or another, and doctors say that most of the time it's because your skin is too dry. Solution? Use a moisturizer.

WHY ARE THERE LOTS OF BALD MEN AND ONLY A FEW BALD WOMEN?

Alopecia, the medical term for loss of hair, is common in both men and women. Generally, women do not have hair loss as severely as men do, and women who do lose hair usually do so after menopause. The National Alopecia Areata Foundation estimates that there are nearly three million men, women, and children in this country with some degree of alopecia areata. It is a fairly common condition which in most cases is temporary.

Factors that promote hair loss in both men and women are poor circulation, acute illness, surgery, radiation, skin disease, sudden weight loss, iron deficiency, diabetes, thyroid disease, chemotherapy drugs, stress, poor diet, and vitamin deficiency. A study in the New England Journal of Medicine reported that men who are bald have a risk of heart disease three times greater than men who do not go bald. Apparently, the underlying biochemical imbalance which causes alopecia also increases the risk for heart disease.

Hormones are thought to play a major role in male hair loss. Men have higher levels of male hormones like testosterone, which are thought to increase alopecia in those who are susceptible. The American Hair Loss Council reports that 1 of every 7 women will start losing her hair before she reaches the age of 50, compared to 1 of every 2 men.

ON-LINE HOSPITALS AND HEALTH CARE CENTERS

You can search these sites for information on hospitals and health care centers.

For a variety of hospitals around the country:
   http://www.healthmetro.com/hospital/hospusa.html
Arnold Palmer Hospital in Orlando: http://www.orhs.org/aph.html
Baptist Health Care: http://www.bhcpns.org
Baptist Health Systems in South Florida: http://www.bhssf.org
Baptist Hospital in Miami: http://www.bhssfl.inter.net/bhm/bhm.htm

Bethesda Memorial Hospital in Boynton Beach:
  http://www.bethesdaweb.com
Boca Raton Community Hospital: http://www.brch.com
Cancer centers in Florida:
  http://www.healthmetro.com/hospital/cancer.html
Children's hospitals: http://www.healthmetro.com/hospital/child1.html
Columbia Miami Heart Institute in Miami: http://www.miamiheart.com
Fair Oaks Hospital in Delray Beach:
  http://www.tenethealth.com
Florida Hospital Heartland Division:
  http://www.flhosp-heartland.org
Florida Hospital in Orlando:
  http://www.flhosp.org
Health First in Cape Canaveral:
  http://health-first.org
Heritage Hospital in Lecanto:
  http://www.vero.com/heritagehospital

Homestead Hospital: http://www.bhssfl.inter.net/hh/hh.htm
Indian River Memorial Hospital in Vero Beach: http://www.irmh.com
M.D. Anderson Cancer Center in Orlando: http://www.orhs.org/mda.html
Mariners Hospital: http://www.bhssfl.inter.net/mh/mh.htm
Mayo Clinics and Medical Center: http://www.mayo.edu/
Memorial Healthcare Systems in Hollywood: http://www.mhs.net/
Moffit Cancer Center, USF, in Tampa: http://www.moffitt.usf.edu/
Mount Sinai Medical Center in Miami Beach:
  http://www.MountSinaiMiami.org/
Naples Community Hospital:
  http://www.naples.net/health/nch/nchhcs2.htm
Naval Hospital in Pensacola: http://www.nh_pens.med.navy.mil/
North Broward Hospital District: http://www.nbhd.org/
Orlando Regional Medical Center: http://www.orhs.org/ormc.html
Palms of Pasadena Hospital in St. Petersburg:
  http://www.tenethealth.com/PalmsPasadena/
Pinecrest Rehab Hospital in Delray Beach:
  http://www.tenethealth.com/Pinecrest/
St. Vincent's Health Systems in Jacksonville: http://www.baptist-
  stvincents.com
Sarasota Memorial Hospital: http://www.smh.com/
Seven Rivers Community Hospital in Crystal River:
  http://www.tenethealth.com/SevenRivers/
Shands Hospital at the University of Florida in Gainesville:
  http://www.hsc.ufl.edu/shands/sth.htm
Shriners Hospital for Crippled Children in Tampa: http://shriners.com/
South Miami Hospital: http://www.bhssfl.inter.net/smh/smh.htm

South Seminole Hospital in Longwood: http://www.orhs.org/sseminol.html
St. Cloud Hospital in Orlando: http://www.orhs.org/stcloud.html
Tallahassee Memorial Regional Medical Center: http://www.tmrmc.com
University of Florida Health Systems: http://www.hsc.ufl.edu/hs/ufhs.htm
USF Health Service Center in Tampa:
  http://www.med.usf.edu/hschome.html
Wuesthoff Health Systems in Rockledge: http://www.iu.net/wmh/

SIAMESE TWINS

Siamese twins are formed when monozygotic twins, those arising from a single fertilized egg, fail to completely separate from each other during the process of cell division. In a regular pregnancy, a single fertilized egg will undergo cellular division, the cells eventually differentiating into distinct organs and tissues. In the case of identical twins, a set of circumstances not entirely understood causes a separation of cells early in the division process, before actual differentiation begins, and the two halves then go on to form complete fetuses. Siamese twins, however, separate late in the division process, perhaps even after differentiation of cells has begun, and thus form into two fetuses with certain tissues or cell masses shared between them.

YOUR EARS

Noise is measured in decibels, and if your ears are bombarded with enough decibels, you can have permanent ear damage. Experts say anything over 90 decibels can be harmful, so avoid noises that reach that level. A kitchen blender clocks in at 75 to 80 decibels, a steam kettle 70 to 90, a vacuum cleaner 60 to 85, and a loud conversation 60 to 80. Mowing a lawn with a gas mower produces 90 decibels, and a snowmobile (rarely seen or heard in Florida) produces up to 100. Standing close to a video arcade game with explosive sounds goes to 120, and a jackhammer at a 10-foot distance is 125 decibels.

There are limits to exposure to these noises. For example, you can listen to a handheld power drill for several hours without any dangerous effects, but a gunshot near your ear can reach more than 140 decibels, and the tolerance time for a noise like that is zero! The noise at an average rock concert can be tolerated for less than ten minutes. After that, you're at risk.

THE FAT STORY

If you spend any time at the beach, it's important how you look. With the right diet, you can stay trim, but you've got to work at it. Floridians spend about 50 percent of their food money at restaurants because most Floridians agree—cooking ain't fun! When you and your spouse walk into a Florida restaurant looking for something good and nutritious to eat, you may spot some entrees marked low-fat, light, or healthy, or with little red hearts alongside the dish description indicating it's probably good for you. But remember—low-fat doesn't mean low in calories, and it's those calories that put on extra weight.

Until recently, what restaurants claimed on their menus wasn't governed by any state or federal agency, but in May 1997 the Food and Drug Administration stepped in and said that any claims must meet certain standards. For example, a serving of low-fat mashed potatoes or low-fat ice cream can contain no more than three grams of fat per serving to earn the low-fat title. If a restaurant offers low-fat dishes, it must provide information on those meals' nutrition content if you request it.

How to Look Good in a Bathing Suit

Florida means beaches, and beaches mean bathing suits, and bathing suits mean different things to different people. If they mean body image to you, then you're either happy with how you look in a bathing suit or unhappy. If you're happy, you can stop reading right now and go out and buy yourself a cheeseburger and some fries. If you're not happy and you're overweight and have bulges in the wrong places, here are some tips on how to slim down—hopefully in time for the next beach season.

The first step to successful weight management is, experts say, to make a lifestyle change. Whether you want to take off a few pounds, maintain your weight, or simply

increase your energy, what you eat will basically determine how you look and feel. Eat too much and you'll probably be unhappy about how you look in a bathing suit.

Successful weight-loss programs are complex, but there are some simple steps. Always discuss your weight problem with a doctor first. Then determine how much you'd like to weigh. Take the desired weight and multiply by 13. If you want to weigh 120 pounds, then multiply 120 by 13: The result, 1,560, is your daily calorie limit. To lose weight just standing around doing nothing, you'll have eat fewer than 1,560 calories a day. If you eat 1,560 calories a day and exercise, you can lose weight. It's a good idea to avoid anything under 1,300 calories a day without a doctor's recommendation.

A recent study showed that aroma has a lot to do with your desire to eat or not eat. Sniff a plate of bacon and eggs and you want to eat. Sniff a garbage can and you don't. That's why aromatherapy is a hot, new subject.

Losing Weight

Losing weight isn't easy unless you're one of those people who can eat anything without gaining weight. The two main factors in losing weight are diet and exercise, and most people don't like either. Here are some tips to get motivated:

• When it comes to cutting fat and calories from your diet, start slowly: Eat less red meat rather than eliminate it entirely, for instance

- Don't buy cookies, chips, and other high-fat snacks: If they're not in the house, you can't eat them anytime you want
- Have fresh fruits and cut-up vegetables handy so you can grab them when you get hungry
- Before you eat anything, think a minute: Are you really hungry or do you just want to put something in your mouth? Eliminate the desire through exercise, or if you must eat something, make sure it's good for you
- View an exercise routine as a lifestyle change, rather than as a temporary program
- Exercise when it feels right: If you're a morning person, hop out of bed and get moving; if you're more alert in the evening, exercise then
- Choose an exercise routine you enjoy so you'll keep doing it—walk with a friend or spouse, join a gym, buy fitness equipment
- Set goals you can meet
- Make small changes rather than huge ones
- Master one exercise before trying another

Don't expect fast results in weight loss or muscle strength. It's taken a while to get out of shape, so it will take a while to get back into shape. If you have a setback, stop, figure out why, and decide what you need to do differently in the future.

ICE CREAM HEADACHE

Do you get a headache from eating ice cream too fast? That's because the cold ice cream chills the blood in the carotid arteries as it goes down your throat. The cooled blood causes arteries feeding into the brain to constrict. As the blood warms, your headache goes away.

ARE YOU OBSESSIVE-COMPULSIVE?

Do you have to wash your hands over and over again after you've eaten Florida oranges? Do you rearrange the furniture when you rent a hotel room in some Florida resort town? Are you overly concerned about germs and other things crawling around while you're on a Florida beach? Are you always worried about being robbed or, worse, killed? You might be obsessive-compulsive if you answer "yes" to any of these questions. If you think you are, you can call the Specialty Clinic Referral Service at the University of Florida at 1-800-749-7424, extension 50615. All calls are confidential.

*The
Sunshine State
Almanac
& Book of
Florida-
Related
Stuff*

FISH

*A*quariums are attractive and colorful additions to home and office, so if you're thinking of installing one, diving the reefs in the Atlantic Ocean and the Gulf to capture your own fish is one option. You deck yourself out in a snorkel, mask, and fins; grab a fish net on a long stick; dive to the bottom; capture little fish; then take them home and drop them in an aquarium. Feed them on a regular basis, and maybe they'll survive the ordeal. Unfortunately for the do-it-yourselfer, there's more to displaying an aquarium than just dropping some fish in a tank of water.

Saltwater aquariums offer you the opportunity to take advantage of the wide variety of tropical fish in Florida. Aquariums are not only interesting and an attractive addition to the home, but having a marine aquarium allows you to observe a number of fascinating fish and invertebrates in a microcosm of the ocean environment. To maintain a marine aquarium, you need to know a little bit about how things work.

Before starting your new hobby, you need the necessary equipment:

1. Nonmetallic tank (salt corrodes metal, so avoid metal rims).
2. Undergravel filter (a plastic tray that covers the bottom of the tank with spaces for air lift columns).
3. Gravel to provide an area for bacteria to colonize (bacteria process waste in the tank). Using gravel made of calcium carbonate helps buffer the system's pH value. Use one to two pounds per gallon or two to three inches on the bottom.
4. Air pump that circulates air through air lift columns, exposing

water to the surface air, keeping the tank oxygenated, and maintaining bacteria in the gravel. Plastic tubing connects the columns to the pump.

5. Heater. The temperature of tropicals should be adjusted to a constant range: 72–78°F. Animals from colder areas outside Florida may require a different range of temperatures.

6. Thermometer.

7. Hydrometer that measures salinity by gauging density. A more expensive refractometer measures the salinity directly, in parts per thousand (ppt).

8. Salt water.

9. Tank cover to reduce evaporation from the tank and to prevent fish from leaping to their death.

10. Light source or heat lamp (optional) to encourage algae and anemone growth.

11. Plastic bucket for mixing the salt water, washing gravel, siphoning old water, etc.

Setting Up Your Aquarium

When you buy your first tank, take it home and rinse it to get rid of any residue. Test the aquarium for leaks by filling it up to the top and letting it sit for 24 hours. Empty the tank before proceeding with the following directions.

Place the filter in the bottom. Rinse the gravel and lay it over the filter. Put the aquarium in its final position before filling with water. Salt water weighs more than 8 pounds a gallon, so even a small, 20-gallon tank can get heavy. Start adding salt water by pouring the water over your hand or a dish to break its flow. Otherwise it will disturb the gravel and leave a pit.

The water will probably be cloudy at first, but will clear within a day. You can add landscaping like plastic plants, shells, coral, etc., but don't add any fish yet.

Although fish and other animals can be added into an established system, a new aquarium must be conditioned first. Temperature and salinity must be constant, but more important is the biological filtration of wastes. Fish and invertebrates produce toxic waste products such as ammonia. Bacteria living in the gravel on the bottom convert these wastes to other products which are more easily tolerated. A new fish will introduce bacteria into the water from its body, so only species that can tolerate higher levels of waste, such as crabs and damselfish, should be put in the tank for the first six weeks while the bacteria population is growing and converting wastes. After this period, more delicate species may be introduced.

It is also possible to "seed" a new tank by taking some gravel from a healthy established tank that already has a large bacterial growth in it. This culture approach will lessen the time needed to condition the water. Whichever conditioning method you use, remember that the bacteria need waste products to start the conversion cycle, so one or two hardy fish should be present from the beginning. Biological filtration can handle only so much, so resist the temptation to overfill your aquarium. A good rule of thumb is to add only one inch of fish per gallon of water. Every month or so, replace some of the water from the tank (15 to 20 percent) with new salt water to reduce the level of nitrate, which eventually becomes toxic.

To avoid thermal shock, the new water should be the same temperature as that which it replaces. If the water level decreases between changes due to evaporation, simply add enough aged tap water to make up the difference. You can do this because the salt does not evaporate.

Fish or invertebrates must be acclimated to their new environment. There are several gradual steps to follow to prevent shock to the fish from different temperatures and kinds of water. The easiest method for home aquarists is to use a shallow plastic bowl and pour the animal into this with its original water. Float this on the surface of the aquarium and the temperatures will begin to equalize. As it floats, add small portions of new water to the bowl every 10 to 15 minutes for at least one and a half hours until the bowl is nearly full and the temperatures are the same. Then, gently scoop the animal out of the bowl and add it to the tank. Discard the water in the bowl. You can also use the plastic bag in which your animal arrived, floating it in the tank. Again, add new water slowly so that both temperature and water quality will equalize.

Collecting a variety of animals presents an interesting picture of marine life but may also pose a feeding problem. Some animals require special foods or are pickier than others, so research and experiment until a suitable diet is found. Most aquarium supply stores can provide you with information on who likes what. A selection of minced raw fish, shrimp, and squid is a good staple diet for most marine life. Sea horses and anemones both love brine shrimp, and some types of fish may also like to nibble on leafy green vegetables.

If the tank has enough sun or artificial light, algae may grow on the sides, which can be beneficial. Leave this green growth on one side of the aquarium so that fish and invertebrates can graze on it. Supplements are also important for marine animals, since not all minerals and vitamins found in ocean water are in synthetic salts. No matter what the diet, resist the temptation to overfeed any animal. Don't leave food in the tank expecting the fish to snack on it later. It's best to feed fish only until they stop eating or for five minutes.

Then clean up any extra food remaining in the tank. Scavengers such as crabs will help you with this.

Commercial sea salts are available for saltwater aquariums. They can be mixed with tap water, then aged and aerated. While full strength sea water is 35 ppt, this strength encourages external parasites, so keeping the level down to 30–32 is best.

CARP FISHING FOR FUN

Most Floridians don't eat carp, so why do so many go carp fishing? They fish for the challenge, and when they land a big one, they throw it back in. There are several advantages to carp fishing. You can do it year-round and the bait is cheap enough—a ball of dough you can make yourself. Carp live almost everywhere in fresh water, and they've been known to get pretty big.

All you need is a sturdy pole, some line, a hook, and some dough bait. A net comes in handy when you're ready to land the fish. If the waters are calm, you might want to add a cork float to your line.

Carp actually suck the bait, tasting it and then nibbling around the hook. They're so cautious, a cork floating in very calm water barely moves, so patience counts. Try to hook them too soon and off they go.

To make carp bait, mix some Wheaties™ cereal and some kind of sweet soda pop into a dough with a consistency that allows you to mold the dough into balls. Make the balls small enough to cover a small treble hook. Another recipe is one cup of water, one cup of cornmeal, three-fourths of a cup of flour, and two teaspoons of sugar. Bring the water and sugar to a boil, add the cornmeal and flour, and stir over low heat for about five minutes. Cover and cook for about 30 minutes.

Carp like potatoes, so potato balls might catch a big one. Take two peeled and grated potatoes, half a teaspoon of salt, one tablespoon of cornmeal, and two table-

spoons of sweetener and mix with enough water to make stiff dough. Carp have a sweet tooth, so any kind of sweetener mixed in with the dough bait will work. Carp also like cooked whole grains, carrots, boiled parsnips, corn, green and lima beans, marshmallows, and gumdrops.

How to Set a Fish Hook

Fish with tough mouths like tarpon require that every bit of slack be taken out of the line. The most common mistake of most anglers—usually resulting in a fish not being hooked—is their failure to first tighten the line before setting the hook.

Visualize a garden hose lying in loose curves on the lawn. A good yank on one end won't even move the other end unless the hose is first pulled straight. So remember, when the strike occurs, drop the rod tip, reel until you feel the weight of the fish, and then lift up and strike sharply to ensure a good set of the hook.

FRESHWATER FISH

Florida has 3 million acres of freshwater lakes and 12 thousand miles of streams and rivers. From those waters, more than 200 different species of freshwater fish have been collected. These include several rather rare native fishes and 73 species of nonnative fishes (fish that come from outside of the United States and would not have been found in Florida without human intervention). The species that most people tend to think about are the larger fish that are used by people for recreation or food.

Scientific Name	Common Name
Acantharchus pomotis	mud sunfish
Acenser brevostrum	shortnose sturgeon
Acenser oxyrhynchus	Atlantic sturgeon
Adinia xenica	diamond killish
Aequidens pulcher	blue acara
Agonostomus monticola	mountain mullet
Alosa aestivalis	blueback herring
Alosa alabamae	Alabama shad
Alosa chrysochloris	skipjack herring
Alosa mediocris	hickory shad
Alosa sapidissima	American shad
Ameiurus natalis	yellow bullhead
Ameiurus nebulosus	brown bullhead
Ameiurus serracanthus	spotted bullhead
Amia calva	bowfin
Ammocrypta asprella	crystal darter
Ammocrypta bascia	Florida sand darter
Anabas testudineus	climbing perch
Anchoa mitchilli	bay anchovy
Anguilla rostrata	American eel
Aphredoderus sayanus	pate perch
Archosargus probatocephalus	sheepshead
Arius felis	hardhead catfish
Astronotus ocellatus	Oscar
Awaous tajasica	river goby
Badiella chrysoura	silver perch
Barbus conchonius	rosy barb
Barbus gelius	golden barb
Barbus sp.	tinfoil barb
Barbus tetrazona	tiger barb
Belonesox belizanus	pike killish
Betta splendens	Siamese fighting fish
Callichthys sp.	callichthys
Carassius auratus	goldfish
Carcharhinus leucas	bull shark
Carpiodes cyprinus	quillback
Carpiodes veler	highfin carpsucker
Centrarchus macropterus	flier
Centropomus enserus	swordspine snook
Centropomus parallelus	fat snook
Centropomus pectinatus	tarpon snook
Centropomus undecimalis	snook
Cichla ocellaris	butterfly peacock

Scientific Name	Common Name
Cichla temensis	speckled peacock
Cichlasoma bimaculatum	black acara
Cichlasoma citrinellum	Midas cichlid
Cichlasoma cyanoguttatum	Rio Grande cichlid
Cichlasoma labiatum	red devil
Cichlasoma meeki	femouth cichlid
Cichlasoma nigrofasciatum	convict cichlid
Cichlasoma octofasciatum	Jack Dempsey
Cichlasoma salvini	yellowbelly cichlid
Cichlasoma trimaculatum	three-spot cichlid
Cichlasoma uropthalmus	Mayan cichlid
Clarias batrachus	walking catfish
Colis labiosa	thick-lipped gouraim
Colis lalia	dwarf gouraim
Colossoma bidens	pacu
Colossoma brachypomum	pacu
Colossoma macropomum	pacu
Colossoma nigrinnis	blackfin pacu
Corydoras sp.	corydoras
Ctenopharyngodon idella	grass carp
Ctenopoma nigropannosum	two-spot ctenopoma
Cynoscion nebulosus	spotted seatrout
Cyprinodon variegatus	sheepshead minnow
Cyprinus carpio	common carp
Danio (Brachydanio) rerio	zebra danio
Danio malabaricus	giant danio
Dasyatis sabina	Atlantic stingray
Diapterus plumieri	striped mojarra
Dormitator maculatus	fat sleeper
Dorosoma cepedianum	gizzard shad
Dorosoma petenense	threadfin shad
Elassoma evergladei	Everglades pygmy sunfish
Elassoma okefenokee	Okefenokee pygmy sunfish
Elassoma zonatum	banded pygmy sunfish
Eleotris picta	spotted sleeper
Eleotris pisonis	spinycheek sleeper
Elops saurus	ladyfish
Enneacanthus chaetodon	blackbanded sunfish
Enneacanthus gloriosus	bluespotted sunfish
Enneacanthus obesus	banded sunfish
Ericymba buccata	silverjaw minnow
Erimyzon sucetta	lake chubsucker
Erimyzon tenuis	sharpfin chubsucker

Scientific Name	Common Name
Esox americanus	redfin pickerel
Esox niger	chain pickerel
Etheostoma (Ulocentra) sp.	orangeside darter
Etheostoma davisoni	Choctawhatchee darter
Etheostoma edwini	brown darter
Etheostoma fusorme	swamp darter
Etheostoma histrio	harlequin darter
Etheostoma okaloosae	Okaloosa darter
Etheostoma olmstedi	tessellated darter
Etheostoma parvinne	goldstripe darter
Etheostoma proeliare	cypress darter
Etheostoma stigmaeum	speckled darter
Etheostoma swaini	gulf darter
Eucinostomus argenteus	spotfin mojarra
Floridichthys carpio	goldspotted killish
Fundulus chrysotus	golden topminnow
Fundulus cingulatus	banded topminnow
Fundulus confluentus	marsh killish
Fundulus escambiae	starhead minnow
Fundulus grandis	gulf killish
Fundulus heteroclitus	mummichog
Fundulus jenkinsi	saltmarsh topminnow
Fundulus lineolatus	lined topminnow
Fundulus olivaceus	blackspotted topminnow

Scientific Name	Common Name
Fundulus pulvereus	bayou killish
Fundulus seminolis	Seminole killish
Fundulus similis	longnose killish
Gambusia affinis	western mosquitofish
Gambusia holbrooki	mosquitofish
Geophagus brasiliensis	pearl eartheater
Geophagus surinamensis	redstriped eartheater
Gobioides broussoneti	violet goby
Gobionellus boleosoma	darter goby
Gobionellus shufeldti	freshwater goby
Gobiosoma bosci	naked goby
Gobiosoma robustum	code goby
Gymnocorymbus ternetzi	black tetra
Harengula jaguana	scaled sardine
Helostoma temmincki	kissing gourami
Hemichromis bimaculatus	jewelfish
Heterandria formosa	least killish
Hoplias malabaricus	tahira
Hybognathus hayi	cypress minnow
Hybopsis aestivalis	speckled chub
Hybopsis winchelli	clear chub
Hypostomus plecostomus	suckermouth catfish
Ichthyomyzon gagei	southern brook lamprey
Ameiurus brunneus	snail bullhead
Ameiurus catus	white catfish
Ictalurus furcatus	blue catfish
Ictalurus punctatus	channel catfish
Jordanella floridae	flagfish
Labeo chrysophekadion	black sharkminnow
Labidesthes sicculus	brook silverside
Lagodon rhomboides	pinfish
Leiostomus xanthurus	spot
Lepisosteus oculatus	spotted gar
Lepisosteus osseus	longnose gar
Lepisosteus platyrhincus	Florida gar
Lepisosteus spatula	alligator gar
Lepomis auritus	redbreast sunfish
Lepomis cyanellus	green sunfish
Lepomis gulosus	warmouth
Lepomis humilis	orangespotted sunfish
Lepomis macrochus	bluegill
Lepomis marginatus	dollar sunfish
Lepomis megalotis	longear sunfish

Scientific Name	Common Name
Lepomis microlophus	redear sunfish
Lepomis punctatus	spotted sunfish
Leporinus fasciatus	banded leporinus
Leptolucania ommata	pygmy killish
Lucania goodei	bluefin killish
Lucania parva	rainwater killish
Lutjanus griseus	gray snapper
Macropodus opercularis	paradisefish
Megalops atlanticus	tarpon
Menidia beryllina	inland silverside
Metynnis lpincottianus	silver dollar
Microgobius gulosus	clown goby
Micropogonias undulatus	Atlantic croaker
Micropterus coosae	redeye bass
Micropterus notius	Suwannee bass
Micropterus punctulatus	spotted bass
Micropterus salmoides	largemouth bass
Micropterus sp.	bass
Minytrema melanops	spotted sucker
Morone chrysops	white bass
Morone hybrid	sunshine bass
Morone saxatilis	striped bass
Moxostoma carinatum	river redhorse
Moxostoma poecilurum	blacktail redhorse
Moxostoma sp.	greyfin redhorse
Mugil cephalus	striped mullet
Mugil curema	white mullet
Nocomis leptocephalus	bluehead chub
Notemigonus crysoleucas	golden shiner
Notropis atrapiculus	black shiner
Notropis baileyi	rough shiner
Notropis callitaenia	bluestreak shiner
Notropis chalybaeus	ironcolor shiner
Notropis chrysocephalus	striped shiner
Notropis cummingsae	dusky shiner
Notropis emiliae	pugnose minnow
Notropis harperi	redeye chub
Notropis hypselopterus	sailfin shiner
Notropis leedsi	bannerfin shiner
Notropis longostris	longnose shiner
Notropis maculatus	taillight shiner
Notropis petersoni	coastal shiner
Notropis signinnis	flagfin shiner

Scientific Name	Common Name
Notropis sp.	blackmouth shiner
Notropis texanus	weed shiner
Notropis venustus	blacktail shiner
Notropis welaka	bluenose shiner
Notropis zonistius	bandfin shiner
Noturus funebris	black madtom
Noturus gyrinus	tadpole madtom
Noturus leptacanthus	speckled madtom
Opisthonema oglinum	Atlantic thread herring
Orthopristis chrysoptera	pigfish
Osteoglossum bicrhosum	arowana
Oxydoras niger	thorny catfish
Paralichthys lethostigma	southern flounder
Perca flavescens	yellow perch
Percina caprodes	logperch
Percina nigrofasciata	blackbanded darter
Percina ouachitae	saddleback darter
Petromyzon marinus	sea lamprey
Platydoras costatus	Raphael's catfish
Poecilia hybrid	black molly
Poecilia latinna	sailfin molly
Poecilia reticulata	guppy
Poecilia sphenops	liberty molly
Pomoxis annularis	white crappie
Pomoxis nigromaculatus	black crappie
Pterodoras granulosus	(no common name)
Pterophyllum scalare	angel fish
Pterygoplichthys multadiatus	radiated ptero
Pylodictis olivaris	flathead catfish
Sciaenops ocellatus	red drum
Semotilus atromaculatus	Creek chub
Serrasalmus humeralis	pambeba
Serrasalmus nattereri	caribe
Serrasalmus rhombeus	white panha
Stizostedion canadense	sauger
Strongylura marina	Atlantic needlefish
Strongylura notata	redfin needlefish
Strongylura timucu	timucu
Syngnathus scovelli	gulf pipefish
Oreochromis (Tilapia) aurea	blue tilapia
Tilapia hybrid	red tilapia
Tilapia mariae	spotted tilapia
Tilapia melanotheron	blackchin tilapia

Scientific Name	Common Name
Tilapia mossambica	Mozambique tilapia
Tilapia sparrmani	banded tilapia
Tilapia zilli	redbelly tilapia
Trichogaster leeri	pearl gourami
Trichogaster trichopterus	blue gourami
Trichopsis vittata	croaking gourami
Trinectes maculatus	hogchoker
Umbra pygmaea	eastern mudminnow
Xhophorus helleri	green swordtail
Xhophorus maculatus	southern platyfish
Xhophorus variatus	variable platyfish

JELLYFISH

Jellyfish are not fish. They are invertebrates, relatives of sea anemones and corals. Other animals that resemble jellyfish, like the Portuguese man-of-war, are often called jellyfish, but they're not. They're just close relatives.

Jellyfish are made up of three main parts: the round umbrella-like bodies which they use to propel themselves through the water with a pulsating motion; the tentacles that sting and immobilize prey; and the arm, sometimes called a flap, that is used to eat their prey. Jellyfish are 95 percent water and use their nerve cells to move and react to food and danger. They have no heart, brains, eyes, or bones. Simple sensors tell them whether they are heading up or down, into the light or away from it.

Known to have existed 650 million years ago, they predate even the first sharks on the planet. Many of them are almost transparent, a convenient camouflage when there are no places to hide from predators. They sometimes use their pulsing ability to move vertically. As they are carried with the current, they are both prey and predator, catching small animal organisms, fish eggs, and other jellyfish in a net of tentacles. Tiny "harpoons" in the stinging cells of the tentacles paralyze their prey. This stinging quality is well known to Florida swimmers.

More about Jellyfish

Although jellyfish look harmless, they are in fact very efficient predators. They are able to stun or kill their prey with stinging cells called cnidocytes. Each cnidocyte contains a tiny harpoon called a nematocyst that, when triggered by touch or chemicals, not only shoots into the prey but causes the other cells in the area to activate as well. A toxin is released which stuns or kills the prey. The potency of the toxin varies greatly among different kinds of jellyfish. That is why some jellyfish are only annoying, and others, like the box jellyfish, are extremely dangerous.

If you are stung, apply vinegar or alcohol immediately to keep the nematocysts from being fired. Next, apply a paste of water and meat tenderizer to the skin. The meat tenderizer will break down the proteins that make up the jellyfish toxin and provide some relief from the pain.

THE OCEAN SUNFISH

This strange fish, popular off the Florida coast, can grow up to ten feet long and weigh more than a ton. It's actually taller than it is long because of its fins. Its dorsal and anal fins are located in the rear part of the body. These fins appear joined by the caudal fin. The body is silver gray, the fins are dark, and the body is flat and round like a disk.

This is a pelagic fish. When spotted near the coast, it is probably looking for a cleaning by wrasses, which are more abundant close to the coast. The sunfish feeds on animal plankton, algae, squid, and small fishes like eel larvae. It has been observed lying flat near the surface. Some people think it does so to get some sunlight while others think this behavior is a sign of illness or near-death. Still others think the fish is looking downward for prey or predators. Juvenile sunfish are about one inch long with small fins. The sunfish has a very small brain compared to its size: A 450-pound specimen may have a brain that's the size of a nut and weighs only 4 grams.

STARFISH

Starfish (they're not really fish) are also called sea stars. They can regenerate body parts. If the arm is part of the central disc, it can regenerate the entire body. If you cut off only the tip of an arm, that tip will not regenerate, but the animal will grow another arm.

Scientists report they have seen a single arm nearly eight inches long with small, half-inch arms growing off it that would eventually become a whole new sea star. If you cut a sea star into quarters, each piece will grow into a whole new sea star. As long as a piece has part of the central disc, it should regenerate into a whole organism. If you cut a starfish in half, and then let it grow into a whole one before cutting it in half again, the cycle will go on indefinitely.

COMMON FISH OF THE FLORIDA KEYS

Blue Marlin (*Makaira nigricans*)—cobalt blue on top shading to silvery white on bottom; upper jaw elongated in form of spear; dorsal fin and pointed at front end; pectoral fin and anal fin pointed; lateral line reticulated (interwoven like a net), difficult to see in large specimens; no dark spots on dorsal fin; body covered with embedded scales ending in one or two sharp points. Found offshore. The largest of the Atlantic marlins have been known to exceed 2,000 pounds and reach a length of 12 feet or more.

Sailfish (*Istiophorus platypterus*)—dark blue on top, brown-blue laterally, silvery white underbelly; upper jaw elongated in form of spear; first dorsal greatly enlarged in the form of a sail, with many black spots, its front squared off, highest at its midpoint; pelvic fins very narrow, reaching almost to the anus; body covered with embedded scales, blunt at end; lateral line curved over pectoral, then straight to base of tail. Found offshore in waters near the Gulf Stream. Sailfish measuring seven feet in length are common.

Shortfin Mako (*Isurus oxyrinchus*)—deep blue back and white underside; underside of sharply pointed snout white; lunate tail with similarly sized lobes; lateral keel at the base of the tail; origin of first dorsal entirely behind base of pectoral fins; second dorsal fin slightly in front of anal fin; slender; recurved teeth with smooth edges. Found offshore and often seen near the surface. Commonly 6 to 8 feet in length weighing 200 to 300 pounds.

Bonefish (*Albula vulpes*)—silvery color with bluish or greenish back; slender, round body; snout long, conical, aiming downward

and overhanging lower jaw; dark streaks between scales on upper half of body and faint cross-bands extending down to lateral line; extremities of dorsal and caudal fins shaded with black. Found primarily in shallow waters less than one foot deep, usually over lush grass flats or white sand. Size ranges from three to five pounds.

Tarpon (*Megalops atlanticus*)—back dark blue to green or greenish black shading into bright silver on the sides; may be brownish gold in estuarine waters; last ray of dorsal fin extended into long filament; one dorsal fin; huge scales; mouth large and points upward. Found primarily near shore, although adult fish spawn offshore where the ribbonlike larval stage of the fish can be found. Weigh 40 to 50 pounds.

Permit (*Trachinotus falcatus*)—gray, dark or iridescent blue above, shading to silvery sides, in dark waters showing golden tints around breast; small permit have teeth on tongue (none on pompano); no scutes; dorsal fin insertion directly above that of the anal fin; 17 to 21 soft dorsal rays; 16 to 19 soft anal rays. Found offshore on wrecks and debris, near shore on grass and sand flats and in channels. Weigh around 25 pounds.

Red Grouper (*Epinephelus morio*)—brownish red; lining of mouth scarlet-orange; blotches on sides in unorganized pattern; second spine of dorsal fin longer than others; pectoral fins longer than pelvic fins; squared-off tail; margin of soft dorsal black with white at midfin; black dots around the eyes. A bottom-dwelling fish associated with hard bottoms and reefs.

Dolphin (*Coryphaena hippurus*)—bright greenish-blue above, yellow on sides, with capability of flashing purple, chartreuse, and a wide range of other colors; body tapers sharply from head to tail; irregular blue or golden blotches scattered over sides; anterior profile of head on adult males is nearly vertical; head of females more sloping; the single dark dorsal fin extends from just behind the head to the tail; anal fin margin concave and extending from anus to tail. Found offshore in warm waters. Average weight to 30 pounds. *Note*: This is not the marine mammal.

Mutton Snapper (*Lutjanus analis*)—olive green on back and upper sides, all fins below the lateral line having reddish tinge; bright blue line below eye, following contour of operculum; anal fin pointed; small black spot below dorsal fin; V-shaped tooth patch on roof of mouth. Inshore species found near grass beds, mangroves, and canals. Larger adults usually found offshore. Weigh about 15 pounds.

Florida Fishing Laws

In Florida, you need a license to fish but not to operate a boat. Licenses are available at bait and tackle shops around the state, along with literature on fishing restrictions and regulations. At press time, the following fees were in effect:

Residents:

Ten-day license	$10
One-year license	$12
Five-year license	$60

Nonresidents:

Three-day license	$5
Seven-day license	$7
One-year license	$30

Lifetime fishing licenses for saltwater fishing are also available to Florida residents. The fees are based on age. Residents over 64 years old receive a free license. Residents aged 13 to 63 pay $300 for a lifetime license; residents aged 5 to 12 pay $225 for a lifetime license. A lifetime sportsman's license—good for freshwater and saltwater fishing, archery, muzzle-load guns, turkey, waterfowl, snook, and crawfish—is also available with fees based on age: over 64, no fee; 13–63, $1,000; 5–12, $700; children under 5, $400.

No fishing license is required if you're over 65 years of age, a member of the armed forces serving in Florida, or a permanently disabled Florida resident. Also, no license is needed for saltwater fishing off a structure attached to the land (a pier, bridge, jetty, etc.). There are a lot of confusing exceptions, so if you have questions, contact the Florida Marine Fisheries Commission at 904-487-0554, the Florida Marine Patrol at 800-942-5367, or call 800-SHARK-8-1.

Here Are Some More Rules

Once you have your license, you should know the state has specific rules about taking saltwater species out of the water. For instance, it's unlawful to harvest, possess, land, purchase, sell, or exchange jewfish, sawfish, saw shark, basking shark, whale shark, spotted eagle ray, and sturgeon. Here's an explanation of the codes listed below:

(A) Must remain in whole condition until landed ashore
(B) Total length—tip of snout to tip of tail
(X) Federal size limits apply
(N) New or additional information provided
(R) Restricted species (Mullet is not a restricted species west of the Ochlockonee River)
(D) Harvest from approved shellfish harvest areas only

African Pompano—size limit: not less than 24"; no closed season; daily bag limit: two per person per vessel. Remarks: No snatch hooking.

Bay Scallops—no size limit; closed season: September 1–June 30; daily bag limit: two gallons whole or one pint meat. Special regulations apply to St. Joe Bay. Restricted harvest areas apply to all other state waters. Call Florida Marine Patrol for latest information.

Billfish—size limit: sailfish 57", blue marlin 86", white marlin 62"; no season; daily bag limit: one. Remarks: Species includes marlin, spearfish, and sailfish.

Black Drum (R, B, A)—size limit: not less than 14" or more than 24"; no closed season; daily bag limit: five; cannot possess more than one over 24".

Black Mullet (R, C)—no size limit; closed season: ten consecutive twenty-four-hour periods beginning at noon on fourth Friday in December; daily bag limit: 50 per vessel or person, whichever is less. Remarks: Regional gear and harvest requirements.

Blue Crab (R)—no size limit; no closed season; daily bag limit: ten gallons whole. Remarks: Illegal to use more than five traps without proper permit. Trap requirements apply. Harvest of egg-bearing blue crab prohibited.

Bluefish (R, A)—size limit: 12" fork; no closed season; daily bag limit: ten.

Bonefish (B)—size limit: 18"; no closed season; daily bag limit: one. Remarks: Cannot buy or sell. Only one in possession.

Cobia (A)—size limit: 33"; no closed season; daily bag limit: two.

Crawfish (R, A)—size limit: more than 3" carapace; closed season: April

1–August 5; daily bag limit: 24 per boat or 6 per person, whichever is greater. Remarks: Trapping under license only. Crawfish stamp is required. Special recreational crawfish license holder bag limit: 50 per vessel. Call Florida Marine Patrol for current information.

Cubera Snapper (R, B)—size limit: not less than 12″ or more than 30″; no closed season; daily bag limit: ten. Remarks: No more than two 30″ or larger per person or vessel, whichever is less. Under 30″ included in aggregate limit.

Dolphin—no size limit; no closed season; daily bag limit: ten. Remarks: 20″ size limit for sale.

Flounder (R, B)—size limit: 12″; no closed season; daily bag limit: ten.

Gray Snapper (mangrove) (R, A, B)—size limit: 10″; no closed season; daily bag limit: five. Remarks: No more than ten snappers aggregate of all snappers with a bag limit.

Greater Amberjack (R, A)—size limit: 28″ fork; no closed season; daily bag limit: three. Remarks: Shall not purchase, sell, or exchange less than 36″ fork length.

Grey Trigger (B)—size limit: 12″; no closed season; no daily bag limit.

Grouper (R, A, B)—size limit: 20″; no closed season; daily bag limit: five aggregate of all species. Remarks: Includes yellowfin, red, black, gag, yellowmouth, scamp. Harvest of Nassau prohibited.

Hogfish (R)—size limit: 12″ fork; no closed season; daily bag limit: five.

King Mackerel (R)—size limit: 20″ fork; no closed season; daily bag limit: two. Remarks: Bag limit in Gulf-Atlantic fishery reduced to one when federal waters closed to harvest.

Lane Snapper (R, A, B)—size limit: 8″; no closed season; bag limit: no more than ten snappers aggregate of all snappers with a bag limit.

Mutton Snapper (R, B)—size limit: 16″; no closed season; daily bag limit: ten. Remarks: Included in snapper aggregate.

Oysters (D)—size limit: 3″. Closed season: June, July, August in Dixie, Wakulla, and Levy Counties; July, August, September in all other areas. Daily bag limit: two bags per person or boat, whichever is less per day. Remarks: Apalachicola Bay has summer and winter areas. Check with Marine Patrol for legal locations.

Permit (R)—size limit: not less than 10″ or greater than 20″; no closed season; daily bag limit: no more than ten per any combination with pompano. Remarks: No more than one 20″ or larger. No snatch hooking.

Pompano (R, A)—size limit: not less than 10″ or greater than 20″; no closed season; daily bag limit: no more than ten per any combination with permit. Remarks: Prohibits sale greater than 20″. Must be landed whole.

Red Drum (redfish) (A, B)—size limit: not less than 18″ or more than 27″; no closed season; daily bag limit: one. Remarks: Gigging, spearing, snatching prohibited. Cannot buy or sell native redfish.

Red Porgy (B)—size limit: 12″ on Atlantic Coast; no closed season; no daily bag limit.

Red Snapper (R, A, B)—size limit: 14″ on Gulf Coast, 20″ on Atlantic Coast; no closed season; daily bag limit: two. Remarks: Bag limit. No more than ten snappers aggregate of all snappers with a bag limit.

Schoolmaster (R, A, B)—size limit: 10″; no closed season; daily bag limit: ten. Remarks: Bag limit. No more than ten snappers aggregate of all snappers with a bag limit.

Sea Bass (B)—size limit: 8″; no closed season; no daily bag limit.

Shad—no size limit; closed: March 15–November 15; daily bag limit: ten. Remarks: Hook and line only.

Shark—size limit: none; no closed season; daily bag limit: one per person or two per vessel, whichever is less. Remarks: Also see protected species. Practice of finning prohibited.

Sheepshead (R, A, B)—size limit: not less than 12″; no closed season; daily bag limit: ten. Remarks: No snatch hooking.

Snappers (all other) (R, A, B)—size limit: 12″; no closed season; daily bag limit: ten aggregate of all snapper having a bag limit. Remarks: Includes blackfin, cubera under 30″, dog, mahogany, queen, silk, and yellowtail.

Snook (A, B)—size limit: not less than 24″ or more than 34″; closed: December 15–January 31, June, July, August. Daily bag limit: two. Remarks: Cannot possess more than one over 34″. Cannot buy or sell. Snook stamp required.

Spanish Mackerel (R, A)—size limit: 12″; no closed season; daily bag limit: ten. Remarks: Transfer of Spanish mackerel to other vessels prohibited.

Speckled Hind (R, N)—no size limit; no closed season; daily bag limit: one per person per vessel. Remarks: Not counted in grouper aggregate bag limit.

Spotted Sea Trout (Spotted Weakfish) (R, A, B)—size limit: East and Southwest Region: not less than 15″ or greater than 20″; Northwest Region: not less than 15″ or greater than 24″; closed season: East and Southwest Region: November 1–December 31; Northwest Region: February 1–February 28. Daily bag limit: East and Southwest Region, five; Northwest Region, seven. Remarks: May possess one over regional size maximum, does count towards bag limit.

Stone Crab (R)—size limit: two 3/4″ claws; closed season: May 15–October 15; daily bag limit: one gallon claws. Remarks: Trapping under permit only. Cannot possess whole crab.

Tarpon—no size limit; no closed season; daily bag limit: two. Remarks: Cannot buy or sell. Requires $50 tarpon tag to possess or kill.

Tripletail (R, A, B)—size limit: not less than 15″; no closed season; daily bag limit: two. Remarks: No snatch hooking.

Vermilion Snapper (R, A, B)—size limit: 8″ on Gulf Coast, 10″ on Atlantic Coast; no closed season; daily bag limit: ten (Atlantic). Remarks: Not counted in snapper aggregate bag limit.

Weakfish—size limit: not less than 12″; no closed season; daily bag limit: four.

FLORIDA'S FISH

All the waters surrounding Florida are home to more than a thousand species of fish. More than 40 of these are so important to the state that they're regulated. Game fish (fish that cannot be sold commercially) include sailfish, bonefish, tarpon, redfish, snook, and permit over a certain length.

Here's a list of sport fish commonly caught by Florida anglers.

Almaco jack	Fantail mullet	Sand seatrout
American shad	Fat snook	Sandbar shark
Atlantic sharpnose shark	Florida pompano	Scalloped hammerhead
	Gag	Scamp
Atlantic croaker	Gray snapper	Schoolmaster
Atlantic spadefish	Greater amberjack	Sheepshead
Banded rudderfish	Gulf flounder	Shortfin mako
Bank sea bass	Jewfish	Silk snapper
Black sea bass	King mackerel	Silver seatrout
Black grouper	Ladyfish	Silver perch
Black drum	Lane snapper	Spanish mackerel
Blackfin snapper	Lesser amberjack	Spotted seatrout
Blue runner	Longbill spearfish	Striped (black) mullet
Blue marlin	Mahogony snapper	Swordfish
Bluefish	Mutton snapper	Swordspine Snook
Bonefish	Nassau grouper	Tarpon Snook
Bonnethead shark	Palometa	Tarpon
Cero	Permit	Vermilion snapper
Cobia	Queen snapper	Weakfish
Common snook	Red snapper	White marlin
Crevalle jack	Red grouper	White grunt
Cubera snapper	Red drum	Yellowfin grouper
Dog snapper	Rock sea bass	Yellowmouth grouper
Dolphin	Sailfish	Yellowtail snapper

SPEARFISHING IN FLORIDA

Florida law says you cannot spearfish within 100 yards of a public beach or pier or from any bridge where public fishing is allowed. You also cannot spearfish within 100 yards of a jetty that is above the water's surface except at the 500-yard mark of an exposed jetty that extends more than 1,500 yards from the shoreline.

It is unlawful to spear any ornamental reef fish like trumpet fish, porcupine fish, sturgeon, dorsal fish, parrotfish, angelfish, sea horses, and puffers in certain Florida counties and in any waters under the jurisdiction of the State Division of Recreation and Parks.

LOBSTER HUNTING

You can never spear lobster in Florida. The season for lobster is August 6 to March 31. A mini-season is open on the last consecutive Wednesday and Thursday in July. All lobster must be taken whole and remain in whole condition until you reach land. No egg-bearing females may be taken. The use of devices such as spears, gigs, grab hooks, and similar devices is prohibited. You must have a measuring device and measure each lobster before removing it from the water.

STONE CRABS

Stone crab season is October 16–May 14. Legal claws may be taken, but live crabs must be released. It is unlawful to remove claws from an egg-bearing female. Claws must be at least 2.75 inches. Stone crab may not be trapped unless you have a permit for trapping. You cannot use devices such as spears, gigs, grab hooks.

HOW TO CLEAN A FISH

After you catch a fish or buy one whole, there are a few steps to transform a whole fish into what winds up on your plate. Most first-time fish cleaners say it's not as messy as one might think, although it is a little messy by some standards.

First, cover your work area with plenty of newspaper or heavy paper bags. Have a plastic bag handy for the guts, bones, etc. (Seal well before disposing.) Wash the fish to remove any slime. With a sharp knife, cut off the pectoral fins on both sides of the fish. Not all fish need scaling. If you're not sure, run the blade of the blunt knife at almost a 90-degree angle to the body from tail end to head. If the scales are thick and come up easily, you need to remove them. Continue until the body is smooth.

The dorsal fin is that large, tough, spiny fin that runs along the backbone, and the pectoral fin is smaller, more flexible, and attached to either side of the body. Cut along the length of each side of the dorsal fin (the one on the top). Remove it and the connecting bone by giving a quick pull from tail end to head. This step isn't always necessary, but it does eliminate those tiny, annoying bones that can ruin a meal. Cut the head off right below the gills. Cut the tail where it joins the body. To prepare a fish for cooking whole, it is not necessary to remove the head, tail, or dorsal bones. It is necessary, however, to remove the gills.

Using the sharp knife, drive the blade point into the vent (the small anal opening near the tail where the body begins to widen). Cut right through the belly all the way to the gills. Remove the guts from the cavity with a spoon, and scoop out the dark reddish-brown kidney line that lies along the backbone. It's important to cut out all parts of the gills. If you don't have a sharp knife, kitchen shears will do the job. These can be used to remove the gills, cut off the head and tail, and snip open the cavity.

Now you're ready to throw the fish on the grill, in the oven, or in the frying pan.

*The
Sunshine State
Almanac
& Book of
Florida-
Related
Stuff*

HOBBIES

*F*lorida is the ideal place to raise exotic pets such as snakes, lizards, and monkeys. The weather is favorable, and chances are good any outdoor pet will enjoy the Sunshine State—especially compared to places like Newark and Cleveland. But exotic pets are, well, exotic and require special care, often beyond the average pet lover's abilities. If you've had experience only with cats, dogs, and goldfish, hosting an exotic pet will be an entirely new experience.

Before you consider buying an exotic pet that will spend its life with you, first determine if you have enough room for the pet.

Does the pet need some kind of special cage?

Are you willing to take care of the pet on a daily or even an hourly basis? This includes not only feeding and grooming the pet but providing it with companionship and attention and cleaning up.

Can you afford to not only buy the pet but pay for the pet's upkeep, which might include trips to the vet, special medicines and grooming products, special foods, etc.

How will you care for the pet when you're away from home? Do you have (reliable) friends or relatives who will pet-sit for you?

What will you do with the pet if it becomes unmanageable or the novelty wears off?

Learn as much as you can about a particular pet species and the pluses and minuses of owning one. Some pets live longer than humans, so if it outlives you, it's going to need care after you're gone. A parrot can live 80 years; a turtle more than 100. Visit the library or access information from the Internet and learn everything you can about the exotic pet you're considering. Most of all, try to control the impulse to buy an exotic pet until you've considered every angle.

HOW TO BUY A PET BIRD

Florida is the perfect home for pet birds. The mild climate allows you to keep birds outdoors part of the year, and you can house them in some of the fanciest cages available anywhere. Some cages in brass sell for as much as $5,000, but if you're a budget bird buyer, you can find a cage for as little as $20. Make sure the cage is big enough so the bird can move around unhampered.

Deal only with a reputable pet shop that will guarantee the bird for at least two weeks. Get the guarantee in writing. Immediately after buying the bird, take it to a vet for an examination. Ask the vet about the overall condition of the bird and if there are any problems that might arise in the future. If the vet gives the bird a clean bill of health, keep it. If it needs shots or treatment, call the pet shop and see if they will pay the bills. If you spent over $100, they might pay all or part of the bill.

What's the best bird for you? First, decide what you want in a bird. Do you want the bird to talk, to cuddle, to be independent? How much time can you devote to the bird? How much time are you home? How much noise can you tolerate? Cockatoos, for instance, want attention from every member of the family. They're noisy and are often described as drama queens. Some birds are nippy and prefer one person, so other family members are likely to be ignored. Lovebirds, sold in pairs, are quiet and—other than a slight cooing when the cage is uncovered—are hardly noticeable. Parrots are popular but don't know instinctively how to be good pets. It's up to their owners to teach them the rules. Both parrots and macaws are noisy and have driven new bird owners to drink. They're aggressive and not nice around children. Parrotlets are domineering and so are not a good choice if this is your first bird. Goffins cockatoos are expensive, costing about $750–$900. They aren't great talkers, but they do have a sweet disposition. They need lots of attention and toys to play with. Outside the cage, they'll get into everything, so they should never be left unsupervised.

The bottom line is shop carefully if you expect to live with the bird for years to come. Discuss what you're looking for in a pet with shop owners and let them make some suggestions. Check with friends who have or have had pet birds and get their advice. Pick up a book on birds as pets at the library or bookstore and get a pet bird education.

FLORIDA JUGGLING CLUBS

Even if you can't juggle four tennis balls, a watermelon, and a chain saw at the same time, you're welcome to drop in on any of the Florida-based juggling clubs and get some tips on how it's done. You may become a member, learn the skill, and pass your knowledge on to other fledgling jugglers. Locations and times are always changing, so call first if you plan on attending one of their meetings. Here's where to go to meet with the juggling crowd and sign up:

The Tallahassee Juggling Club usually meets on Sundays 3–6 P.M. (later in the summer months) on the Union Green, Florida State University, and in front of Thagard Health Center behind the pool when the weather is good. Information: Jay Schroer, 904-222-3364; John Kilgo, 904-644-5392 or 904-893-8469; or Gregory Cohen, 904-385-6463

First Coast Jugglers meet Wednesdays 8:10 P.M. at the University of Jacksonville. Information: Mickey Cecil, 904-725-6198.

Ultimate Freestyle Juggling Team meets Tuesdays and Thursdays 12:45–4 P.M. at the Plaza of the Americas, Newel Drive and Union Drive at the University of Florida. Information: Keith Helfrich, 352-373-3696, or Neil Swartz, 352-336-9029.

UCF Jugglers meet Sundays 2–5 P.M. on the University of Central Florida (Orlando) campus. Information: Randy Cabral, 407-273-7024.

Tampa Bay Jugglers Club meets Wednesday 7–9 P.M. at the Port Tampa Recreation Center at 4719 Prescott Street, Port Tampa. Information: Ed Kosco, 813-527-1716, or Dan Amyx, 813-839-4517.

Jugglers in Paradise meet Tuesdays 7:30 P.M. at the Center for the Arts, 333 Tressler Drive, Stuart 34994. Information: Martinez, 561-223-9678.

South Florida Jugglers. Information: Fran Guerra, 912 S. 26th Avenue, Hollywood 33020.

Grove Juggling Exchange meets Thursdays 7:30–9:30 P.M. at the breezeway of the Student Union at the University of Miami in Coral Gables. Information: David Landowne, 305-661-4847, or Roger Katchen, 305-663-0331.

POLICE, FIRE DEPARTMENT, AND MEDICAL SERVICES SCANNING

Scanning is the hobby of listening to local frequencies used by police, airports, taxi services, TV and radio stations, road crews, and other businesses. Even fast-food businesses are broadcasting out there somewhere. Check the person taking orders in the take-out window—if he's wearing a headphone and microphone, he's transmitting your order to another employee on the premises.

Scanner frequencies differ from AM and FM radio stations in that they do not transmit continuously. A scanner scans the frequencies and stops only when it reaches an active frequency. When that signal ceases, the scanner continues scanning the remaining channels.

Cellular phones transmit on the 800–900 MHz frequencies, but it's against the law to listen in, so most scanners today come with the 800–900 MHz frequencies excluded. Scanners range in price from $50–$400, depending on their features. Almost all scanners cover the frequencies used by medical services, fire departments, and the police, and often this is where the action is, so you can listen in to find out what's going on around your city.

Most medical services around the state of Florida (ambulances,

hospitals, emergency medical teams) transmit and send messages on 155.160; 155.205; 155.220; 155.280; 155.340; 155.400; 462.975; 463.000; 463.175.

Statewide, the police broadcast at 45.060; 45.100; 45.220; 45.420; 154.665; 154.680; 154.920; 154.950; 460.150; 460.250; 460.275; 460.300; 460.350. The Department of Transportation uses 47.140; 47.260; 47.300; 156.180.

Here are some region-specific frequencies:

In the Miami area, police use 151.070; 154.100; 154.770; 154.920; 155.670; 156.090; 460.375; 470.862. The fire department broadcasts on 153.905; 154.340; 460.525; 460.550.

In Orlando, police broadcast at 460.050, 460.100, 460.125, 460.150, 460.175, 460.275, 460.400, 460.425, 460.450. Fire departments broadcast at 153.890, 154.280, 154.430, 154.370; 154.430; 460.575; 460.600; 460.625. For miscellaneous city service transmissions, scan 46.520; 46.560; 153.755; 153.845; 154.085; 155.025.

In Tallahassee, police broadcast at 154.725; 155.190; 460.025; 460,075; 460.125; 460.175; 460.200; 460.225; 460.275; 460.300. Fire departments broadcast at 153.890; 154.190; 154.310; 154.385; 154.445.

In Tampa and the St. Petersburg area, police broadcast at 154.650; 154.785; 155.010; 155.190; 158.730; 453.550; 453.700; 453.750; 453.800; 453.800; 453.875; 460.075;

460.125; 460.175; 460.350. Fire departments broadcast at 46.120; 151.145; 151.220; 153.830; 154.130; 154.160; 154.175; 154.220; 154.250; 154.280; 154.340; 154.355; 154.430.

FROG HUNTING

Permits are required to sell or possess for sale any live amphibian or carcass, skin, or any body parts of amphibians native to the state of Florida. Frogs may be taken throughout the year by gigs, clubs, blow gun, hook and line, hand, or gun during daylight hours. A commercial freshwater fish dealer's license is required to take for sale or to sell frogs. The gopher frog (*Rana capito*), pine barrens tree frog (*Hyla andersonii*), and Florida bog frog (*Rana okaloosae*) are listed as species of special concern and are thus protected from the taking, possessing, and selling of whole animals, body parts, and eggs.

THEY CALL THEM CRAZY

There are more than one hundred businesses in Florida that use the word "crazy" in their names. Here are some:

Crazy About Pets in Fort Lauderdale
Crazy Colors in Miami
The Crazy Cow Restaurant in Hialeah
Crazy Daisy Florida in Tamarac
Crazy Dave's Auto Parks in Kissimmee
The Crazy Dog Scuba Shop in Mount Dora
Crazy Eddie's Action Auction in Sunrise
Crazy Horse Hair Styling Salon in Venice and Englewood
Crazy Mary's Grocery Store in Okeechobee
Crazy Papa's Gas Station in Bradenton

BEER

Florida breweries are turning out kegs of beer by the thousands. Annual output ranges from a couple of hundred barrels (Spanish Springs Brewery in Lady Lake) to eight thousand barrels from the Williamsville Brewery in Fernandina Beach. Of course, Anheuser-Busch leads them all with more than seven million barrels a year. Here are just a few of the Florida breweries and their annual capacities:

Blue Anchor Pub
10550 St. Augustine Road
Jacksonville
Capacity: 400 barrels

Hops of Mandarin
9826 San Jose Boulevard
Jacksonville
Capacity: 800 barrels

Ybor City Brewing
2200 North 20th Street
Tampa
Capacity: 70,000 barrels

Hops of South Tampa
327 North Dale Mabry
Tampa
Capacity: 800 barrels

Stroh Brewery Company
1111 30th Street
Tampa
Capacity: 1,700,000 barrels

Hops of Palm Harbor
33086 U.S. Highway 19 North
Palm Harbor
Capacity: 400 barrels

Killian Bayer Brewing
1000 Charleston Avenue South
Fort Meade
Capacity: 50,000 barrels

Sarasota Brewing
6607 Gateway
Sarasota
Capacity: 2,000 barrels

Hops of Clearwater
18825 U.S. Highway 19 North
Clearwater
Capacity: 800 barrels

Coppers Brooker Creek
   Grille & Taproom
36221 East Lake Road
Palm Harbor
Capacity: 100 barrels

Dunedin Brewery
1368-A Spaulding Road
Dunedin
Capacity: 364 barrels

Treasure Coast Brewing
2851 SE Monroe
Stuart
Capacity: 3,000 barrels

Brewing Terminology

Microbrewery: a brewery that produces fewer than one million barrels of beer annually and packages all of its beer for sale off the premises.

Large Brewery: a brewery that produces more than one million barrels of beer annually.

Beer Marketing Company: a company that puts its own label on beer that is brewed for the company by a brewery.

Homebrew: a brew produced by a private individual from his or her own home.

GO FLY A KITE

Kites date back more than 3,000 years, when they were made from bamboo and silk in China. From China, the kite found its way to Europe and the Americas. In the nineteenth century, kites were used for sci-

entific experiments. Today they're used for everything from military applications to just plain fun.

Benjamin Franklin is often referred to as the father of the kite, experimenting with kites to investigate atmospheric conditions and electricity. Alexander Graham Bell also conducted studies involving kites. For 40 years between the 1890s and 1930s, box kites consisting of two or more connected open-ended boxes were used to send meteorological instruments aloft to measure wind velocity, temperature, barometric pressure, and humidity. On November 12, 1894, Lawrence Hargrave was lifted from the ground by a train of four kites hooked together. This was simply one experiment in his quest for a stable lifting surface which could eventually be powered and used as a means of transportation. Hargrave was doing his utmost to invent the airplane!

Hargrave developed several styles of kites and gliders, refining and developing the concept of curved surface wings and also inventing the rotary engine. He never patented any of his inventions, preferring instead for them to be made available for the advancement of mankind. He made scathing attacks on people who experimented in secrecy with the intention of profiting from their inventions, accusing them of trying to exploit humanity.

Nine years after Hargrave got off the ground, Samuel Franklin Cody crossed the English Channel on a vessel towed by kites.

In the late nineteenth and early twentieth centuries, kites were used for lifting military observers high off the ground so they could observe the location and activity of enemy forces. During World War II, kites were also used as gunnery targets. Civilians found the French military kites fun to fly because of their high lifting power and stability.

Beginners need forgiving kites that will stay aloft despite any mistakes. Some kites respond instantly to every little movement of the hand and are not recommended for beginners. One of the best places to fly a kite is on the beach. The sand is a safe place for launching and landing a kite, and there are usually few power lines in the area. But be careful not to run over sunbathers as you prepare to launch.

What's the Right Kite?

Not all kites will fly in all wind conditions," says Alicia Skidmore of Aerial Dynamics, a kite shop in Seaside. "A delta kite, for example, will fly best in five- to ten-mile-an-hour winds. The most popular single-line (one-string) kites you'll find in kite stores are delta, parafoil, dragon, cellular, diamond, and box kites. For the beginner, delta kites are the easiest to fly. They're in the shape of a triangle and range in size from four to nine feet. The delta kite can be flown with or without a tail and is generally very stable in light to moderate winds. To launch a delta, you stand with your back to the wind and slowly release the kite line until it reaches the height you desire. If the kite starts to fall, simply tug on the string and the kite should shoot up into the air."

Parafoils are a popular style of kite for adults and children. Designed after a parachute, the parafoil requires very little upkeep. It has no breakable parts and can be packed into a case for transportation to and from the beach. Parafoils come in a variety of sizes, the most popular commonly called the pocketfoil, which can be flown in 5- to 15-mile-an-hour winds. The bigger the kite, the more wind you'll need.

Dragon kites fly with the grace and ease of a bird. Varying in size from 25 to 150 feet long, the kite requires more wind speed than a delta or parafoil. If you have a helper, he or she can hold the tail while you hold the top and string.

"When there are high winds, a cellular or box kite is a good choice," Alicia says. "These kites dance in the sky and quickly gather crowds as they dart through the air. They're easy to launch: Just stand with your back to the wind and let the kite line go, and up she goes."

For the more adventurous, consider a stunt kite. Each stunt kite has a quality that makes it different from other stunt kites. Flying a stunt kite requires patience and persistence. Having a helper comes in handy. The helper can hold the kite steady while you launch the kite lines. Once the lines are straight, the launch is fairly easy. Tug quickly on the line and the kite will ascend into the air. But your job isn't over once the kite is aloft. Keeping the kite in the air requires skill and determination, but it's well worth it. A stunt kite is one of the most enjoyable kites to fly. With a little bit of practice, you can perform stunts that will draw crowds.

Kite Safety Precautions

Kite flying is great fun, but you and your kite can become a nuisance to other people. Buzzing people's heads and running through the sand may be fun for you, but it's not fun for people trying to enjoy their day at the beach. Choose a spot away from the crowds.

* Don't fly close to roads—landing a kite in a road could cause a serious accident.
* Keep away from overhead power lines.
* Don't fly near airports.
* Don't fly your kite in winds stronger than those recommended.
* Although it is unusual for dogs to attack kites, make sure that there are no dogs around when you launch or land your kite.

*The
Sunshine State
Almanac
& Book of
Florida-
Related
Stuff*

FOOD

WINES AND SEAFOOD—
WHAT'S BEST WITH WHAT?

Wine and food have been enjoyed together for centuries, mainly because wine enhances the enjoyment and flavor of food. Foods that rely on simple flavors need straightforward wines with clean fruit flavors that don't overpower the dish. Richer foods go well with the richer and more complicated wines, such as those with an oak treatment. Foods containing tasty sauces also need richer and more complex wines.

For seafood dishes, look for wines that are dry (no sugar left in after fermentation) and ripe with good acid levels. The wines can be made with or without oak, but they should be low in tannin, as they will generally accompany more delicate flavors. For grilled fish, look for pure flavors of fruit, simple but not strong and overpowering. You might try Riesling, Sauvignon Blanc, or Pinot Grigio. The Rieslings of Australia and Germany are good choices and are not too sweet. Alsace also makes a good wine for grilled fish. Pinot Grigio from Italy has the clear fruit flavors and acid that work so well with fish. As the dish becomes more complicated—oysters, crab, or lobster—the wine needs some added flavors. Sauvignon Blanc can handle these extra flavors well, as can the aged Semillons of Australia and the white blends of Bordeaux of France (Semillon and Sauvignon Blanc), where small amounts of oak are used. You can also try Chardonnay, either lightly wooded or with no oak treatment at all. These are available from the United States (Oregon), France, Australia, and especially New Zealand.

Full-flavored seafood dishes cooked in or with a rich sauce, as well as chargrilled fish, require a simple wine, like flavored Chardonnay wines that have been fermented in the barrel. Look for White Burgundy or the best wines from Australia and California. To this group can be added the rosé style wines of the South of France, such as Tavel or Beaujolais. These wines are very low in tannin, very soft and easy to drink, and can be lightly chilled.

Finally, don't ignore Pinot Noir. Its soft but rich flavors and low tannin match rich seafood dishes, especially if the seafood has been charcoal grilled.

Zinfandel, a red wine with a ripe, berry taste, goes well with salmon and full-flavored seafood dishes. Muscadet has always been looked upon as the quintessential wine to be consumed with oysters and shellfish. Light and refreshing, with a hint of spritz, it should be drunk when it is young and fresh. A good Chardonnay has great character and complex flavors: full-bodied with hints of apple, pear, and tropical fruit. Enjoy with salmon, lobster, shrimp, and monkfish. A good-quality Fumé Blanc is one of the outstanding white wines from California. Rich and floral fruit flavors balanced with a crisp finish make this a great wine to be enjoyed with shellfish, pasta, and salmon. Brut champagne, Winston Churchill's favorite, is delicate and fresh with lots of apple and dough flavors. It has great body with a creamy texture and a smooth, buttery finish. It is an excellent value and ideal with lobster and any shrimp dish.

Grayton Beach Grouper Soup
1 pound grouper fillets
1 teaspoon paprika
Non-stick cooking spray
Two 15-ounce cans tomato sauce
8 ounces sliced, fresh mushrooms
1 teaspoon ground thyme
1 teaspoon ground marjoram
1 teaspoon ground savory
1 cup chopped green onions

Cut fillets into approximately 2"-by-2" pieces and combine with paprika. Lightly oil large skillet with cooking spray. Brown fish on medium high until it flakes easily when tested with a fork. Remove from heat, set aside, and keep warm. In the same skillet, combine tomato sauce, mushrooms, thyme, marjoram, and savory and simmer on medium/low heat until mushrooms are tender. Divide tomato sauce mixture evenly into four soup bowls; add fish and top with green onions. This recipe yields four servings with 301 calories, 3 grams of fat, and 80 milligrams of cholesterol.

ROAD FOOD

Lots of people like a good hamburger, especially when they're driving around Florida on vacation. Nutritionists say you can eat yourself right out of your bathing suit if you don't watch the calories and fat, so here's a warning list you can use—or ignore.

Burger King Hamburgers
Double Whopper with Cheese: 960 calories, 63 grams of fat
Whopper: 640 calories, 39 grams of fat

McDonald's Hamburgers
Big Mac: 530 calories, 10 grams of fat
Quarter Pounder: 420 calories, 21 grams of fat
Regular hamburger: 270 calories, 10 grams of fat

Wendy's Hamburgers
Big Bacon Classic: 580 calories, 30 grams of fat
Plain Single: 360 calories, 16 grams of fat
Jr. Bacon Cheeseburger: 380 calories, 19 grams of fat

ROOT BEER

Root beer foams because the molecules of carbon dioxide lower the surface tension so the liquid can spread out over a wider area. When root beer is whipped or stirred, air gets into the mixture, forming bubbles. Eventually the bubbles fizz out and everything quiets down.

In the non-hamburger sandwich category, Subway offers a six-inch-long cold-cut sandwich trio on white bread (362 calories, 13 grams of fat).

SQUIRREL-EATING TIPS

Should you eat squirrel . . . even cooked? A Harvard Medical School study says no. Mad squirrel disease dates back to the 1900s, when settlers in Florida served up squirrel dishes and people started getting sick. The actual recipes are long forgotten, but the study showed that squirrel gravy (made from squirrel brains) is a major cause of Creutzfeldt-Jakob, or mad cow, disease.

HOW TO OPEN A COCONUT

Coconuts look like they're designed to be as difficult as possible to open. Professional coconut-openers say this is how to do it: Buy a good coconut, one that's hairy and has no cracks. When you shake it, you should be able to feel and hear liquid sloshing around inside. To get inside the coconut and retrieve the liquid and meat, you'll need a clean screwdriver, a cup or glass, a heavy knife or cleaver, and a hammer or mallet. You can drink the liquid, but it's not the "coconut milk" of recipes, which is an infusion of grated coconut meat in boiling water or milk.

To collect the liquid, find the three eyes of the coconut on the smaller end of the husk. Tap the end of the screwdriver about two inches into one of the eyes until it penetrates the husk. Remove the screwdriver and pour out the liquid. Tapping two eyes will help drain it more quickly.

Place the coconut on a flat surface and find a point about a third of the way down the husk from the smaller end. Take the knife and give that spot a light whack with the back of the knife blade. Rotate the nut and hit it again on the opposite side, the same distance from the small end. Do this several times.

If you did it right, you'll find a natural fracture point that will become apparent as you lightly whack the nut. Once you see the fracture develop, insert the tip of the knife into the crack and pry upwards. The coconut should separate easily so you can get at the meat inside.

A Few Facts about Key West Cooking

The uniqueness of Key West cooking comes from various influences. Through them all can be traced the history of the island. The Conch style is a blend of the English cooking style with a style brought by the Conchs, who migrated here from the Bahamas. They developed recipes like "duff," which is a tropical plum pudding using fruits like papaya and guava. It's been said that the Conch diet is "grits and grunts," but actually they have invented scores of interesting dishes.

Orange Eggnog

Here's how to make orange eggnog for 16 people:

2 quarts milk
Orange sections
6 oz. orange juice concentrate
1½ cups sugar
12 eggs, separated

Heat milk in large, heavy saucepan. Beat egg yolks with one cup sugar. Stir in about one cup hot milk. Quickly stir in remaining hot milk and cook, stirring constantly, over very low heat until mixture thickens and coats a metal spoon. Remove from heat and add vanilla. Chill. Stir in undiluted orange concentrate. Pour into punch bowl. In separate bowl, beat egg whites until foamy. Add remaining ½ cup sugar, two tablespoons at a time, and continue beating until mixture stands in stiff peaks. Float heaping tablespoons of meringue on top of eggnog. Garnish with orange sections.

The Cuban population is another marked influence. Their style comes from Spain and makes a rich blend with native Key West foods. Bollos, guava shells and cream cheese, molletes, paella (which is like arroz con pollo but more elaborate), and good, strong Cuban coffee are just a few of the things one ought to try while visiting Key West. Key lime pie is the most famous local recipe. While everybody loves it, nobody knows where it came from.

How to Make Really Authentic Key Lime Pie

Key lime pie, a custard pie concoction, dates back to the 1800s when limes were one of the few fresh products available in Key West. Key limes are sensitive to cold—to date no Key limes have been successfully grown in the United States above the southern tip of Florida.

The ingredients for an eight-inch pie are as follows:

3 eggs
12 oz. sweetened condensed milk
4 oz. Key lime juice
sugar
pie crust of your choice (Most
  bakers prefer a graham cracker
  crust.)

Put egg whites in a large mixing bowl and set aside. Combine the egg yolks, milk, and juice and mix thoroughly. The acid in the juice will thicken the milk and eggs and produce a custard. Add sugar to the egg whites and beat until stiff. Spoon the custard into the pie crust and spread it evenly. Spoon the beaten egg whites on the top of the custard and spread evenly. Refrigerate. Before serving, put the pie under a hot broiler for a few minutes until the egg whites are slightly browned.

Another recipe calls for blending one can of sweetened condensed milk with two egg yolks and a half cup of Key lime juice (you can substitute regular limes) and putting the ingredients into an eight-inch graham cracker crust.

Chill and serve with a garnish of whipped cream, a slice of lime, or a sprig of mint.

Gourmet pie makers in the Keys say Key lime pie is never green, so don't add food coloring. After researching various Key lime pie recipes for *The Sunshine State Almanac,* we found that while recipes vary slightly, they all include sweetened condensed milk, eggs, and Key lime juice.

If you don't have time to make an authentic pie, here's a quick recipe invented by Key Westers who are constantly on the run.

4 eggs
14-oz. can condensed milk
½ cup Key lime juice
Graham cracker pie shell

Separate three egg whites. Beat four egg yolks and one egg white until thick. Add milk, beat again. Add lime juice, beat again. Separately beat three egg whites until they peak. Fold into the above mixture, but do not beat. Pour into baked pie shell. Refrigerate and enjoy!

FLORIDA SUN TEA AND THE MICROWAVE SOLUTION

Some Floridians take advantage of the hot weather to do everything from spending a day at the beach to using the heat to make iced tea. The formula is simple. Put three family-size tea bags in a gallon jar and fill with water. Put the cap on loosely, and put the jar out in the sun. Three hours later, remove the tea bags and serve over ice. Of course, in this hectic world, three hours is often not available. For the twenty-first-century version of almost-instant iced tea, put two liters of water in a uncovered microwave-safe plastic pitcher. Toss in one family-size tea bag. Microwave for ten minutes. Remove the tea bag and serve over ice.

The Ultimate Cup of Tea

When the chill is in the air in northern Florida (where temperatures reach below freezing during the winter months), a cup of hot tea is a welcome pleasure. To do it right, you don't just drop a tea bag into a cup of hot water and drink it. The English—the world's number one tea drinkers—say there's only one way to prepare a cup of tea.

Use loose tea instead of tea bags. Fill the teapot with hot water from the tap so it's preheated and won't cool off the boiling water you'll be using in a minute or two. Pour the water out and set the teapot aside.

Add one teaspoon of tea leaves for every cup. Pour boiling water over the tea leaves. Steep three to five minutes, and do not stir. Three minutes is recommended

for average strength, five minutes if you like it strong. Steeping takes into account three things: 1) caffeine, 2) coloring, and 3) flavor. Strain the tea directly into a cup and serve. If milk is used, warm it in advance. Perfect temperature? 133°F.

Of course, if time is important (and don't tell the British this!), fill a cup with cold water, pop it in the microwave for three minutes on high, take it out, drop a tea bag in it, stir, and serve. Use the string on the tea bag to squeeze it before discarding.

THE MOST EXPENSIVE COOKIE RECIPE IN THE WORLD

The story goes like this: Three tourists are out shopping and go to a famous restaurant in Miami for lunch. Each has a salad, a glass of wine, and coffee. When the dessert tray is rolled around, each person chooses a chocolate chip cookie. They all agree it is the best cookie they have ever tasted and ask the waitress if they can have the recipe. The waitress goes into the kitchen and returns, saying the chef said he couldn't give them the recipe, but he would sell it to them for two fifty. Cheap enough, they think, and put the check and the cost of the recipe on a credit card. Thirty days later, they receive a bill for three salads ($26), three glasses of wine ($9), three coffees ($6), and one chocolate chip cookie recipe ($250). They call the restaurant and complain, saying they thought the chef meant $2.50, not $250. The restaurant refuses to refund their money, so to get even, they post the cookie recipe on every Internet site likely to be visited by food lovers.

Versions of this story have been bouncing around since the early 1930s and are the result of someone's overactive imagination. It started out at the Waldorf Astoria's restaurant in New York 60 years ago, flashed across the country, hopped the Atlantic to restaurants in France, Switzerland, and England, and landed in Miami a few years ago. It has appeared in magazines, on radio and TV, and in newspapers, and most experts agree the story is a myth. But several well-known restaurants have complained about the bad publicity that resulted when they were said to have charged for the recipe. Recently Neiman-Marcus' restaurant in Dallas was hit. To stifle the rumor, they posted their recipe for chocolate chip cookies on the Internet for everyone to see. And, they added, there's no charge.

Here's the recipe from the Miami restaurant:

½ cup unsalted butter, softened
1 cup brown sugar
3 tablespoons granulated sugar
1 egg
2 tablespoons vanilla extract
½ teaspoon baking soda
½ teaspoon baking powder
½ teaspoon salt
1¾ cup flour
1½ teaspoons instant espresso powder, slightly crushed
8 ounces semisweet chocolate chips

Cream the butter with the sugars until fluffy. Beat in the egg and the vanilla extract. Combine the dry ingredients and beat into the butter mixture. Stir in the chocolate chips. Drop by large spoonfuls onto a greased cookie sheet. Bake at 375° for 8 to 10 minutes or 10 to 12 minutes for a crispier cookie. Makes 12 to 15 large cookies.

NUTRITIONAL FACTS ABOUT FLORIDA GRAPEFRUIT

A medium grapefruit (5.3 oz./154 g) provides:

60 calories
0 fat
0 cholesterol
0 sodium
230 mg potassium
16 g total carbohydrate
6 g dietary fiber
4 g soluble fiber
1 g insoluble fiber
10 g sugar

It also provides (as percent of daily requirement):

Vitamin A	15%
(100% as beta carotene)	
Vitamin C	110%

Thiamin	4%
Riboflavin	2%
Niacin	2%
Calcium	2%
Iron	0%
Vitamin B6	4%
Folic Acid	6%
Phosphorous	2%
Magnesium	4%
Copper	2%
Pantothenic Acid	2%

FLORIDA GRITS

When early colonists arrived in the southern part of the United States, Native Americans made hominy by soaking their corn in a solution of lye made from wood ashes. Ashen grits were made to preserve the grain through the winter.

Modern-day or supermarket grits are processed hominy corn treated in an alkaline solution so that the hulls and germ float to the surface. These grits are the grits served routinely at thousands of restaurants. Once bleached, the corn is dried, enriched (some of the nutrients lost in the processing are added back in), and ground—often too fine for many people's tastes.

Most grit enthusiasts say coarsely ground, whole-grain grits are the best grits you can find. They taste like freshly ground corn and when cooked resemble creamed corn, although they're somewhat starchier. They can be used like pasta or rice as a side dish or as a main dish. Most grit cookers like to cook their grits for a long time because the longer they cook, the creamier they become. Grits can be put in a slow cooker overnight; when morning rolls around, you have a delicious pile of grits. But if you're in a hurry, you can easily cook grits in a half hour if you're willing to watch the pot and stir occasionally.

Cooked grits can then be enriched with egg, poured into a well-seasoned cast-iron skillet or greased baking pan, and refrigerated. The chilled grits are then unmolded, cut into portions, dusted with flour or cornmeal, and pan-fried like polenta.

Grits invite a host of accompaniments. Any sauce or gravy that you would put on pasta or rice is ideal. If you plan to serve grits plain, a little stock made from meat trimmings from the main course is a welcome addition if stirred in near the end of cooking.

Basic Grits
1 quart water
2 tablespoons butter
Salt to taste
1 cup stone-ground whole-grain
  grits

Bring the water, butter, and salt to a boil in a stockpot. Gradually add the grits. Return to a boil, then reduce to a simmer. Cook the grits, stirring occasionally so they don't stick or form a skin, about 25 minutes. When they're creamy and to your liking, turn the heat down to its lowest setting and cover it while you prepare the rest of the meal.

Basic Grits Cakes
1 cup grits
2 eggs
2 tablespoons heavy cream
2 teaspoons water
¼ cup unbleached all-purpose
    flour, cornmeal, corn flour, or
    bread crumbs
Peanut oil for frying

As soon as the grits are done, put one egg into a medium mixing bowl with the cream and stir well to combine. Quickly add some grits to the egg and cream, beating well with a wire whisk so that the egg doesn't curdle. Dump the mixture into the grits pot and whisk all together well. Turn the grits out into a greased nine-inch cake pan and cool to room temperature. Refrigerate until firm.

When you're ready to cook, heat some oil in a heavy pan over medium-high heat. Preheat the oven to its lowest setting. Place a rack over a sheet pan and put it in the oven. Remove the grits from the refrigerator and turn them out onto a cutting surface. Beat the remaining egg with the water in a pasta bowl to make a wash. Cut the grits into eight wedges, then gently lift each one up and dip it in the egg wash, then in the flour, cornmeal, or bread crumbs. Sauté or deep-fry until golden brown, then transfer to the rack in the oven to drain.

FOOD SAFETY HOTLINE

The U.S. Food and Drug Administration has a toll-free food information line for consumers. It is located in the Center for Food Safety and Applied Nutrition in Washington, D.C. The hotline offers information to consumers in English and Spanish, 24 hours a day, 7 days a week. More than 20 recorded informational messages are offered, and almost 75 publications may be mailed or automatically faxed to callers. Information is available on safe seafood purchasing, handling, cooking, and storage, as well as on nutrition, labeling, economic fraud, additives, pesticides, contaminants, and general food safety. Public affairs specialists are available from noon to 4 P.M. Eastern Time, Monday through Friday, to answer specific questions. The FDA Food Information Hotline: 800-332-4010 (or 202-205-4314 in the D.C. area)

HOW TO REMOVE A TOUGH JAR LID

If a jar lid won't twist off on your first try, screaming won't help, so you'll have to use more brains than brawn. Here are some hints on how to remove a tough jar lid without getting frustrated.

Wash your hands with a mild detergent and dry them thoroughly on a clean towel. Often our hands have a natural, oily residue which makes it difficult to get a good grip on slick, metallic things.

Wash the jar. Jars, especially those lurking at the back of the shelf over the stove for weeks or months, may have accumulated an oily residue from kitchen grease and smoke. Paying particular attention to the lid, rinse the jar under warm water to loosen and remove any oily residue. Use a drop or two of liquid detergent if the jar feels particularly greasy, and dry thoroughly with a clean towel.

First try: Rinse the jar lid under hot water, turning the jar as you hold it under the water. Get a clean, dry kitchen towel. Hold the jar firmly in one hand and drape the towel over the lid. Put your hand on top of the towel and twist the lid off.

Second try: Leverage is important, but not everybody knows how to maximize his or her own body leverage. For maximum leverage, hold the jar in your dominant hand at about chest level. The back of your hand should be facing out away from you. Hold your palm along the side of the jar (not covering the lid), and line up the thumb and index finger parallel to the lid. Wrap the thumb of your non-dominant hand around the side of the lid that's facing you, and curl your fingers around to the opposite side.

Wedge the lid firmly in your hand. Try to turn the lid by moving your hands in opposite directions at the same time. Your dominant hand (on the jar) will move clockwise, and your non-dominant hand (and the lid) will move counterclockwise. Elbows up, relax, and take a deep breath. As you exhale, grip tightly while turning your hands. Don't strain yourself now, but do remember that it's just a jar, and you're going to get this thing off no matter what it takes.

Third try: Turn the jar upside down (but at a slight angle) and rap the corner of the lid with a large knife. No knife? Rap it on a hard kitchen counter or surface with a similar edge. Be careful not to break the jar or damage the surface. Try to twist the lid off.

Fourth try: Set the jar on the counter and hold it steady with one hand. Using the handle of a knife (watch your fingers!), rap the rim of the

jar lid twice on the edge. Turn the jar around 90 degrees and do it again. These raps should break the seal, and you can now twist the lid off. For real tough lids, you might have to rap the sides of the lid every inch or so before the lid twists off.

Give up? If brute force isn't your game, look in kitchen appliance stores or catalogs and buy one of those lid-removing gadgets. Some look similar to oversized pliers; others look like reversed wedges and mount under your kitchen cabinets. They're cheap and can remove any lid you're likely to encounter.

SATELLITE BEACH SALAD

1 pound calico or bay scallops
1 teaspoon salt
1 teaspoon paprika
1 teaspoon minced garlic
1 teaspoon white pepper
2 cups cooked ziti or other pasta
1 cup chopped chopped water
   chestnuts
1 cup finely chopped celery
1 cup chopped green onions
1 cup Caesar dressing
¼ cup chopped red cabbage
1 cup quartered artichoke hearts

Rinse scallops to remove any remaining shell particles. In large bowl combine salt, paprika, garlic, and pepper and mix well. Spread scallops close together in a single layer on a broiler pan and coat the tops with spice mixture. Broil scallops six to eight inches from heat for six to eight minutes or until they are opaque in the center.

Remove from heat and cool in the refrigerator.

Combine pasta, bell pepper, water chestnuts, celery, onions, and dressing; mix well. Add cooled scallops to the pasta mixture and mix well. Garnish with the artichoke hearts and red cabbage.

SANTA ROSA SHRIMP

1 pound raw shrimp, peeled and
   deveined
2 tablespoons minced garlic
1 tablespoon lime juice
1 teaspoon ground thyme
1 teaspoon salt
White pepper
Non-stick cooking spray
2 cups fresh corn kernels
1 cup chopped green bell pepper
1 cup chopped red bell pepper
1 cup chopped onion
1 large tomato, cut into eight pieces

Drain shrimp of all excess water. In large mixing bowl, combine shrimp, garlic, lime juice, thyme, salt, and white pepper. Mix coating well. Lightly oil large skillet with cooking spray and cook shrimp on medium high for six to eight minutes, stirring occasionally. Remove shrimp from skillet and set aside. Into same skillet add corn, bell peppers, and onions; cook on medium until corn is tender. Add shrimp and tomatoes to skillet and cook until shrimp are opaque in the center. Yields six servings. This dish has 180 calories per serving.

Peppy Seafood Sauce
Here's a great sauce you can use on any type of seafood:

1 cup catsup
1 cup chili sauce
3 tablespoons lemon juice
1 tablespoon prepared horseradish
1 teaspoon Worcestershire sauce
1 teaspoon grated onion
¼ teaspoon salt
¼ teaspoon liquid hot pepper

Combine all ingredients and chill. This recipe yields one cup of sauce or six servings.

FLORIDA ORANGES

Although non-Florida oranges may be bright orange on the outside, they have thicker rinds. Thin-skinned Florida oranges are heavier because they are juicier on the inside. Oranges from Florida also may have a slightly marked exterior. This is known as "wind-scarring," which results from gentle breezes blowing the fruit against the branches. This doesn't affect the orange's taste. When shopping for oranges, look for an orange that's firm with no soft spots.

Don't pass by oranges that are yellow or green-tinted. These oranges are fully ripe, juicy, and sweet-tasting. A medium-sized orange averages about 60 calories and is a major source of Vitamin C. Oranges also contain folate, thiamine, and other nutrients and are a good source of fiber and potassi-

um. They are also sodium-free, cholesterol-free, and fat-free.

From Grove to Glass

In Florida, most oranges bloom in March and April. The early varieties, such as Hamlins and Parson Browns, reach maturity October through January. The mid-season varieties such as the Pineapple Orange reach maturity from December through February. Late-season varieties such as the Valencia matures from March through June.

Most citrus fruit, including oranges, must ripen on the tree. Citrus does not ripen once it's removed from the tree. Florida's grove managers take representative samples of oranges from a particular block of trees, about 40 pieces of fruit per 40-acre block. The juice is squeezed from the sample fruit and tested for two main attributes—brix (soluble sugars) and acid. From these two attributes, the sugar/acid ratio (which determines the flavor of the juice) is determined. Juice must meet minimum standards in order for it to be sold as 100 percent Florida orange juice.

The brix content is determined using a hydrometer to measure the specific gravity, which is then converted to degrees brix. Using a titration method, the percent acid is determined using sodium

In Florida, almost 98 percent of all oranges are harvested by hand.

hydroxide and a phenolphthalein indicator. The ratio of the brix to the acid content can then be calculated. The minimum maturity for oranges varies during the season, but generally it is a minimum of 8.50 brix with a 10 to 1 ratio. Many juice processing plants will have even higher minimum maturity standards.

Once a block is determined to be ready for harvest, a crew of harvesters is sent to pick the entire block of fruit by hand using wooden ladders and canvas sacks. In Florida, almost 98 percent of all oranges are harvested by hand. There are a few experimental mechanical harvesters in use. The most popular is the trunk shaker, a machine that clamps onto the trunk of the tree and violently shakes off the fruit into a catch frame. Currently, there is no cost advantage to using mechanical harvesting instead of hand harvesting.

The pickers dump the fruit into plastic tubs that hold approximately 900 pounds of oranges. A special truck (called a goat) then comes through the grove and, using a hydraulic boom, picks up the tub and dumps it into the back of the goat. The goat then goes outside the block of trees and the body raises up and dumps its load of oranges into a large tractor-trailer that holds about 45,000 pounds of oranges. A truck-tractor then hauls the trailer to the processing plant.

At the processing plant, the trailerload of oranges is weighed on scales to determine the payment to the grower. The trailer of oranges is then unloaded onto a conveyor belt. From this belt, the Florida Department of Agriculture and Consumer Services (FDACS) takes a representative sample to test it for juice content and maturity and to certify the pounds solids per box (the unit that growers' payment is based upon). The fruit is then diverted to storage bins labeled according to the juice specification as determined by FDACS. Oranges are then selected from the bins to enable blending of optimal quality.

The fruit is conveyed by belt through a washing process, then enters the processing plant, where it is graded for bad or damaged fruit. The fruit is then separated by size and sent to the juice extractors. Inside the extractors, before juicing, the peel is pricked to extract the oils found in the peel, then the juice is extracted. The pulpy juice next goes through a finisher (screen) where the pulp and seeds are removed and, along with the peel, are diverted to be used for by-products such as cattle feed. From this point, the juice for not from concentrate (NFC) goes directly into a pasteurizer, and the juice for frozen concentrated orange juice (FCOJ) goes on to the evaporators where most of the water is taken out by vacuum and heat, and then it is chilled. This process also strips out certain essences and oils. The concentrated juice is then piped to the tank farm, where concentrate is stored at about 176°F and separated according to variety and ratio (brix to acid) range.

When FCOJ is ready to be shipped to a customer, such as a juice packager, it is blended from the various tanks to meet the specifications of the customer and USDA requirements. Essences and oils (recovered in the processing process) are reintroduced to enhance flavor. This blending process is the reason that FCOJ has a more consistent quality year-round than fresh juice, or NFC. FCOJ is either put into 55-gallon drums and shipped in a refrigerated truck, or loaded onto a special food-grade insulated tanker truck and delivered to a packaging plant. Some Florida processing plants also have packaging plants at the same site. Many dairies around the country also package orange juice using the same equipment used to package milk.

To make cans of frozen concentrate, filtered water is added to bring the brix level down (about three times more concentrated than fresh juice). It is then put in cardboard cartons, glass containers, or plastic jugs to be sold at retail stores.

TROPICAL FRUIT

Tropical fruit might well be the recipe ingredient of the first decade of the new millennium as chili peppers were the recipe ingredient of the 1980s. Restaurants throughout Florida are adding excitement to their menus with these exotic and flavorful treasures. We have the advantage of being able to get a variety of locally grown tropical fruits. Florida produces more than 24 varieties of tropical fruits—from the well-known mango and papaya to the unusual wax jambu and black sapote. Many of these fruits are available almost year-round in supermarkets and specialty stores.

Every tropical fruit variety is succulent, flavorful, and sweet. Not only are these fruits delicious, but their colors and shapes also contribute to stunning presentations. This helps make Florida's spirited regional cuisine highly distinctive, always fresh, and colorful. Chefs especially enjoy working with the carambola's yellowish, star-shaped slices; mamey's silky, reddish-orange flesh; lychee's deep-ruby skin and pearly-white fruit; and mango's golden-hued flesh. Mango and papaya are among the most versatile of tropical fruits. While both routinely are used in desserts, salsas, fruit salads, sauces, and chutney, it is not uncommon to see them used in a variety of entrees, such as gingered tropical fruit paella or stewed clams and mangos. The familiar plantains are now available in the delicious Hua Mua variety, which produces fruit that is larger in circumference and sweeter than other varieties, adding another dimension to traditional uses. These fruits have intense flavors, so they lend themselves to preparations using less fat.

It is difficult to do justice to all of the tropical fruit varieties here, but possibly the following list will be a modest introduction. Once you've become an expert at working with these exotic wonders of nature, you will find comfort in their easy charms—and so will your dinner guests.

Annona
Barbados cherry
Carambola
Coconut
Guava
Jaboticaba
Jackfruit
Key lime
Kumquat
Litchi
Longan
Mamey
Mango
Monstera
Papaya
Passion fruit
Pummelo
Sapodilla
White sapote
Black sapote
Tahiti lime
Wax jambu

Now try preparing this dish:

Shrimp Banana Guava
  with Coconut
1 cup orange juice
1 cup cilantro, chopped
1 tablespoon lime juice
1¼ pounds large shrimp
1 tablespoon olive oil (for cooking)
Salsa:
1 tablespoon olive oil
2 tablespoons chopped green onion
1 cup chopped papaya
1 cup orange juice
3 bananas (red or fingerling)
Rice:
1 cup coconut milk
1 cup white rice
1 teaspoon salt

To marinate the shrimp, combine orange juice, cilantro, lime juice, and shrimp. Marinate for 30 minutes. For the salsa, combine all ingredients and chill. For the rice, bring the coconut milk to a boil; add rice and salt. Simmer on low heat until done (10 to 15 minutes).

In a large sauté pan, heat one tablespoon olive oil and add the shrimp. Cook shrimp until opaque and remove from heat.

To serve: Add chopped bananas to salsa. Place a mound of rice in the center of the plate, then place six or seven shrimp on top of the rice and garnish with a generous spoonful of salsa and a sprig of fresh cilantro.

WOULD YOU BELIEVE—PINEAPPLES IN FLORIDA?

In south Florida, there's a 20-acre pineapple operation doing quite well, thank you. Pineapples haven't been grown commercially in Florida for the past 80 years, so this marks the first time the Queen Victoria pineapple has been grown in the continental United States. This ain't just your ordinary pineapple. The price is reputed to be about six dollars for a pound and a half. The highest-priced pineapples to date have been priced at about four dollars for a pound and a half. Up until now, the Queen Victoria has been grown only in Madagascar and the French Islands in the Indian Ocean.

HAVING FRIENDS OVER FOR DINNER?—A DRINK GUIDE

If you plan on serving drinks, you should know:

One liter of alcohol equals 22 1.5-ounce drinks

A 750-milliliter bottle of wine equals 6 4-ounce drinks

A 112-liter bottle of wine equals 12 4-ounce drinks

One bottle of champagne equals 6 servings

One case of champagne equals 72 servings

For 50 people, you'll need approximately 25 bottles of wine, or 6 quarts of punch, or 20 bottles of champagne, or 6 bottles of alcohol.

OSTRICH RECIPES

There are only a handful of gourmet ostrich meat cookers in Florida, but those we contacted said to try these recipes if you ever get ahold of a few chunks of ostrich meat.

Boomerang Steaks Marinade
½ cup soy sauce
¼ cup green onions
½ cup orange juice
½ teaspoon ground ginger
1 tablespoon rice vinegar
1 teaspoon garlic, minced
1 tablespoon honey
1 teaspoon smoked sesame oil
2 teaspoons wasabe (Japanese horseradish) or prepared horseradish
2 pounds boomerang ostrich or emu steaks

You can use strip steak, but that's not half the fun. Combine all ingredients and marinate ostrich or emu two hours or overnight. Grill over medium coals.

Ostrich Orzo
1 pound ostrich or emu fajita strips or skirt steak sliced and cut into 1-inch lengths
1 cup orzo(rice-shaped pasta), uncooked
2 teaspoons chopped celery
1 teaspoon salt
½ teaspoon black pepper
Garlic
¼ cup red wine
1 small onion
2 cups chicken or beef broth
1 small green or red pepper, chopped

Season meat with salt and black pepper. Spray a non-stick skillet and add meat, stirring constantly until meat is just brown. Remove meat from pan and add onion, green or red bell pepper, and garlic. Stir mixture for two to three minutes. Do not let garlic brown. Remove vegetable mixture from pan and combine with meat in a one-and-a-half-quart covered casserole dish. Add wine to pan, then return to heat and stir to remove all residue from the skillet. Pour wine with remaining ingredients into dish and bake in a 350° oven for 30 minutes or until orzo is soft. Serves four to six.

Ostrich Patties with Mushroom Sauce
2 pounds ground ostrich
2 teaspoons salt
½ teaspoon grated nutmeg
1 teaspoon black pepper
2 cups fresh bread crumbs
¾ cup fat-free yogurt
2 egg whites

Combine all ingredients for patties. Shape into patties and bake in preheated 300° oven for five to ten minutes depending on size of patties.

Mushroom Sauce
1 small onion, chopped
1 pound mushrooms, sliced
2 tablespoons cider vinegar
1 teaspoon salt
½ teaspoon black pepper
¼ cup fat-free yogurt
¼ cup capers (if desired)

Heat medium sauce pot and spray with oil. Add onions, stir over heat for about two minutes, and add mushrooms. Cook until liquid from mushrooms has evaporated. Add vinegar, salt, and pepper and cook another two to three minutes. Remove from heat and add yogurt and capers, if desired. Do not bring to a boil, as yogurt will separate. Serves six to eight.

Ostrich Skewers
1 tablespoon vegetable oil
⅔ cup sugar
⅓ cup soy sauce
1 small onion
1 pound ostrich or emu

Combine first four ingredients in a blender or food processor and puree. Pour marinade ingredients over meat and marinate two hours or overnight. Remove meat and reserve marinade; thread strips of meat on skewers. Grill over medium heat or broil, basting occasionally with reserved

marinade. Serves 8 to 12 as an appetizer.

Ostrich Stroganoff
1 pound ostrich or emu fajita strips, cut into 1-inch sections, or skirt steak sliced and cut into 1-inch lengths
1 teaspoon salt
½ to 1 teaspoon freshly ground black pepper
Vegetable spray
8 ounces mushrooms, sliced
½ to 1 cup chopped onion
½ teaspoon chopped garlic
3 tablespoons flour
1½ cups beef broth
2 tablespoons tomato paste
2 tablespoons sherry
2 teaspoons dill weed
1 cup fat-free sour cream

Season meat with salt and pepper. Heat a non-stick frying pan. When hot, apply vegetable spray and add meat, stirring constantly, until most of the pink disappears. Remove meat from pan and add mushrooms; when they begin to release liquid, add onions and gar-

lic. Cook this mushroom mixture until liquid has evaporated, then add flour, stirring to coat mixture. Add beef broth all at once, stirring constantly with a wire whisk; bring to a boil. Add tomato paste. Reduce heat and simmer for two to three minutes. Add remaining ingredients and remove from heat. Serve over rice or egg noodles. Serves four to six.

Ostrich Paella
1 pound ostrich steak, cut into 1-inch cubes
¾ cup green onions, sliced
2½ cups chicken broth
½ teaspoon salt
¼ teaspoon crushed saffron
1 pound fresh medium peeled and deveined shrimp
2 tablespoons fresh chopped parsley
¾ pound pork sausage links
¼ clove minced garlic
1½ cups long grain rice
½ teaspoon oregano
¼ bay leaf
1 jar (2 ounces) drained pimento strips

In a large skillet or four-quart Dutch oven, brown the sausage over medium heat. Drain, reserving two tablespoons drippings in Dutch oven, then set aside. Put ostrich, green onion, and garlic in the skillet and cook until ostrich is browned, stirring occasionally. Transfer ostrich to the Dutch oven and add sausage, chicken broth, uncooked rice, salt, oregano, saffron, and bay leaf. Bring to boil.

Reduce heat, cover, and simmer 20 minutes. Add shrimp, pimento, and parsley. Simmer, covered, for 10 to 15 minutes or until shrimp are done. Remove bay leaf prior to serving.

ROASTED CLAMS

Wash two to three pounds of hard clams and place them in a single layer in a roasting pan or on a baking sheet with sides. Roast in a 350° oven for about 10 to 12 minutes, depending on size of clams. When clams are open, remove from oven and serve with cocktail sauce, drawn butter, or the following vinegar dipping sauce.

Vinegar Dipping Sauce
½ cup cider vinegar
1 teaspoon garlic
½ cup green onions, finely chopped
1 teaspoon salt
1 teaspoon freshly cracked pepper
¼ cup tomatoes, finely chopped

Mix all ingredients together. Serve with roasted clams. Yields two to four servings.

Ginger-Honey Amberjack
1 pound amberjack fillets
1 cup honey
2 teaspoons ground ginger
1 red seeded bell pepper, cut into 2-inch strips
1 yellow seeded bell pepper, cut into 2-inch strips

Cut fillets into serving-size pieces, then set aside. Combine honey and ginger and coat fish evenly. Place on oiled grill over medium-hot coals, basting frequently with honey mixture and turning once. Coat bell peppers with honey mixture and grill with fish until tender, turning peppers often to avoid burning. Fish is done when it flakes easily when tested with a fork. This recipe yields 4 servings and contains 474 calories, 2 grams of fat, and 160 milligrams of cholesterol.

SEAFOOD HOTLINE

Should you eat those oysters in Sarasota, that mackerel salad in Jacksonville, or that tuna sandwich in Key West? The U.S. Food and Drug Administration operates a toll-free hotline that can answer your questions about seafood anywhere in the U.S. Taped messages give you information on the latest seafood warnings. For information, call 800-332-4010. If you get the good news, go ahead and eat 'em. Here's a recipe for a popular Florida dish.

Red Hot Oysters
Three dozen oysters in the shell
Hot pepper sauce to taste

Wash oysters thoroughly. Shuck and place oysters on deep half of shell, removing any remaining shell particles. Arrange oysters on baking sheet and top with a teaspoon (or more) of sauce. Bake in preheated oven at 350° for 10 minutes or until edges begin to curl. This recipe makes 6 servings with 60 calories per serving.

OYSTERS—THE BAD NEWS

Last year, it's estimated 20 million Americans ate raw oysters, and a good percentage of them were right here in Florida. For some people, eating raw oysters can cause serious illness or even death.

The cause is a bacterium called *Vibrio vulnificus* that occurs naturally in marine waters and is commonly found in Gulf of Mexico oysters. While not a threat to most healthy people, *Vibrio vulnificus* can cause sudden chills, fever, nausea, vomiting, blood poisoning, and death within two days in people with certain medical conditions. Forty percent of *Vibrio vulnificus* infections from raw oyster consumption are fatal. The bacteria are not a result of pollution, so although oysters should always be obtained from reputable sources, eating oysters from "clean" waters or in reputable restaurants with high turnover does not provide protection. Eating raw oysters with hot sauce or while drinking alcohol does not kill the bacteria.

Certain health conditions put you at risk for serious illness or death from this infection. Unfortunately, some of these conditions have no signs or symptoms, so you may not know you are at risk. These conditions include liver disease, from excessive alcohol intake, viral hepatitis, or other causes; hemochromatosis, an iron disorder; diabetes; stomach problems, including previous stomach surgery and low stomach acid (for example, from antacid use); cancer;

immune disorders, including HIV infection; and long-term steroid use (as for asthma and arthritis).

If you are an older adult, you also may be at increased risk because older people are more likely to have these risk conditions than younger people. If you are or think you may be in any of these risk categories, you should not eat raw oysters. If you drink alcoholic beverages regularly, you may be at risk for liver disease, and, as a result, at risk for serious illness or death from raw oysters. Even drinking two to three drinks each day can cause liver disease, which may have no symptoms. The risk of death is almost 200 times greater in those with liver disease than those without liver disease.

Here are some steps to take if you're an oyster eater:

* Always order oysters fully cooked at restaurants.
* When cooking oysters at home, cook live oysters in boiling water for three to five minutes after the shells open. Use small pots to boil or steam oysters.
* Do not cook too many oysters in the same pot because the ones in the middle may not get fully cooked. Discard any oysters that do not open during cooking.
* Steam live oysters four to nine minutes in a steamer that's already steaming.
* Boil or simmer shucked oysters for at least three minutes or until edges curl.
* Fry in oil for at least three minutes at 375°F.
* Broil three inches from heat for three minutes.
* Bake (as in Oysters Rockefeller) for ten minutes at 450°F.

Still have questions? Call the Food and Drug Administration Seafood Hotline at 800-FDA-4010. They know everything about oysters.

What to Do with Three Dozen Oysters

If you're walking the beach and come across three dozen oysters, here are some suggestions on how to cook them.

Bacon and Cheese Oysters
36 oysters in the shell
½ cup low-fat bacon chips
12 ounces grated low-fat mozzarella cheese
4 fresh jalapeno peppers, sliced thickly

Wash oysters thoroughly. Shuck and place oysters in deep half of shell, removing any remaining particles of shell. Arrange oysters on baking sheet and top each with ½ tablespoon of cheese, a sprinkle of bacon chips, and one slice of pepper. Bake oysters in a preheated oven at 350° for ten minutes or until edges of oysters begin to curl, then serve. Nutritious? You decide. This dish has 240 calories, 6 grams of fat, and 60 milligrams of cholesterol.

Lemon Garlic Oysters
36 oysters in the shell
1 tablespoon salt
6 ounces melted butter
¼ cup lemon juice
1 tablespoon chopped garlic

Wash oysters thoroughly. Shuck and place oysters in deep half of shell, removing any remaining shell particles. Arrange on baking sheet, cover, and refrigerate. Combine remaining ingredients in a sauce pot and simmer on low heat for ten minutes; let cool. Top each oyster with ½ teaspoon of butter mixture and bake in a preheated oven at 350° for ten minutes or until edges begin to brown. This dish has more calories (340) and fat (30 grams) than the bacon and cheese oyster recipe (above). It must be all that butter.

HOW TO COOK AN OCTOPUS

Fried octopus is a popular dish among octopus eaters in Florida. They tend to lean toward octopus recipes from Portugal and Spain, the two major octopus-eating countries in the world.

Precook about two pounds of cleaned octopus meat, drain, and set aside to cool. Cut the meat into large chunks. Mix together three beaten eggs, a quarter of a cup of milk, some finely chopped parsley, some olive oil, and salt and pepper to taste. Don't oversalt—octopus is salty. Dip the octopus into the egg mixture and fry in olive oil in a shallow pan, turning each piece until it's golden brown. Enjoy!

BUTTERMILK CRACKLIN' CORNBREAD

Sift, then measure:
1 cup all-purpose flour
Resift with:
½ tablespoon baking soda
1½ tablespoons baking powder
1 teaspoon sugar
1 teaspoon salt
Add:
¾ cup yellow ground cornmeal
Combine and beat:
1 cup buttermilk
2 eggs
3 to 4 teaspoons melted butter or bacon fat

Preheat oven to 425°. Stir the liquid into the dry ingredients with a few swift strokes. Add ¼ cup salt pork cracklins (skins). Pour the batter into a preheated greased pan and bake the bread for about a half hour.

TEN THINGS TO DO WITH LEFTOVER SPICES

1. Cayenne pepper sprinkled on garbage can lids will keep animals out of the trash.
2. For a relaxing bath, try this: Combine equal amounts of rosemary, peppermint, and lemon thyme in a cloth bag. Hang the bag from the tub faucet while the water is running. After the bath, massage the bag into your skin for an even more sensual experience.
3. A whole bay leaf will keep weevils out of stored flour,

cornmeal, and other grains without flavoring the foods.

4. Mint repels mice. Long stems of it placed along the eaves in your attic will encourage mice to choose a different winter home. A word of warning: Another spice, anise, attracts mice.

5. Rosemary is a symbol of remembrance. Enclose rosemary sprigs in your Christmas cards, birthday cards, etc., for a fragrant reminder.

6. Plant garlic bulbs around the edge of a flower garden to keep animals out of the bed.

7. Cold hands and feet? Sprinkle a small amount of cayenne pepper in socks and gloves to help keep them warm. Warning: Cayenne pepper should not be used in or around any mucous membrane.

8. For natural mouthwash, mix one tablespoon each anise seed, dried peppermint, and rosemary. Double the amounts if using fresh spices. Strain, cool, and refrigerate to be used as needed. Warning: This is not meant to be swallowed.

9. For a refreshing potpourri, add one tablespoon dried peppermint leaves and one tablespoon cinnamon bark pieces to a saucepan of water and simmer.

10. Bouquets of mint, rosemary, and thyme wrapped lightly in cheesecloth and hung in a closet will repel moths.

WHAT'S ORGANIC AND WHAT ISN'T?

Fruits and vegetables grown in Florida are often sprayed with pesticides. Studies show that pesticides can penetrate the outer covering of the fruit or vegetable and be absorbed through the roots. If you peel the product and then wash it, it's estimated that only 25 percent of the pesticides are removed. The rest is consumed by the eater.

The number one pesticide-contaminated fruit is strawberries, followed by cherries, peaches, cantaloupes, apples, apricots, and grapes. For vegetables, the leader is bell peppers, followed by spinach, celery, green beans, and cucumbers.

Some Florida fruits and vegetables are advertised as "organic." Experts say it's best to buy organic produce that is certified by the Organic Trade Association. To earn this title, fruits, vegetables, grains, and nuts have to be grown without the use of any synthetic pesticides on land that has been chemical-free for a period of three years. If the land is free for only two years, the food is labeled "transitional organic." Processed and prepared fruit and vegetable prod-

ucts must include products that are 95 percent organic with no artificial additives or preservatives. Eggs, milk, and other dairy products must come from cows and chickens that are fed organic feeds free of hormones for at least 12 months.

Lighthouse Shrimp with Kiwi-Plum Salsa
1 pound raw peeled and deveined shrimp (with tails on)
2 cups cut onions for kabobs
2 cups cut bell peppers for kabobs
¼ cup vegetable oil
¼ cup soy sauce
¼ cup orange juice
1 teaspoon ground oregano
1 teaspoon black pepper
⅔ cup diced radish

⅔ cup diced plums
⅔ cup diced kiwi

Arrange shrimp, onions, and bell peppers on skewers and set aside. In an eight-ounce container with a lid, combine oil, soy sauce, juice, oregano, and pepper. Cover and shake to mix well. Brush kabobs liberally with oil mixture and place on grill over medium hot coals for six to eight minutes on each side. Baste frequently while grilling. While shrimp are cooking, dice and mix radish, plums, and kiwi. Divide evenly and serve with kabobs. This recipe yields four servings.

Pickled Shrimp
1 pound cooked, peeled, and deveined shrimp
1 cup white vinegar
1 cup chopped red onions
1 cup salad oil
2 tablespoons capers

Combine all ingredients and refrigerate overnight, stirring occasionally. Remove shrimp and onions from the marinade and serve with salad greens or pasta. This recipes yields four servings.

Fried Orange Shrimp
1 beaten egg
1 cup all-purpose flour
1 cup orange juice
1 teaspoon salt
1 pound peeled and deveined shrimp
Oil for deep frying

Combine egg, flour, orange

juice, and salt; mix well. Heat oil to 350°F. Dip shrimp into batter to coat, then place in oil to fry. Cook shrimp approximately one minute or until golden brown. Remove from oil and drain on absorbent paper. This recipe yields 6 servings and has 434 calories, 3 grams of saturated fat, and 252 milligrams of cholesterol per serving.

Rock Shrimp Dreams

1 pound cooked, peeled, and deveined rock shrimp
6 ounces soft cream cheese
1 cup chopped pecans
1 cup drained crushed pineapple
¼ cup chopped ripe olives
1 tablespoon lime juice
6 slices lightly buttered white bread
6 slices lightly buttered wheat bread

Chop rock shrimp. Combine all ingredients except bread; mix well. Spread equal amounts of shrimp mixture on six slices of white bread; cover with remaining slices of wheat bread and cut each sandwich into four pieces diagonally. This recipe yields four servings.

*The
Sunshine State
Almanac
& Book of
Florida-
Related
Stuff*

HOUSE &
GARDEN

*A*ll Floridians know to keep doors closed and screens on windows to keep bugs out of their homes. But many of us carry bugs into our homes accidentally, to live in the perfect bug environment—in and on our houseplants. According to experts, there are any number of freeloading bugs that we hand carry into our homes with plants, including mealybugs, spider mites, aphids, whiteflies, scales, psocids, and even fungus gnat maggots.

Carefully examine any plant you purchase or get from a friend to be sure it is free of pests. It's a good idea to isolate new plants for a couple of weeks before you place them with other plants in your home. During that time you can discover any infestations on the new plants.

Another source of pest infestations could be the soil used for planting or re-potting. Always use sterilized soil and new or sterilized pots for potting.

The most common pests on houseplants are spider mites and mealybugs. Both cause plant damage by sucking the juices from plants. Spider mites measure only one-fiftieth of an inch and are commonly found on the undersides of leaves. If a plant is heavily infested, a fine webbing appears on it. Mealybugs, when mature, are nearly one-eighth of an inch long with soft bodies covered by a white powdery substance. Some species have long wax filaments extending from the rear.

Three other plant suckers are aphids, scales, and whiteflies. Aphids come in many colors, from green to pink to blue, and have pear-shaped bodies with long antennae and two short tubes extending from the rear of the body. Scales can be almost any color and measure from one-eighth to one-third of an inch when mature. They are found all over the plant, on either side of the leaves, and even on twigs and branches. Whiteflies resemble tiny white moths and tend to swarm when disturbed.

Fungus gnat maggots, springtails, and psocids are soil pests that may damage houseplant root systems. All are difficult to detect and very small in size, ranging from the microscopic springtail to the wormlike maggot measuring one-fourth of an inch long.

Here are some treatments you can try to rid houseplants of unwelcome critters. Syringing is spraying plants with a forceful stream of room-temperature water twice a month to remove insects before they settle in. This is best done outside or over a laundry sink where you can get at the underside of leaves where most bugs congregate. To wash a plant, use three tablespoons of mild detergent in a gallon of water and wash the leaves with a soft brush or cloth. To remove aphids, mealybugs, and scales from broad-leafed plants, give your plants a scrubbing twice a year.

A light infestation of mealybugs or aphids can be controlled by swabbing the undersides of leaves with alcohol. But alcohol can burn the foliage, so use with care. You can soak a cigar or pipe tobacco in a quart of water for several days, dilute it to the color of weak tea, and add one tablespoon of mild detergent to wash away aphids.

If only a few bugs are involved, you may be able to remove the pests with a toothpick or tweezers. Slugs, snails, and cutworms can be picked from plants at night when they come out to feed.

In severe cases, pesticide treatments may be necessary. Insecticides and miticides can be purchased at garden supply or hardware stores. However, the Florida Pest Control Association encourages you to use all chemicals with care or better still, hire a professional to do it.

TAKING CARE OF LAWN AND GARDEN BUSINESS

When Florida moves into the summer months, lawns and gardens need constant attention to maintain their health and beauty. One of the most important elements in keeping your yard healthy under the hot sun is watering. It doesn't have to be time-consuming and can even be relaxing if you combine watering with time spent outdoors when the weather is pleasant.

One of the most efficient methods of watering is drip irrigation. This requires a soaker hose that supplies water through porous tubing lying directly on the ground. Since the water is delivered at very low pressure, it is quickly absorbed by the soil with a minimum loss to runoff or evaporation. This is important if the water comes from a city source and is charged to residents. If you keep your grass height to two to three inches, your lawn will need less water and be less susceptible to rot burn.

Keep watering to a minimum by using mulches like bark or pine straw around vegetables, annuals, and shrubs. Keep these areas free of weeds, which compete for water. To minimize evaporation and fungus-related diseases, water only in the early morning. For best growth, water at the edge of the circle formed by the tips of a plant's branches. Water deeply and allow soil to dry slightly between waterings. This aerates the ground and speeds growth.

NUISANCE WATERFOWL

Ducks, geese, swans, and cranes can cause problems near rivers, ponds, and lakes. They feed on crops, grass, and other vegetation; trample plants; and leave droppings. If you have a backyard pond, you might wind up with some uninvited visitors.

Whatever the problem with waterfowl, immediate action is crucial to successful control. A combination of several frightening techniques—scarecrows, noisemakers, flags, balloons, and even dogs—may produce the best results. Scarecrows should be of simple construction and capable of moving in the wind. For large areas, use one for every five acres.

Anything that moves in the wind and makes noise—old cans, farm machinery, pinwheels, streamers, fluorescent traffic cones, and aluminum pie plates—can work. Flags may be the most effective and least expensive control tool. Make two-by-three-foot black plastic flags and mount them on four-foot posts. Put one flag per acre in fields where waterfowl have been feeding, and one per five acres in fields with no damage. Balloons, if properly maintained and frequently moved, can also be effective waterfowl scares. Fill a 2-foot-diameter balloon with helium and anchor it with a 50- to 75-pound monofilament line. A free-roaming dog, trained to chase birds as soon as they land, will discourage waterfowl.

THREE WATER-SAVING TIPS FOR YOUR LAWN

* Water lawns only when necessary, and turn automatic watering systems off if rain is predicted. Always water lawns early in the morning or late in the evening to reduce evaporation.

* Never overwater. The average lawn needs only an inch of water per week. If using automatic sprinklers, adjust them properly so they water only the lawn, not paved areas.

* Don't cut grass too short. Longer grass has better roots, is healthier, and makes better use of water. Mow no more than one-third of the blade height. Leaving cuttings and leaves on the lawn improves water absorption and adds natural fertilizer.

REASONS TO IMPROVE YOUR HOME'S LANDSCAPING

By improving the outside areas around your home, you can do everything from luring birds into the area and cutting your heating and cooling costs to improving your property's value. Strategically placed trees provide shade in the summer and allow the sun to come in during the winter. A yard filled with flowering trees and trimmed bushes looks better than a yard full of weeds. Eye appeal can increase the value of your home when you're ready to sell. Here's what professional landscapers in Florida suggest:

A flowering garden can increase wildlife populations. By carefully arranging your conifer and hardwood trees, you can lower winter heating and summer cooling costs. Trees, shrubs, and properly kept lawns are good for soil conservation and can prevent erosion. Anything that grows is always nice to look at. A neat garden is also a good place for children to play.

With the right vegetation, you can probably double the number of bird species you can lure onto your property. Cherries, strawberries, and crabapples attract birds and are also good to eat. Try keeping a list of what birds visited your property and on what date. You can identify birds with *Florida's Birds* by Kale and Maehr, the best book on the subject. Birds

such as tree swallows, house wrens, brown thrashers, and orioles offer natural insect control.

Native plants need less water to survive, have fewer pests than nonnative plants, are more likely to entice birds and wildlife into the area, and will probably survive better than more exotic plants. For a new landscape project, retain existing native plants since they require no establishment and minimum maintenance. Remove any invasive exotic plants that can easily get out of control. Honeysuckle, Brazilian pepper, Australian pines, and punk trees all use too much water and can overpower native plants.

The best wildlife landscapes require a minimum amount of care.

NATIVE PLANTS THAT ATTRACT WILDLIFE

Gardening for wildlife is rapidly increasing in popularity in Florida. Home landscapes can help offset the habitat loss that occurs in urban areas, allowing a greater variety of wildlife to live nearby. Plants are the key to attracting wildlife to your property. Your plant choices and your landscape design will determine

what animals you will attract. A yard landscaped with wildlife in mind need not appear wild to be effective.

Your choice of plants is one of the most important factors in gardening for wildlife. Wildlife usually does best in landscapes with plants native to the region in which they live. These plants often are better at providing the food and cover required. When planted in the proper location, native plants also require less attention and water.

There are a great many native trees and shrubs to choose from in Florida. Every plant has some value to wildlife, but some are better than others.

Plants listed as "tall trees" (taller than 30 feet at maturity) often are used best as canopy trees. Small trees, measuring less than 30 feet tall, can be used below the canopy when they are shade-tolerant or as low-canopy trees in areas where large trees are not desired or appropriate.

Shrubs, defined as woody plants with a bushy form, are used best near trees. Shade-tolerant shrubs can be planted directly beneath the canopy. Others can be planted at the edge of the shade zone so that they receive ample sunlight.

Some plants produce either male or female flowers. These are known as dioecious. Other plants produce both male and female flowers. These are called monoecious. Monoecious plants can set fruit by themselves. For dioecious plants, you need to have both sexes nearby, and only the female plants produce fruit. Because fruit production is important to a wildlife landscape, remember this when you make your plant choices. Consider the size of the fruit—large fruit may be difficult for small wildlife to use. Also be aware of the season when the fruit ripens, and try to have food available throughout the year.

The best wildlife landscapes require a minimum amount of care. Frequent watering, fertilizing, spraying, and pruning disturbs animals and limits their use of the area. Use plants that are adapted to existing growing conditions. It's important that your landscape be attractive to you as well as fill the needs of the wildlife you wish to attract.

MAKING A LEAF SANDWICH

Fall is a wonderful time to collect leaves. All across northern Florida you can find attractive leaves in various colors and designs. One way to make a leaf collection is to preserve each leaf between two pieces of waxed paper and make a leaf sandwich. This is a great project for children.

You'll need an iron, some towels, enough waxed paper to cover the leaves and, of course, the leaves. Set the iron to the highest setting. While the iron is heating, place a towel on your ironing surface, then place a sheet of waxed paper on top of the towel. Arrange your leaf or leaves on the waxed paper. Place another sheet of waxed paper on top, forming a sandwich. Place a second towel on top of the top sheet and iron for about two to three minutes. Keep the iron moving so you don't have burn spots. Wait about 20 minutes before removing the top towel. The heat from the iron will seal the wax around the leaves. You can label the leaves, place them in a scrapbook or loose-leaf notebook, or hang them in a window using string or colored ribbon.

PRUNING A FRUIT TREE

One of the primary reasons to prune fruit trees is to open the trees up so sunlight can penetrate to the inside branches. Cut the branches that cross or rub against other branches, removing branches that are growing toward the center of the tree. On a sunny day, check to see if the sun is reaching the center of the tree. If not, trim the branches. Determine the correct height for the tree, and trim the higher branches. This is called "topping" the tree. Pruning and topping is required yearly to allow light and air circulation and to control the height and branch growth.

Getting Rid of Fruit-Eating Birds

Once you start feeding birds, you might find they're eating fruit from trees you've planted in your garden. Before you get a chance to enjoy the fruit of your labors, the birds have already had their fill. Barriers are the most effective deterrent. You can make one out of chicken wire or mesh. Hot caps—those opaque plastic "hats" used to cover young plants in the spring to prevent freezing—work well. An inverted crate can keep most birds away from small plants. Placing feeders filled with sunflower, millet, nectar, and peanuts nearby may also distract birds.

BUILDING A BACKYARD POND

Not every Florida home has a view of the water. If one does—and that water is the Atlantic Ocean or the Gulf of Mexico—you can figure the house sells for top dollar. The next step down from ocean- and gulf-front is canals, lakes, rivers, and ponds. If you don't have any of these, you can create your own water view by building a backyard pond, even if you're miles away from a natural water flow. Lily Water Gardens (800-999-5450) sells liners that will keep the water in place and will last as long as 20 years.

First, figure out how large a liner you need. Liners are rectangular, so determine the pond's length, width, and depth. If the pond will be about 18 inches deep, add 4 feet to the rectangle's length and width. Add 5 feet for a 2-foot depth, 6 feet for a 30-inch depth, and 7 feet for a 3-foot depth.

Outline the desired area with a garden hose or large rope. Oval shapes are most popular. Mark your outline with cuts using a shovel and begin

digging from the inside out, leaving shelves if you plan to add underwater potted plants. Most water gardens are 14 to 24 inches deep. Check your excavation's top level. This is critical to ensure that water does not pour over one side and leave your liner exposed on the other.

Each liner comes with instructions. Just follow the directions step by step. Lay your liner in place, smoothing out any wrinkles. Begin filling your new "pond" with water, smoothing out any more wrinkles. Take a break. It might take hours to fill up the pond.

When the pond is nearly full, trim the excess liner and nail the flaps in place with #10 nails. This is explained in the instructions. The pond pictured will have stone coping around the sides to cover any of the liner that still shows.

Koi and Your Backyard Pond

The common carp and goldfish are distant cousins to the koi, a popular fish from Japan, where koi usually live in lushly landscaped, outdoor fish ponds. Their Japanese name is *nishikigoi*. They were bred in Japan more than 200 years ago. They'll thrive in any backyard pond as long as the pond provides adequate water oxygenation and filtration. Koi can grow to a length of 24 to 36 inches, depending on the size of the pond, the amount of aeration, and the method of feeding. It is not uncommon for a small koi to grow two to four inches a year in a backyard pond.

If you're interested in stocking your pond with koi, here are some buying tips from the experts. Check the fishes' swimming movements. Do they look active and healthy? Check the gill movements. Are they moving slowly and regularly? Avoid koi with white spots, redness on the skin (which could be a parasite infection), raised scales, cloudy eyes, fin rot, and lacerations.

To transport koi, check the plastic bags they will be carried in to ensure they are large enough to contain the fish. Bags should be well-oxygenated with at least two parts oxygen to one part water. Explain to the dealer how long you think it might take to get your fish to your pond. Put the bag in a comfortable and secure place in your car, away from heat.

Upon arrival at home, don't release the fish into your pond immediately. Let the bagged koi float on the pond for an hour to equalize temperature inside and outside the bag. Avoid putting stress on the fish before releasing them into a new home.

Quarantining new fish will avoid importing diseases into your pond. Depending on the time they've been with the dealer, some koi need longer times to adjust to their new environment. They eat poorly and lie at the pond's bottom, not actively swimming. The quarantine period will allow you to determine if the koi are sick and need treatment. In that case, call the shop or individual from whom you bought the fish.

FISH DINNERS FOR WILDLIFE

When you add freshwater fish like koi to your pond, they might attract herons, pelicans, cormorants, osprey, kingfishers, diving ducks, and egrets passing through the neighborhood. One solution is a physical barrier that's effective but somewhat unsightly. For small ponds, complete screening with bird netting may be effective. Properly spaced monofilament lines suspended over a pond may exclude gulls (every four feet), mergansers (every two feet), and herons (every foot). Perimeter fences provide some protection from wading birds.

Stocking Your Backyard Pond with Flowers

Water lilies are a beautiful addition to any backyard pond. With a minimum of care, hardy water lilies attain a diameter of about three feet. Tropicals vary in size. Stems grow to the depth of the water, and blooms are produced on the surface of the water from spring until late summer. Water lilies shade the shallow areas of the pond, retarding algae growth. You can safely cover 60–70 percent of your pond's

surface with water lilies.

The hybrid water lily is not to be confused with its wild counterpart, the native pond lily. The native pond lily, if left unchecked, will overcome the shallows of a pond with endless lily pads and few flowers. The hybrid water lily will attain a diameter of about three feet. The leaf growth may thicken, but the plant will not spread across the pond to areas where it is not wanted. It continually produces from one to three glorious blooms per plant once the plant is well established. It will bloom through the summer, with each blossom lasting three to four days, opening in the morning and closing in the afternoon.

Plant requirements are quite simple. Select an area of the pond that receives at least six hours of direct sunlight daily. The water should be still (away from any fountains or jets). Place the lily in a container filled with about five gallons of heavy topsoil. Avoid humus, peat moss, or light loamy soils. Plant the lily in the container.

Leave the crown of the plant level with the top of the container. Top the container with about one-half inch of gravel. Now you are ready to put the lily in the pond. Slowly lower the container into the water. Ideally, 6 to 12 inches of water should cover the top of the container.

Your lily will live for many years with proper care. Do not use broadleaf weed killers in or near the pond. Copper sulfate and some other algae killers may also prove harmful. Do not let the lily tuber freeze solid during the winter. In late fall, lower the container to the bottom of your pond to a maximum depth of three feet. When the water warms up in the spring, return the plant to the shallows, and watch it grow.

Lotus are hardy perennials which should be planted in the spring in a large container with rich garden soil and placed in shallow water (two to four inches above soil). The very fragrant lotus blooms in warmer climates from morning to mid-afternoon for six to eight weeks in early June. Lotus need five to six hours of sunlight daily.

A wide variety of marginals and bog plants are available throughout the season. All can be purchased from nurseries specializing in water plants.

HOUSING OPTIONS IN FLORIDA

If you're considering settling down in Florida, here are some good reasons for considering a new house. New home pricing is competitive, based on the number of new homes being built in an area. New homes usually come with some kind of warranty that everything inside is going to work for at least a few years, and if something doesn't work, the contractor will fix it for free. New appliances are always nicer than old appliances, and they're state-of-the-art. Home builders build in areas that are often better located than neighborhoods with used homes, so you might find something you like on a golf course or on the water.

Builders of new homes often offer a variety of floor plans, giving you the opportunity to include an extra bathroom, a double garage rather than a single garage, different carpeting, and other custom features. Almost all new homes are made with new materials like fire-retardant shingles, better insulation, and energy efficiency features, while older homes used what was best when they were originally built.

Almost all used homes will need repairs sooner than a new home, so maintaining a new home over a period of time usually costs less than repairing an existing home. Banks like to finance new homes, so you might find financing easier to get on a new home than on an old home.

Buying a Home—How Much Can You Afford?

Planning on buying a home in Florida? The Fannie Mae Foundation reports that in June 1998, the average price for a three-bedroom, two-bath home on a 75- by 125-foot lot in Miami was $135,000; in Fort Lauderdale, $136,500; in Marathon in the Florida Keys, $195,000; in Orlando, $96,500; in Tampa, $92,400; in Naples, $165,000; in Pensacola, $87,000; and in rural areas away from the tourist crowds, as low as $65,000. For waterfront locations, add 30 percent.

As a general rule, Fannie Mae says you should not commit more than 25 percent of your gross monthly income for mortgage payments. If you earn $5,000 a month, your mortgage payment should be no more than $1,250. Assuming an interest rate of 8 percent and a 30-year loan, your borrowing power tops out at $170,000.

A free booklet on buying your first home is available from the Fannie Mae Foundation at 800-659-7557. Or log on to http://www.quickenmortgage.com and enter your yearly income, monthly debt, the current interest rate, and the amount you can afford on a down payment; the computer will tell you how much you can safely afford to spend on a house.

HOW WE GET ELECTRICITY—SIMPLIFIED

The electricity that reaches your home comes from the power company. In Florida and across the United States, it's 60 Hz. The power arrives at your home as 240 volts. Then it's divided into two 120-

volt signals which are 180 degrees out of phase with each other. Most of the electrical appliances in your home run on 120 volts (television, hair dryer, electric mixer, etc.), while some require 240 volts (clothes dryer, electric stove, etc.)

The power comes into your home to a metal box which contains fuses or circuit breakers. Each fuse or circuit breaker limits the amount of current that can be drawn from all the outlets it feeds. If you exceed that amount, the fuse blows out or the circuit breaker trips, disconnecting the power from the outlets. It does this to protect the wires inside the walls from overheating. Under ideal conditions, and as long as you don't overload any circuits, you'll never have to worry about fuses or circuit breakers. Just pay your electric bill on time, and you'll always have electricity.

BEATING THE HIGH COST OF STAYING COOL AND KEEPING WARM

You can cut utility costs considerably by planting trees, shrubs, and hedges around your home. The Florida Department of Energy reports you can save as much as a quarter of your annual home energy use for heating and cooling by carefully positioning trees in your yard. An eight-foot deciduous tree costs about the same as an awning large enough to cover a window and produces almost the same results. The tree will let in

Not all ceiling fans are created equal.

some winter sun to cut down on your heating and lighting costs, but will block the sun when it blooms in the summer, reducing the cost of keeping the home cool.

Take this test: Go to a park or wooded area when the temperature is high and feel the difference between an unshaded, open area and a shaded area under trees. Air temperatures in shady areas can be as much as 9 or 10 degrees cooler than unshaded areas and as much as 25 degrees cooler than nearby roads.

Consider installing a ceiling fan to circulate both heated and cooled air. During the warm months, a ceiling fan moves the air-conditioned air around a room. During the winter months, the fan reclaims lost heat from the ceiling area.

Not all ceiling fans are created equally, however. Check to see how much air is circulated, how quiet the fan is, whether the fan blades wobble, and how long the fan will last. The greater the angle of the blade, or blade pitch, the more air movement you get. Cheap fans compromise on blade pitch because the more pitch the blades have, the more power the fan needs to operate. Inexpensive fans can be noisy because of non-precision ball bearings and poor engineering. Cheap blade materials can cause the fan to wobble, and lack of quality control in the manufacturing process can cause the blades to have different pitches. It always pays to buy something of quality.

How to Cool Off Your Body

When your body temperature is at 98.6 degrees and you're exposed to heat, your body's cooling system flips the "on" switch. Blood vessels dilate, sweat glands run on "high," and more blood gushes to the surface of your skin. Avoiding the heat and drinking lots of fluids is one way to get some relief. In Florida, most people get uncomfortable when the temperature is over 80 degrees and the humidity creeps over the 65 percent mark. The high-cost solution? Turn on the air conditioning. The low-cost solution? Avoid big meals, and limit your movements. Turn on a fan. Of course, all fans do is move hot air around, so spray yourself with a water mist so the air can cool off your skin.

FIGURING YOUR PROPERTY TAXES

Most of the taxing jurisdictions in Florida get about one-third of their revenue from property taxes. In Florida, that amounts to billions of dollars a year. Nobody likes the idea of paying taxes, but it's part of the state's survival plan, and there's not much we can do about it. There are options available to contest the appraisal of a home and, hence, the amount of taxes paid. The first step is to contact the county tax office and find out the procedure. If you can prove your home's appraisal was too high compared to similar homes in the area, you can request a new appraisal and perhaps pay less in taxes.

It's easy to figure out your annual property and school taxes if you know the millage rate and who's taxing what. Taxes are paid on the appraised value of your home, not the market value. In all cases, the appraised value is less than the market value. The home we use in the example below sold for $181,000 and was assessed for tax purposes at $143,149.

Florida has a Homestead Exemption law that says the first $25,000 of value on a home is exempt from municipal and county taxes—if you qualify. Homeowners have to live in the home as of January 1 of the year in which they are applying for exemption. To apply, you have to show tax officials your Florida voter's registration (assuming you vote), state driver's license (assuming you drive), vehicle registration (assuming you own a vehicle), the recorded deed for the property, a copy of your electric bill dating back to January 1, and your Social Security number. Don't forget to double-check your tax bill after you've received your exemption to be sure the appraised value has been reduced. If you're eligible for the Homestead Exemption, take the appraised value of your home and subtract $25,000. In our example, the assessed value was $143,149 minus $25,000, for a taxable value of $118,149. If you're not eligible for the exemption, you pay taxes on the entire $143,149.

Multiply the millage rate (center column; varies from county to county) by $118,149 (taxable value of the home in our example) to figure total tax for each item. To figure your taxes, contact the property appraiser in your tax district for your millage rates. Numbers are rounded to the nearest whole dollar.

Item	Millage Rate	Total Tax
County	5.63	$665
School RLE	6.56	$776
Water management	.5	$6
Mosquito spraying	.39	$47
Miscellaneous	.5	$72
Total taxes		$1,566

Home Improvements

I f your Florida home is (pick one): too small, too old, too ugly, or you want an extra bathroom, a swimming pool, or a deck overlooking the ocean, don't despair. Florida contractors are standing by to do the work if you can pay the bills. Just remember—stay conventional and avoid any bizarre improvements. A purple widow's walk with no railing that's accessible only by climbing a rope will do little to increase the value of your home.

How much do improvements cost? Here's an estimate of costs around Florida, compiled by National Financial Services, a major supplier of financing for home improvements in the Southeast. These 1996 figures (the date of the last study) also include how much you can expect to recover from your investment if you decide to sell your house. Of course, prices will vary depending on your location, the cost of materials in that area (higher in Key West than in, say, Jacksonville), and the size of the improvement. Make sure your contractor is licensed to work in Florida.

* Adding a pool: $12,000–$25,000 (recovery: about 80 percent) unless the people interested in buying your house don't want a pool; then it could hinder a sale.
* Adding a deck: $4,000–$8,000 (recovery: about 40 to 60 percent).
* Adding a bathroom: $15,000 (recovery: about 80 percent) but could actually increase the value of the home.
* Adding a garage: $10,000–$15,000 (recovery: about 80 percent) but could actually increase the value of the home.
* Adding a new room: $20,000–$30,000 (recovery: about 75 percent).
* Enclosing a porch: $8,000–$12,000 (recovery: about 80 percent).

HURRICANE SURVIVAL TIPS FROM THE EXPERTS

The hurricane season in Florida lasts from June 1 to November 30. Determining exactly when hurricanes are a threat is not an exact science, so the danger period can fluctuate.

Being prepared for a hurricane is the key to your own survival and minimal damage to your property. If you live in a hurricane-prone area, keep an adequate supply of food and emergency equipment on hand. This includes enough canned food to last four to five days, a hand can opener, battery-powered radio, extra batteries, and emergency cooking equipment like a camp stove with fuel to operate it. You'll need about one gallon of water per person per day if your water supply is cut off. A battery-powered TV also comes in handy if local stations are still on the air. Don't forget flashlights, candles, matches, a kerosene lamp, fire extinguisher, and a first aid kit. A camera comes in handy to record any damage. Refill any prescriptions and clear the area around your house of outdoor furniture, potted plants, trash cans, and other non-stationary items.

If the National Weather Service announces a hurricane "warning," expect hurricane conditions within 24 hours. Know your evacuation routes, and don't wait until the last minute to leave the area. Decide where you will go and how you will get there. Choose a hotel or motel or home of a friend, and lay the groundwork prior to any trouble. As a last resort, you can always go to one of many local shelters, so know where they are. Listen for weather updates on the radio or TV.

Fill the bathtub and large containers with water. Turn your refrigerator and freezer to the coldest setting. The colder food is before a possible power failure, the longer it will last. You might want to purchase a 50-pound block of dry ice, which should keep food safe without power for two days or more in an 18-cubic-foot freezer filled with food. Dry ice registers minus 216°F, so wear gloves or use tongs when handling it. Wrap it in brown paper for longer storage, and separate it from direct food contact with a piece of cardboard. Fill a partly empty freezer with crumpled newspaper to cut down on air currents, which cause dry ice to dissipate.

Flooding often accompanies hurricanes. If you live in an area subject to floods, be ready to raise refrigerators or freezers by putting cement blocks under their corners. If you keep canned goods and other foods in a basement or low cabinets, move them higher.

Floodwaters may carry silt, raw sewage, oil, or chemical waste. If foods have been in contact with floodwaters, throw them away.

BUYING A SWIMMING POOL

The temperature's creeping toward the 100 degree mark, the air conditioner is working overtime, and the ceiling fans are whirring overhead. If you had a swimming pool, you could step outside for a dip and cool off. Don't have a pool? You might consider buying one. There are several things you should think about before laying down your money.

What type of pool do you want (and can you afford)? How big should it be? Where are you going to put it? How much work is it to maintain, and how much does that cost?

The least expensive pool is an above-ground pool. They're not permanent, so you can take them with you when you move. They're easy to install—you can do it yourself. They're well suited to small backyards.

In-ground pools are the most expensive type of pool. They add value to your home should you decide to sell it, and they'll last longer than an above-ground pool. In-ground pools come in fiberglass, concrete, and vinyl. Fiberglass pools come in one piece and can be dropped into an excavation hole and completed in a week or two. Sizes are limited, but they're almost maintenance-free. They use fewer chemicals than other pools, and they're easier to clean because of their super-slick surface. Poured concrete pools are the most common type of pool in Florida. They take longer to install and require more maintenance than fiberglass pools.

A vinyl-liner pool is furnished to the installer in kit form. After excavation, the panel walls are bolted or fastened together and supported at the bottom by a concrete footing. The vinyl liner is spread over the interior of the pool and

covers the excavated floor and paneled walls. It is connected to the top of the panel walls by a vinyl rib at the outside edge of the liner. It's held in place by the weight of the water. Construction time for vinyl-liner pools is typically one to three weeks.

In Florida, an in-ground pool measuring about 30 feet long costs about $10,000–$15,000 plus the cost of any decking and landscaping.

How to Clean a Very Dirty Pool

You've probably seen some badly neglected pools in Florida. It's estimated there are about 800,000 above-ground and in-ground pools around the state, and some are badly in need of attention. The best solution is to avoid the problem in the first place by checking your pool's chemicals at least once a week and removing all floating and bottom debris whenever you see it. If your pool has gone beyond that point, here are some suggestions to turn an ugly, neglected, contaminated, greenish, moldy-looking pool filled with debris into a work of aquatic art.

First, remove all of the debris from the pool with a net. Don't vacuum at this point or put in any chemicals. This cleanup will initially stir up the water and make it look worse, but things will settle in a few hours or overnight.

When all of the debris is removed, brush the bottom and sides to loosen dirt and mold. You can now vacuum using the vacuum that came with the pool. Then backwash the pool according to instructions that came with your pool filtering system. If instructions aren't available, you can get advice from your local pool supply store.

Adjust the pH and alkalinity levels of the water using whatever chemicals your pool chemical supplier suggests. If you're unsure, take a sample to your local pool store and have them determine what you need to get the pool back in shape chemically. Unless everything is within the proper levels, the water will never clear.

Now, shock the pool. Shocking involves super-chlorinating the water to kill off any bad stuff that shouldn't be there. If your pool is very dirty, it may need lots of liquid chlorine over a period of days before the water clears. Start by adding three or four gallons, and if you see no results overnight, add three or four more gallons the next day. Continue this process until you notice the water changing color to either cloudy white, light green, or clear. Generally speaking, the more chlorine you add, the more quickly the water will clear.

Run the filter 24 hours a day, and backwash often (three or four times a day). Green or cloudy water will quickly clog a filter, so you may have to backwash your filter many times a day until the pool clears. Remember, you cannot backwash a pool filter too much. The more you run your pool and the more you backwash the filter, the faster the pool will clear up.

If you have a diatomaceous earth (D.E.) filter, remember to add new D.E. to the skimmer closest to your filter after each backwashing. A D.E. filter is more work than a sand filter, but the D.E. filter will clear a green pool about twice as fast as a sand filter. If you follow these instructions and your pool does not clear up within four or five days, your filter may not be functioning properly. Have it checked out by a professional.

REVERSE MORTGAGES

Many Floridians over the age of 65 are looking seriously at reverse mortgages. Here's how they work. If you're over 65 and own your home, you can borrow money now and have someone pay it back when (gulp!) you're deceased.

A reverse mortgage allows homeowners to borrow money without making monthly payments. When the owner dies or the title to the property changes hands (usually through a sale or by heirs inheriting the property), the loan is due and can be paid off or the property can be sold and the loan settled.

Depending on which lender you go to, you'll have a choice of how you'll get the money from the loan proceeds. You can get equal monthly payments for a fixed period of time that you select, monthly payments for as long as you occupy the home as your principal residence, a line of credit that you can draw on whenever you want, or a line of credit plus equal monthly payments for a fixed period you select.

The maximum amount that can be borrowed is based on the age of the youngest borrower, the interest rate, and the market value of the home. For example, a person who is 75 and owns a home worth $150,000 can receive about $50,000 in cash. If you're considering something like this, experts say it pays to shop around. Different companies offer different amounts and have different rules.

The Department of Housing and Urban Development (HUD) has been encouraging lenders to offer such loans to the public, so at least the government thinks this method of raising money during your senior years has some merit. The Federal Housing Administration (a branch of HUD) has been offering insurance on qualified Home Equity Conversion Mortgage (HECM) loans, helping to offset any potential losses that could occur to lenders. Fannie Mae has also encouraged lenders to offer reverse mortgages through its Home Keeper program. Fannie Mae is a shareholder-owned corporation that buys mortgage loans from lenders, so lenders can use the money to make even more home loans to the public.

HOW TO BUY A MOBILE HOME

Mobile homes are popular in Florida because of their cost, the availability of mobile home parks throughout the state, and the mild climate here. Officially, a mobile home is a dwelling built on an integral chassis in a factory, transportable in one or more sections, eight feet or more in width.

You buy a mobile home like you buy everything else: compare costs and shop around for the best buy, comparing floor plans, square footage, energy efficiency, construction method, and inside and outside decor. Beware of a new mobile home that does not display a label certifying code compliance. All single-family mobile homes must bear a certification label which is displayed on the rear of the home.

If you purchase a new mobile home from a dealer, the dealer must be licensed with the Division of Motor Vehicles, Department of Highway Safety and Motor Vehicles. Used mobile homes may be sold by licensed dealers, real estate brokers (if the land is included in the sale), or private owners. The choice of a mobile home dealer is as important as the selection of any home, since you'll be relying on the dealer's expertise and future service. You can call the Division of Consumer Services, Department of Agriculture and Consumer Services, 800-342-2176, and your local Division of Motor Vehicles office to see if complaints have been filed against a mobile home dealer, the nature of those complaints, and if the problems were resolved.

In Florida, a mobile home is a motor vehicle and requires a certificate of title as proof of ownership, just as your car or truck does. There is a separate title document for each section of your mobile home, so there is one title document for a single-wide mobile home and two title documents for a double-wide. If your mobile home has been paid in full, you will receive the title(s) from Tallahassee. If there is a lien on your home, the lienholder will receive the title and hold it until the lien amount has been paid.

If you own the land on which your mobile home is located and the home is permanently affixed to the land, you must declare the home to be "real property" and have it placed on the tax rolls of your county. Your taxes are then be paid in the same way as conventional taxes are paid. If you rent the land on which your home is located or if your home is not permanently affixed to your land, you must purchase and display a decal each year for each section of your mobile home. If you are uncertain as to whether your home is permanently affixed to the land, contact your county property appraiser, who will make this determination.

If your mobile home is real property, failure to place it on the county real property tax rolls may result in back taxes and penalties being assessed against you, so it is important to make sure your mobile home is classified properly.

How to Choose a Mobile Home Park

If you decide to live in a mobile home, you need a place to put it. You can buy some land and plunk it down there (if zoning laws permit) or live in a mobile home park. Among your choices are renting the lot, buying the lot, or moving into a co-op park. If the park is your solution, visit various parks in the area where you plan to live and compare what they have to offer. In each case, prior to agreeing to anything, be sure you read and understand the terms of the lease and the rules and regulations of the park. If possible, talk to some of the park residents about their experiences with the park and its management.

If you're leasing a lot, find out the amount of rent, what it includes, and how often it is raised. Under Florida law, the park must notify the tenants, in writing, of any changes in fees, charges, rules, or regulations at least 30 days prior to the implementation date. The Florida Mobile Home Landlord and Tenant Act (FMHLTA) applies to tenancies in which a mobile home is placed upon a rented lot in a mobile home park of ten or more lots.

For a comprehensive information packet on manufactured housing communities in Florida, contact the Florida Manufactured Housing Association, 115 North Calhoun, Suite 5, Tallahassee 32302, 904-222-4011.

Dealing with High Winds

When high winds blow through town, often the first thing to leave the ground is an unanchored mobile home. In Florida, all mobile homes are required to be tied down in accordance with the specifications provided by the manufacturer. In the case of a used home and in the absence of the manufacturer's tie-down instructions, the home must be tied down in accordance with the specifications provided in Department of Highway Safety and Motor Vehicles Rule 15C-1.10. Each county is responsible for ensuring compliance with tie-down regulations.

JUST-IN-CASE THINGS TO KEEP AROUND THE HOUSE

To be prepared for every possible calamity, consider keeping these items handy:

* A Yellow Page phone directory—just in case you need professional help for something you can't do yourself. Once you find good professional help that's reasonably priced, ask for a business card and keep it handy. Eventually, you'll have enough names and phone numbers to solve most problems you're likely to encounter around the house.

* A roll of duct tape—just in case you have to cover a crack in a window or door, repair a broken table leg, or stop a pipe from leaking temporarily. Not very pretty or permanent but functional. If plumbing is a constant problem, get some plumber's putty. You can stuff it in a small hole or crack to stop leaks.

* A can of WD-40—just in case you have to stop something from squeaking or lubricate things that get stuck. You can also use it to remove those annoying price tags stores cement to their products. Just spray on some WD-40, wait a few minutes, and peel off the sticker.

* A jar of assorted size nails, screws, nuts, and bolts—just in case you have to fix something that requires a nail, screw, nut, or bolt.

* A basic tool kit—just in case you need a hammer, screwdriver, or wrench. Throw in a pair of pliers and a small ladder, too.

* A toilet plunger—just in case you have to unstop a plugged-up sink or toilet.

* A smoke detector—A must. It will warn you if there's a fire in the house. While you're at it, include a carbon dioxide detector as well.

* A fire extinguisher—Another must—just in case the smoke alarm goes off. There are different extinguishers for different types of fire (wood, grease, electrical, etc.), so buy several.

* A volt tester—just in case you want to find out if that outlet is feeding electricity to your refrigerator, oven, microwave, TV, VCR, computer, hair dryer, electric toothbrush, etc.

* A tape measure—just in case you want to measure something like the area for a rug you're buying, the height of a table, or a picture frame.

Ten Ways to Save Water around the House

* Use water-saving, flow-restricting shower heads; low-flow faucets; and special toilet flushing devices to reduce the amount of water used.

* When buying washers and dryers, choose models that have water-saving features.

* A gallon or half-gallon milk jug filled with water and placed in the toilet tank, where it doesn't interfere with the flushing mechanism, will save water on each flush.

* When building or remodeling a home, have contractors install only low-flush toilets and other water-saving devices.

* Use the kitchen dishwashers and laundry room clothes washer only when you have a full load.

* Use the garbage disposal sparingly—it wastes water when you flush the sink.

* Fix any leaks. A drippy faucet can waste 20 gallons a day; a leaky toilet up to 500 gallons a day. Check for leaks. Put a few drops of food coloring in the toilet tank. If color appears in the bowl within a few minutes, you have a leak.

* Avoid running water in the sink. Shut off water while brushing teeth, shampooing, washing dishes, or shaving. A closed tap while you brush your teeth can save five gallons of water every minute. Take shorter showers.

* Wash cars with hoses with shut-off nozzles and use a bucket.

* Water your lawn sparingly. Chances are the amount of water you're currently using is too much.

The
Sunshine State
Almanac
& Book of
Florida-
Related
Stuff

LEGAL

*A*ll files maintained by the Department of State, Division of Licensing, are subject to public disclosure under the Florida Public Records Law. All you have to do is ask in the proper manner. Most requests involve filling out paperwork and paying a small fee, if applicable. You can get information on concealed weapon or firearm license applications, copies of sweepstakes applications, computer-generated lists of licensee data, certificates under seal, and custodian of record statements.

The government doesn't open all files to all people. You cannot get data on criminal justice reports, or the name, address, telephone number, and photograph of some applicants or licensees, former law enforcement personnel, Supreme Court justices and certain judges, private investigators, and recovery agents, to name a few.

You can make your request for information by writing to Division of Licensing, Office Box 6687, Tallahassee 32314 or by calling 850-488-6982. The fax number is 850-488-2789. You will be notified of the cost to provide the information requested within three workdays of receipt of your request. To inquire about the status of an application or to determine if an individual or company holds a license with the Department of State, Division of Licensing, call 850-488-5381.

SEXUAL PREDATORS AND OFFENDERS

A Florida law, effective July 1996, requires the Florida Department of Law Enforcement to maintain an updated list of registered sexual predators in the state after a court has made a written finding designating someone as a sexual predator as defined by Florida statute.

The law in Florida requires certain sexual offenders to register with the state and the information to be made available to the public. Sexual predator and sex offender information is accessible as a public record of the Florida Department of Law Enforcement. It's available on the Internet at http://www.fdle.state.fl.us.

This database includes individuals' names, addresses, and county locations. Although the information is updated on a regular basis, it can change quickly. It is possible that information provided on this site may not reflect the current residence, status, or other statistics regarding an individual.

The Florida Department of Law Enforcement has also established a toll-free hotline at 888-FL-PREDATOR (888-357-7332) that allows the public to request information 24 hours a day, 7 days a week, about sexual predators living in their communities and around the state. If you believe that any of the information found on FDLE records is in error, contact FDLE's Criminal Justice Information Systems Help Desk at 904-488-4931.

DEPARTMENT OF REVENUE FAX-BACK SERVICES

If you need tax returns, registration forms, brochures, and other Department of Revenue publications, they're now available at the touch of a fax button. The system's fax-on-demand is a fully automated service that's available 24 hours a day, 7 days a week. Copies of more than 150 tax forms and documents are available, including forms and information on sales, estate, real property, and intangible personal property taxes.

To use the service, call Tallahassee at 904-922-3676 from a fax machine. A taped message explains how to retrieve a docu-ment using the four-digit identification code assigned to each document. If callers don't know the identification codes for the documents they wish to retrieve, they can first retrieve a document index that lists codes for every document available. Callers can retrieve up to five separate documents per call.

HOW TO GET A COPY OF A FLORIDA BIRTH CERTIFICATE

The Office of Vital Statistics (Box 210, Jacksonville 32231) supplies copies of birth certificates by mail. To order, call 904-359-6911 or 904-359-6922. The OVS is also online at http://fcn.state.fl.us/hrs_hsi/ public_html/vitals/vitals.html.

THE TAXPAYER'S BILL OF RIGHTS

In 1991, Florida became one of the first states to adopt the concept of a Taxpayer Rights Advocate. The idea sprang from discussions between the Department of Revenue and various private-sector groups about the need to help taxpayers resolve problems that hadn't been corrected through normal administrative procedures. The Taxpayer Rights Advocate is not a substitute for the department's normal administrative procedures for appealing a tax assessment. However, the program can provide help if a taxpayer feels all the issues in the case weren't properly addressed. You can contact the Taxpayer Rights Advocate Office at 904-488-2321 in Tallahassee.

WHAT TO DO IF YOU GET ARRESTED

Situation: you're cruising along Interstate 75 at eighty miles an hour in a car without license plates and a broken taillight. The exhaust pipe is spitting out black smoke, and the rear bumper is dragging along the ground, sending sparks flying. You haven't slept in 68 hours, so you're weaving back and forth trying to stay awake. A police car pulls up in back with lights flashing, but you don't see it, so you continue, pushing the speed up to 90 miles an hour so you'll get where you're going a lot faster. When you glance in the rear view mirror and spot the flashing lights, you jam on the brakes to stop. Two of the four slick, no-tread tires blow out. You almost lose control as the car skids down the road, crashing into an empty school bus. Fortunately, no one is hurt.

When the officer finds your driver's license expired in 1986, you'll probably take a trip in the backseat of a police car. When you're arrested in Florida, the police take you to the local booking office and feed your name into computers that scan their memory banks in Florida and around the country. If the system finds your name, you're really in trouble. You could

be a multiple offender or wanted for some other crime. If you're clean, you're still in trouble. Procedures vary from county to county, but speeding and driving without a license are serious crimes in every county in Florida.

If there was a person in the car with you, you could get a ticket and a court date and be released. If you're alone, you could get a ticket, a court date, and a taxi ride home, or you could be locked up for the night to see a judge in the morning. In some counties, bonds are established, and you could be released on bond and given a court date. If you don't have any cash on you, start thumbing through the local Yellow Pages in search of a bondsperson. If you're lucky, you'll find someone willing to put up the money to guarantee you'll show up at a future hearing or trial. If it's a lot of money, the bondsperson will probably ask you to put up something of value to cover the bond, so it helps if you own a house or a big yacht.

If the bond is $50,000, you pay the bondsperson $5,000 in cash, and he or she puts up the $50,000 bond. You get your wallet or purse, shoes, and belt back, and you're free to go—but only temporarily. You'll be expected to show up in court on the date of your hearing. While you're free on bail, you can travel anywhere the court says you can, but there might be some restrictions on crossing county lines. If you show up at your hearing, the bondsperson keeps the $5,000 for services rendered. If you skip town, the bondsperson loses the $50,000 and usually gets real angry. If the bondsperson holds the deed to your house or yacht, he or she will attach it or have the court sell it to get the $50,000 back. If only your yacht is attached and is worth only $1,000, the bondsperson might call in a recovery specialist called a bounty hunter. Now you've got even bigger problems.

How to Get a Lawyer

Lawyers don't come cheap. Back in June of 1997, the American Bar Association published a fee chart, comparing lawyers' hourly fees in different areas of the country. In the Southeast, partners in law firms charged clients an average hourly fee of $183, a 5 percent increase over the previous year. Intellectual-property lawyers charge an average of $207 an hour, the highest rate in the industry. Lawyers specializing in taxation charged an average of $201 an hour; bankruptcy lawyers, $198 an hour; corporate lawyers, $187 an hour; and estate planning and probate lawyers, $178 an hour. Lawyers in the study said people seeking lawyers should remember that you get what you pay for.

The best way to locate a lawyer you can afford is to ask friends or relatives who have had previous dealings with local lawyers. You can also call a local lawyer and ask about the charges for a consultation and handling a case. Who's available can be found in the Yellow Pages of your telephone directory. The Florida Bar Lawyer Referral Unit in Tallahassee at 800-342-8011 (in Florida) or 904-561-5844 (outside Florida) can refer you to lawyers in your area by type

WHAT'S THE DUI CAPITAL OF FLORIDA?

The 1997 Florida Traffic Crash Facts Standard Summary, an annual report published by the Florida Department of Highway Safety and Motor Vehicles, classified Duval County as the DUI Capital of Florida, with 551 people being arrested for driving under the influence more than 6 times! Duval County beats out number two Hillsborough County, followed by Pinellas, Orange, Dade, Polk, Palm Beach, Broward, Escambia, and Bay Counties.

of case. The referrals have agreed to provide up to 30 minutes of over-the-phone consultation time for a maximum billing of $15.

Legal Aid and Legal Services offices are available in most communities for low-income residents who cannot afford an attorney.

REGISTER TO VOTE AT YOUR DRIVER'S LICENSE OFFICE

You can register to vote while applying for or renewing your driver's license. An examiner will ask you if you wish to register to vote (or change your address or party affiliation) and will provide you with documentation of registration at the time you receive your license. Your official registration card will be mailed later from your local supervisor of elections office. Take advantage of this great service—it's free. You can also register to vote on the Internet at the following address: http://election.dos.state. fl.us/voterreg/regform.htm.

HOW TO REGISTER YOUR CAR

If you're a new Florida resident and need to register your car, here's what to do. First, get automobile insurance from a company licensed to do business in Florida. Visit an insurance agent (check the Yellow Pages of your telephone directory) and shop around for the best price on the coverage you need. Take proof of insurance along with the car's title to your local county tax collector to register the car.

ORGAN AND TISSUE DONATION

The Agency for Health Care Administration and the Department of Highway Safety and Motor Vehicles offers you the chance to give someone the gift of life. On your Florida driver's license or identification card, you can indicate your desire to donate organs and tissues and an optional monetary donation to help maintain a statewide registry of organ and tissue donors.

Your organ donation can save the lives of those suffering from organ failure, bone problems, blindness, or serious burns. If you choose to make a donation, be sure to discuss your decision with your next of kin. For more information on the state's Organ and Tissue Donor Education Program, write to the Agency for Health Care

Administration, 2727 Mahan Drive, Tallahassee 32308.

For further information, contact The Living Bank (800-528-2971). This is a national registry and referral service for people wanting to donate their tissues and vital organs for transplantation. It informs the public about organ donation and transplantation. By completing a donor card in the presence of your family and having them sign as witnesses, you ensure that your organ and tissue donation is your commitment to sharing life. Remember to carry it in your wallet or purse at all times. Or contact the following agencies.

National Marrow Donor
   Program
800-MARROW-2
Sponsored by the National
   Heart, Lung, and Blood
   Institute and the Department
   of the Navy. Offers information on becoming a bone
   marrow donor.

United Network for Organ
   Sharing
800-243-6667
804-330-8507 (Fax)
Offers information and referrals for organ donation and
   transplantation. Answers
   requests for organ donor
   cards.

WHO'S WHO IN FLORIDA EXECUTIONS?

Here's a list of people executed in Florida in the last 20 years:

John Spenkelink, 30, executed May 25, 1979, for the murder of a traveling companion in a Tallahassee hotel room.

Robert Sullivan, 36, executed November 30, 1983, for the shotgun slaying of a Homestead hotel-restaurant assistant manager.

Anthony Antone, 66, executed January 26, 1984, for masterminding the October 23, 1975, contract killing of a Tampa private detective.

Arthur F. Goode III, 30, executed April 5, 1984, for killing a nine-year-old in Cape Coral on March 5, 1976.

James Adams, 47, executed May 10, 1984, for beating a Fort Pierce rancher to death with a fire poker during a 1973 robbery attempt.

Carl Shriner, 30, executed June 20, 1984, for killing a 32-year-old Gainesville convenience-store worker who was shot five times.

David L. Washington, 34, executed July 13, 1984, for the murders of three Dade County residents during a ten-day span in 1976.

Ernest John Dobbert Jr., 46, executed September 7, 1984, for the 1971 killing of his nine-year-old daughter.

James Dupree Henry, 34, executed September 20, 1984, for the March 23, 1974, murder of an 81-year-old civil rights leader.

Timothy Palmes, 37, executed November 1984, for the stabbing death of a Jacksonville furniture store owner. He was a co-defendant with Ronald John Michael Straight, executed May 20, 1986.

James David Raulerson, 33, executed January 30, 1985, for gunning down a Jacksonville police officer on April 27, 1975.

Johnny Paul Witt, 42, executed March 6, 1985, for killing, sexually abusing, and mutilating his victim on October 28, 1973.

Marvin Francois, 39, executed May 29, 1985, for shooting six people during a drug house robbery in Miami on July 27, 1977.

Daniel Morris Thomas, 37, executed April 15, 1986, for shooting a University of Florida associate professor, raping the man's wife, and shooting the family dog on New Year's Day, 1976.

David Livingston Funchess, 39, executed April 22, 1986, for the December 1974 stabbing deaths of a 53-year-old and 56-year-old during a holdup in a Jacksonville lounge.

Ronald Michael Straight, 42, executed May 20, 1986, for the stabbing deaths of two people during a Jacksonville lounge holdup.

Beauford White, 41, executed August 28, 1987, for his role in the July 27, 1977, shooting of eight people, six of whom died, during the robbery of a small-time drug dealer in a Miami suburb.

Willie Jasper Darden, 54, executed March 15, 1988, for the September 1973 shooting of a man in Lakeland.

Jeffrey Joseph Daugherty, 33, executed March 15, 1988, for the March 1976 murder of a hitchhiker in Brevard County.

Theodore Robert Bundy, 42, executed January 24, 1989, for the rape and murder of a 12-year-old at Lake City at the end of a cross-country killing spree.

Aubry Dennis Adams Jr., 31, executed May 4, 1989, for strangling an eight-year-old child on January 23, 1981, in Ocala.

Jessie Joseph Tafero, 43, executed May 4, 1990, for the February 1976 shooting deaths of a Florida highway patrolman and a Canadian constable from Kitchener, Ontario.

Anthony Bertolotti, 38, executed July 27, 1990, for the September 27, 1983, rape and stabbing death of a woman in Orange County.

James William Hamblen, 61, executed September 21, 1990, for the April 24, 1984, shooting death of a man during a robbery at the victim's lingerie shop.

Raymond Robert Clark, 49, executed November 19, 1990, for the April 27, 1977, shooting murder of a scrap metal dealer in Pinellas County.

Roy Allen Harich, 32, executed April 24, 1991, for the June 27, 1981, sexual assault, shooting, and slashing death of a woman near Daytona Beach.

Bobby Marion Francis, 46, executed for the June 17, 1975, murder of Titus R. Waiters, a drug informant, in Key West.

Nollie Lee Martin, 43, executed May 12, 1992, for the 1977 murder of a 19-year-old George Washington University student, who was working at a Delray Beach convenience store.

Edward Dean Kennedy, 47, executed July 21, 1992, for the April 11, 1981, slayings of two men, one a Florida highway patrol trooper, after escaping from Union Correctional Institution.

Robert Dale Henderson, 48, executed April 21, 1993, for the 1982 shootings of three hitchhikers in Hernando County. He also confessed to twelve murders in five states.

Larry Joe Johnson, 49, executed May 8, 1993, for the 1979 slaying of a service station attendant in the small north Florida town of Lee in Madison County. Veterans groups claimed Johnson suffered from post-traumatic stress syndrome.

Michael Alan Durocher, 33, executed August 25, 1993, for the 1983 murders of his girlfriend, her daughter, and his six-month-old son in Clay County. Durocher also was convicted in two other killings.

Roy Allen Stewart, 38, executed April 22, 1994, for beating, raping, and strangling a 77-year-old woman in Perrine in Dade County on February 22, 1978.

Bernard Bolander, 42, executed July 18, 1995, for killing four men in Dade County whose bodies were set afire in car trunk on January 8, 1980.

Jerry White, 47, executed December 4, 1995, for the slaying of a customer in an Orange County grocery store robbery in 1981.

Phillip A. Atkins, 40, executed December 5, 1995, for the molestation and rape of a six-year-old Lakeland boy in 1981.

John Earl Bush, 38, executed October 21, 1996, for the 1982 slaying of the heir to the Evinrude outboard motor fortune. The victim was working in a Stuart convenience store when she was kidnapped and killed.

John Mills Jr., 41, executed December 6, 1996, for the fatal shooting of a Wakulla man and burglary of the man's home.

Pedro Medina, 39, executed March 23, 1997, for the 1982 slaying of an Orlando schoolteacher.

The Death Penalty in Florida

Electrocution is Florida's only method of execution. The electric chair was constructed in 1923 when the Florida Legislature authorized electrocution as the official method of capital punishment. Before that, executions had been carried out by counties, usually by hanging. The chair was originally located at Union Correctional Institution but was moved to Florida State Prison in 1962. Frank Johnson was the first inmate executed in the electric chair in Florida on October 7, 1924.

On June 29, 1972, in Furman v. Georgia, the U.S. Supreme Court struck down the death penalty in the United States. At that time, Florida had not carried out an execution since May 12, 1964. The death sentences of 95 men and 1 woman were commuted to life in prison as a result of the Furman decision. The Florida Legislature revised the death penalty statutes in December 1972. These statutes were upheld by the U.S. Supreme Court on July 2, 1976, in Proffitt v. Florida. John Spenkelink was the first Florida inmate executed in the post-Furman era on May 25, 1979. To date, more than 200 inmates have been executed in the electric chair.

The Electric Chair Controversy

The executions of Jesse Tafero on May 4, 1990, and Pedro Medina on March 25, 1997, created problems for the state. During both of these executions, flames erupted under the headgear. Incorrect use of sponges in the headgear was ultimately blamed for the problems. For the Tafero execution, a synthetic sponge, which was substituted for a natural sponge, ignited. In the Medina execution, one of the two sponges located inside the execution headpiece had not been soaked in a saline solution.

As a result, activists are questioning the effectiveness of the state's electric chair. According to them, the 74-year-old chair is cruel and unusual punishment and needs to be retired. Lawyers for the state of Florida say that all the problems associated with the chair have been corrected.

The options are few. Either declare the chair functional—not cruel and unusual—and go on with the executions, or disagree and find another method of execution. Some opponents vote for execution by lethal injection, and that option is being considered by the state legislature. Florida voters seem to lean toward the chair. Some ask that Florida consider execution by firing squad: it's quick (10 seconds), inexpensive (1 bullet), and 100 percent effective.

Death Row Statistics

At this writing, there are 380 inmates on death row in Florida: 374 men (219 white, 135 black, 20 other) and six women (4 white, 2 black). Fifty-four of the men are housed at Florida State Prison; the rest, at Union Correctional Institution. The six women on death row are housed at Broward Correctional Institution. The death chamber is located at Florida State Prison in Starke. Nationwide, there are more than 3,350 people on death row, and fewer than 2 percent of them are women.

Execution—How Do They Do That?

Approximately one hour prior to an execution, the inmate's head and right calf are shaved. A patch on the chest is shaved for the placement of a stethoscope. The inmate then showers and returns to a holding cell. The superintendent reads the death warrant, and an electrolytic gel is applied to the inmate's head and right calf.

The inmate is led into the death chamber and is strapped into the electric chair. Chin, chest, arm, wrist, waist, and leg straps are secured. A metal headpiece covers a leather hood. The hood, made at the prison, is lined with wool and has a bronze rod with a copper wire mesh screen brazed to it on the inside. A natural sponge is sewn with cotton twine onto the copper screen. Natural sponges, which have been soaked overnight in salt water, are placed at the contact points in the headgear and on the leg.

The executioner is a private citizen who is paid $150 in cash. The executioner is present in the death chamber behind a screen. Information as to the identity of the executioner and the execution team is confidential. The electricity for executions is provided by the institution's emergency generator. According to the Florida Depart-ment of Corrections, the cycle is two minutes or shorter in duration, with cycle voltage and amperage levels peaking on three occasions. The maximum current is 2,000 volts and 14 amps.

The cost of one execution by electrocution is $2,225 and is divided as follows: executioner's fee

$150; last meal $20; suit and shirt $150; funeral home fee $525; and security overtime $1,380.

The electric chair used in Florida is a three-legged oak chair constructed by inmates and is known as "Old Sparky." Executions usually take place at 7 A.M. Administrative shift change occurs at 8 A.M. By scheduling executions for 7 A.M., the institution is relatively quiet and secure. Inmates are still in lock-down from the previous night.

The History of Old Sparky

Florida's electric chair has always created some controversy, and the question "Should we or shouldn't we?" is always under discussion.

Electric chairs have been grabbing headlines since they were first designed in the late 1800s as an alternative to hanging. Although the stated reason for their development was that it was a more humane way of executing people, the actual reason is a bit more insidious. At that time, electricity was ready to become the universal power source that it is today. Thomas Edison and George Westinghouse were the two major players in the struggle to control electrical utilities. Technical and economic circumstances at the time made Westinghouse's AC current superior to Edison's DC current. Edison, therefore, had to resort to some Machiavellian manipulations to ensure his domination of the wired world.

Edison's strategy was to convince everyone that Westinghouse's AC current was unsafe and unpredictable. He hired scientists to travel around and give public demonstrations of this by electrocuting cats, dogs, and horses with AC current. He lost the struggle when a New York state prison switched from hanging to an electric chair powered by a Westinghouse AC generator.

The School of Mines at Columbia University administered a series of DC shocks to a large Newfoundland mix dog. They reported that after the initial shock, the dog was in agony but not dead. A charge of 330 volts AC finally did the job. Over the next few months, they killed two dozen dogs, two calves, and a 1,230-pound horse. The New York Times reported " . . . alternating current will drive the hangman out of business."

The History of Old Sparky—Part Two

In January 1889, the world's first electrical execution law went into effect, and the term "electro-cution" was coined to describe the new practice of execution by electricity. The superintendent of New York prisons arranged to buy Westinghouse AC generators to power the state's electric chair. Three generators were purchased for about $7,000. In March 1889, William Kemler, from Buffalo, New York, killed his girlfriend, Tillie Ziegler, with an ax and was sentenced to die by electrocution. He was almost bumped out of first place on the execution list by another killer, Joseph Chappleau, convicted of poisoning his neighbor's cows, but Chappleau's sentence was later commuted to life imprisonment, and Kemler jumped back to the top of the list.

In the meantime, Edwin Davis designed the chair that would be used in prisons across the country. It was tested using huge slabs of meat and closely resembles the chairs in use today. All of Kemmler's attempts to beat the chair were futile, and he was executed on August 6, 1890. The first application of current didn't work, and Kemmler didn't die until the current was fired up a second time. The New York Herald reported that strong men fainted and fell like logs on the floor as they witnessed the execution. Even George Westinghouse said they could have done much better with a hatchet.

In 1896, Ohio introduced electrocution, and in 1898, Massachusetts followed suit. New Jersey joined the rolls in 1906, Virginia in 1908, and North Carolina in 1910. Soon thereafter, at least 20 states were using electric chairs, making it by far the most popular means of execution.

AVOIDING SCAMS

One of the most frequent consumer rip-offs in Florida is the door-to-door sale scam. The nice weather offers con men (and con women) year-round access to front doors, so they can operate without worrying about snow and inclement weather. Of course, not every door-to-door seller makes misrepresentations, but enough do that it is wise to be forewarned and understand your rights.

Products frequently misrepresented by door-to-door salespeople include home improvements such as siding and storm windows, funeral service contracts, books, and magazine subscriptions. There are some specific legal definitions on door-to-door sales that determine what is covered by the law and what is not.

A door-to-door sale (Florida law calls it a home solicitation transaction) takes place whenever a consumer purchases goods or services at a place other than the merchant's place of business for more than $25 payable in cash or installments. But there are exceptions.

The sale of insurance and farm equipment is not regulated by this law. Real estate purchases under $100 made at a place other than the merchant's place of business are not covered by this law, nor are sales where an attorney or broker assists in the transaction.

The solicitation must be made in person (not over the phone) in order for the law on door-to-door sales to apply. This law does not protect you if you negotiated the sale at the merchant's business establishment, and the door-to-door sale is the result of those negotiations.

Now that you know the confusing rules, here are some tips on protecting yourself. Be suspicious of anyone who tries to sell you something by playing on your emotions. For example, some sellers will suggest you are shirking your responsibilities to your family if you don't buy their product or service.

Be suspicious of salespeople who tell you they are selling their service or product at the lowest price, who claim that their competitors do poor-quality work, or who say they have done other work in your city or neighborhood but refuse to give you the names of some past customers.

Ask how you will get your money back if the salesperson doesn't deliver or if the product is defective. If you buy from a reputable local business, you can always take the product back. If you buy from a fly-by-night seller, chances are you'll never see him or her again.

Don't be a victim. Don't be pushed into signing a contract or giving your money to a salesperson unless you're sure you want the product. Take time to think about it. You should always do some comparison shopping. Remember, any time you get a once-in-a-lifetime offer, you should be suspicious. If it's a legitimate offer, it will be there tomorrow.

Donating to Charities—Watch Out!

You may get a letter or a phone call. You see starving kids on television, or someone knocks on your door. Their needs are pressing, and their stories are convincing. You reach for your checkbook, wallet, or credit card. Stop! Sit down, take a deep breath, and think about what you're doing.

Give, but give wisely, and know how to ask the right questions. In Florida, the charity business is thriving, and its main contributors are retirees who have come to Florida to enjoy the good life. Most have a comfortable income, and with enough persuasion, they're prime candidates for the contribution pitch.

First, determine who wants your money. If you're familiar with the charity, get its full name, address, and telephone number. Many small charities have names that are similar to well-known charities, and you could be misled.

Ask whether the organization is listed as a tax-exempt public charity by the IRS and whether your donation will be tax deductible.

How will the organization use your donation? Dramatic, heart-rending descriptions of the sick, the underprivileged, and the needy may get your attention, but you should know as much as you can about the cause before you make a donation. Find out the planned use of your money. Does it go directly to the cause, or is a high percentage of donations spent on administration, salaries, and promotion? Ask them to mail you written information that includes a breakdown of how much is spent on salaries, administration of the program, and fund raising.

Watch out for high-pressure phone calls. A legitimate charity will be glad to give you the time to make a decision. Most honest charities don't offer prizes to entice you to give a donation. Dishonest individuals often avoid using the mail to solicit contributions, because mail fraud is a federal crime.

Never give your credit card number over the phone. Don't respond to letters saying you have pledged money when you haven't. Never give cash. Always write a check in the name of the charity so you'll have a record of your donation. Before you give a significant gift, check with an attorney.

Finally, you can check with your local Better Business Bureau, the Philanthropic Advisory Service at 703-267-0100, the National Charities Information Bureau at 212-929-6300, or the American Institute of Philanthropy at 314-454-3040.

In November 1997, the Chronicle of Philanthropy, a charity-monitoring publication, rated the Salvation Army the most honorable and popular charity organization in the United States. Last year, the Salvation Army received more than $1 billion in contributions, compared to $480 million for the American Red Cross.

FLORIDA'S LEMON LAW

When someone buys or leases a new motor vehicle in Florida, he or she should receive a Lemon Law rights booklet that explains consumers' rights and gives steps to follow to resolve problems. The booklet also contains a toll-free number for the Florida Lemon Law Hotline and a form consumers can use to notify the manufacturer of

Florida Better Business Bureaus

Better Business Bureau
5830 142nd Avenue North
Clearwater 34620
727-854-1154

Better Business Bureau
Gainesville 32600
352-378-0406

Better Business Bureau
4900 Bayou Boulevard
Pensacola 32503
850-494-0222

Better Business Bureau
1950 Southeast Port Saint Lucie
  Boulevard
Port St. Lucie
561-337-2083

Better Business Bureau of
  Central Florida
1011 North Wymore Road
Winter Park
407-621-3300

Better Business Bureau of
  Northeast Florida
7820 Arlington Expressway
Jacksonville
904-721-2288

Better Business Bureau of South
  Florida
16291 Northwest 57th Avenue
Hialeah
305-625-0307

chronic defects. After the third repair for the same problem, the consumer gives notice to the manufacturer to afford a final opportunity to repair the vehicle. Upon receipt of notice, the manufacturer has ten days to direct the consumer to a repair facility, and then up to ten days from delivery of the vehicle to fix it.

The consumer is eligible for relief if the problem still exists after the fourth attempt and if the vehicle is out of service for repair for a cumulative total of 30 or more days, provided notice was given after the vehicle was out of service 15 or more days and the manufacturer or its authorized service agent had at least one opportunity to inspect or repair the vehicle.

If the manufacturer does not provide a refund or a replacement vehicle, consumers can invoke their rights through arbitration programs. The consumer must file a claim for arbitration within six months after the expiration of the Lemon Law rights period. The dispute must be submitted for arbitration to a manufacturer-sponsored program, if that program was certified by the state when the consumer acquired the vehicle. The manufacturer's warranty explains how and where to file a claim with a certified program.

If you think this is your kind of justice, call the Lemon Law Hotline at

800-321-5366 or 904-488-2221 (out of state). They'll let you know if the manufacturer has a state-certified program. The dispute must be submitted to the Florida New Motor Vehicle Arbitration Board and the Office of the Attorney General if the manufacturer does not have a certified program, the certified program fails to render a decision in 40 days, or the consumer is dissatisfied with the certified program's decision.

Once a case is approved for arbitration before the board, a hearing will be scheduled within 40 days. A panel of three arbitrators hears the case at one of ten regional sites around the state. Hearings are held during normal working hours and are conducted in accordance with Florida's Open Meetings Law. At the hearing's conclusion, the board renders an oral decision, which is subsequently reduced to writing and mailed to the consumer and the manufacturer. If the board determines the vehicle is a lemon, the consumer is awarded either a replacement vehicle or a refund, including collateral and incidental charges, less an offset for the consumer's use of the vehicle. The case is dismissed if the board rules in favor of the manufacturer. Decisions of the board are final unless an appeal is filed with the circuit court within 30 days. If the award is not appealed, the manufacturer must comply within 40 days of receipt of the written decision.

If you're ready to file a complaint, here's where to start. Report the problem to the dealer within the first 18 months or 24,000 miles, whichever occurs first. Take the vehicle to the dealer for repairs three times for the same problem. Obtain a written repair order from the dealer for each repair examination of the vehicle. Notify the manufacturer in writing, by certified or registered mail. Get a receipt. Take the vehicle back to the dealer for the final attempt at repairs. If the problem is not corrected, file for arbitration by applying to the manufacturer-sponsored arbitration program.

Contact the Lemon Law Hotline if no decision is rendered within 40 days or if you're dissatisfied with the decision.

GETTING REVENGE!

If you buy something you feel has been misrepresented, keep your receipt. Take it back to the store and politely explain the problem to a sales clerk. If he or she doesn't give you a refund, ask to speak to the store manager. Be polite and don't use a loud voice. If you don't get any satisfaction from the manager, tell him or her, "I'm going to call my lawyer!" If you don't have a lawyer, say it anyway. If you have a lawyer, he or she can write a letter for you, probably for a fee, or you can do it yourself. Write a letter to the store manager explaining the problem. Include copies of any receipts, credit card charges, etc. Have the letter typed—it looks more professional. After your signature block, type cc: (the symbol for "copy to"), and send a copy to the company's president. You can get the address by calling the store. If you charged the purchase, call your credit card company and contest the charge. They will usually put a hold on paying the company until the problem is resolved. If all else fails, consider small claims court.

GETTING YOUR VOICE HEARD IN TALLAHASSEE

As a Floridian, one of your biggest responsibilities is to help elect the legislators who represent you and the state's more than fourteen million other residents. But your role in the democratic process of government doesn't end at the polls. By sharing your opinions and ideas with your representatives and senators in Tallahassee, you help them decide what to do about the issues and pending legislation that affect us all. They value your suggestions and encourage you to express them.

Your legislators receive a huge number of phone calls and letters from their constituents, so it's difficult for them to personally read and respond to each one. Here are some tips on how to voice your opinions effectively.

Know who your legislators are and how to contact them. If you don't know who represents you, you can find out by calling the local courthouse.

Understand the legislative process. Even the most basic understanding of the process will help you effectively express your ideas.

Contact your legislator about a particular issue before the legislature takes action on it. Most matters coming before the legislature are well publicized before session and mentioned in your newspaper.

You can get in touch with your representatives by using a variety of communication methods. You might choose to telephone, write, e-mail, fax, or visit your legislator. You might also choose to give testimony at public hearings held by the legislature. (To give testimony, you need to contact the appropriate committee secretary before the hearing to sign up.)

Tell your legislator what effect you think a particular bill, if it becomes law, will have on you, your children, your business, or your community. Be concise and specific.

Be polite, even if you disagree strongly with the legislator you are addressing. Lawmakers cannot please everyone. Your communication will be more effective if you are reasonable in your approach.

Suggest a course of action and offer assistance. Don't make promises or threats.

Keeping in Touch

When writing your legislator, address letters to members of the House of Representatives as:

The Honorable John Doe
Florida House of Representatives
The Capitol
Tallahassee, Florida 32399-1300

Address letters to senators as:

Senator Jane Doe
The Capitol
Tallahassee, Florida 32399-1100

Make sure you spell all names correctly and use the right address. Type or print legibly. Sign your name and give your address, so recipients can respond to your letter.

Keep letters, e-mail, and faxes brief—one page is best. Long, rambling letters are likely to be ignored. Identify your issue or opinion at the beginning of the letter. Don't bury your main point under trivial text. Cover only one issue per letter. If you have other concerns, write another letter. Back up your opinions with supporting facts.

Avoid abbreviations or acronyms, and don't use technical jargon. Rather than impressing your reader, such terms will only frustrate him or her. Don't send the same letter to more than one legislator. Personalized letters have more impact.

When telephoning or visiting your legislator, plan your call or visit carefully. Keep to the point and discuss only one issue. Organize your thoughts ahead of time and make notes to help you stay on track. Make an appointment. Don't just drop by your legislator's office and expect him or her to drop everything to see you. Call or write for an appointment as soon as you know when you are going to be at the Capitol. Prepare a one-page fact sheet concerning your issue to give to your legislator. This will help him or her better retain what you present.

VICTIM COMPENSATION

If you're the victim of a crime, or a crime resulted in the death of a family member, you may be eligible for assistance with bills, compensation for lost wages as a result of injuries, or other compensation from the Bureau of Victim Compensation in Tallahassee.

The program provides monetary help to innocent victims who incur medical bills or funeral expenses as a direct result of a crime. You are eligible if you received personal injury or if you are a survivor of someone who was killed as the result of a felony or misdemeanor crime punishable under federal or state law. The crime must be reported to law enforcement within three days, and you must not have contributed in any way to any injuries.

Benefits include compensation for lost wages or loss of support for persons dependent on a deceased victim, payment of funeral expenses, and reimbursement for medical treatment, loss of property, or disability.

To apply for victim compensation, you must complete appropriate forms and mail them to the Bureau of Victim Compensation. Forms are available through hospitals, law enforcement agencies, and the State Attorney's office. If you need help in obtaining or completing the forms or need additional information, contact the Victim Advocate hotline or call the State Attorney's office at 941-335-2700. The toll-free Victim Services Information and Referral Hotline is 800-226-6667.

*The
Sunshine State
Almanac
& Book of
Florida-
Related
Stuff*

SPORTS

A BRIEF HISTORY OF JAI ALAI

*T*he origins of jai alai are obscure. Over three centuries ago, in the Basque area of Spain's Pyrenees Mountains, a game called *pelota vasca* (Basque ball) was developed. Some versions were played at festivals and were called *jai alai,* or merry festival. In northern Spain, the game was played outdoors using the walls of churches as the first playing courts. Jai alai is considered the world's fastest ball game.

Jai alai came to Cuba from Spain in 1898 and was successfully introduced as a professional game in Miami, Florida, in 1926. Jai alai is a unique sport played in various places throughout the world. Though its birthplace is the Basque region, there are more jai alai frontons, or playing courts, in Florida than any place in the world. World Jai Alai, the leading organization in the sport, has three Florida frontons. The rules are similar to those of handball and tennis, with the basic requirement being to return the ball in one continuous motion.

Each point is started by serving the pelota (ball). The server must bounce the ball behind the serving line and, with the cesta (basket), hurl the ball to the front wall so that when it rebounds, it bounces between lines on the court. If it does not, it's called an under- or overserve, and the other team receives a point.

To score a point, the ball must be caught on the fly or first bounce, then thrown in one fluid motion. All three walls are in play, and the red lines on the court are out of bounds.

Like handball or squash, jai alai players share the court with the opposition. If a player blocks another's line to the ball on the catch or to the wall on the return, the judges may rule interference if they deem that the ball was "playable." Under Division of Pari-mutuel Wagering rules of jai alai, the player or team scoring the designated number of points first is the winner. Official place and show positions are awarded to the player or team having the greatest number of points behind the winner.

Jai Alai Terminology

Faja (red sash) is the traditional belt worn by the players. It's a bright red sash with yellow tassels. In Europe, the color of the belt determines the post.

The wicker basket used to catch and throw the ball is custom-made and fitted to each player. It's made from reeds found in the Pyrenees Mountains of Spain. The frame is made of steam-bent chestnut. The hand is inserted into a leather glove and held in place by a wraparound. A professional basket costs about $200; a full-time professional uses about 15 a year.

Shoes are rubber-soled professional athletic footwear providing maximum traction on the concrete floor and side walls.

The Pelota

The pelota is considered one of the most lethal balls in any sport. About 75 percent the size of a baseball and harder than a golf ball, its speed has been clocked at over 180 miles an hour. *The Guinness Book of World Records* calls it the world's fastest ball. The ball is made of hand-wound Brazilian rubber with two goatskin covers. Pelotas cost more than $150 each and must be re-covered after 15 minutes of play.

Jai Alai—Place Your Bets

Jai alai betting is simple. Like picking a horse or dog to win a race, the bettor picks a team to win a game. A typical jai alai game lasts about 15 minutes. The skill and agility of the players allows for some handicapping, but the speed and tricky action of the ball introduces an element of luck into the equation.

BIKE TRAILS

If you like to pedal your way through the wilds, there are designated bike trails at several Florida state parks, including those listed below.

Big Bend Region Parks
Tallahassee–St. Marks
    Historic Railroad State
    Trail

North-Central Region Parks
Gainesville-Hawthorne State Trail
Gold Head Branch State Park
Paynes Prairie State Preserve

Northeast Region Parks
Little Talbot Island State Park
Ravine State Gardens

Central Region Parks
Tosohatchee State Reserve

Southeast Region Parks
Fort Pierce Inlet State Recreation
    Area
Jonathan Dickinson State Park

South Region Parks
North Shore State
    Recreation Area
Oleta River State Recreation
    Area

out Florida. The best-organized trails can be found at Florida state parks. Here you'll find self-guided trails maintained by the state so you can learn more about the state's natural and cultural resources on your own. There are trails available for all interest and fitness levels.

Along with the many miles of walking and hiking trails found in Florida's state parks, the Florida Park Service also administers a network of recreational, scenic, and historic trails to encourage bicycling, canoeing, hiking, horse-

HIKING TRAILS

Recreational, scenic, and historic trails encourage all sorts of activities.

There are literally thousands of miles of hiking trails winding through-

back riding, walking, and jogging. Eventually this trail system, authorized by the Florida Recreational Trails Act of 1979, will link trails with other state, national, and community parks and forests.

For specific information about any trail, contact the Florida Recreational Trails System, 3900 Commonwealth Boulevard, Tallahassee 32399, 904-487-4784.

EQUESTRIAN TRAILS

Some of Florida's state parks provide equestrian trails through some of the most scenic parts of the state. Several have staging areas/corrals and overnight camping for horses and riders. Prior to bringing a horse into the park, you'll need proof of a recent negative Coggins test.

Big Bend Region Parks
Econfina River State Park

Florida Caverns State Park
Tallahassee–St. Marks Historic
  Railroad State Trail

North-Central Region Parks
Gainesville-Hawthorne State Trail
O'Leno State Park
Paynes Prairie State Preserve
San Felasco Hammock State
  Preserve

Northeast Region Parks
Amelia Island State Recreation
  Area

West Region Parks
Fort Cooper State Park
Little Manatee River State
  Recreation Area

Central Region Parks
Highlands Hammock
  State Park
Lower Wekiva River
  State Preserve
Rock Springs Run
  State Reserve
Tosohatchee State Reserve
Wekiwa Springs State Park

Southeast Region Parks
Jonathan Dickinson State Park

Southwest Region Parks
Myakka River State Park

RAILS TO TRAILS

The Florida Rails to Trails program buys and develops abandoned railroad corridors for public use, enjoyment, and appreciation. The Tallahassee–St. Marks Historic Railroad State Trail stretches 16 miles south of Tallahassee to St. Marks. In 1997, nearly 100,000 cyclists, hikers, and horseback riders enjoyed the trail.

The 12-mile Gainesville-Hawthorne Rail Trail connects the quiet country town of Hawthorne with bustling Gainesville in north central Florida. Along the 41-mile Withlacoochee State Trail in central Florida lies the Withlacoochee State Forest, Inverness, Citrus Springs, and Gulf Junction, the northern trailhead, south of Dunnellon. The General James A. Van Fleet State Trail is 29 miles of scenic beauty in central Florida, from Polk City through Bay Lake to the town of Mabel.

SPORTING LICENSES BY MAIL

You can order a Florida hunting and fishing license as easily as you can order flowers delivered to your home. The service is open to sportspeople anywhere in the United States and Canada. Operators are online 24 hours a day year-round. The cost is the cost of the license plus $3.95, and you can use your credit card.

Call toll-free 888-HUNT-FLORIDA (888-486-8356) for hunting licenses and 888-FISH-FLORIDA (888-347-4356) for fishing licenses.

Don't Shoot!

It's illegal to shoot a deer at night and to fire a gun from a county, state, or federal highway in Florida. The State Game and Fresh Water Fish Commission

It's a crime to tackle Robo-Deer.

used to use a cardboard cutout of a deer to catch illegal hunters, but eventually the fake deer had so many bullet holes in it and was so rain-soaked, it fell apart. Now, in some counties, the commission is using Robo-Deer, a life-size replica with a moving head and tail, to catch poachers and hunters who use bright spotlights to kill deer at night. It is placed near the road so it can be seen from the highway. So far, well over 100 arrests have been attributed to Robo-Deer.

One day, according to the commission, the driver of a pickup truck stopped by the side of the road, flashed a spotlight at the Robo-Deer, then revved his engine and sped in the deer's direction. Game officials watching the scene from a distance thought the driver was attempting to run over the deer. Instead, he jammed on his brakes when he was 20 feet away, leaped out of the truck, and tackled the deer with knife in hand. The deer fell over, the head fell off, and game officials, somewhat slowed by their laughing, arrested the guy.

If you're hunting illegally in Florida and see a deer by the side of the road moving only its head and tail, the commission suggests you holster your gun. If you don't and you get involved with Robo-Deer and game officials, you can be charged with a second-degree misdemeanor, serve 60 days in jail, and pay a fine of up to $500.

SAILBOARDING

Kelly Moore, a professional sailboarder currently ranked number one in the U.S., turned her favorite sport into a crusade for clean waters when she became the first woman to sailboard across the Florida Gulf

Stream. The 9-hour ordeal had Moore voyaging 60 miles, from Bimini in the Bahamas to Fort Lauderdale, Florida, to raise money and awareness for marine and coastal pollution education.

"With legislation threatening to repeal the Clean Water Act and eroding safeguards for our public waters, the future of our oceans and rivers is very much at stake," says Moore. "I just couldn't stand by and do nothing while industrial and municipal polluters help congressmen craft bills that are a formal assault on the health and safety of our marine ecosystems."

Moore realized marine waters were in peril after she hit patches of raw sewage while sailboarding. She also witnessed fellow sailboarders undergo hospitalization after contracting an unknown bacterial infection linked to polluted waters. "I had to make a statement for my own peace of mind with the hopes that the 'domino effect' would place greater pressure on our elected officials," says Moore.

SURFING

In *The Surfer's Guide to Florida* by Amy Vansant (Pineapple Press), the author lists the best surfing spots in each area of the state. In the northwestern Panhandle, you can find good surfing spots from Perdido Key down to Mexico Beach. East Coast surfing conditions are good or bad up and down the coast, depending on the wind and the ground swells. Overall, surfing conditions are based on cold fronts and storms that have been known to create waves as big as ten feet or more.

GETTING YOUR BOATING EDUCATION

Visitors and residents of Florida spend a lot of time on the water. The more they know about boating do's and don'ts, the more likely they are to have a pleasant experience. Start your education by contacting the United States Power Squadrons (USPS) at 800-828-3380. They offer a course on safe boating. Instruction is free with a nominal charge for a student workbook and chart. The course is offered at more than 500 locations around the country.

The United States Coast Guard Auxiliary also teaches several boating courses. They can be reached at 800-368-5647. The United States Safe Boating Institute offers courses at locations around the state: call 800-336-BOAT.

Florida Boater Education Law

Effective October 1, 1996, before operating a vessel with a motor of ten horsepower or more in Florida, anyone born after September 30, 1980, will be required (1) to have successfully completed a boating education course approved by the National Association of State Boating Law Administrators (NASBLA); or (2) to have passed a course equivalency or temporary certificate examination. He or she also must have a boating education ID card and a photo ID card.

The age requirement will increase one year each October 1st for the five years following 1996. In 1997, the age requirement was seventeen; in 1998, eighteen; and so on. By the year 2001, all persons 21 years of age will be required to take this course.

The fee for the course or examination is currently two dollars, with an optional one-dollar fee for the contractor. The law does provide for some exemptions to the boating education requirements. You don't have to take the course if you are licensed by the U.S. Coast Guard as a master of a vessel; are operating a boat on a private lake or pond; are accompanied in the vessel by a person who is exempt and 18 years of age or older; or are a non-resident and have proof of completing a NASBLA approved course in another state and are visiting Florida for 60 days or less in a boat registered outside the state.

To supplement the many courses offered by the U.S. Coast Guard Auxiliary, the U.S. Power Squadrons, and the NASBLA, the department will be expanding its use of the "How to Boat Smart" correspondence course. This course has a test in the back of the book which can be completed and returned to the department to be graded and scored. The test requires an 80 percent passing score. A certificate and boater safety identification card will be issued to those successfully completing the course. For further information, contact the Boating Safety Section, Mail Station 665, 3900 Commonwealth Boulevard, Tallahassee 32399.

Boating Accidents

Every year, more than 1,000 people die in boating accidents. Nine out of ten drown, and about half of all accidents are alcohol-related. A person who is tipsy is more likely to fall overboard. Once a person is in the water, the alcohol reduces the body's ability to protect against the cold. There are cases where a drunk person has fallen overboard and, confused, has swum down into the water rather than up to the surface and has drowned.

Always wear a Coast Guard–approved life jacket that fits well. When buying a life jacket, put it on, adjust all the straps, and make sure it's comfortable. Do the same for all family members—especially children. There are several types of buoyancy devices. The Type I life preserver is bulky but offers the best flotation. It's best for open-water boating and can turn most unconscious people face up in the water. A Type II is a yoke-type, less bulky than Type I and more comfortable to wear. It will also hold an unconscious person's head up. Type III are vest-style, designed only for calm-water boating. The wearer will have to be able to hold his or her face out of the water. Type IV are throwable devices like life rings and floating cushions. Type V are special-use devices, approved only for the activities listed on the label. Some are approved specifically for white-water rafting, board sailing, etc. When fully inflated, they have the flotation performance of a Type II or better.

What to Do When Caught in a Thunderstorm

Thunderstorms in Florida and over its coastal waters are frequently unpredictable. Even with the best weather reports, along with constant and accurate observations of climatic conditions, boaters still can be caught in open waters in a thunderstorm. Then, with or without a lightning protection system, it is critical to take additional safety precautions to protect people on the boat. Stay in the center of the cabin if the boat is so designed. If no enclosure like a cabin is available, stay low in the boat. Don't stand up and be a human lightning rod. Always keep your arms and legs in the boat, and never dangle them in the water. Stop fishing, water skiing, scuba diving, swimming, or other water activities when there is lightning or even when weather conditions look threatening. Disconnect and do not use or touch the major electronic equipment, including the radio, for the duration of the storm. Lower, remove, or tie down the radio antenna and other protruding devices if they are not part of the lightning protection system.

If possible, avoid making contact with any portion of the boat connected to the lightning protection system. Never be in contact with two components connected to the system at the same time. For example, the gear levers and spotlight handle are both connected to the system. Should you have a hand on both when lightning strikes, the possibility of an electrical current passing through your body from hand to hand is great. The path of the electrical current would be directly through your heart—a very deadly path!

Canoe Safety

You can learn how to get in and out of a canoe without getting wet—if you practice.

Always keep your center of gravity low, and move deliberately and slowly. Transfer your weight from the dock to the bottom center of the canoe, and move into your sitting or paddling position. For maximum control, always kneel in the canoe if there are no seats. To get out of the canoe, just reverse the steps. If the canoe capsizes, relax and hold onto it. If you go underwater, stay under the canoe until you're free of any obstacles, then surface and stay with the canoe until help arrives. If you're far offshore, stay with the canoe and move toward shore by kicking your feet. Hold on with your hands and arms, and don't attempt to get back in the canoe.

Sixty-Three Places to Get Your Canoe Wet

Alapaha Rise in Westlake (near Perry)

Alexander Springs in Astor Park in Ocala National Forest

Beckton Springs in Vernon (near Holmes)

Black Springs in Kynesville (near Springfield)

Blue Hole Spring in Marianna

Blue Spring in Bronson (near Chassahowitzka)

Blue Spring in Madison Bonnet Springs, Luraville (seven miles east of Madison)

Blue Spring in Mayo (near Perry)

Blue Spring in Orange City

Blue Springs in High Springs (fifteen miles northwest of Gainesville)

Branford Spring in Branford (near Chassahowitzka)

Chassahowitzka Springs in Homosassa Springs

Crystal River Springs in Crystal River

Crystal Springs in Zephyrhills

Cypress Spring in Vernon

Eureka Springs in Tampa

Fanning Springs in Fanning Springs (thirty miles southwest of Gainesville)

Fern Hammock Springs in Astor

Fletcher Springs in Hatchbend (eight miles south of Branford Springs)

Gainer Spring in Bennett (twenty miles north of Panama City)

Ginnie Springs in High Springs

Glen Julia Springs in Mount Pleasant (six miles northeast of Quincy)

Guaranto Springs in Rock Bluff Landing

Hart Springs in Wilcox

Holgon Springs in Adams

Homosassa Springs in Homosassa

Ichetucknee Springs in Fort White

Indian Springs in Greensboro

Juniper Springs in Astor

Kini Springs in Bethel

Lime Springs in Ellaville

Lithia Springs in Lithia

Manatee Springs in Chiefland

Morrison Springs in Redbay

Natural Bridge Springs in Woodville

Newport Springs in Newport

Otter Springs in Wilcox

Peacock Springs in Luraville

Pitts Springs in Bennett

Ponce de Leon Springs in Barberville

Ponce de Leon Springs in Ponce de Leon

Rainbow Springs in Dunellon

Rock Bluff Springs in Bell

Salt Springs in Salt Springs

Silver Glen Springs in Salt Springs

Silver Springs in Ocala

Springboard Springs in Marianna

St. Marks Springs in Woodville

Sun Springs in Wilcox

Suwanee Springs in Live Oak

Telford Springs in Luraville

Troy Springs in Branford

Turtle Springs in Hatchbend

Vortex Blue Spring in Ponce de Leon

Wacissa Springs in Wacissa

Wakulla Springs in Wakulla Springs

Waldo Springs in Perry

Warm Springs in Venice

Weeki Wachee Springs in Weeki Wachee

Welaka Spring in Welaka

Whitewater Springs in Palatka

Williford Springs in Bennett

FLORIDA DIVE CLUBS

Diving rule number one: never dive alone. If you're visiting and ready to take a dip, you might find an experienced diving buddy at any of these Florida dive clubs:

Adventure Divers in Fort Lauderdale, 800-752-6386
American Diving Headquarters in Key Largo, 800-634-8464
Association of Black Scuba Divers in Winter Park, 407-657-6032
Barnacle Busters of Gainesville, 904-372-8775
BC Buddies in Inverness, 352-860-7307
Blue Dolphin Dive Club in Orlando, 407-859-2173

Bottom Time Dive Club in Eustis, 352-787-7611 or 352-787-3523
Brendal's Dive Shop and Tours in Fort Lauderdale, 800-780-9941
Bud 'n Mary's Dive Center in Islamorada, 800-344-7352
Central Florida Pleasure Divers in Orlando, 407-365-8502 or 407-836-8990
Central Florida Scuba Nuts in Fanning Springs, 352-463-7111
Central Florida Underwater Photography Club in Casselberry, 407-699-0863
Clearwater Dive Association, 813-442-9931
Club Med in Madeira Beach, 813-398-6875
Coral Reefers Dive Club in St. Cloud, 407-932-4326 or 407-348-5124
Crazy Dog Dive Club in Mount Dora, 352-357-5888
Deep Six Watersports (several locations along the East Coast), 800-732-9685
Denizen, Inc. in Pompano Beach, 800-874-6888
Depth Perception in Jupiter, 800-346-6749
Diver's Den in Panama City, 800-272-4777
Diving Solutions in West Palm Beach, 800-797-7771
Fantasy Scuba Headquarters in Destin, 800-326-2732
Hammerhead Dive Club in Largo, 813-539-0227
InnerSpace Explorers in Tampa, 813-837-9400
Key West Pro Dive Shop in Key West, 800-426-0707
Lauderdale Divers in Fort Lauderdale, 800-654-2073
Loggerhead Dive Club in Lakeland, 813-533-8432

Kissimmee Divers Club in Orlando, 407-933-5090
Martin Dive Club in Orlando, 407-351-1514
Moby Nick's AquaHolics in Tarpon Springs, 813-942-6635
Ocala Dive Club, 352-236-6699
Orlando Otters in Altamonte Springs, 407-260-8956
Rainbow Reef Dive Center in Islamorada, 800-457-4354
Rampage Dive Charter in West Palm Beach, 800-525-0876
Reef Preservers in Largo, 813-585-0938
Reef Seeker Dive Club in Winter Haven and Lakeland, 941-859-4558
Sea-Js Dive Association in Largo, 813-585-DIVE
Sea Bunnie in Clearwater, 813-585-6736 or 813-577-8425
Sea Salts Dive Club in Clearwater, 813-539-3999
Sport Divers in Miami, 800-327-0244
Suncoast Reef Rowdies in Pinellas Park, 813-447-1714
Suncoast Scuba Club in Brandon, 813-671-5653
Sunshine Fin Dive Club in Bay Pine, 813-360-4250 or 813-823-7323
Tackle Shack Divers in Pinellas Park, 813-546-5080
Tampa Trident Club in Tampa, 813-971-3368
Tilden's Pro Dive Shops in Marathon, 800-223-4563
Two-Dive Club in Clearwater, 813-443-5819
Underseas, Inc. in Big Pine Key, 800-446-5663
University of Central Florida Dive Club in Orlando, 407-382-8007
USF Scuba Club in Tampa, 813-974-5303
YearRound Divers Society in Casselberry, 407-332-1222

FLORIDA'S BEACH FLAG WARNINGS

On major beaches around the state, swimming conditions are indicated by a series of warning flags. The warning are posted for several reasons: undertows, jellyfish, or worse . . . sharks! A blue flag indicates safe swimming conditions. A yellow flag means swim with caution. A red flag indicates dangerous conditions, so stay out of the water.

SHARK ATTACKS

Thanks to modern medicine and the speed with which it's delivered, most people don't die from shark attacks today. Years ago, it sometimes took hours to get someone bitten by a shark from the beach to a hospital. Today, Emergency Response Teams are on the scene in minutes, and they're equipped to handle any emergency.

Sharks generally attack surfers and occasionally lone swimmers or waders. Sharks tend to avoid

A red flag means stay out of the water!

groups of people, so stay with other swimmers, and stay as close to the shore as you can. Don't splash around. Sharks interpret this as a sign of a wounded fish and often attack. Never swim at night. Be cautious of areas near sandbars and areas leading from waist-high water to open water. Don't wear jewelry that's shiny and reflective. Sharks have been known to attack a swimmer's foot because of contrasting skin colors—suntanned on top, white on the sole.

Sharks have several basic types of attacks. For bathers near shore, the shark dashes in, bites, then retreats when it realizes the person is not a fish. This usually results in gashes and slashes. In deep water, a shark will bump into a surface swimmer or scuba diver, circle slowly, then dash in and bite, holding on and turning its head from side to side. This can result in serious injury and even death. In Florida, most shark attacks are from blacknose and blacktip sharks.

SCRATCH, SCRATCH

If you're swimming and suddenly get the itch, you probably ran into some of those tiny sea creatures that inhabit Florida waters. Crab larvae resemble body lice and are almost invisible to the naked eye. They use their pincers to sting swimmers and leave a pinpoint wound. Hop in the shower, and you'll probably wash them away.

Schistosomes, or body flukes, are found in both fresh and salt water. They burrow into the skin of swimmers and then die, causing reddish welts and itching. You feel the itch shortly after you leave the water. Under the worst conditions, the itch can last for two weeks. Over-the-counter antihistamine and hydrocortisone creams will provide relief.

Jellyfish larvae are present from May to June. They cause itchy dermatitis that often lasts a week or more. Loose-fitting bathing suits can trap more of these creatures than tight-fitting ones. The treatment is the same as for *schistosomes* dermatitis.

FLORIDA TIDES

Tides play an important role in the behavior and feeding activity of fish, especially those inhabiting areas near the shore. Bait fish and crustaceans follow tidal flow into the mangroves to seek food and refuge from predators. Game fish follow and intercept their prey in the passes, creeks, and shoreline edges. Fishermen need to be familiar with the tides to be where the game fish are and to navigate near the shore without grounding their boats.

RIPTIDES

Most of Florida's coastline is made up of beaches—some accessible, some not. The beaches are made of loose sand and gravel, contoured over the years by tides, waves, and currents. When waves break along the shoreline, they can produce a current or riptide that flows out toward open waters. Since most riptides are narrow—15 to 75 yards wide—a swimmer can swim away from one by swimming parallel to the shore, then toward the beach. The big problem is panicking and trying to fight the tide.

Sometimes you can detect an area where riptides are common by the discoloration in the water and the wave length and width. Look for small whitecaps, churning waters, and low wave heights. When swimming in areas with a history of riptides, pay attention to the flags posted (red means stay out of the water), and swim only in areas where you can touch bottom with your feet.

The
Sunshine State
Almanac
& Book of
Florida-
Related
Stuff

WATER

WHAT'S HAPPENING TO OUR WATER?

Contrary to popular belief, most of the water on Earth is unpolluted. Many people rely on wells drilled into the ground for their water, and this water has generally remained untainted by human activity. In some of Florida's agricultural areas, there is concern that pesticides may leach through sandy soils and contaminate some of this underground water. In other parts of the state, there is concern that too much water has been drawn out for irrigation and that the wells will eventually go dry. The good news is that water can be cleaned by filtering, boiling, or chemical treatment, so drinking water supplies are safe most of the time.

So, while some of the water on Earth may be polluted by natural bacteria or by agricultural or industrial waste, there's always enough clean water around for us to use without concern.

WATER, WATER EVERYWHERE, BUT NOT A DROP TO DRINK

Floridians tend to take things like water for granted. Hey, we're surrounded by it, so why not? Salt water is something we have plenty of, but what about drinking water? Just turn on the tap, and there it is, all you want! Nothing is more fundamental to life than pure drinking water, and protection of Florida's drinking water is one of the state's basic, most important priorities.

Most of us in Florida drink water that is pumped from the ground— our valuable groundwater in the vast freshwater aquifers that lie under most of the state. For most of us, the water we drink every day is our most direct contact with Florida's natural environment. Unfortunately, there are many ways for our water supplies—both surface and ground—to become contaminated by runoff from the frequent, heavy rains in Florida that carry oils and grease from our streets and parking lots and fertilizers and pesticides from our lawns and farmlands. Other possible sources of contamination include septic tanks, underground petroleum storage tanks, poorly designed or leaking solid waste landfills, and spills of toxic and hazardous materials.

Florida has more than 80 stringent ground and surface water quality standards. Coupled with management and regulatory programs that protect drinking water wells and well fields, protect the water supply from chemical and petroleum spills, and prevent wastes injected into the ground from entering potable drinking water aquifers, these standards help to ensure that our drinking water is safe. Efforts like these show the importance we in Florida place on protecting our drinking water.

Florida's primary drinking water standards establish maximum contaminant levels or treat-ment techniques for 18 inorganic chemicals and 54 organic chemicals, including volatile organic compounds, turbidity, microbiological contaminants, and radionucleides. These substances all may cause health problems, and limiting them in drinking water is a step toward protecting human health.

Nitrates, for example, are used in fertilizers and are found in sewage and wastes from farm animals. An article in *Health and Environmental Digest*, published by the Freshwater Foundation, reports that nitrates in drinking water have been linked to blue baby syndrome. Nitrates deprive babies of oxygen and can cause problems with developing nervous systems. There is also concern that long-term exposure to nitrates in water may cause cancer in adults.

Because private well water supplies are not regulated by federal or

state agencies, people who use well water should have their water tested periodically for nitrates and coliform bacteria, particularly if there are small children in the home; if the well is shallow (20–30 feet deep); or if the well is close to a source of contamination, such as a septic system, animal feed lot, or barn. Furthermore, experts suggest that you have your well water tested if there has been any work done on your well or well head or if there has been a change in the odor, color, or taste of your water.

Water Shortages

Pollution isn't the only threat to our water supplies. In many areas of Florida, rapid growth is outstripping the readily available supplies of quality drinking water. Because of increasing evidence of local and regional water shortages—at least for parts of the year—state agencies and local governments sometimes undertake a number of actions to conserve water supplies.

One common approach to water conservation is to restrict the use of water for nonessential uses, such as watering lawns, washing cars, or filling swimming pools. Some communities offer free or inexpensive add-on devices that conserve water. Items such as flow regulators for showers are available at any hardware store.

Water management districts urge Floridians to landscape their yards with native plants, which generally require less water than emerald-green turf lawns and exotic shrubbery imported from other parts of the United States or the world.

Some coastal communities are looking to enhance their water supplies through such activities as desalinization—removing salt from seawater or brackish groundwater and using it for drinking water. This is an expensive option, however, and is probably the solution of last resort for most communities. A growing and more readily available option is reuse of treated wastewater—especially for such nonpotable uses as yard and landscape watering and irrigation for golf courses and some agriculture.

Groundwater and Pollution

Florida's groundwater is stored in the cracks and spaces between soil and rock particles below the ground. It is one of the state's most vital natural resources—and the source of drinking water for 95 percent of the state's population. Floridians use about 4.6 billion gallons of groundwater per day.

Groundwater is a part of what can be called the oldest recycling program—the hydrologic cycle. The hydrologic cycle involves the continuous movement of water between the earth and the atmosphere. As water falls to the earth in the form of rain and snow, much of it runs into surface water bodies, evaporates, or is used by plants. The rest of the water soaks into the ground until it reaches the water table. The water table is the top of the saturated zone, or the area in which all interconnected spaces in rocks and soil are filled with water. The water in the saturated zone is called groundwater. Where the water table occurs at the ground's surface, groundwater discharges into marshes, lakes, springs, or streams.

Groundwater is stored under many types of geologic conditions. An aquifer is an area where groundwater exists in sufficient quantities to supply wells or springs. Aquifers are either confined or unconfined. If the aquifer is sandwiched between layers of relatively impermeable materials, it is called a confined aquifer.

Confined aquifers are generally found at greater depths than unconfined aquifers, and the water within them can be pumped to the surface or may rise to the surface by a natural pressure called artesian pressure. In contrast, unconfined aquifers are not sandwiched between layers of impermeable materials, and their upper boundaries are generally closer to the surface.

Groundwater protection is cru-

Groundwater is the source of drinking water for 95 percent of Floridians.

cial to Florida. High rainfall and the state's unique geology—a thin, permeable soil cover; high water table; porous limestone formations; and the high potential for saltwater intrusion—make our groundwater extremely vulnerable to contamination.

The threats to groundwater can come from many sources, both natural and man-made. Nature can change the quality of our groundwater through severe weather, droughts, and contamination that enters through sinkholes. Unfortunately, human activity is the main contributor to groundwater contamination.

The water that runs off impervious surfaces such as streets and parking lots contains many pollutants. These include oils, grease, heavy metals, and coliform bacteria. Storm water enters groundwater directly through sinkholes and drainage wells and indirectly in areas with very sandy soils or where porous limestone is at or near the surface.

Because of its climate and diverse agricultural and urban pest problems, Florida is one of the nation's largest users of pesticides. Where groundwater is very vulnerable to pollution, contamination can occur from even normal use of some pesticides. Homeowners contribute to this type of groundwater pollution with the chemicals they apply to lawns and gardens. Fertilizers can add nitrates to groundwater.

Approximately one-fourth of all homes in Florida rely on septic systems to dispose of wastes. If these systems are improperly built or poorly maintained, they can contaminate groundwater with bacteria, nitrates, viruses, synthetic detergents, and household chemicals. Additionally, between 50,000 and 60,000 underground storage tanks store a variety of materials, including gasoline, fuel oil, and chemicals. Over time, exposure to the elements can cause the tanks to corrode and leak, contaminating groundwater. Hazardous wastes are a major threat to Florida's groundwater as well. Many industries in Florida create hazardous wastes such as used oils and grease, reactive wastes, heavy metals, and solvents as part of their manufacturing processes.

The major environmental threat from landfills is groundwater contamination. Water enters landfills, seeps (leaches) through the layers of garbage, becomes polluted, and then goes on to contaminate groundwater. Today, landfills are constructed with clay or synthetic liners and leachate collection systems to help keep polluted water from entering groundwater.

Impoundments or reservoirs often are used to store untreated wastewater from factories. Toxic chemicals in the wastewater can leach through the bottom of unlined impoundments and end up in wells that provide drinking water.

Before there were community water supply systems, most people relied on wells for their drinking water. In many rural areas, this is still the case. If a well is improperly built or is abandoned without being properly sealed, it can act as a direct channel for contaminants to reach groundwater.

Many toxic materials are transported throughout the state by truck, train, and airplane. Every day, accidental chemical or petroleum spills occur and, if not handled properly, can result in contamination. There are also many instances of contamination from illegal dumping of hazardous or harmful wastes.

The Department of Environmental Protection (DEP) is charged with protecting, conserving, and restoring Florida's valuable groundwater. The DEP achieves its mission by direct administration of programs, supervision of the five water management districts, and delegation of its powers to its district offices and to local governments.

Florida's comprehensive groundwater rule puts the state in the forefront of efforts to protect groundwater. The rule establishes minimum water-quality criteria designed to prevent the introduction of toxic and cancer-causing materials into water supplies.

The way you and your family dispose of products you use at home can contribute to the contamination of your community's groundwater. Products like motor oil, pesticides, leftover paints or paint cans, mothballs, flea collars, weed killers, household cleaners, batteries, and medicines can be harmful to the environment. Never pour toxins like these down the drain or on the ground. Many areas have local amnesty days when you can dispose of contaminants. To find out about or to request an amnesty day, call your local public works department.

For further information on Florida's groundwater management programs, boot up your computer, set the modem to 8-N-1, and call the Department of Environmental Protection's Ecosystem Management and Environmental Education BBS at 800-217-2934.

*The
Sunshine State
Almanac
& Book of
Florida-
Related
Stuff*

WEATHER

E verybody talks about Florida's wonderful weather and climate, so what is climate? Climate is defined as a composite of the long-term prevailing weather that occurs at a given location. It is the normal weather pattern that we know will probably occur year after year with some small variations, barring any severe weather like hurricanes. Our sense of a place's climate leads us to expect that temperatures at a particular time of year will fall within a certain range, that they are unlikely to rise above or fall below certain extreme values, that enough rain will fall at certain times of year to sustain crops, and so on. Even the exceptions to these patterns often occur with some regularity, so hurricane season pops up once a year, and we can expect so many inches of rain during other times of the year.

It is this regularity that makes climate so important, because it creates the long-term conditions that allow ecosystems to evolve and survive. For human societies, this reliability is equally important for such basic activities as agriculture and settlement. When climates change, all species, including humans, must either adapt or migrate if they are to avoid major stress.

Ultimately, climate is a consequence of the way the atmosphere redistributes the sun's energy. Because the intensity of solar radiation changes with latitude, the tropics are heated much more intensely than the poles. It is this imbalance that drives the complex pattern of atmospheric and oceanic motions that redistribute heat and moisture from one part of the globe to another and cause our weather.

Local regional climates are highly influenced by latitude, altitude, topography, and the proximity of large water bodies such as oceans. Globally, climate is affected by complex interactions involving the sun, land, sea, air, the earth's ice cover, its plants, and all other life forms.

In March 1998, when it was 74 degrees in Miami, it was:

50 degrees in London
48 in Vancouver
60 degrees in Athens
54 degrees in Paris
81 degrees in San Juan
76 degrees in Sydney
37 degrees in Toronto
52 degrees in Beijing
43 in Chicago and Boston

EVERYTHING YOU WANTED TO KNOW ABOUT WEATHER TERMINOLOGY

Temperature conversions: To convert temperatures from Fahrenheit to Celsius, subtract 32 degrees, multiply by 5, and divide by 9. To convert Celsius to Fahrenheit, multiply by 9, divide by 5, and add 32 degrees.

One **knot** is one nautical mile per hour or about 1.5 statute miles per hour.

One **meter** is 39 inches.

One **kilometer** (km) is .62137 of a mile.

A **weather advisory** is issued when forecast conditions are expected to cause general inconvenience or concern but do not pose a serious enough threat to issue a weather warning. An advisory will often precede a warning.

Air mass is a large, horizontal body of air with a uniform distribution of moisture and temperature.

Atmosphere is a mass of air held close to the earth by gravity. The atmosphere is subdivided into four sections: the troposphere (from the earth's surface to an altitude of about ten kilometers); the stratosphere (from 10 km to 50 km); the mesosphere (from 50 km to 80 km); and the thermosphere (anything beyond 80 km).

Atmospheric pressure is a force exerted by the weight of the atmosphere, also known as barometric pressure. The internationally recognized unit for measuring this pressure is the kilopascal.

Aurora (aurora borealis) is a luminous, radiant emission from the upper atmosphere over middle and high latitudes, centered around the earth's magnetic poles. These silent fireworks are often seen on clear winter nights in a variety of shapes and colors. They are also referred to as the northern lights.

Backing is a counterclockwise change in wind direction. For example, from east to west, through north. Backing is the opposite of veering.

Blizzard is a severe snowstorm lasting three or more hours. It is characterized by low temperatures, strong winds, and poor visibility due to blowing snow. True blizzard conditions are most common on the prairies of the United States and have never occurred in Florida.

Cirrus is high, white patches of cloud composed of ice crystals, found at altitudes of 6,000 meters or higher. Fine and delicate in appearance, their shape and texture are often described as looking like mares' tails. In forecasts they are referred to as high cloud.

Climate is the prevalent or

characteristic meteorological conditions, and their extremes, of any place or region.

Cloud is a visible cluster of tiny water and/or ice particles in the atmosphere above the earth's surface.

Condensation is the physical process by which vapor becomes liquid or solid. Condensation is the opposite of evaporation.

Cumulonimbus is a large, fairly dense cloud, frequently with an anvil-shaped top. These clouds produce heavy rain showers, lightning, thunder, and sometimes hail or tornadoes. The entire cloud can be seen only from a distance.

Cumulus are fair-weather clouds with broad horizontal bases, producing no precipitation and rarely covering more than one-half of the sky.

Cyclone is a closed counterclockwise movement of air around a low-pressure center, usually called a low. The term is frequently misused to describe a tornado.

Dew: As the surface of the earth cools at night, warm moist air near the ground is chilled and water vapor in the air condenses into droplets on the grass and other objects. Dew is particularly heavy on clear nights, when the earth cools rapidly. When a blanket of cloud insulates the earth, the cooling rate is slower.

Dew point is the temperature to which air must be cooled to become saturated by the water vapor already present in the air.

Draft is a small gusty current associated with the abrupt vertical movement of air, for example, updrafts and downdrafts.

Drizzle is precipitation from stratus clouds consisting of numerous minute, fine water droplets which appear to float. In drizzle, the droplets are much smaller than in rain.

Eye is a roughly circular area of comparatively light winds and fair weather found at the center of a severe hurricane. It is usually referred to as the eye of the storm.

Flurry is precipitation in the form of snow from a convective cumulus-type cloud. Flurries are characterized by the suddenness with which they start and stop, by their rapid changes in intensity, and usually by rapid changes in the appearance of the sky.

Fog consists of tiny water droplets or, under very cold conditions, ice crystals or ice fog that reduces visibility. It's generally found in calm or low wind conditions.

Fog bank is a well-defined mass of fog observed in the distance, most commonly at sea. This does not apply to patches of shallow ground fog which usually occur over land at night or early in the morning.

Forecast provides a description

of the most significant weather conditions expected during the current and following day. The exact content depends upon the intended user, such as forecasts for farmers or mariners.

Freezing rain is rain which freezes on impact to form a coating of ice upon the ground and on the objects it strikes. A freezing rain warning is issued if more than four hours of continuous freezing rain or seven hours of freezing drizzle are expected.

Freezing spray occurs when a combination of low temperatures and strong winds cause sea spray to freeze on a ship's superstructure or on other structures either in the sea or near the water's edge. A freezing spray warning is issued whenever moderate or heavy ship icing is expected.

Front is the boundary between two different air masses. A cold front is the leading edge of an advancing cold air mass, and a warm front is the trailing edge of a retreating cold air mass.

Frost is water vapor which deposits directly as a solid on a surface colder than the surrounding air and which has a temperature below freezing. It is not frozen dew. A killing frost is one severe enough to end the growing season.

Gale is a strong wind. A gale warning is issued for expected winds of 34 to 47 knots (65-100 km/h) over the water.

Gulf Stream is a warm, relatively swift, and narrow ocean current that runs up the east coast of North America, south of Newfoundland, and into the North Atlantic. If you go up high enough in a Miami Beach condo, you can see it!

Gust is a sudden, brief increase in wind speed, generally lasting less than 20 seconds.

Hail is precipitation in the form of lumps of ice, mainly associated with thunderstorms. Hail size usually ranges from small pea-size to cherry-size but has been observed as large as oranges.

Halo: In ages past, the huge rings or halos around the sun or the moon were thought to portend everything from storms to great personal disasters. They are the optical result of the refraction of light from the sun or moon by ice crystals in the very high clouds (9,000 meters) called cirrus or cirrostratus. On occasion, only two bright spots on either side of the sun can be seen. These are known as sun dogs and are caused when the ice crystals occur in a certain uniform arrangement.

Haze is fine dust or salt particles dispersed through a portion of the atmosphere, reducing visibility. Haze is distinguished from fog by its bluish or yellowish tinge.

Humidity is a measure of the water vapor content of the air. Usually relative humidity is expressed as a percentage of total possible moisture content.

Hurricane is a tropical storm with wind speeds from 65 knots (120 km/h) to 240 knots (460 km/h) that can be thousands of square kilometers in size. Such systems usually have a life span of several days.

Intermittent rain is rain which starts and stops repeatedly, although not as abruptly or as frequently as showers.

Isobar is a line on a weather map or chart connecting points of equal pressure. The large concentric lines on television or newspaper weather maps are isobars.

Jet Stream is an undulating band of strong high-altitude winds which may occasionally exceed 400 km/h. Pilots flying at high altitudes often search out the jet stream to speed up eastbound flights.

Kilopascal is an internationally recognized unit used by the Atmospheric Environment Service for measuring atmospheric pressure.

Leeward is located on or moving toward the side toward which the wind is blowing.

Lightning is any and all of the various forms of visible electrical discharge produced by thunderstorms.

Low is an area of low atmospheric pressure that has a closed counterclockwise circulation in the Northern Hemisphere. It is also known as a cyclone.

Marine wind warnings or **small craft warnings** are issued if winds are forecast to be in the range of 20 to 33 knots inclusive. A **gale warning** is issued if winds are forecast to be in the range of 34 to 47 knots inclusive. A **storm warning** is issued if winds are forecast to be in the range of 48 to 63 knots inclusive. A **hurricane force wind warning** is issued for winds of 64 knots or greater.

Mist consists of microscopic water droplets suspended in the air which produce a thin grayish veil over the landscape. It reduces visibility to a lesser extent than fog.

Normal is long-term average value of a meteorological element for a certain area, usually averaged over 30 years. For example, temperatures are normal for this time of year.

Outlook intends to provide, in very general terms, an indication of the trend in the weather for one to three days beyond the current forecast.

Ozone is a pungent-smelling, slightly bluish gas which is a close chemical cousin to molecular oxygen. About 90 percent of the earth's ozone is located in a natural layer far above the surface of the globe, in a frigid region of the atmosphere known as the stratosphere. In this outer region it protects the Earth and its inhabitants from the harmful effects of ultraviolet radiation from the sun.

Prevailing wind is the wind direction most frequently observed during a given period.

Probability of precipitation is a forecast that estimates the chance of encountering measurable precipitation at some time during the forecast period. Measurable means at least 0.2 millimeters of rain or the water equivalent of snow. For example, a 40 percent probability of rain today means there are four chances in ten that it will rain.

Rainbows occur when sunlight is refracted and then reflected by raindrops. The raindrops act like a prism, breaking the light into the colors of a rainbow, with red on the outer edge and blue on the inner. On occasion, the light can be reflected from both the front and back of the raindrops and two rainbows are visible, with the color bands in the second opposite to those in the primary rainbow. Rainbows can be seen when the sun is shining and the air contains water spray or raindrops. This condition occurs frequently during or immediately following showers. Rainbows are always observed in the portion of the sky opposite the sun. The sun, the observer's eye, and the center of the rainbow arc always fall in a straight line.

Relative humidity is the ratio of water vapor in the air at a given temperature to the maximum amount which could exist at that temperature. It is usually expressed as a percentage.

Report: A weather report is a statement of the actual weather conditions observed at a specific time at a specific site.

Ridge is an elongated area of relatively high pressure extending from the center of a high-pressure region. Ridge is the opposite of a trough.

Sea breeze occurs during the daytime in warm sunny weather when the air over land is heated more rapidly than the air over an adjacent water surface. As a result, the warmer air rises, and relatively cool air from the sea flows onshore to replace it. At night, the air over the land cools faster than that over the nearby ocean and causes the air circulation to be in the opposite direction—a land breeze. Land breezes are usually weaker than sea breezes and have a less noticeable effect on the temperature.

Shower is liquid precipitation from a convective cumulus-type cloud. Showers are characterized by the suddenness with which they start and stop, by their rapid changes in intensity, and usually by rapid changes in the appearance of the sky.

Small craft warnings are issued when winds over the coastal marine areas are expected to reach and maintain speeds of 20–33 knots inclusive.

Squall is a strong, sudden wind which generally lasts a few minutes, then quickly decreases in speed. Squalls are generally associated with severe thunderstorms.

The saying, "The wind goes down with the sun," is especially true in the warm season.

Temperature. In general, temperature is the degree of hotness or coldness measured against some definite scale by means of a thermometer.

Thunderstorm is a local storm, usually produced by a cumulonimbus cloud, and always accompanied by thunder and lightning.

Tornado: A tornado appears as a violent, funnel-shaped wind vortex in the lower atmosphere with upward spiraling winds of high speeds, spawned by severe thunderstorms. The tornado usually appears from a bulge in the base of a cumulonimbus cloud. It has a typical width of tens to hundreds of meters and a life span of minutes to hours. In area, it is one of the least extensive of all storms, but in violence, it is the world's most severe. More tornadoes occur in the United States than in any other country.

Trough is an elongated area of relatively low pressure extending from the center of a low-pressure region. A trough is the opposite of a ridge.

Turbulence is the vertical motion of the air, at times violent, which can cause the up-and-down movement of a plane.

Veering is a clockwise change in wind direction. For example, from east to west through south. Veering is the opposite of backing.

Virga are wisps or streaks of precipitation falling out of a cloud which evaporate before reaching the ground.

Warm front is a front that moves in such a way that warmer air replaces colder air.

Wave, in meteorology, is the intersection of warm and cold fronts.

Weather is the state of the atmosphere with respect to heat or cold, wetness or dryness, calm or storm, clearness or cloudiness. Weather is the meteorological day-to-day variations of the atmosphere and their effects on life and human activity. It includes temperature, pressure, humidity, clouds, wind, precipitation, and fog.

Weather warnings are announcements separate from and supplementary to routine forecasts issued to warn of weather conditions that may endanger lives, property, and the welfare of the general public. Warnings are broadcast by the National Weather Service. They are issued for snowstorms, blizzards, heavy blowing snow, heavy rains, frost, cold waves, freezing rain, severe thunderstorms, and strong winds, according to thresholds established for local and regional public needs.

Wind is the horizontal movement of air relative to the earth's surface.

Relative Humidity

There are places in Florida where the relative humidity reaches 98 percent now and then. Would we all drown if the humidity reached 100 percent? No. The relative humidity is the amount of water vapor in the air compared to the amount of water vapor that the air can hold. When the air is holding as much water as it can, we refer to that as 100 percent humidity. No matter how high the humidity is, the actual amount of water present in the air is minimal. At 86 degrees, for instance, the air can only hold three or four percent water vapor, hardly a threat.

EARTHQUAKES IN FLORIDA

Most people believe earthquakes in Florida are as uncommon as hurricanes in Alaska. It is true that most of the state has little chance of experiencing a damaging earthquake—it lies in the zero earthquake risk zone, a term that means no damage expected from earthquakes.

Yet, minor shocks have occurred in the state, and one of these caused damage. Three additional shocks of doubtful seismic origin also are listed in earthquake documents.

The first, and strongest, shock in Florida's known history occurred near St. Augustine, in northeastern Florida, in January 1879. Residents of the nation's oldest permanent settlement, founded by Spain in 1565, reported that heavy shaking knocked plaster from walls and articles from shelves. Similar effects were noted at Daytona Beach, fifty miles south. At Tampa, the southernmost point of the affected area, the trembling was preceded by a rumbling sound at 11:30 P.M. Two shocks were reported in other areas, at 11:45 P.M. and 11:55 P.M. The tremor was felt through north and central Florida and at Savannah, Georgia.

In January 1880, Cuba was the center of two strong earthquakes that sent severe shock waves through the town of Key West. The tremors occurred at 11 P.M. on January 22 and at 4 A.M. on the 23rd. At Buelta Abajo and San Cristobal, Cuba, many buildings collapsed, and some people were killed.

The next tremor to be felt by Floridians also was centered outside the state, in Charleston, South Carolina, in August 1886. The shock was felt throughout northern Florida, ringing church bells at St. Augustine and severely jolting other towns along that section of the east coast. Jacksonville residents felt many of the strong aftershocks that occurred in September, October, and November of 1886.

On June 20, 1893, Jacksonville experienced another slight shock, apparently local, that lasted about ten seconds. Another minor earthquake shook Jacksonville at 11:15 A.M. on October 31, 1900. It caused no damage.

A sudden jar caused doors and windows to rattle at Captiva in November 1948. The apparent earthquake was accompanied by sounds like distant heavy explosions.

On November 18, 1952, a slight tremor was felt by many residents at Quincy, a small town about 20 miles northwest of Tallahassee. Windows and doors rattled, but no serious effects were reported. One source notes, "The shock interfered with the writing of a parking ticket."

The three Florida shocks of doubtful seismic origin rumbled through the Everglades at La Belle and Fort Myers in July 1930, Tampa in December 1940, and the Miami/Everglades and Fort Myers areas in January 1942. Most authorities attribute these incidents to blasting, but a few people contend they were seismic.

FLORIDA'S GLOBAL CHANGES

Some call it global warming. Others say it's the greenhouse effect. Still others think in terms of sea-level rise. Whatever they call it, it could have dire effects on Florida. Most scientists now agree that it seems likely that some degree of climate change will affect our lives and the geography of Florida over the next century. Not everyone believes in the global change—but enough do to make some predictions.

Because of the increased load of greenhouse gases in the atmosphere, the world is getting warmer and will continue to warm into the next century. A warming world will cause changes in the global weather and rainfall patterns, affecting the world's agriculture and weather. In a warmer world, the intensity of storms here in Florida is likely to increase, and sea levels are sure to increase.

Humans are a major cause of climate change. The change results from everyday human activity like burning fuel and releasing industrial, chemical, and agriculture toxins into the air. These activities send carbon dioxide and other greenhouse gases into the atmosphere. Add to this the gases from decaying vegetation, volcanoes, swamps and marshes, and evaporation from bodies of water, and you can see the problems.

The Earth is already warming. Over the past century, scientists have recorded a gradual overall warming of the earth by one degree centigrade. And so far, the 1990s are the warmest decade in recorded history. In fact, 1995 was the warmest year on record. Climate models indicate the likelihood that temperatures will rise between 1.5 and 4.5 degrees centigrade over the next 100 years. That range of temperatures, however, clearly indicates the amount of uncertainty still associated with the modeling of global climate. For comparison purposes, the global surface temperature of the Earth during the last Ice Age (some 18,000 years ago) was only 5 degrees centrigrade lower than it is today. Glaciers high in the Peruvian Andes are melting at a rate of 99 feet a year as the rate of global warming increases.

At the opposite end, the freezing level in the Earth's atmosphere—the height where the air temperature reaches zero degrees centigrade—has been gaining altitude since 1970 at the rate of nearly five feet a year.

The warming of the Earth causes the sea to rise through thermal expansion of ocean waters and through the shrinking of ice caps and glaciers. Scientists have recorded a rise in sea levels of about 6 inches over the last 100 years.

According to the U.S. Global Change Research Information Office, an increase in the Earth's average temperature of about 3.5 degrees Fahrenheit, too little to melt most polar ice, would result in an increase in sea level of 8 to 30 inches. This would flood many coastal areas. Higher sea levels could also cause more damage from storm surges associated with hurricanes. For Florida, rising seas could mean the destruction of coral reefs and other coastal ecosystems like mangrove swamps and coastal marshes, as well as the intrusion of salt water into our drinking water aquifers.

Climate changes in Florida and around the world can also affect agriculture, bringing heat waves and drought to some areas, rain and flooding to others. On the other hand, fewer frosts and warmer weather might extend the growing season for some areas, possibly resulting in improved agricultural yields.

Global precipitation trends between 1900 and 1994 reveal a general tendency toward more precipitation at higher latitudes (north and south toward the poles) and less precipitation at lower ones (a wide band around the equator). Because Florida is a peninsula almost completely surrounded by water, little change has occurred.

Two thousand of the nation's top economists, including six Nobel Laureates, say all this is a matter of concern. Florida, with its low coastlines, especially in its populous southeast and western coasts, and the state's susceptibility to tropical storms and hurricanes, is among the areas in the United States that needs watching.

THE NATIONAL WEATHER SERVICE

The National Weather Service provides a continuously updated weather forecast for Florida and its coastline via the VHF/FM channels WX1 (162.550 MHz), WX2 (162.400 MHz) and WX3 (162.475 MHz).

HURRICANES

When a tropical storm's winds reach 74 miles an hour, the storm is upgraded to a hurricane. A hurricane warning is an indication that a hurricane is expected in a specific area within 24 hours.

Category 1 Hurricane—central pressure of 28.94 inches or more and wind speeds from 74–94 miles an hour. Four- to five-foot storm surges are common.

Category 2 Hurricane—pressure of 28.50 to 28.93 inches with winds from 96–110 miles an hour. Storm surges from six to eight feet.

Category 3 Hurricane—pressure of 27.91 to 28.49 inches with winds from 111–130 miles an hour and 9- to 12-foot storm surges.

Category 4 Hurricane—pressure of 27.17 to 27.90 with winds from 131–155 miles an hour. Hurricanes Andrew, Hugo, and Hazel were Category 4 hurricanes with storm surges from 13 to 18 feet.

Category 5 Hurricane—pressure less than 27.17 inches with winds higher than 155 miles an hour and storm surges higher than 18 feet.

Since record-keeping began, only two Category 5 hurricanes have hit the United States. On Labor Day of 1935, more than 400 people were killed by a hurricane in the Florida Keys. In 1960, Hurricane Camille killed 256 people in Mississippi.

Hurricanes stop becoming hurricanes and become typhoons at the longitude line 180 degrees west of the international date line. The hurricane season in the Pacific differs from Florida's hurricane season in that it has a different start date. In Florida, the start date is June 1, while the Pacific hurricane season starts on May 15. Both end November 30. Surprisingly, there are more storms in the Pacific than in the Atlantic.

Hurricane Names

One theory of naming hurricanes is that it was started by a radio announcer who sang "Every little breeze seems to whisper Louise" when issuing a hurricane warning. After a rash of hurricanes and typhoons (in the Pacific), the United Nations weather experts who name storms decided to retire the names Andrew, Hugo, and Mike because of their negative reputation. The name Andrew will be replaced by Alec and Hugo by Humberto. Typhoon Mike, which swept through the Philippines, causing more than $350 million in damage and killing hundreds, has been retired without a replacement.

The National Weather Service gives each storm a name from one of six lists that are rotated every six years. The 1994 list, for example, will be used again in the year 2000. Names are given when a disturbance intensifies into a tropical storm with rotary circulation and wind speeds over 30 miles an hour. The names on the lists are agreed upon by nations involved in the World Meteorological Organization.

Hurricane Deaths

The deadly force of hurricanes can be seen in the tragic loss of so many lives. Below is a listing of hurricanes in this century that have caused 25 or more deaths, with the most destructive listed first. When hurricanes occurred before names were introduced, their geographical region is indicated.

Hurricane	Deaths
Louisiana (1893)	2,000
Florida (1928)	1,836
South Carolina and Georgia (1893)	1,000–2,000
Georgia and South Carolina (1881)	700
Florida Keys and south Texas (1919)	600–900 (more than 500 of these lost on ships at sea)

New England (1938)	600
Florida Keys (1935)	408
Hurricane Audrey—southwest Louisiana and north Texas (1957)	390
Northeastern United States (1944)	390 (344 of these lost on ships at sea)
Louisiana (1909)	350
Louisiana/New Orleans area (1915)	275
Texas/Galveston area (1915)	275
Hurricane Camille—Mississippi and Louisiana (1969)	256
Florida/Miami area (1926)	243
Hurricane Diane, northeastern United States (1955)	184
Southeast Florida (1906)	164
Mississippi, Alabama, and Florida (1906)	134
Hurricane Agnes—northeastern United States (1972)	122
Hurricane Hazel—the Carolinas (1954)	95
Hurricane Betsy—Florida and Louisiana (1965)	75
Hurricane Carol—northeastern United States (1954)	60
Florida, Louisiana, and Mississippi (1947)	51
Georgia and the Carolinas (1940)	50
Hurricane Carla—Texas (1961)	46
Southern California (1935)	45
Texas (1909)	41
Texas (1932)	40
South Texas (1933)	40
Hurricane Hilda—Louisiana (1964)	38
Southwest Louisiana (1918)	34
Southwest Florida (1910)	30
Hurricane Connie—North Carolina (1955)	25
Louisiana (1926)	25

Hurricane Preparation—Taking Inventory of Your Home

You never plan to lose your valuables and other belongings in a hurricane, but if one comes along and damages your home and its contents, would you be able to accurately report what you lost and how much it's going to cost to replace it? Your insurance company will want to know this, and if you plan to deduct any damages on your income tax, so will the Internal Revenue Service.

It's a lot easier to do an inventory of your home now rather than to sit down afterward with your family and try to remember a lifetime worth of purchases. You can start by planning an inventory day sometime this week. Walk around the house and write down each item of value, serial numbers (available on the back of the item), date purchased, where purchased, and the cost. Estimate each item's current value based on age and usage.

Inventory everything: furniture, appliances, carpeting, contents of your closets, jewelry, electronics, etc. Sheets, pillowcases, linens, blankets, etc., can be combined into one entry, as can dishes, pots and pans, etc. Do the garage, the attic, the basement, and exterior of the home, including the cost of landscaping, fencing, etc.

It's easier if you make this a family project and have different family members provide information while you take notes. You can walk around with a tape recorder in your hand and transcribe the inventory to paper when you're done. If you have a camera, take photos of the more valuable items. Store the list and any photos in a safe place, and ask a friend or relative to hold a copy of everything for safekeeping. Better yet, store your inventory in a safe-deposit box.

The easiest way to record your possessions is with a video camera. If you don't have one, borrow one from a friend or rent one for the day. Walk around the house putting each item on video and explain what it cost, when it was bought, and its estimated current value. This is another way the family can participate. Have children explain the contents of their rooms.

Important documents should be photocopied. Keep one copy in your home and the original in a safe-deposit box. This is a good idea whether you're preparing for a hurricane or not. Floods, fire, theft, and other mishaps can result in the loss of these documents. Important items include, but are not limited to, the paperwork on the house (escrow, title, deed, insurance policy); personal papers (birth certificates, medical history, passports, insurance certificates, credit card numbers, will, etc.); automobile documents (certificates of ownership, finance contracts, registrations, insurance policy, driver's licenses); financial papers (account numbers for checking and savings accounts, certificates of deposit, stocks, bonds, other significant investments); and tax records, including copies of the first two pages of your state and federal returns for the past five years. Complete returns with appropriate receipts and canceled checks should be kept in a separate file box.

Most policies limit the amount

> *It's a lot easier to inventory your home's contents before disaster strikes.*

of reimbursement for theft of valuable items such as jewelry, furs, silverware, and guns. If you have some particularly valuable items in these categories, you may need to purchase additional coverage called a floater. These types of policies cover each item individually and are usually quite inexpensive. For example, $10,000 worth of coverage on computers and electronics not covered in the home policy costs about $100–$150 a year. Your insurance agent can help you determine whether your property is adequately protected.

These tips will be beneficial only if you make use of them now. By inventorying your personal possessions before a disaster strikes, you will save yourself much frustration later.

SOLAR ENERGY—FLORIDA'S UNTAPPED RESOURCE

Our sun is a giant nuclear fusion reactor running on hydrogen. Each second, it converts 564 million tons of hydrogen to 560 tons of helium through the fusion process. The loss of four million tons of mass equates to 91,000,000,000,000 gigawatt hours of energy (a gigawatt is equal to 1,000,000 kilowatts). This is more energy in one second than six billion nuclear power plants would produce in a year.

The sun's energy is an enormous and constant energy resource, but because of the Earth's protective atmosphere, only a small amount of the total energy produced by the sun reaches Earth. If all of the sun's energy could reach the Earth, we'd really be in trouble!

Astronomers have determined that the sun's energy has remained relatively constant over the last century and that this "solar constant" will continue to be 1.35 kilowatts per square meter (±3.5 percent) for about the next four billion years.

Even in the North, the solar energy available is impressive. On a sunny summer day in the Northeast, for example, the states there receive about 196,000 gigawatt hours of solar energy. This is more than all the electric power plants in the states would produce in a year. With all of this potential energy, it is no wonder many people find solar energy a useful, environmentally friendly, and economical energy source to heat their homes and businesses, as well as their water.

In Florida and elsewhere, we are able to use this vast resource primarily in three ways: passive solar heat, active solar heat, and photovoltaics. The first two energy sources involve collecting the heat produced by the sun for use in heating living or working space or water. Photovoltaics use the light produced by the sun (or any light source) to generate electricity directly. Sunlight striking a photovoltaic or solar cell causes a voltage and current to be created in a semiconductor that can be used just like the electrical energy from a battery or DC generator.

Passive solar buildings, designed with large areas of glass facing south, are popular for interior heating of homes and buildings. The warmth of the sun passes through the glass and provides interior heat. To enhance the solar gain, thermal storage is often added in conjunction with the southern exposure. Thermal storage devices can be as simple as dark-colored floor tile to help store the heat or as complex as hollow walls filled with water. As a general rule, the darker the color of the material and the greater the density, the better it stores heat.

Pools and hot-water heaters can be heated by solar energy through a series of pipes that are exposed to the sun. The water is pumped from the pool or heater through the pipes and back into the pool/heater. Check the water inside a plastic garden hose that has been lying in the sun and you can see how this works.

FLORIDA'S WEATHER: 1998–2000

Starting in 1999, temperatures from November through March 2000 will average near normal with below-normal rainfall, especially in February. The period will start with relatively cool temperatures. April and May will bring near- to below-normal temperatures, except in the north, where temperatures will average two degrees above normal.

Precipitation will be near normal, although continued dry weather in the south will be a prelude to an unusually dry summer. While temperatures from June through August 2000 will be near normal, precipitation will be relatively light with substantially less thunderstorm activity than usual. The hottest period for Florida as a whole will occur in the second week of August. September and October will be warmer than normal, especially in the northeast and along the Panhandle. Rainfall in central Florida will be above normal.

FLOODS

The "wall of water" type of flash flood, common in the western United States, is rare in Florida because of our relatively flat terrain. However, serious flooding can occur near rivers and streams, in coastal areas, and in urban areas. This flooding can cause severe personal inconvenience, damage to property, and even loss of life. Recent construction in previously uninhabited areas of Florida has led to exposure from flooding through a rise in ground water. Particularly after heavy periods of rain, these areas revert to their swampy origins, causing isolation of residences and businesses, damage to roadways and utilities, and contamination of water supplies for weeks and sometimes months.

Before purchasing property, carefully research its flood potential. Due to recent construction, records may not be available or may not adequately reflect the current risk of flooding. Learn your vulnerability to flooding by determining the elevation of your property. If the property is prone to flooding, buy flood insurance—a separate policy from your homeowner's policy. Ask property owners nearby about the record of flooding in the area.

Have a NOAA Weather Radio with tone alert on hand. During heavy rains, monitor it for flood warnings, watches, or statements. Stay tuned to local radio and television stations.

If you live in a flood-prone area, keep materials like sandbags, plywood, plastic sheeting, plastic garbage bags, and lumber available. Keep your automobile fueled. Keep a stock of food requiring little or no cooking and no refrigeration. If you have to cook, you can always cook on an outdoor barbecue. Keep a portable radio, emergency cooking equipment, lights, and flashlights in working order. Keep some extra batteries.

During a flood, avoid driving into water of unknown depth, especially during periods of low visibility. Moving water can quickly sweep your vehicle away. Standing water deep enough to cover wheels can cause cars to float—possibly into a canal, river, or lake. If warned by local officials to leave, quickly evacuate the area to avoid being cut off by flood water. Package important documents in waterproof containers and take them along. If time permits, move furnishings to safe ground; fill tanks to keep them from floating away; grease immovable machinery. Carry cash if possible.

After the flood, test all drinking water for potability. Wells should be pumped out and the water tested before drinking. Don't use fresh food that has been in contact with flood waters. Restrict children from playing in flooded areas. Hidden sharp objects and open storm drains are a safety hazard. If kids do play in standing water, bathe them as soon as possible and watch for signs of infection or disease.

Never handle live electrical equipment in wet areas. All electrical equipment should be checked and dried before returning to service. Unclog storm drains. Standing water breeds mosquitoes, which carry disease. Use flashlights, not lanterns or torches, to examine buildings; flammables may be inside. Report broken utility lines to appropriate authorities.

Before buying property, carefully research its flood potential.

AVERAGE MEAN TEMPERATURES AROUND FLORIDA (°F)

	Jan	Feb	Mar	Apr	May	Jun	Jul	Aug	Sep	Oct	Nov	Dec
Pensacola	52	54	57	64	72	78	82	82	81	74	64	55
Panama City Beach	55	53	57	63	69	70	80	80	80	73	65	55
Tallahassee	53	55	57	63	71	77	81	81	80	74	63	55
Gainesville	57	57	59	63	71	77	80	81	80	74	66	56
Jacksonville	55	56	59	65	72	78	82	83	81	75	66	56
Tampa	62	61	63	69	75	80	82	82	81	79	71	63
Orlando	62	61	63	69	74	80	81	83	82	78	72	64
Naples	66	65	67	72	75	79	81	82	82	80	74	68
Miami Beach	69	69	70	74	76	79	82	83	82	81	76	71
Key West	71	70	72	76	79	82	84	84	83	82	77	73

FLORIDA—LIGHTNING CAPITAL OF THE WORLD

Step outside in the middle of a rainstorm and your chances of getting hit by lightning are about 600,000 to 1, obviously in your favor, but there are never any guarantees. Last year, more than 1,000 people were stuck by lightning, mostly during thunderstorms. If you are struck, your chances of dying are about ten to one. People who have been struck by lightning report numbness in their limbs, memory loss, depression, and often permanent nerve damage.

Every day, lightning strikes more than eight million times on the planet Earth, causing more than $2 billion in damages. The area around Tampa is considered the Lightning Capital of the United States, if not the world, probably because of its proximity to water and the moisture in the air. In fact, 8 percent of all injuries and deaths from lightning occur in Florida. When you see those thunderstorm clouds overhead and hear the first rumble, it's time to seek shelter. Get away from the water. Since lightning seeks out the tallest object in the area, don't be that tallest object. Stay away from trees and open fields and beaches. If someone is struck by lightning and not killed, you might find that person prone on the ground and not breathing. Administer CPR and call 911 as quickly as possible.

Thunder and Lightning

You can't have thunder without lightning. When a cloud builds up a charge, the top has a positive charge while the portion facing the earth has a negative charge. With all of this electrical energy on the earth side of the cloud, the energy heads

toward the ground. Since the ground normally has a positive charge and the underside of the cloud a negative charge, when the lightning strike begins, little pulses of electricity head toward the earth at a speed of about one-eighth the speed of light. The air is ionized and becomes an excellent conductor of electricity. The stroke produces the light and enough heat to expand the air and produce the sound of a thunderclap.

Lightning Speed

I f you see lightning and hear thunder, you can calculate the distance between you and the lightning by measuring the time that it takes to hear the thunder. This is true because the laws of physics say the speed of light is so fast that you see the lightning flash instantly while the sound moves much more slowly. Sound travels one mile in about five seconds, so if you hear the thunder one second after you see the lightning, it's about one-fifth of a mile away.

WIND

W ind is an important element in Florida. It accompanies tornadoes and hurricanes and dictates whether boaters can head out to open waters. During violent storms, it's often the major cause of damage. Wind is a fluid current set up by differing areas of pressure. If there are a high-pressure area in the atmosphere and a neighboring low-pressure area, air will flow between the two to try to equalize the pressures. That air flow is what we call wind. High air pressure means there are more molecules of air (O_2, N_2, etc.) piled up there than in an area of low pressure. Thus the molecules "flow downhill" to the area of low pressure. We feel this change as wind because molecules have mass and if we bump into them, we feel it.

*The
Sunshine State
Almanac
& Book of
Florida-
Related
Stuff*

WILDLIFE

*F*rogs and toads are members of the class Amphibia, the first backboned animals to live on land. The word is derived from the Greek word *amphibios,* which means "double life." Most frogs and toads have two stages in their life cycle: larvae (tadpole) and adult. There are approximately 80 known species in the United States. Of these, 22 frog (and 4 additional subspecies) and 5 toad species are native to Florida.

Frogs look different from toads in several ways. Most toads (except the eastern narrow mouth toad) have dry, warty skin, whereas frogs have moist, smooth skin. Most toads also have a pair of parotid glands bulging out from behind their eyes. These glands produce a bufotoxin that protects them from being eaten by most animals. Frogs do not possess these glands, and there are no poisonous frogs in Florida. All toads have these glands, but most are too small to severely affect people and pets. The one exception is the nonnative marine toad, which is large enough (six inches long) to release toxin amounts that can cause skin irritations, make people seriously ill, and kill dogs and cats. This toad, *Bufo marinus,* has been imported into Florida. Its venom is purported to be one of the ingredients in the concoction used by voodoo practitioners in Haiti to produce zombies.

Frogs and toads have evolved characteristics that allow them to survive on land. Adult frogs and toads have a keen sense of smell. This is controlled by a smell-taste organ called the Jacobson's organ in the nasal passages. Frogs and toads have a wide range of vision and are sensitive to movement. They cannot turn their heads, but their large, bulging eyes give them excellent side vision to see potential predators. Frogs and toads also have a well-developed outer ear. This circular tympanic membrane is located behind their eyes.

Frogs and toads live in a wide variety of habitats throughout Florida. Adults of many species spend considerable time in dry upland habitats and migrate to wetlands only during the breeding/egg-laying season. When tadpoles metamorphose into adults, their body structure and breathing organs change. The tail disappears, legs form, the mouth enlarges, lungs replace gills, and other organs transform to adapt to a life that includes breathing air, eating different food items, and living on land as well as in the water.

Frog Food

All adult frogs and toads are predators and feed on a wide variety of insects. They have large mouths and long, sticky tongues that they use to capture prey. Their hunting style is to sit and wait for their food to come to them. When an insect moves within range, a frog or toad turns its body (if necessary), lunges forward, and shoots its tongue through the air. It will also pursue slower prey on the ground. Its feeding response is triggered by the movement of its prey. Because frogs and toads swallow their prey whole, they have little need for teeth. They also lack throat muscles to help them swallow, so they push their food into their stomachs with their upper head muscles and eyes. Tadpoles are herbivores (plant-eaters) and feed mostly on algae, which they filter from the water.

> *Venom from* **Bufo marinus,** *a poisonous non-native toad, may be used by voodoo practitioners to create zombies.*

The Sex Life of Frogs

Frogs and toads move to ponds, lakes, streams, and ditches to breed. Males move to the pond first and begin calling. Usually, this activity takes place on rainy nights when the barometric pressure is falling. Once a female arrives, she selects her mate and breeding begins. When the male and female come close together, the male clasps the female around the waist with his forelegs. This clasping, known as amplexing, stimulates hormones in the female that cause her eggs to be released into the water. When this occurs, the male releases sperm, fertilizing the eggs. The eggs remain inside a gelatinous mass until hatching. Amphibian eggs must remain in a moist environment, because they have no protective shell. Toads lay their eggs in single strands, while chorus frogs lay eggs in broken strands, and other frogs lay eggs in large clumps.

Frog Nuisance Problems

Homeowners who live near water may hear a variety of types of calls throughout the year. Frogs and toads will be attracted to any body of water for breeding, including bird baths and swimming pools. If you are bothered by this, there is little you can do other than to make the water inaccessible with materials like screening and netting. If the noise is interrupting your sleep, you may want to consider closing the windows or turning on a fan or some other noise-making device that is less disturbing but will drown out the frog calls.

THE ENDANGERED SPECIES ACT

To prevent wildlife extinction, the U.S. Congress passed the Endangered Species Act (ESA) in 1973. The ESA has two categories for species whose survival is in trouble. Endangered species are in danger of becoming extinct because only a very small number of them are left. Threatened species are likely to become endangered, too, if they are not protected.

Two agencies determine which species need to be put on the Endangered and Threatened Wildlife and Plants list. The Fish and Wildlife Service is responsible for all land species, sea turtles when they nest on beaches, and fish that swim from salt to fresh waters, such as salmon. The National Marine Fisheries Service is responsible for all marine life. Private citizens with the proper scientific information can also petition for a species to be listed.

There are now more than 1,117 species on the endangered list. Half of those are found in the United States. Scientists have identified almost 4,000 more species in the U.S. that are waiting to be put on the list! Sadly, some have already become extinct in the meantime. Most of the species listed are mammals, birds, and plants because more research has been completed on them. Invertebrates (animals without backbones: arachnids, clams, crustaceans, insects, snails) make up 90 percent of all species on earth, but only 85 species are listed.

After a species is listed, the next step is to prepare for a recovery plan to increase the population. This can include buying more habitat or breeding the species in captivity for future release. Unfortunately, it is a slow process. Often, there is not enough money or people to do all the needed work. Only one-third of all species listed have recovery plans.

The American alligator and the eastern population of brown pelicans are two species that have made successful comebacks thanks to recovery plans that worked. The bald eagle has also made a good recovery. Endangered red wolves were successfully reintroduced to Alligator River National Wildlife Refuge in North Carolina in 1988. Not long ago, black-footed ferrets, once thought to be extinct, were reintroduced to Wyoming. And at least 50 black-footed ferrets will be released in the wild every year. It's against the law to harm endangered species. People caught stealing, injuring, or killing endangered and threatened species can be fined up to $20,000 or sentenced up to one year in jail.

To control the trade in wildlife and wildlife products, the international treaty CITES was signed in 1975. CITES is short for Convention on International Trade in Endangered Species of Wildlife Fauna and Flora. One hundred and eighteen countries, including the United States, have signed this treaty. Species and species products listed in CITES cannot be bought or sold for profit.

ENDANGERED AND THREATENED SPECIES OF SOUTH FLORIDA'S NATIONAL PARKS

T hreatened, endangered, and extinct are words that have become all too common in our twentieth-century vocabulary. The natural process of species evolution, taking hundreds and thousands of years, has accelerated rapidly since the turn of the century. Today, because of man's desire for land and raw materials, his continued pollution, and his indiscriminate hunting, many plant and wildlife species are on the brink of extinction.

Nowhere is man's impact on other species more evident than in south Florida. Drainage of wetlands, alteration of overland water flow, and hunting have all contributed to species decline. The Everglades area, once known for abundant bird life, has seen its wading bird population decline drastically since the turn of the century. The Florida panther, once common throughout the state, today is on the verge of extinction. Within Everglades National Park, Biscayne National Park, Big Cypress National Preserve, and Fort Jefferson National Monument, there are 16 endangered and 6 threatened wildlife species. The mere physical boundaries of a national park do not guarantee a species' survival.

Maintaining harmony between progress and wilderness areas requires research, legislation, and public awareness. For the last decade, the South Florida Research Center at Everglades National Park has been studying how changes occurring outside the parks influence the fragile areas within their boundaries. Research going on today may lead to a brighter future for many species.

Legislation such as the Endangered Species Act of 1973 has also afforded some measure of protection for wildlife. The Act provided for the classification of wildlife species as "endangered" or "threatened" and mandated legal protection for species so listed. In justification for such protection, the Act also recognized that the various species of fish, wildlife, and plants have aesthetic, educational, historical, and scientific value.

ENDANGERED PLANTS

The list of endangered plant species in Florida is constantly changing. At last count, there were 54 species on the list, ranging from pigeon wings to pawpaw. In alphabetical order, here's the latest list of Florida's endangered plants.

American chaffseed (*Schwalbea americana*)
Apalachicola rosemary (*Conradina glabra*)
Avon Park harebells (*Crotalaria avonensis*)
Beach jacquemontia (*Jacquemontia reclinata*)
Beautiful pawpaw (*Deeringothamnus pulchellus*)
Britton's beargrass (*Nolina brittoniana*)
Brooksville bellflower (*Campanula robinsiae*)
Carter's mustard (*Warea carteri*)
Chapman rhododendron (*Rhododendron chapmanii*)
Cooley's meadow rue (*Thalictrum cooleyi*)
Cooley's water-willow (*Justicia cooleyi*)
Crenulate lead-plant (*Amorpha crenulata*)
Deltoid spurge (*Chamaesyce deltoidea ssp. deltoidea*)
Etonia rosemary (*Conradina etonia*)
Florida bonamia (*Bonamia grandiflora*)
Florida golden aster (*Chrysopsis floridana*)
Florida perforate cladonia (*Cladonia perforata*)
Florida skullcap (*Scutellaria floridana*)
Florida torreya (*Torreya taxifolia*)
Florida ziziphus (*Ziziphus celata*)
Four-petal pawpaw (*Asimina tetramera*)
Fragrant prickly-apple (*Cereus eriophorus var. fragrans*)
Fringed campion (*Silene polypetala*)
Garber's spurge (*Chamaesyce garberi*)
Garrett's mint (*Dicerandra christmanii*)
Gentian pinkroot (*Spigelia gentianoides*)
Godfrey's butterwort (*Pinguicula ionantha*)
Harper's beauty (*Harperocallis flava*)
Highlands scrub hypericum (*Hypericum cumulicola*)
Key tree-cactus (*Pilosocereus robinii*)
Lakela's mint (*Dicerandra immaculata*)
Lewton's polygala (*Polygala lewtonii*)
Longspurred mint (*Dicerandra cornutissima*)
Miccosukee gooseberry (*Ribes echinellum*)
Okeechobee gourd (*Cucurbita okeechobeensis ssp. okeechobeensis*)
Papery whitlow-wort (*Paronychia chartacea*)
Pigeon wings (*Clitoria fragrans*)
Pondberry (*Lindera melissifolia*)

Pygmy fringe-tree (*Chionanthus pygmaeus*)
Rugel's pawpaw (*Deeringothamnus rugelii*)
Sandlace (*Polygonella myriophylla*)
Scrub blazingstar (*Liatris ohlingerae*)
Scrub buckwheat (*Eriogonum longifolium var. gnaphalifolium*)
Scrub lupine (*Lupinus aridorum*)
Scrub mint (*Dicerandra frutescens*)
Scrub plum (*Prunus geniculata*)
Short-leaved rosemary (*Conradina brevifolia*)
Small's milkpea (*Galactia smallii*)
Snakeroot (*Eryngium cuneifolium*)
Telephus spurge (*Euphorbia telephioides*)
Tiny polygala (*Polygala smallii*)
White birds-in-a-nest (*Macbridea alba*)
Wide-leaf warea (*Warea amplexifolia*)
Wireweed (*Polygonella basiramia*)

EXOTIC PLANTS

Florida is unwilling host to hundreds of exotic plants and is threatened with invasion by scores of others. An exotic or nonindigenous species is a plant which is not native to Florida but which may survive and reproduce here, displacing native species and altering native ecosystems. In some cases, exotic species seem to cause little or no obvious damage, appearing only as weeds in our gardens or along roads.

But plants like the *Melaleuca*, or Brazilian pepper, for example, push out native plants and animals, reduce biodiversity, destroy ecosystems, and drink up our water supplies. They are cause for economic as well as ecological concern.

Here are some of the most notorious of Florida's exotic invaders and their effects on Florida's natural systems:

Australian pine covers more than 373,000 acres and can quickly colonize, displacing native species.

Hydrilla covers 100,000 acres. It produces a dense mat at the surface, shading out bottom vegetation, creating low dissolved oxygen levels and affecting animal life.

Brazilian pepper covers 703,504 acres. Birds spread the seeds of this invasive species. It displaces native understory plants and affects bird population densities.

Cogon grass has established itself in at least 27 Florida counties. Its dense growth can affect the intensity of fires.

Chinese tallow is a native of China. It invades bottomland hardwood forests and wetlands and may replace native species. Its leaf can be toxic to aquatic invertebrates.

Torpedo grass covers 17,544 acres. It displaces native vegetation along waterfronts and has little or no habitat value.

Kudzu covers more than two million acres in the Southeast and crowds out native vegetation.

Tropical soda apple forms dense single species stands in agricultural and pasture lands, ditch banks, and roadsides. It threatens natural areas with invasion.

Water hyacinth covers 1,680 acres. In the 1950s, water hyacinth covered more than 120,000 acres of Florida waterways. It shades out bottom areas and depletes oxygen.

Catclaw mimosa covers less than a thousand acres in five locations in South Florida, but it is a distinct threat to the Everglades, where it could obstruct water flow.

These are only a few of the more than 1,000 alien plant species that have become established in Florida, infesting more than 1.5 million acres of land.

ENDANGERED SPECIES

The Florida Game and Fresh Water Fish Commission's list of species that are threatened, endangered, or of special concern is constantly changing. This list includes creatures big and small that fly, crawl, swim, and wiggle their way around the state. Here are their scientific and common names.

Ajaia ajaja	Roseate spoonbill
Ammodramus maritimus juncicolus	Wakulla seaside sparrow
Ammodramus maritimus mirabilis	Cape Sable seaside sparrow
Ammodramus savannarum floridanus	Florida grasshopper sparrow
Aphelocoma coerulescens	Florida scrub-jay
Aramus guarauna	Limpkin
Campephilus principalis	Ivory-billed woodpecker
Charadrius alexandrinus tenuirostris	Southeastern snowy plover
Charadrius melodus	Piping plover
Cistothorus palustris griseus	Worthington's marsh wren
Cistothorus palustris marianae	Marian's marsh wren
Columba leucocephala	White-crowned pigeon
Dendroica kirtlandii	Kirtland's warbler
Egretta caerulea	Little blue heron
Egretta rufescens	Reddish egret
Egretta thula	Snowy egret
Egretta tricolor	Tricolored (Louisiana) heron
Eretmochelys imbriccata imbratica	Atlantic hawksbill turtle
Eudocimus albus	White ibis
Eumeces egregius egregius	Florida Keys mole skink

Eumeces egregius	Bluetail mole skink
Eumops glaucinus floridanus	Florida (Wagner's) mastiff bat
Falco peregrinus tundrius	Arctic peregrine falcon
Falco sparverius paulus	Southeastern American kestrel
Felis concolor coryi	Florida panther
Gopherus polyphemus	Gopher turtle
Graptemys barbouri	Barbour's map (sawback) turtle
Grus americana	Whooping crane
Grus canadensis pratensis	Florida sandhill crane
Haematopus palliatus	American oystercatcher
Haliaeetus leucocephalus	Bald eagle
Heraclides aristodemus ponceanus	Schaus' swallowtail butterfly
Kinosternon bauri	Striped mud turtle
Lepidochelys kempi	Atlantic ridley turtle
Liguus fasciatus	Florida tree snail
Macroclemys temmincki	Alligator snapping turtle
Mustela vison evergladensis	Everglades mink
Mycteria americana	Wood stork
Myotis grisescens	Gray bat
Myotis sodalis	Indiana bat
Neoseps reynoldsi	Sand skink
Neotoma floridana smalli	Key Largo woodrat
Nerodia fasciata taeniata	Atlantic salt marsh snake
Odocoileus virginianus clavium	Key deer; toy deer
Orthalicus reses	Stock Island tree snail
Oryzomys argentatus	Silver rice rat
Oryzomys palustris sanibeli	Sanibel Island rice rat
Pandion haliaetus	Osprey
Pelecanus occidentalis	Brown pelican
Peromyscus gossypinus allapaticola	Key Largo cotton mouse
Peromyscus polionotus allophrys	Choctawhatchee beach mouse
Peromyscus polionotus niveiventris	Southeastern beach mouse
Peromyscus polionotus peninsularis	St. Andrews beach mouse
Peromyscus polionotus phasma	Anastasia Island beach mouse
Peromyscus polionotus trissyllepsis	Perdido Key beach mouse
Picoides borealis	Red-cockaded woodpecker
Pituophis melanoleucus mugitus	Florida pine snake
Podomys floridanus	Florida mouse
Polyborus plancus audubonii	Audubon's crested caracara
Pseudemys concinna suwanniensis	Suwannee cooter
Rostrhamus sociabilis	Snail kite
Rynchops niger	Black skimmer
Sciurus niger avicenniam	Big Cypress (mangrove) fox squirrel

Sciurus niger shermani	Sherman's fox squirrel
Sorex longirostris eionis	Homosassa shrew
Speotyto cunicularia	Burrowing owl
Sterna antillarum	Least tern
Sterna dougallii	Roseate tern
Stilosoma extenuatum	Short-tailed snake
Storeria dekayi victa	Florida brown snake
Tantilla oolitica	Miami black-headed snake
Thamnophis sauritus sackeni	Florida ribbon snake
Sylvilagus palustris hefneri	Lower Keys marsh rabbit
Tamias striatus	Eastern chipmunk
Trichechus manatus	West Indian (Florida) manatee
Ursus americanus floridanus	Florida black bear
Vermivora bachmanii	Bachman's warbler

WILDLIFE VIOLATIONS

The Florida Game and Fresh Water Fish Commission has installed toll-free telephone lines so residents of the state can report violations or suspected violations of wildlife. The telephones operate 24 hours a day, 7 days a week, and you can remain anonymous. If your information results in an arrest, you will be eligible for a reward usually ranging from $50 to $1,000, based on the severity of the case. It is important to report violations as soon as possible and provide as much detail as you can about the descriptions of violators, their vehicles, license tag numbers, description of people involved, time of day, location, etc. Examples of frequently reported violations include illegal hunting, killing, or capturing of protected species and fishing by illegal means.

Lake City	800-342-8105
Lakeland	800-282-8002
Ocala	800-342-9620
Panama City	800-342-1676
West Palm Beach	800-432-2046

Cellular phone customers throughout most of the state can make a free call to the Game and Fish Water Fish Commission by dialing *GFC.

WOOD IBIS AND WHOOPING CRANE, FLORIDA.

How to Identify Water Hyacinth

Water hyacinth is a free-floating plant which grows up to three feet in height. It has thick, waxy, rounded, glossy leaves that rise well above the water surface on stalks. The leaves are broadly ovate to circular, four to eight inches in diameter, with gently incurved sides. Leaf veins are dense, numerous, fine, and longitudinal, and leaf stalks are bulbous and spongy.

At the top of its thick stalk is a single spike of 8 to 15 showy flowers. The flowers have six petals, purplish blue or lavender to pinkish, the upper petals with yellow, blue-bordered central splotches. Water hyacinth reproduces vegetatively by short runner stems (stolons) that radiate from the base of the plant to form daughter plants. It also reproduces by seed. Its roots are purplish black and feathery. Water hyacinth may be confused with frog's-bit (*Limnobium spongia*).

Water hyacinth is a nonnative pest species which grows in Florida's waterways, depleting oxygen and crowding out native plants. A huge program to eradicate water hyacinth has been somewhat successful.

Wetland Nightshade

Wetland nightshade (*Solanum tampicense*) is also known as aquatic soda apple and is an invasive non-indigenous plant spreading over the wetlands of Florida. The weed is believed to have come from Mexico and Belize. First noticed in Florida in 1983, wetland nightshade has spread into many wetland areas in southwest Florida.

The flowers of wetland nightshade are white and yellow, and tomato-like (it is in the same botanical genus as edible tomatoes). Its fruits are pea-sized berries, in clusters of up to 11 berries. The berries turn from green to orange to deep red as they ripen. Wetland nightshade leaves are elongate, measuring up to six inches long and two inches wide with indented edges and prickles on the veins. Sprawling stems are up to one-half inch wide and 6 to 15 feet long and are covered in curved prickles. The prickles snag and interlock so that these plants can form impenetrable thickets that can cover small trees and bushes to a height of 15 feet.

Poisonous Plants

Poison ivy, poison oak, and poison sumac are the three most common urushiol-containing plants in the United States, and you can find all three right here in Florida. The common poison ivy (*Toxicodendron radicans*), in six subspecies, thrives from southern Maine to Florida and as far west as Nebraska, Kansas, Oklahoma, and Texas. It can also be found near the Mexican border in eastern Arizona and western New Mexico. Humid weather and rich damp soil favor its spread, but it can persist in what might seem rather daunting circumstances.

Poison oak is a woody plant that grows in dry barren areas from southern New Jersey to northern Florida and as far west as California. Poison oak has adapted to a wide range of habitats, from rich loam soil to rock crevices, and can be found from sea level to about 5,000 feet.

"Leaflets three, let it be!"

Poison sumac is usually found along the margins of swamps and bogs where the soil is acidic and wet. The shrub can grow to 20 or more feet high and is never found in the vinelike form of its ivy relatives. Poison sumac shrubs in dry soil are stunted but just as poisonous as the larger version. They look innocuous and poison the unwary.

The key to protection from urushiol is the ability to recognize and avoid the plants that carry the poison. Remember "Leaflets three, let it be!" when you're near any strange vegetation. Poison ivy and poison oak have three-leaflet stems. The two-side or lateral leaflets appear to be symmetrical and grow close to the stem, while the end leaflet is distinct and alone.

Poison sumac can have 7, 9, 11, or 13 leaflets which grow in symmetrical pairs close to the stem—except for the one at the end. The odd number of leaves, the symmetrical pairing, and the isolated end leaflet should allow you to group poison sumac with its evil relatives and avoid it.

In the rare instance where contact with urushiol-bearing plants cannot be avoided, take extreme precautions to prevent direct or indirect contamination. Ordinary work trousers tied at the boot mouth, a long-sleeved shirt, and

gauntlet-type gloves will usually protect against direct contamination of the skin, but protection against indirect contamination requires great vigilance. A casual wipe of a contaminated glove against the head can cause the characteristic rash, and a breath of smoke from burning urushiol-containing trash can inflame the mouth, nose, throat, and lungs.

Clothing and tools can remain contaminated for years after being in contact with a urushiol-producing plant. Washing contaminated clothing and contaminated surfaces with copious amounts of cold water is the easiest way to get rid of urushiol.

PALM TREES

Palm trees grow in places that are warm and have a lot of sunshine. They're a symbol of warm sunny places like Florida, California, the Caribbean islands, and tropical paradises. They like to live in states where they can get lots of water. Florida has a lot of water, so Florida has a lot of palm trees. One species of palm tree's fruit is the coconut, a hard-shelled fruit containing coconut milk that some people enjoy drinking.

Most fruits and their seeds are carried by animals, birds, or the wind, and this accounts for their introduction into new areas. But the coconut is too big to be carried around by animals and birds, so the coconut palm has devised an interesting way to get its seed from one place to another. It likes areas with water so the seeds can be carried by currents to other areas. Because the coconut is hollow and floats, it can assist in the relocation. After a trip, the coconut washes up on shore, spits out some seeds, and starts growing again.

TROPICAL HARDWOOD HAMMOCKS

Along both coasts of southern Florida, scattered throughout the Everglades, and especially in the Florida Keys, there exist dense, vine-entangled forests called tropical hardwood hammocks. Geologists believe their origin dates back some 110,000–120,000 years, when coral reefs were exposed by receding ancient seas. Deprived of its life-giving sea water, the living coral soon died, leaving slowly fossilizing limestone behind to support some of Florida's—even North America's—rarest plant and animal communities.

Struggling for existence on the same rocky substrate as the tropical hardwood hammocks is another rare plant community known as pine rocklands. Dominated by hardy south Florida slash pines, the pine rockland community inhabits fossilized coral limestone where frequent ground fires are the norm. The different burning frequencies of hammocks and pinelands play a major role in maintaining the natural balance between these linked but distinctly different habitats. Without fire, the hammock understory would eventually take over the pineland and change it into a hardwood hammock.

The tropical hardwood hammock is a self-maintaining community that usually remains untouched by fire or flood. These tiny "islands" support more than 20 species of broad-leafed trees, shrubs, and vines, most of which are native to the West Indies. Subject to thin soils and relatively low rainfall in a tropical climate, tropical hardwood hammocks form a low canopy beneath which is a dense, sometimes impenetrable tangle of shrubs and vines. Hidden in the hammocks are some of Florida's rarest and most beautiful animal life.

Historically, tropical hammocks were found as far north as Cape Canaveral on the Atlantic coast and to the mouth of the Manatee River on the Gulf coast. These more northerly hammocks had unique characteristics all their own. Today, most of the northern hammocks have been destroyed, leaving only remnant stands in south Florida, mostly in the Florida Keys.

The connection between wildlife and wild land is finally being realized by many Floridians. The tropical hardwood hammock and its inhabitants are inseparably linked, just as all of Florida's wildlife depends on suitable habitat for survival.

In south Florida, there are hammocks at John D. MacArthur Beach State Park, Gumbo Limbo Nature Center in Everglades National Park, Hugh Taylor Birch St. Recreation Area, and Fern Forest Nature Center in Coconut Creek. Also, visit Collier-Seminole State Park, South Florida Hammocks/Castlellow Hammock Park, Charles Deering Estate, Crane Point Hammock, Everglades National Park/Gumbo Limbo Trail and Mahogany Hammock Trail, John Pennekamp Coral Reef State Park, Lignumvitae Key State Botanical Site, National Key Deer Wildlife Refuge/No Name Key, and Bahia Honda State Recreation Area in the Florida Keys.

SAW PALMETTO—MIRACLE DRUG OR WEED?

Deep in the steamy heart of Florida, amidst sand pine scrub and in the undergrowth of other flat woodland areas, grows the saw palmetto plant, or *Serenoa repens*. Saw palmetto is a low-growing palm whose berries have been cherished by herbalists and natural medicine practitioners for years, while the shrub has been reviled by ranchers and developers for being persistent and undesirable. Now, as international awareness of the therapeutic properties of saw palmetto grows, the plant has become a valuable commodity.

Saw palmetto, sometimes known as sawtooth palm or windmill palm, grows in the southeastern United States from South Carolina to southern Mississippi. It grows naturally in every county of Florida. Saw palmetto palms grow in dense clumps and have broad, fanlike leaves. The berries are sheltered inside the thick foliage on small stems attached to the trunk. The hard saw teeth for which the plant is named run along the petiole, or leaf stalk, making collection of the protected berries dangerous and difficult. The hardy, compact saw palmetto is very fire-resistant, and it often grows in areas which are naturally prone to fire.

Saw palmettos flower from December to March, bearing deep purple berries between April and October. These berries produce a juice, the taste and smell of which have inspired hot debate. One herbalist at Frontier Herbs has claimed that the fruity, pungent saw palmetto is "the worst herb I've ever tasted," while others find the flavor deep and satisfying, like a fine wine. To make saw palmetto berries into powder, whole berries are dried and ground cryogenically (at subzero temperatures) so that their active constituent fatty acids are preserved from the heat and friction which occur in a conventional grinding process.

Saw palmetto has been used for centuries. Native Americans, perhaps as far back as pre-Mayan civilizations, used the berries for food and medicine. Early American botanists noted that animals fed these berries grew sleek and robust. Saw palmetto is useful as a nutritive tonic, supporting healthy appetite and smooth digestion. Saw palmetto berry also tones the urethra, and it may be used to uphold the healthy function of the thyroid gland and urinary system. In one of its more exotic uses, saw palmetto has been employed as an ingredient in love potions. Much of the recent attention paid to saw pal-

metto in the United States and Europe has focused on its properties in relation to the prostate gland.

A study sponsored by Pfizer, Inc., the Pharmacia-Upjohn Company, and the Cytogen Corporation in 1996 indicated that the most promising agent for benign prostatic hyperplasia is an extract of saw palmetto. Good prostate health can be threatened by the hormone dihydrotestosterone (DHT). DHT is converted from the male hormone testosterone in the prostate, particularly in men over 50. One of the effects of DHT is to cause prostate cells to multiply, which induces the prostate to become larger. Saw palmetto inhibits the functioning of DHT by preventing it from binding to prostate cells. Furthermore, it actually prevents the conversion of testosterone into DHT in the prostate. This remarkable herbal action makes saw palmetto a superior supplement in maintaining normal, healthy prostate function.

Studies demonstrating these therapeutic properties have caused the demand for saw palmetto berries to escalate dramatically. This has produced something of a saw palmetto boom in parts of Florida. Raiders who sneak into cultivated fields and wild areas to poach the valuable berries can earn handsome profits in the marketplace. However, in addition to hurting those growers and landowners who are being robbed, this situation may be upsetting the delicate balance of some of the area's ecosystems. Saw palmettos are an important source of food and shelter for a number of wildlife species. Among these is the very rare Florida panther, which often makes its den in tall stands of mature saw palmettos. Research is currently being conducted at the University of Florida to determine the effect of saw palmetto harvesting on the black bear, a threatened species in Florida.

ST. JOHN'S WORT—NATURE'S WONDER DRUG?

St. John's wort has been known as klamath weed, tipton weed and goatweed over the years, and it has a history dating back to the ancient Greeks. The word wort means "herb" in old Anglo-Saxon language. It grows like a shrub, sometimes looking like a small tree. It can be found in wet flatwoods and around cypress ponds. In Florida, it grows in the northwest Panhandle. The leaves are small, the flowers yellow with five petals.

The fruit is oval shaped and contains a small seed. For centuries it's been said to have magical powers. The red oil glands on the leaves were rumored to be drops of blood dating back to the beheading of John the Baptist. By coincidence, the herb is most potent sometime around late June, approximately the date of the Feast of St. John.

The leaves contain many translucent oil glands that look like holes (hence the species name *perforatum*, which describes the apparent perforations). The bright red color in these glands is produced by the pigment hypericin. The plant produces clusters of yellow flowers from June to September. Each of these flowers has five petals with black dots at the edges. If you crush the petals between your fingers, they also produce hypericin. The herb has a strong acrid flavor and an aroma reminiscent of turpentine.

St. John's wort is regarded among some ranchers and others as a nuisance and a noxious weed. Others cherish the colorful perennial, whose green leaves and bright yellow flowers make for a stunning splash of summer color. Those who cultivate the herb typically germinate and plant the seeds in early May or late April.

It is the bright red pigment, hypericin, that is regarded as the key constituent in St. John's wort, though there are dozens of other active ones. Hypericin may be found throughout the plant, but is typically found in greatest concentration in the yellow flowers.

Hypericin concentration is typically highest when the flower buds are full but not quite open.

St. John's wort has long been associated with magic, and it was regarded as having power over evil spirits. The genus name *Hypericum* is derived from two Greek words—*hyper*, meaning "over," and *eikon*, meaning "apparition." Early Christians and pre-Christians saw power in the bright, sun-yellow flowers and stamens—the power, as they saw it, to ward off encroaching darkness and evil apparitions. In pre-Christian religious practices in England, St. John's wort was used in many ceremonies and rituals. Bringing the flowers into the house on midsummer's eve would protect against the evil eye; sleeping with a sprig of the plant under one's pillow on St. John's Eve would ensure a vision of the saint and his blessing.

St. John's wort has been used as

Leatherbacks are the largest living turtles in the world.

a health enhancer since the time of the ancient Greeks. It was favored by both Galen and Paracelsus, two of the great Greek healers and scientists, for purposes for which it is still employed today. Externally, the oil of St. John's wort may be used as a reinforcing balm for the skin. Internally, St. John's wort is a specific for the nervous system, and it is used to support nerve tissues throughout the body. The herb induces hypotension in blood vessels, thereby increasing blood flow. It is often used by those who are experiencing high degrees of stress or mental burnout. It is also used as a general support to the nervous system. It usually is not appropriate for those who suffer from severe depression.

THE LEATHERBACK TURTLE

The leatherback turtle is easily distinguished from other oceanic turtles by its

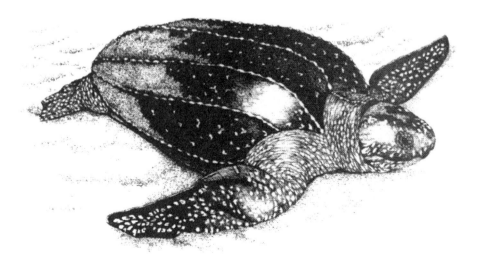

smooth leather-skinned carapace, or shell, which has seven prominent longitudinal keels. The carapace varies from brown to black, as do the head and neck. The flippers are black but may have some white blotches. The plastron, or breastplate, is white with some black blotching.

Leatherbacks are the largest living turtles in the world, weighing as much as 250 pounds. The throat of this species is lined with backward-pointing spines, an adaptation that enables it to feed extensively on jellyfish. Leatherbacks can be harmed by ingesting man-made debris that looks like jellyfish. Many people have stopped releasing helium balloons into the air because of this.

Leatherback turtles are listed as endangered in Florida. For many years their eggs have been dug out of nesting sites on sandy beaches in Florida and throughout the southern United States and Mexico. In many cases, the adults are captured and used for food, and their skins and shells are used commercially.

GREEN TURTLES

The green sea turtle was listed as endangered/threatened on July 28, 1978. The breeding populations off Florida and the Pacific coast of Mexico are listed as endangered, while all others are threatened. Total population estimates are unavailable because of wide, year-to-year fluctuations in the numbers of nesting females, the difficulty of conducting research on early life stage, and the long generation time. But estimates are that there are from 200 to just over 1,000 females nesting on U.S. beaches. The number of nests has increased on Hutchinson Island in Florida, although nesting levels have been low on other nesting beaches.

Adult green turtles may reach a size of 30 to 40 inches long and weigh 300 to 400 pounds. The carapace is smooth and is colored gray, green, brown, and black. The plastron is yellowish white. Hatchlings weigh about 25 grams and are about 50 millimeters long. Hatchlings are black on top and white on the bottom. Age at sexual maturity is estimated at 20 to 50 years.

The greatest cause of decline in green turtle populations is commercial harvesting of eggs for food. Other turtle parts are used for leather and jewelry, and small turtles are sometimes stuffed for curios. Incidental catching during commercial shrimp trawling is a continuing cause of death.

Other activities are major causes of the green turtle's decline. Development of beachfront property results in the loss of dry nesting beaches, preventing females from getting to nesting sites. Artificial lighting can cause both hatchlings and adults to become disoriented. Turtle hatchlings are attracted to light, ignoring or coming out of the ocean to go towards a light source, increasing their chances of death or injury.

Repeated mechanical raking of

nesting beaches by heavy machinery can result in compact sand and causes tire ruts which may hinder or trap hatchlings. Rakes can penetrate the surface and disturb or uncover a nest.

Nighttime use of a beach by humans disturbs nesting females. Use of off-road vehicles and automobiles on beaches is always a problem. The invasion of a nesting site by nonnative beach vegetation can lead to increased erosion and destruction of nesting habitat. Trees shading a beach can also change nest temperatures, altering the natural sex ratio of the hatchlings.

Green turtles have been known to eat a wide variety of marine debris such as plastic bags, plastic and Styrofoam pieces, tar balls, balloons, and plastic pellets. Effects of consumption include interference in metabolism or gut function, even at low levels of ingestion, as well as absorption of toxic byproducts.

Several thousand vessels are involved in hook and line fishing for various coastal species, and catching turtles is not uncommon. Significant numbers of turtles are killed by gill and net fisheries off the eastern coast of central Florida.

*The
Sunshine State
Almanac
& Book of
Florida-
Related
Stuff*

VACATION

*T*ourism is big business in Florida. Some areas report that tourism contributes more to the local economy than business and industry combined. But vacationing in Florida isn't always cheap. What with the cost of transportation, hotels and motels, dining out, admissions, souvenirs, and other expenses, even budget travelers are feeling the pinch. One solution is knowing in advance where you're going and what's available when you get there. If you know the accommodation options and who charges what, what attractions are available in the area, what is free to visitors, where the best (and most reasonable) dining spots are located, and what events are planned during your stay, you can keep your expenses to a minimum.

You can get this type of money-saving information free from many Florida sources. Most popular tourist areas have a chamber of commerce and/or tourist office that will send you a couple of pounds of free vacationing material just for asking. Somewhere in that pile of vacation stuff, you'll find free road maps, hotel and restaurant guides, and what-to-do information. You can plan in advance what you're going to do when you get there. In some packages, you'll find coupons good for discounts and two-for-one admissions. Palm Beach County offers a discount booklet good for $500 worth of discounts at hotels, restaurants, and attractions. You can get a free copy by calling 800-554-7256.

You can locate the cheapest restaurants in the state in *Cheap Eats— 4,000+ Places To Eat On A Budget* (Pilot Books, 800-79-PILOT). The ultimate guide to accommodations is *Where To Stay In Florida, Volume Two* (Hunter Publishing, 908-225-1900), which lists more than 5,000 hotels, motels, resorts, bed and breakfasts, inns, and condominium rentals, with

information on facilities and rates. Pineapple Press (800-746-3275) publishes a series of Florida books that can introduce you to what's going on around the state: try *Visiting Small-Town Florida*; *Historic Traveler's Guide To Florida*; *Guide to the Lake Okeechobee Area*; and the series of *Exploring Wild Florida* books.

TOLL-FREE TOURIST INFORMATION

Call these toll-free telephone numbers to get free tourist information:

Beaches of Fort Walton	800-822-6877
Big Pine Key in the Florida Keys	800-872-3722
Brevard County	800-USA-1969
Cape Coral	800-226-9609
Florida Keys and Key West	800-A-KEYS
Fort Lauderdale-Broward County	800-322-8263
Kissimmee-St. Cloud	800-327-9159
Lauderdale by the Sea	800-699-6764
Lee County Tourist Council	800-533-4753
Lee Island Coast	800-533-4753
Marco Island and the Everglades	800-788-6272
Polk County	800-828-7655
St. Petersburg/Clearwater	800-345-6710
Sarasota and the Gulf Islands	800-522-9799

HOUSEBOATING—VACATIONING AFLOAT

If you're Florida-bound and looking for a unique vacationing experience, you can climb aboard a houseboat and cruise the waterways, stopping along the way to fish and swim and anchoring overnight in the mangroves or on the beach. The idea of exchanging highway travel for waterway travel appeals to many visitors, and living aboard a houseboat eliminates the cost of paying rent in hotels and motels and dining out. Rental houseboats come equipped with full kitchens, air conditioning, a couple of bedrooms, and some nautical extras like deck furniture and a marine radio. Renting a houseboat isn't particularly cheap, but you can rent one for about what you would spend on a first-class oceanfront hotel room or condo.

"The average family of four [or two couples vacationing together] can travel and live comfortably in our smallest model, the thirty-eight-footer," says Tim Garry of Houseboat Rentals of Florida in Marco Island. "The rental rates include everything you need to be comfortable. All houseboats are equipped with reliable Volvo engines, TVs, full kitchen and bath, sleeping accommodations for two to eight, swim platform, and a rubber dingy for off-the-boat exploring."

When you arrive at your destination each night, you can nudge the nose into a cove and tie up to a dock or a tree (for free) and settle down. With a well-placed cast of the fishing line, you might even pull dinner out of the ocean. If you like a little more civilization, you can pull into a marina and have dinner at a local restaurant. Rates vary with location and the size of the houseboat, but statewide averages for a 38-footer is $500 to $700 for three nights/four days or $1,000 to $1,300 for a full week, with discounts available for two people.

TEN PLACES TO RENT A HOUSEBOAT IN FLORIDA

Flamingo Marina
Flamingo Lodge
Flamingo 33034
800-600-3813

Florida Houseboat Rentals
21616 West Cape Coral
    Parkway
Cape Coral 33914
941-945-BOAT

*Holiday Cruise Houseboat
    Rentals*
16457 130th Avenue North
Jupiter 33478
800-862-8645 or 561-743-9286

Holly Bluff Marina
2280 Hontoon Road
DeLand 32720
800-237-5105 or 904-822-9992

Hontoon Landing
2317 River Ridge Road
DeLand 32720
800-248-2474 or 904-734-2474

*Houseboat Rentals of South
    West Florida*
4800 Molokai Drive
Naples 34112
941-775-2003

*Houseboat Vacations of the
    Florida Keys*
85944 Overseas Highway
Islamorada 33036
305-664-3111 or 305-664-4009

Houseboats of Florida
654 Bamboo Court
Marco Island 33937
800-880-9276
Miller's Suwannee Houseboats
Box 280
Suwannee 32692
800-458-BOAT or 904-542-
    7349

*Smilin' Island Houseboat
    Rentals*
Box 3003
Key Largo 33037
305-451-1930

YOUR PLACE OR MINE?—HOME EXCHANGE

If you're interested in visiting Florida, France, Japan, or South America (among other places), there are homeowners around the world interested in visiting your hometown, and, if you both agree, they'll move into your house and you'll move into theirs. It's called home exchanging, and thousands of families do it every year. If you live in Florida, you can vacation anywhere in the world. If you live anywhere in the world, you can vacation in Florida rent-free.

It's a great way to spend an extended period of time in one area and eliminate the high cost of staying in hotels and dining out while away from home. There are no hotel bills, and you can cook in. Some homeowners will let you use their cars or boats, too. If you have children, vacationing in a fully equipped home is more comfortable than squeezing into a hotel room, and there may be other children living next door. Your exchange partners will often introduce you to their neighbors— great local tour guides.

There are usually no limits on how many times you can exchange your home, so you can travel to one destination this year and another next year. It's not always necessary to have a home in a popular vacationing area. There are home exchangers who are only interested in staying in an area where relatives live or in using a home as a base from which to research a local college or job.

Swapping homes isn't for everybody, but for those who are adventurous and want to take advantage of the opportunity, there are options almost everywhere. During the planning stages, you're in contact with your exchange partner and you can work out the details.

To get started, list your home with one of the home exchange services listed below and explain what you have to offer, when it's available, and your preferred exchange locations. Once your home is listed in their catalog, you can thumb through the pages, find a home you're interested in, and contact the other homeowner. Addresses, phone numbers, and e-mail addresses are listed, so you'll have no trouble making contact.

If you're Florida-bound, currently

Spend a few weeks or months in a loft apartment in Paris.

there are home exchanges in Sanibel and Captiva, Fort Myers, Fort Lauderdale, Marathon in the Florida Keys, Sarasota, Treasure Island, and other locations. On Big Pine Key, you can move into a waterfront home with three bedrooms and two baths, boat dock, screened porch, and air conditioning. In Fort Myers, there's a two-bedroom, two-bath home with screened balcony overlooking the Gulf of Mexico. Located directly on the beach and across the street from a golf course, it's available anytime but December through April.

Looking over the European options, there are homes in France available in the town of Chamonix at the foot of Europe's highest mountain. One has three bedrooms and one and a half baths and is close to the borders of Italy and Switzerland. The owners are interested in staying on the northwest coast of Florida. In Paris, there's an apartment with a loft within walking distance of several Paris landmarks. It has three bedrooms, two baths, fireplace, Macintosh computer, and washer/dryer. A car is included.

If you're interested in this low-cost solution to the high cost of getting away from it all for an extended period of time, sign up and start packing your bags.

Discovery Holiday Exchange
Box 16
Tenterden, TN30 6ZT
England
44 (0) 7050 374 729

Fair Tours Home Exchange
Postfach 615
9001 St. Gallen, Switzerland
http://www.gn.apc.org/fair-tours

Home Exchange International
Box 30085
Santa Barbara, California 93130
http://www.west.net/
  ~prince/he

The International Home
  Exchange Network
385 Great Bay Woods
Newmarket, New Hampshire
  03857
603-659-2542
http://www.magicnet.net/home
  xchange/index.html

International Home
  Exchange Service
Box 3975
San Francisco, California 94119
415-535-3497

Internet Home Exchange
24 Big Rock Road
Rye Beach, New Hampshire
800-815-0395
http://www.nethom
  exchange.com

Teacher Swap Home Exchange Service (for teachers only)
Box 454
Oakdale, New York 11769
516-244-2845

BOB LEONARD'S LIST OF THE BEST HISTORIC HOTELS IN FLORIDA

The best historic inns in Florida are not necessarily the best value nor the most attractive inns, but they are nice places to stay when you're away from home. This list is for vacationers who want to share a sense of history and adventure while visiting a new area of Florida.

The **Florida House Inn** (22 South Third Street, Fernandina Beach 32034, 904-261-3300). This 11-room, 2-story inn is the oldest continuous (1857) hotel in Florida and was the staging area for travelers when Fernandina Beach was the Florida arrival point for ocean vessels. Today, you can sit in a whirlpool in the room where Cuban patriot Jose Martí plotted ways to recapture a cargo of Cuban-bound weapons confiscated by U.S. Customs. There are two restaurants, a cocktail lounge, and information available on touring the historic downtown district.

St. Francis Inn (279 St. George Street, St. Augustine 32084, 904-824-6068). In a city with dozens of fine bed and breakfast inns, this 1790 structure has had more notable visitors and tenants than any other. Van Wyck Brooks wrote the Pulitzer Prize–winning *The Flowering of New England* in the

delightful cottage. Rent it or one of the efficiencies (handy for couples) or one of the 11 rooms. Lots of restaurants nearby.

Belleview Mido Resort Hotel (25 Belleview Boulevard, Belleair 34617, 813-442-6171). This 1897 Henry B. Plant hotel overlooking Clearwater Bay is the last of the huge Victorian resorts built by the great railroad emperors. The 292-room structure (largest wooden hotel in the world) is surrounded by a golf course and offers a shuttle to the Gulf beaches.

The **Gibson Inn** (Market Street and Avenue C, Apalachicola 32329, 850-653-2191). This 1907 inn near

the Apalachicola River and the historic district has been popular with travelers and tourists for years. There are 30 rooms in the 3-story structure, as well as a restaurant.

The **Biltmore Hotel** (1200 Anastasia Avenue, Coral Gables 33134, 305-445-1926). The 1925 pride of George Merrick's booming development, this 278-room palace served as a military hospital in World War II. Now it has been restored to capture the excitement of the Florida Land Boom. The golf course location, the great dining areas, and what was once the world's largest pool are all top-notch. Expensive, but less costly than time machine travel.

Riverside Hotel (620 East Las Olas Boulevard, Fort Lauderdale 33301, 954-467-0671). At the turn of the century, when people like Frank Stranahan were trading with the Seminoles, this 109-room hotel on the New River was the place to stay. If you want to recapture those days, a stay here among the lush vegetation, only a short stroll away from Fort Lauderdale's Historic District and great cultural centers, is a good bet. Nice restaurant, refrigerators, and heated pool.

Herlong Mansion (402 Northeast Cholokka Boulevard, Micanopy 32667, 352-466-3322). This 12-room, 1845 manor house is just down the road from one of Central Florida's rustic antique villages. You'll recognize the streets where Michael J. Fox walked the pig in the film *Doc Hollywood*, but you might be shocked to see whirlpools and efficiencies in this old masterpiece.

BOB LEONARD'S LIST OF THE BEST LITERARY SITES IN FLORIDA

Here's a collection of Florida's hottest literary sites where writers of note resided, hung out, and contributed to the American literary scene:

Marjorie Kinnan Rawlings House in Cross Creek, located north of Ocala on County Road 325, four miles west of US 301. A state landmark, the farmhouse and citrus grove of the author of *The Yearling* and *Cross Creek* maintain the rural atmosphere of Rawlings' works. Her rustic typewriter sits on a well-lit tabletop, and her personal belongings fill the rooms. Open daily except for holidays, the attraction offers guided tours of the rooms of the one-story house for a small fee. You can walk around the property and take a stroll down dirt paths where you might even encounter a deer. Some of the locations from her books are within walking distance of the grounds. A restaurant down the road serves some of Rawlings' favorite dishes.

Marjorie Kinnan Rawlings is buried at the Island Grove Antioch Cemetery off US 301 on SE 3C Road. Her beach house stands at 6600 Broward Street in Crescent Beach, Florida.

The **Ernest Hemingway** House, 907 Whitehead Street, Key West. Despite the commercialization of Hemingway's presence in Key West and a fairly high admission price, fans of Hemingway will enjoy a visit to the 1851 stone Spanish colonial–style residence where the author lived from 1931 to 1961. It was in his studio above the pool house where Hemingway wrote *A Farewell to Arms, Death in the Afternoon,* and his only Florida-based novel, *To Have and Have Not.* Hemingway lived here with his second wife, Pauline, and sons Patrick and Gregory. The guides are knowledgeable, and the tour allows visitors to browse around Hemingway's artifacts. On the estate's grounds, one might encounter one of the many six-toed cats, descendants of Hemingway's favorite pets.

Zora Neale Hurston Sites in Eatonville, located north of Orlando off Interstate 4 on Florida Highway 438A. Born in 1901 in one of America's oldest all-black towns, Zora Neale Hurston moved to New York City, where she became a star of the Harlem Renaissance. Her famous novels, *Mules and Men* (1935) and *Dust Tracks on a Road* (1942), were the stories of her Florida childhood. Though her house, which stood on the block of West, Lime, People, and Lemon Streets, is gone, you can still capture the spirit of her writings while driving around the community. The Zora Neale Hurston National Museum of Fine Arts is located at 227 East Kennedy Boulevard near City Hall, where her father served as mayor.

Hurston lived at one time at 791 West King Street in St. Augustine. She died in poverty and is buried in the Garden of Heavenly Rest, North 17th Street and Avenue South, Fort Pierce. Her gravestone was donated 13 years after her death by Alice Walker, author of *The Color Purple.*

Harriet Beecher Stowe Home Site, 12447 Mandarin Road, Mandarin. The author of *Uncle Tom's Cabin* came to this small hamlet with her husband, Calvin, in the winter of 1867. They loved the area so much that they built a house, started a church, and organized many civic groups. During the days of steamboating on the St. Johns River, the Stowe homestead was a major attraction to vacationing Northerners. Sometimes Mrs. Stowe obliged by coming out on her dock. The house is gone, but across the street is the 1869

> *The Hemingway House has one of the few basements in south Florida.*

Community Club (once the Freedmen's Bureau office), where she volunteered. Down the road is a replica of the church the Stowes formed (the original was destroyed by a hurricane). The Carriage House of the Stowe estate remains as a converted residence. One of Florida's oldest towns, Mandarin is a restful and wonderful Victorian masterpiece.

Jack Kerouac Apartments, 5155 Tenth Avenue North and 5169 Tenth Avenue North, St. Petersburg. The great novelist (1922–1969) of the Beat generation came to Florida to be with his mother. Despite poor health, he remained a literary icon for *On the Road* (1957) and *The Dharma Bums* (1958). He avoided most public interviews and spent his days researching at the University of South Florida Library (Tampa) and sharing views with professors at the Wild Boar Tavern on North Nebraska Avenue. He died October 20, 1969, at St. Anthony's Hospital in St. Petersburg.

John D. MacDonald, Berth F18, Bahia Mar Yacht Basin, Fort Lauderdale. There never was a Berth F18 at Bahia Mar, but in honor of the most prolific American mystery writer in modern times, the people of Fort Lauderdale set up a berth and marker for detective Travis McGee and the Busted Flush.

In truth, MacDonald's main residence was down a private Siesta Key (Sarasota) lane, at 1430 Point Crisp. Further north on the key, at 4105 Shell Road, lived his writing pal MacKinlay Kantor, winner of the Pulitzer Prize for *Andersonville*.

Tennessee Williams House, 1431 Duncan Street, Key West. The great playwright (1911– 1983) came to Key West in the winter of 1949 and, after enjoying the company of the island's literary society for several years, purchased this humble residence. Williams fit into Key West's individualistic population very nicely and was a popular guest at the piano bar of the old Tradewinds Boarding House at DuVal and Caroline. The *Rose Tattoo* (1956) was his most notable local production.

Erskine Caldwell House, 1831 Oak Creek Drive, Dunedin. The Georgian author of *Tobacco Road* and *God's Little Acre* obtained this large house in the Spanish Oaks section as his longtime winter home.

Robert Frost Winter Homes, 8101 Southwest 53rd Avenue, South Miami, and 410 Caroline Street, Key West. The great American poet (1874–1963) loved his winter days in Florida. In Key West he lived in a small cottage behind the main house. He finally constructed Pencil Pines, his Miami winter residence.

> *There never was a Berth F18 at Bahia Mar; the people of Fort Lauderdale set up a berth and marker for detective Travis McGee and the Busted Flush.*

John Dos Passos House, 1401 Pine Street, Key West. The great historian (1896–1970) of *The 42nd Parallel* (1930) and *Mid-Century* (1961) was part of the Hemingway circle of writers in Key West.

The **Walter Farley** Collection, Venice Public Library, 300 Nokomis Avenue South, Venice. If you are in the Venice-Sarasota area and loved the book or movie *The Black Stallion*, you might want to visit the Farley Children's Wing, where Farley (1915–1989) left his Smith-Corona typewriter, his riding equipment, and the original manuscript of the popular novel.

KIDS' RESORTS AND SPECIAL PLACES

Florida has long been the family-fun destination of choice for people the world over. There are activities and attractions to suit all age groups, but some places specialize in catering to kids. So if you're planning a trip with kids in tow, give them a call, get information on the programs, and make your reservations.

Amelia Island Plantation
3000 First Coast Highway on
   Amelia Island
904-261-6161
Daily children's program, for ages 4 to 12, includes golf, tennis, and field trips. Children's evening dinner parties. Golf, tennis, racquetball, fishing, bicycling, swimming, and pristine beach. Villas include a kitchen, living room, and balcony.

Boca Raton Resort and Club
501 East Camino Real in Boca
   Raton
561-395-3000
Daily children's program for ages 3 to 17, plus tennis clinics on clay courts for kids as young as 6. Other amenities include a fitness center, private beach, marina, and championship golf. Discount packages available.

The Breakers
1 South County Road in Palm
   Beach
561-655-6611
This is a historic hotel featuring week-long summer camp packages for children, including programs on the culinary arts, etiquette, and money management. Daily supervised activities are available for kids 3 to 17.

Buena Vista Palace Resort and Spa
1900 Buena Vista Drive in Lake
   Buena Vista
800-327-2990
Arcade, kids' contests, organized games, clubhouse, water slide, and extensive children's programs year-round.

Cheeca Lodge in Islamorada in the
   Florida Keys
800-327-2888
Eco-tours to nearby islands, fishing, snorkeling, and scuba. Children's programs emphasizing outdoor activities for kids ages 6 to 12.

Club Med Sandpiper Bay
3500 Morningside Boulevard in
  Port St. Lucie
800-258-2533
Free child care for babies as young
  as four months old. On-site circus for older children features
  juggling, a flying trapeze, and
  clown lessons. Water skiing, sailing, tennis, and golf.

The Colony Beach & Tennis Resort
1620 Gulf of Mexico Drive on
  Longboat Key
941-383-6464
Tennis programs, shell crafts, scavenger hunts, and swimming in
  the pool for children ages 3 to 17.

Disney Hotels in Lake Buena Vista
407-934-7639
Children's programs and golf, tennis, hiking, and horseback riding.

Disney's Vero Beach Resort
9250 Island Grove Terrace in Vero
  Beach
800-359-8000
A Disney resort that delights parents, teens, even toddlers.
  Children's programs in the
  morning and evening for ages 6
  to 12. Spiral water slide and
  water attractions for youngsters.
  Teen program includes a day
  with a member of the Vero Beach
  Dodgers professional baseball
  team and a family trip to the
  game. Evening campfire and
  sing-along. For parents, scuba
  lessons, tennis, croquet, volleyball, a fitness center, massages,
  and bike rentals.

Doral Golf Resort and Spa
4400 Northwest 87th Avenue in
  Miami
305-592-2000
Daily children's program includes
  tennis, fishing, golf, arts, crafts,
  and games. For children ages 4 to
  12. Five golf courses, fifteen tennis courts, and spa and fitness
  center.

The Fontainebleau Hilton
4441 Collins Avenue in Miami
  Beach
305-538-2000
Volleyball, dancing, and a host of
  other fun activities for ages 5 to
  17. Teen programs feature beach
  olympics, kite flying, video
  games, and trips to Parrot Jungle,
  the Miami Seaquarium, and
  other attractions.

Four Seasons Resort
2800 South Ocean Boulevard in
  Palm Beach
561-582-2800
Free children's program for ages 3
  to 12 includes an assortment of
  activities such as water olympics,
  scavenger
  hunts,
  and crab
  races.
  There are
  water
  sports,
  golf, and
  tennis for
  parents,
  so every-
  body gets
  enter-
  tained.

Grenelefe Golf & Tennis Resort
3200 State Road 546 in Haines City
800-237-9549
Daily children's program with Ping-Pong, mini-golf, and basketball, plus private babysitting evenings. Daily children's program.

Hawk's Cay Resort and Marina
Mile Marker 61 on Duck Key in the Florida Keys
800-432-2242
Dive trips, glass-bottom boat tours, kayak excursions, parasailing, and lessons about the environment for kids and adults. The Island Pirates Club is for kids ages 5 to 13. Wednesday, Friday, and Saturday evening programs for kids include movie and pizza.

Hilton at Walt Disney World Village
1751 Hotel Plaza Boulevard in Lake Buena Vista
407-827-4000
Children's program nightly.

Holiday Inn Maingate East
5678 Irlo Bronson Memorial Highway in Kissimmee
800-366-5437
Daily children's program for kids ages 3 to 12. Children's private restaurant section and a tuck-in from the hotel's mascot.

Holiday Inn SunSpree Resort
715 South Gulfview Boulevard on Clearwater Beach
800-465-4329
Daily children's program for ages 3 to 12. Evening programs with dinner.

Holiday Inn SunSpree Resort 2711 South Ocean Drive on Hollywood Beach
800-237-4667
Children under 18 stay and eat free. Daily activities for children ages 5 to 12. Rooms have refrigerators and microwaves, and there's a nearby deli and convenience store.

Holiday Inn SunSpree Resort
1617 North First Street on Jacksonville Beach
800-590-4767
Children stay and eat for free. Children's program from Memorial Day through the end of August. Rooms include refrigerators and microwaves.

Holiday Inn SunSpree Resort
13351 State Road 535 in Lake
  Buena Vista
800-366-6299
Restaurant for kids, plus mascots to
  tuck them in at night. Daily
  supervised activities program for
  kids ages 2 to 12.

Hotel Royal Plaza
1905 Hotel Plaza Boulevard in Lake
  Buena Vista
800-248-7890
Free activities throughout the day
  for children ages 5 to 12. Private
  babysitting available.

Indian River Plantation
555 Northeast Ocean Boulevard in
  Stuart
800-444-3389
Beaches, an 18-hole golf course,
  tennis, swimming, and a popular
  kids' camp with children's daytime and evening programs.

Innisbrook Hilton Resort in
  Tarpon Springs
813-942-2000
Tennis, golf, movies, swimming,
  nature walks, and other supervised activities for ages 4 to 12.

Marco Island Hilton Beach Resort
560 South Collier Boulevard on
  Marco Island
941-394-5000
Daily and nightly children's programs. Health club, spa, and
  rentals of assorted boats, sails,
  and boards for water fun.

Marriott at Sawgrass Resort
1000 TPC Boulevard on Ponte
  Vedra Beach
904-285-7777
Children's program includes
  indoor activities and visits to the
  nearby beach. Open to children
  ages 3 to 12. Evening dinner program. Tennis, golf, a health club,
  and spa for parents.

Marriott's Bay Point Resort
4200 Marriott Drive on Panama
  City Beach
800-874-7105
Themed activities with kids' program for guests ages 5 to 12.
Marriott's Casa Marina Resort
1500 Reynolds Street in Key West
800-235-4837
Free children's program for kids
  ages 6 to 12.

Marriott's Orlando World Center
World Center Drive in Orlando
800-621-0638
Daily children's program, games,
  arts and crafts, and other activities for children ages 4 to 12.
  Tennis, mini-golf, golf, and pool
  complete with waterfalls and
  slides.

Marriott's Resort and Golf Club
400 South Collier Boulevard on
  Marco Island
800-438-4373
Educational program includes
  Everglades tour and a visit to the
  zoo or aquarium for ages 5 to 12.
  Wading pool, two playgrounds,
  and mini-golf.

Naples Bath and Tennis Club
4995 Airport Road North in Naples
800-225-9692
Day summer camp includes two
  hours of tennis lessons daily,
  swimming, volleyball, and more
  for kids ages 4 to 14.

Naples Beach Hotel & Golf Club
851 Gulf Shore Boulevard North in
  Naples
800-237-7600
Free Beach Klub daily for kids ages
  5 to 12. Golf, nature walks,
  shelling excursions, water sports,
  five restaurants, free transportation to downtown Naples, and an
  orchid house with more than
  3,000 plants. A free tennis, volleyball, and golf clinic every
  Saturday for kids ages 11 to 16.
  Children under 18 stay free with
  parents.

Palm Island Resort
7092 Placida Road in Cape Haze
800-824-5412
Daily hour-long activities on this
  private island include fishing,
  nature tours, shell hunts, bike
  riding, tennis, and water sports.

Pink Shell Beach Resort
275 Estero Boulevard on Fort
  Myers Beach
800-237-5786
Children's program features a different theme every day, plus a special
  teens' program.

Radisson Marco Island
600 South Collier Boulevard on
  Marco Island
800-333-3333
Daily children's program occupies
  youngsters 3 to 12. Activities for
  teens ages 12 to 16.

Radisson Sandpiper Beach Resort
6000 Gulf Boulevard in St.
  Petersburg
800-333-3333
Daily program for children ages 2
  to 12. Evening dinner programs.

Radisson Suite Resort on Sand Key
1201 Gulf Boulevard in Clearwater
800-333-3333
Shell hunts, face painting, volleyball daily for children ages 4 to
  12. Dinner program three
  evenings a week.

Registry Resort and Spa (formerly
  Bonaventure)
250 Racquet Club Road in Weston
800-247-9810
Daily children's program. Activities
  include games, swimming, and
  crafts. Lunch is included.
  Additionally, there's an evening
  dinner program, golf, tennis, racquetball, famous spa, and spa
  restaurant.

Ritz-Carlton
100 South Ocean Boulevard in
 Palm Beach
800-241-3333
Ritz Kids entertains guests ages
 four and up. Weekend evening
 pizza parties, golf, tennis, boating, and well-earned massages for
 parents.

Ritz-Carlton Amelia Island
Amelia Island Parkway on Amelia
 Island
800-241-3333
Ritz Kids for children 4 to 14 provides a full day or evening of
 games, crafts, and fun. Kids' programs include lunch or dinner.
 Golf, tennis, horseback riding,
 spa, and a cooking school for
 parents.

Ritz-Carlton Hotel
280 Vanderbilt Beach Road in
 Naples
941-598-3300
Free hour-long kids' program daily,
 plus Ritz Kids program. Themed
 dinner parties for kids every
 Saturday evening. Also, private
 babysitting for children of all
 ages.

Saddlebrook
5700 Saddlebrook Way in Wesley
 Chapel
813-973-1111
Kids Club features games for children to age 12, nature walks,
 crafts, and visits to nearby attractions.

Sandestin
 Beach
 Hilton
 Golf and
 Tennis
 Resort
4000
 Sandestin
 Boulevard
 South in
 Destin
904-267-
 9500

Children's program features swimming and games during the day
 and movies in the evening.

Sanibel Harbour Resort & Spa
19260 Harbour Pointe Drive in
 Sanibel Harbour
813-466-4000
Kids' Klub for ages 5 to 12 includes
 movies, pool games, and crafts
 daily and on weekend evenings.

Sanibel Inn
937 East Gulf Drive on Sanibel
 Island
800-554-5454
Programs for kids ages 3 and older
 include environmentally con-
 scious landscaping, bird and butterfly gardens, use of native vegetation, tennis, kayaking, and
 bicycling.

Seaside Cottage Rental Agency in
 Seaside
800-277-8696
Camp Seaside, for kids ages 5 to 12,
 includes daily art classes, croquet,
 archery, swimming, and more
 (with lunch). Evening programs
 Wednesday and Saturday.

Sheraton Bal Harbour Beach Resort
9701 Collins Avenue in Bal Harbour
800-999-9898
Harbour Kids Club teaches new crafts and games at various programs.

Sheraton Key Largo Resort
97000 South Overseas Highway in Key Largo
800-826-1006
Tennis, parasailing, water skiing, sailboarding, sailing, and diving at nearby John Pennekamp Coral Reef State Park. Daily children's programs include snorkeling lessons and hikes along a nature trail. For kids ages 5 to 12.

Sheraton Key West
South Roosevelt Boulevard in Key West
800-452-3224
Coral Reef Kids Club has Wednesday, Friday, and Sunday evening programs. Activities include face painting, storytelling, treasure hunts, and movies. Also offered during the day on weekends. Fitness center, bicycle rentals, free transportation downtown, snorkeling trips, and sunset sails.

Sonesta Beach Hotel
350 Ocean Drive in Key Biscayne
305-361-2021
Daily children's program features trips to area attractions, including MetroZoo and Seaquarium, for guests ages 5 to 13. Free, except for meals and admission to attractions. Jet skiing, kayaking, and tennis too.

South Seas Plantation on Captiva Island
800-227-8482
Daily and nightly programs for kids ages 3 to 11 include outdoor sports and lessons in local wildlife and conservation. New nature center with aquarium and touch tanks educates youngsters about marine life.

Sundial Beach Resort
1451 Middle Gulf Drive in Sanibel
800-237-4184
Daily children's program for kids ages 3 to 12 and Tiny Tots Tennis for kids as young as 4.

TradeWinds Resort
5500 Gulf Boulevard in St. Petersburg
800-345-6461
Activities for kids ages 3 to 12. Funniest Kids videos, dinners, crafts, and travel away from the hotel.

Westgate Lakes Resort
10000 Turkey Lake Road in Orlando
407-352-8051
Free children's program is offered Tuesday through Saturday for children
ages 4 to 12. Pizza parties Tuesday and Thursday evenings.

PACK YOUR BAGS

Florida has several cruise ports from which you can sail to exotic locations. If you need some help deciding what to take, here's a list of things you can consider taking on a casual cruise. If it's not casual, consider adding a tux for him and a floor-length evening gown for her.

Men	*Women*
Bathing suit	Bathing suit
Belt or suspenders	Belt
Sports jacket	Casual jacket
Suit	Suit
3 dress shirts	3 blouses
2 ties	
3 casual shirts	3 skirts
3 pairs of shorts	3 pairs of shorts
3 pairs of socks	3 pairs of socks
2 pairs of slacks	2 pairs of slacks
1 pair of dress pants	
1 pair of dress shoes	1 pair of dress shoes
1 pair of casual shoes	1 pair of casual shoes
1 pair of sneakers	1 pair of sneakers
Sweater	Sweater
Windbreaker	Windbreaker
Raincoat	Raincoat
Handkerchiefs	Handkerchiefs
Pajamas/robe/slippers	Lingerie/robe/slippers
1 set of underwear	1 set of underwear
for each day of the cruise	for each day of the cruise
Fanny pack	Fanny pack

Also
Camera/film/extra batteries, notebook or diary, pocket calculator, alarm clock, personal items (razor, soap, makeup, reading glasses, etc.)

THE MEDICAL POWER OF ATTORNEY

I f you're an unmarried couple (him/her, him/him, or her/her) planning a trip to Florida, you might want to carry a Medical Power of Attorney—just in case.

If you or your traveling partner is injured, hospitals won't allow an unrelated friend or companion to participate in treatment decisions unless you have this document. It gives each of you the power to speak on the other's behalf. Make two copies (one for you, one for the other party), fill in the names and an expiration date, and have the document notarized. To save you the $50 attorney's fee, we've reproduced the document below.

MEDICAL POWER OF ATTORNEY

KNOW ALL MEN BY THESE PRESENT THAT I

_____ OF _____

hereby   CONSENT   and   APPOINT

_____ as my true and lawful attorney-in-fact, for me and in my name to give medical authorization should I be incapacitated and not able to give same myself, and to bind me thereby in as full and ample a matter as I myself could do, where I personally authorized and signed the same.

I HEREBY AUTHORIZE my said attorney-in-fact to affix my seal to all and every kind of instrument which he/she may think in any way necessary or proper, hereby ratifying and confirming whatever my said attorney-in-fact may do with regard to the foregoing power conferred to him/her.

This POWER OF ATTORNEY shall be in full force and effect from _____ to _____.

_____

(Signature)

SIGNED, SEALED AND DELIVERED
IN THE PRESENCE OF:

_____

_____

BOB LEONARD'S LIST OF THE BEST-VALUE PLACES TO STAY AT DISNEY WORLD

This list assumes that you aren't a millionaire and don't want to stay outside the Walt Disney World area (where you could probably rent a three-room house with a pool for the cost of the best rooms at Disney). Here are some options:

Shades of Green (open only to active and retired military personnel and their families, the National Guard, and Department of Defense employees). The United States Armed Forces Recreation Center operates this 288-room former Disney Inn, and you'll find it hard—make that impossible—to beat their prices. The complex is surrounded by Disney's best golf courses, and a morning stroll will bring you a view of the local deer population. The only problem, besides the limited access, is that visitors are not eligible for Disney's transportation, so they have to rely on the hotel's little bus fleet.

Wilderness Lodge is one of the newer and less obvious hotels, a 7-story, 728-room complex with a rustic lakeside setting facing Fort Wilderness. Resembling a Great Northwest Park property, the lodge has two good-value, quality restaurantsm, Artist Point and the Whispering Canyon Cafe. It isn't as bustling as Grand Floridian and Contemporary and doesn't have the crowds of day visitors that are always disrupting the public facilities. The rooms are relatively small, but if you're gone all day, that's no big problem. You can take the boat to Magic Kingdom or a bus to Epcot and elsewhere.

Treetop Villas (villas at Disney Institute) are 3-bedroom octagonal houses on stilts. They are quite expensive but can accommodate eight to ten people, so you can split the cost. The Seasons Dining Rooms offer great values. You'll have to travel by car or by bus to get to the theme parks.

Dixie Landings. There are 2,048 mansion and bayou guest rooms in this huge complex, but unlike nearby Port Orleans and the less costly Caribbean Beach, Dixie Landings has a more rustic personality. The 2-story Alligator Bayou rooms by Ol' Man Island have wonderful tin roofs. The food court and Boatwright's Dining Hall are acceptable. The rooms are small, and the facilities, like all of Disney's moderately priced places, have family wear and tear. Bus transportation prevails, although a riverboat goes to Disney Village and Pleasure Island.

Fort Wilderness Resort and Campground. If you own or plan to rent an RV, this is one of the best campgrounds in the world. Seven hundred acres of preserved forest hide four hundred trailer and three hundred tent sites. Disney has a full program at Fort Wilderness, and recreational facilities are quite complete: heated pools, grocery, cafeteria, riding stables, canoes, boats, and fitness trail. If you get sites 100 to 500, you also get cable-TV hookup. Obviously, if you don't like camping, this isn't for you.

FLORIDA'S CHEAP! PLACES

If you're on a budget, living cheaply is one solution to the high cost of everything from dining out to having your car repaired. Florida has a variety of cheap places, and their owners are not shy about using cheap in the names so you know you're getting a bargain. There's Cheap Dave's Auto Salvage in Orlando and even a Cheap Cheapo Movers in Miami. Here are some other "cheap" businesses that would appreciate your patronage.

Cheap Charlie's Antique Emporium in Orlando, 407-841-2923
Cheap Charlie's Wrestling Supplies in Miami, 305-279-4920
Cheap Frills in New Port Richey, 813-848-1522
Cheap J & R in Fort Lauderdale, 954-741-5154
Cheap Jack Dollar Store in Mount Dora, 352-735-4715
Cheap Printing in Palm Coast, 904-445-5110
Cheap Shot Sporting Goods in Miami, 305-225-5300
Cheap Travel in St. Augustine, 904-825-1911
Cheap-Es Auto Parts and Salvage in Apopka, 407-884-9481
Cheaper Beeper in Miami, 305-651-0014
Cheaper Beepers USA in Fort Lauderdale, 954-748-3384
Cheaper Car Sales in Daytona Beach, 904-238-0620
Cheaper Carpet in Tampa, 813-238-4724
Cheaper Costs Auto Repair in Fort Lauderdale, 954-522-1088
Cheaper Mini Movers in Lauderdale Lakes, 954-486-5528
Cheaper Mobile Home Movers in Perry, 904-584-2492
Cheaper Towing in Ocala, 352-622-5886
Cheapo Auto Glass in North Miami, 305-681-1010
Cheapo Taxi in Marathon, 305-743-7420
Cheapscapes in Naples, 941-591-2071
Cheapside Discount Distributions in Hollywood, 954-923-5486
Cheapskates in Fort Lauderdale, 954-748-4411

HOT-AIR BALLOONING

Viewing Florida from the sky is a unique way to see the state. Hot-air balloon rides will do the trick. Hot-air balloons are baskets dangling beneath a balloon (called an envelope) that drift with the wind. The balloon is inflated by spreading it out on the ground and using a small fan to blow air into the envelope. A burner is used to heat the air inside, and as the heat rises, the balloon lifts off the ground. The balloon can have a volume of one hundred thousand cubic feet and be sixty to seventy feet in length.

You can't steer a hot-air balloon, so you basically go where it wants to go. Since winds blow in different directions at different altitudes, the balloon can rise and fall while the pilot looks for winds blowing in a specific direction. The best time to get off the ground is early in the morning, just after sunrise, or a couple of hours before sunset. At these times the winds are fairly stable, and the balloon tends to go straight up rather than left and right. Of course, you don't want to drift out to sea, so keeping an eye on the wind direction is one of the most important things to do while hot-air ballooning. Ideally, you'll stay aloft for an hour or two, depending on how much propane is carried aboard to keep the envelope inflated. When the trip is over, you come down gently and the balloon is recovered by a chase team that has been following the balloon's progress from the ground.

The Balloon Federation of America grew out of this country's balloon movement in 1961. It's the largest balloon organization in the world, with nearly 5,000 members in the U.S. and 25 foreign countries. If ballooning sounds like your kind of up-in-the-air adventure, contact Mark Chapdelaine at Balloons Over Florida (561-334-9393 or 800-887-2965).

TRAVELING WITH YOUR PET

Are you traveling to or from Florida with your pet or taking your pet on vacation? Here are some traveling tips from the experts:

First, consider leaving pets at home. Most hotels and resorts don't allow pets, so this will limit where you can stay during your trip. But if you insist on taking your pet, when traveling by car, use a carrier in the back seat. If you have rear seat belts, secure the carrier. You can let the pet out of the cage occasionally if there is a second person in the car who can supervise the release while you drive. Take along your pet's toys. If the pet gets carsick, a little honey can ease its discomfort. Take along some cleanup supplies just in case.

Work out a system when one person is out of the car and the other person is in the car with the pet loose. Knock on the window when you return so the person inside the car can hold the pet when you open the door.

Exercise the pet occasionally while traveling and try to give the pet a good dose of exercise before you leave. Hopefully, the animal will get tired and sleep.

If your hotel or motel allows pets, keep the pet in a carrier or on a leash when you're outside the room. Carry a flashlight for night walks and some sealed plastic bags for cleanup. You can also put a couple of ice cubes in a plastic bag, and when they melt, voilà—water!

Some airlines will allow pets to fly with you in the cabin as long as the carrier fits underneath the seat.

TOLL-FREE FLORIDA (AGAIN!)

Pounds of brochures, booklets, pamphlets, and directories are available from any of the regional tourist offices around the state. The offices listed below not only provide free literature, but the phone call is free as well.

Big Pine Key and the Lower Keys Chamber of Commerce on Big Pine Key
800-872-3722

Bradenton
800-4-MANATEE

Chamber of Commerce of Cape Coral
800-226-9609

Clearwater/St. Petersburg
800-345-6710

Daytona Beach Area Convention and Visitors Bureau
800-544-0415

Hollywood Florida Chamber of Commerce
800-231-5562

Lauderdale by the Sea Chamber of Commerce
800-699-6764

Lee County and Fort Myers Visitor and Convention Bureau
800-237-6444

Manatee and Palmetto Convention Bureau
800-248-4299

Miami Convention and Visitors Bureau
800-4-MIAMI

New Smyrna Beach, Edgewater, and Oak Hill Chamber of Commerce
800-541-9621

North Palm Beach Tourism Advisory Group
800-854-3747

Okaloosa County and Fort Walton Beach Tourist Development Council
800-322-3319

Orlando
800-643-9493

Orange County Convention Bureau
800-345-9845

Panama City Chamber of Commerce
800-553-1330

Pensacola Beach Chamber of Commerce
800-635-4803

Sarasota Area Visitors Service
800-522-9799

South Walton Tourist Development Council
800-822-6877

Tallahassee Area Convention and Visitors Bureau
800-628-2866

Tampa Visitors Information
800-826-8358

Volusia County
800-541-9621

AIRLINES SERVICING FLORIDA

Air Canada	800-776-3000
Air South	800-247-7688
American Airlines/American Eagle	800-433-7300
Avianca Airlines	800-284-2622
Aviateca Airlines	800-327-9832
Bahamas Air	800-222-4262
Canadian Holidays	800-666-1401
Canadian Airlines International	800-426-7000
Carnival Airlines	800-824-7386
Comair	800-354-9822
Continental Airlines/Continental Express	800-525-0280
Delta Airlines	800-221-1212
Eastwind Airlines	800-644-3592
Gulfstream International Airlines	800-992-8532
L.T.U.	800-888-0200
Laker Airways Ltd.	800-331-6471
Midway Airlines	800-446-4392
Midwest Airlines	800-452-2022
Northwest Airlines	800-225-2525
Sprint Airlines	800-772-7117
Sun Country Airlines	800-359-5786
Trans World Airlines	800-221-2000
United Airlines	800-241-6522
USAir and USAir Express	800-428-4322

TOURIST FACTS

Give or take a few million, Florida had about 43 million visitors in 1997. One of ten came from the New York area. Visitors arriving by air usually vacation in south Florida, while car travelers choose the Northwest area. Air visitors spend an average of a $110 a day, while car visitors spend just under $64 a day.

Five Touristy Things to Do in Central Florida:
1. Head for the sky on a balloon tour with Aerial Adventures of Orlando in Kissimmee (407-944-1070), Orange Blossom Balloons in Lake Buena Vista (407-239-7677), or Rise and Float Balloon Tour in Orlando (407-352-8191).
2. Go skydiving with Phoenix World Skydive Center in Lake Wales (941-678-1003).
3. Take a cruise with Riverside Romance (800-423-7401) or St. Johns River Cruises (407-330-1612), both in Sanford.
4. Take an airboat tour at Black Hammock Fish Camp at Winter Springs

(407-365-2201) or Gator Ventures Airboat Rides at Oviedo (407-365-3976).

5. Head off on a nature tour with Swampland Tours in Okeechobee (941-467-4411).

Twelve Touristy Things to Do in East Central Florida:
1. Drift up in the clouds over Tampa with Big Red Balloon by Fantasy Flights (800-44-TAMPA).
2. Take a dinner cruise with Casablanca Cruises in Tarpon Springs (813-937-2274).
3. Belly up to the felt tables on a casino cruise with Tarpon Springs Cruises in Tarpon Springs (813-937-2274) or with Empress Cruise Lines in St. Petersburg (800-486-8600).
4. Dine out aboard the Lady Anderson in St. Petersburg (800-533-2288) or the Starlite Majesty in Clearwater (813-462-2628).

5. Put on your hiking shoes and take a nature tour at the Myakka State Park and Wilderness Preserve in Sarasota (941-365-0100).
6. Sign up for a paddle-boat cruise on The Starlight Princess in Tampa (813-595-1212), the Seafood Shack Showboat in Cortez (941-794-3766), or the Marina Jack II dinner boat in Sarasota (941-366-9255).
7. Paddle off on a canoe tour with Canoe Outpost in Wimauma (813-634-2228).
8. Roar off on an airboat tour from Perico Harbor in Bradenton (941-730-1001).
9. Take an overnight sailing trip to Venice or Egmont Key out of Regatta Point Marina in Palmetto (941-746-4288), or take a half- or full-day cruise out of Marina Drive in Holmes Beach (941-887-1977).
10. Ride the rails on a diesel locomotive from the Florida Gulf Coast Railroad Museum in Parrish (941-653-4984).
11. Tour the Manatee River on a pontoon boat out of Regatta Point Marina in Palmetto (941-722-5675).
12. Try some backwater fishing and a sightseeing trip with Snead Island Chargers (941-722-5675).

Eight Touristy Things to Do in Northeast Florida:
1. Take a historic walking tour at the Amelia Island Museum of History (904-751-8116).
2. Sail off on a dinner and casino cruise with Star Dancer Dinner and Casino Cruises (904-277-8980).
3. Go sightseeing aboard the St. Augustine Sight-Seeing Train (904-829-6545), or take a sightseeing trip on the water with St. Augustine Scenic Cruise (904-824-1806).
4. Visit the brewery at Busch Brewery Tours in Jacksonville (904-751-8116).
5. Ride the water taxi with Water Taxi and Boardwalk Tours in Jacksonville (904-396-4900).
6. Gamble the night away on a casino cruise with LaCruise in Jacksonville (800-752-1778).
7. Take a paddleboat tour with Riverwalk Cruise Lines in San Marco (904-389-0797).
8. Head for the sky on a balloon tour with Outdoor & Balloon Adventures in Jacksonville (904-739-1960).

Ten Touristy Things to Do in Northwest Florida:
1. Shop and look at the live animals (including alligators) at Alvin's Big Island & Tropical Department Store in Panama City Beach (850-234-3048).
2. Head for a tour of Shell Island and the lagoons off the Gulf of Mexico on a do-it-yourself pontoon boat ride with Ragin' Rentals in Panama City Beach (850-234-0294).
3. Take a sightseeing tour with Island Star Sightseeing (850-235-2809), or hop aboard the glass-bottom boat tour out of Treasure Island Marina (850-234-8944), both in Panama City Beach.
4. Go parasailing with Coastal Parasailing in Panama City Beach (850-233-0914).
5. Take a nature tour at Florida Caverns State Park in Marianna (850-482-9598).
6. Ride the glass-bottom boats at Wakulla Springs State Park in Wakulla Springs (850-922-3633).
7. Tour The Zoo in Gulf Breeze (850-932-2229).
8. Take a historic tour with Mission San Luis in Tallahassee (850-487-3711), or sign up for a guided tour with Tours with a Southern Accent

(800-365-9108), Gulf Coast Excursions (904-984-5895), and Lake Talquin Tours (904-877-3198).

9. Take a dive tour with Hydrospace Dive Shop in Panama City Beach (850-234-3063).

10. Fly off on a pontoon airplane for a sky-view of the Panhandle (850-234-1532).

Eight Touristy Things to Do in Southeast Florida:

1. Take a luxury cruise aboard Palm Beach Cruise Line in Riviera Beach (800-841-7447), tour the Intracoastal Waterway in Palm Beach (407-930-8294), or go sightseeing on the Intracoastal in Palm Beach Gardens (407-775-2628).

2. Take a seaplane ride with Island Air Tours in Palm Beach.

3. Tour an authentic Native American village with the Hallapattee Seminole Indians in Boynton Beach (407-734-4800).

4. Take a nature tour at Loxahatchee National Wildlife Refuge in the northern Everglades (407-734-8303).

5. Hop aboard an airboat for a water tour with Loxahatchee Airboat Rides, climb aboard the Louie's Lady Riverboat for a trip along the Intracoastal Waterway and Jupiter Island (407-744-5550), or sail on a catamaran, *Manatee Queen*, out of Jupiter for an afternoon, evening, or sunset cruise (407-744-2191).

6. Ride a swamp buggy through the Everglades and Seminole Indian Park in Seminole (305-257-3737), or visit the Miccosukee Indian Village and take an airboat ride in Miami (305-223-8380).

7. Go sightseeing aboard the Moby Duck amphibious vessel along the Intracoastal Waterway and beaches (954-777-DUCK), take a casino cruise with Hollywood Casino Cruises out of Hollywood (954-929-3800), or explore our sensitive ecology aboard a narrated boat ride with Tidewater Tours (954-929-5353).

8. Take a reef tour at Biscayne National Underwater Park in Homestead (305-230-1100), sign up for a tour of the Keys with Emerald Transportation in Key Largo (305-852-1468), or tour the Everglades by boat from Key Largo (305-451-4540).

WHAT'S GOING ON AROUND FLORIDA IN JANUARY

Bunnell
Tree City U.S.A.
904-437-7500

Coconut Creek
Carnival in the Snow
954-968-3880

Eatonville
Zora Neale Hurston
  Day
407-647-3307

Fellsmere
Frog Leg Festival
407-571-0116

Fort Myers
Southwest Florida and
  Lee County Fair
941-543-8368

Key West
Monroe County Fair
305-296-2454

Miami Beach
Art Deco Weekend
305-672-2014

Naples
Collier County Fair
941-455-1444

New Smyrna
Indian River Native
904-424-0860

Oklawaha
Ma Barker vs. the FBI
352-687-3660

Palatka
African-American
  Festival
904-325-9901

Palmetto
Manatee County Fair
941-722-1639

Plantation Key
Upper Keys Seafood
  Festival
305-852-0643

St. Petersburg
International Folk Fair
813-327-7999

St. Petersburg
Native American
  Powwow
800-683-7800

Sarasota
International Circus
  Festival
941-351-8888

West Palm Beach
South Florida Fair
561-793-0333

White Springs
Stephen Foster Day
904-758-1555

Winter Haven
Florida Citrus Festival
941-967-3175

WHAT'S GOING ON AROUND FLORIDA IN FEBRUARY

Brighton
Arts, Crafts, and
   Rodeo
941-763-4128

Brooksville
Heritage Days
352-799-0129

Coconut Grove
Arts Festival
305-447-0401

Cortez
Fishing Festival
941-794-1249

Crystal River
Manatee Festival
352-795-3149

Dade City
Pasco County Fair
352-567-6678

Davie
Florida Westfest
954-581-0790

Eatonville
Zora Neale Hurston
   Day
407-647-3307

Eustis
Washington's Birthday
352-357-3434

Everglades City
Seafood Festival
941-695-3941

Fort Lauderdale
Greek Festival
954-761-3378

Fort Lauderdale
Irish Fest
800-882-3746

Fort Lauderdale
Sistrunk Historical
   Festival
954-357-7514

Fort Myers
Edison Festival of
   Lights
941-334-2999

Fort Myers
Greek Festival
941-481-2099

Fort Myers
Southwest Florida and
   Lee County Fair
941-543-8368

Fort Pierce
Saint Lucie County
   Fair
561-464-2910

Grant
Grant Seafood Festival
407-723-8687

Hialeah
Annual Spring Festival
305-828-9898

Hollywood
Florida Renaissance
   Festival
954-776-1542

Hollywood
Seminole Powwow and
   Rodeo
800-683-7800

Homosassa
Rodeo
352-247-2332

Jacksonville
Scottish Highland
   Games
904-641-0650

Key West
Festival of the Seas
305-296-2454

Kissimmee
Osceola County Fair
407-846-6046

La Belle
Swamp Cabbage
   Festival
941-675-0125

Lake Buena Vista
Mardi Gras
407-934-7781

Lake City
Battle of Olustee
904-758-1312

Lake Mary
Renaissance Festival
407-380-9151

Lake Wales
International Carillon
  Festival
941-676-1408

Lake Wales
Mardi Gras
941-638-2686

Lakeport
Sour Orange Festival
941-946-1627

Moore Haven
Chalo Nitka Festival
941-946-0440

Mount Dora
Mount Dora Art
  Festival
352-383-0880

New Smyrna Beach
Black Heritage Festival
904-428-6225

Ocala
Youth Fair
352-629-1255

Orlando
Central Florida Fair
407-295-3247

Ortona
Cane Grinding Festival
941-946-0818

Plant City
Florida Strawberry
  Festival
800-448-2672

Rubonia
Mardi Gras Festival
941-729-8397

St. Augustine
Menendez Day
800-653-2489

Sarasota
Medieval Fair
941-351-8497

Sarasota
Project Black Cinema
941-953-6424

Sarasota
Sunshine State
  Bluegrass Festival
941-639-3646

Sebring
Highlands County Fair
941-382-2255

Sebring
Roaring '20s Festival
941-471-5104

Tampa
Gasparilla Pirate Fest
813-273-6495

Tampa
Florida State Fair
813-621-7821

Venice
Italian Feast and
  Carnival
941-493-6344

West Palm Beach
Seafood Festival
561-655-5522

Ybor City
Fiesta Day
813-248-3712

Zolfo Springs
Pioneer Days
941-773-2161

WHAT'S GOING ON AROUND FLORIDA IN MARCH

Arcadia
De Soto County Fair
941-494-5678

Auburndale
Bluegrass Champion-
  ships
941-967-4307

Barberville
Florida Multicultural
  Festival
904-749-2959

Bonita Springs
Tomato Seafood
  Festival
941-334-6881

Boynton Beach
Great American Love
  Affair
561-375-6240

Bradenton
Heritage Days and
  Festival
941-741-4070

Bradenton
Hunsader Farms
  Spring Festival
941-727-7580

Brooksville
Spring in the Woods
  Festival
352-683-3700

Bunnell
Cracker Day
904-437-7464

Bushnell
Sumter County Fair
352-793-2750

Cape Coral
Celebrate Cape Coral
941-549-6900

Chokoloskee
Seminole Indian Day
941-695-2989

Clewiston
Hendry County Fair
941-983-9282

Coconut Creek
Tri-City Fair
305-972-0818

Davie
Florida West Fair
800-962-2420

Daytona Beach
Bike Week
904-255-0981

Englewood
Spring Celebration
941-474-3262

Estero
Koreshan
  Archaeological Fair
941-992-0311

Eustis
Heritage Days
352-357-8555

Fanning Springs
Suwannee River Fair
352-486-5131

Floral City
Strawberry Festival
352-726-2801

Fort Myers
Buckingham Historical
  Days
941-694-7116

Fort Myers
Spring Festival
561-879-6035

Fort Pierce
Saint Lucie County
  Fair
561-464-2910

Fort Pierce
Spring Craft Fair
407-860-0092

Fort Pierce
Treasure Coast Blues
  Festival
561-468-3488

Fort Walton Beach
Cajun Crawfish
  Festival
904-243-3585

Fort Walton Beach
International Festival
904-244-8191

Haines City
Haines City Heritage
  Days
941-422-3751

High Springs
Heritage Days
352-454-4201

Homestead
Asian Arts Festival
305-595-1353

Homosassa Springs
The Florida Gathering
813-272-3473

Indiantown
Spring Festival
561-597-4555

Inverness
Citrus County Fair
904-726-2993

Jacksonville
Festival and Feast
904-630-5320

Key West
Conch Blowing
  Contest
305-294-9501

Kissimmee
Annual Bluegrass
  Festival
800-473-7773

Lake Placid
Pioneer Week
941-465-1771

Lake Worth
Finlandia Days
407-586-3713

Largo
Renaissance Fair
612-445-7361

Lehigh
Acres Spring Festival
941-368-4825

Live Oak
Suwannee County Fair
904-362-7366

Live Oak
Suwannee Spring
  Festival
904-364-1683

Marathon
Seafood Festival
305-743-5417

Miami
Calle Ocho
305-644-8888

Miami
Carnaval
305-644-8888

Miami
Dade County Youth
  Fair
305-223-7060

Miami
Italian Renaissance
  Festival
305-757-5136

Milton
Scratch Ankle
904-623-6726

Moore Haven
Chalo Nitka
941-946-0440

Mount Dora
Antique Boat Festival
352-383-2165

Mulberry
Mulberrry Jubilee
941-425-4414

Naples
Seafood Festival
941-434-3238

Ocala
Brick City Festival
352-629-5801

Ocala
Ocala Cracker Country
  Days
352-236-5401

Okeechobee
Speckled Perch Festival
941-763-6464

Oldsmar
Oldsmar Day Festival
813-855-4233

Orange City
Frontier Days
904-668-7799

Orlando
Central Florida Fair
407-295-3247

Palatka
Azalea Festival
904-328-0098

Palatka
Putnam County Fair
904-329-0318

Pinellas Park
Pinellas County Fair
813-541-6941

Plantation
Scottish Festival and
  Games
305-757-6730

Punta Gorda
Bluegrass and National
  Clogging
941-369-3646

Punta Gorda
Seafood Festival and
  Boat Show
941-369-1188

Safety Harbor
Seafood Festival
813-725-1562

St. Augustine
St. Johns County Fair
904-824-8142

St. Petersburg
Family Day Festival
813-384-0027

St. Petersburg
International Folk Fair
813-327-7998

Sanford
St. Johns River Festival
407-322-2212

Sanibel
Shell Fair
941-472-2155

Sarasota
Sarasota County Fair
941-365-0818

Sarasota
Sarasota Jazz Festival
941-366-1552

Sebring
Seminole and Pioneer
  Festival
941-385-4262

Sneads
Golden Daze River
  Festival
904-663-4767

Sorrento
Derby Day
352-383-8801

Spring Hill
Italian Festival and
  Carnival
352-596-5125

Tallahassee
FAMU Spring Sports
  Carnival
904-599-5365

Tallahassee
Food and Fun Fair
904-878-3247

Titusville
Bluegrass Festival
407-267-4198

Wauchula
Hardee County Fair
941-773-2164

Winter Park
Annual Sidewalk
  Festival
407-672-6390

Zephyrhills
Founders Day
813-782-1913

WHAT'S GOING ON AROUND FLORIDA IN APRIL

Belle Glade
Black Gold Jubilee
407-996-0100

Bradenton
Florida Heritage
 Festival
941-747-2072

Bradenton
Plastic Bottle Boat
 Regatta
941-747-2072

Bradenton
Seafood Festival
941-747-2372

Bronson
Annual Hoedown
352-486-1003

Brooksville
Hernando County Fair
352-796-4552

Bunnell
Flagler County Fair
904-437-7464

Callahan
Timberfest
904-879-1441

Cape Coral
Best of Southwest
 Festival
941-574-0801

Carrabelle
Waterfront Festival
904-697-2885

Chiefland
Ol' Fashioned River
 Party
352-493-6072

Clearwater
Sun 'n Fun Festival
813-562-4800

Clewiston
Brown Sugar Festival
941-98-8405

Coral Gables
Merrick Festival
305-447-9299

Crescent City
Annual Catfish Festival
904-698-2114

Dade City
Will McLean Music
 Festival
352-465-7208

Debary
Debary Festival
407-668-6843

DeLand
Balloon Rally
904-736-1010

DeLand
Cracker Day
904-822-5778

DeFuniak Springs
Chautauqua Festival
904-892-9494

Dunedin
Highland Games
813-733-6240

Dunnellon
Boomtown Days
352-489-2320

Eustis
Lake County Fair
352-357-7111

Fort Lauderdale
Seafood Festival
954-463-4431

Fort Lauderdale
South Florida Black
   Film Festival
954-698-5680

Gainesville
Farm and Forest
   Festival
352-334-3288

Green Cove
Springs Clay County
   Fair
904-284-1615

Hastings
Potato and Cabbage
   Festival
904-692-1420

Holiday
Cracker Festival
813-849-1627

Immokalee
Annual Harvest
   Festival
941-657-3237

Jacksonville
River City Kids Day
904-2022566

Jacksonville
World of Nations
   Celebration
904-630-3520

Jacksonville Beach
Cajun Crawfish
   Festival
904-378-0708

Jacksonville Beach
Festival Weekend
904-247-6268

Jacksonville Beach
Springing the Blues
   Festival
904-249-3972

Key West
Conch Republic
   Independent
   Celebration
305-296-0213

Kissimmee
Jazz Festival
407-846-6257

Leesburg
Spring Festival
352-365-0053

Live Oak
Spring Bluegrass
   Festival
904-364-1683

Live Oak
Suwannee River
   Country Jam
904-364-1683

Madison
Down Home Day
904-973-2788

Melbourne
Vietnam Vets Reunion
407-632-4928

Miami
Area Dade Heritage
   Days
305-358-9572

Miami
Springs River Cities
   Festival
305-887-1515

Milton
Santa Rosa County
   Fair
904-623-5055

Orlando
International Fringe
   Festival
407-648-0077

Palmetto
Children's Parade
941-747-2072

Pensacola
Reggae Festival
904-434-6211

Pompano Beach
Seafood Festival
954-941-2940

Punta Gorda
Punta Gorda Days
941-766-3482

Punta Gorda
Sons of Italy Festival
941-639-2222

St. Augustine
Easter Parade
904-829-2992

St. Augustine
Minorcan Day
904-829-2992

St. Petersburg
Festival of States
813-898-3654

St. Petersburg
Mainsail Art Festival
813-893-7734

St. Petersburg
Pioneer Jamboree
813-866-6401

Seminole
Bluegrass and Arts
   Festival
813-392-3331

Starke
Bradford County
904-224-5012

Tallahassee
Food and Fun Fair
904-878-3247

Tallahassee
FSU Flying High
   Circus
904-644-6277

Tallahassee
Hot Air Balloon
   Classic
904-878-0892

Tallahassee
Smokin' Big Bend
   B-B-Q
904-414-9800

Tampa
Storytelling Festival
813-931-2106

Tarpon Springs
Arts and Crafts
   Festival
813-937-109

Titusville
Indian River Festival
407-267-3036

Valparaiso
Saturday in the Park
904-678-2615

Waldo
Waldo Railroad Days
904-468-1001

West Palm Beach
Multicultural
   Storytelling
561-659-5980

West Palm Beach
Sunfest
561-659-5992

Wewahitchka
Tupelo Festival
850-397-4331

White Springs
Stephen Foster
   Storytelling Festival
904-397-4331

WHAT'S GOING ON AROUND FLORIDA IN MAY

Atlantic Beach
Dancing in the Streets
904-247-5800

Arcadia
Watermelon Festival
941-494-5131

Archer
Awolowo
352-495-9305

Archer
Haile Homestead
  Spring Gala
352-495-1044

Archer
Levy-Yulee Day
352-495-1044

Barberville
Wheels in Motion
904-749-2959

Bostwick
Blueberry Festival
904-325-7016

Bristol
Gregory Home Tour
904-643-2074

Bunnell
May Music Festival
904-437-7767

Chiefland
Spring Festival
352-493-1679

Chipley
Historic Day
904-638-6130

Clearwater
Fun 'n Sun Festival
813-562-4800

Cocoa Beach
Beach Fest
407-452-5352

Coconut Grove
Coconut Grove Bed
  Race
305-624-3714

Coconut Grove
Goombay Festival
305-372-9966

Crestview
Old Spanish Trail
  Festival
904-689-6783

Dade City
Native American
  Powwow
352-583-3388

Destin
Mayfest
904-837-6241

Downing
Park Spring Fair
904-658-5200

Fanning Springs
Red Belly Day
352-498-3310

Fernandina Beach
Isle of Eight Flags
  Shrimp Festival
904-261-3248

Fort Lauderdale
Cajun/Zydeco
  Crawfish Festival
305-761-5934

Fort Myers
Israel Family
  Independence Day
941-481-4449

Fort Myers
Offshore Grand Prix
  Festival
941-454-7500

Fort Walton Beach
Billy Bowlegs Festival
904-244-8191

Fort Walton Beach
Firefighters Fun
  Family Fly-In
904-244-5373

Green Cove
Spring Memorial Day
   Festival
904-529-2200

Havana
Old-Time Havana Day
904-539-5017

High Springs
Pioneer Days
904-454-3120

Homestead
Great Sunrise Balloon
   Race
305-275-3317

Jacksonville
Kuumba African Arts
   Festival
904-353-2270

Jacksonville Beach
Teen Fest
904-249-3868

Jay
Harvest Festival
904-675-6823

Juno Beach
Turtle Time Fest
561-627-8280

Jupiter
Seafare
561-747-6639

Korona
Country Sunshine
   Festival
904-437-6183

Lake City
Alligator Festival
904-758-1310

Lakeland
Mayfaire-by-the-Lake
941-688-7743

Largo
Living History Week
813-582-2123

Live Oak
Balloon Classic
904-364-1683

Live Oak
Suwannee Bicycle
   Festival
904-362-3071

Marathon
Pirates Festival
800-262-7284

Marianna
Spring Jubilee
904-482-2523

Masaryktown
Arts, Crafts, & Music
   Festival
813-849-2020

Melbourne Beach
Founders Day Festival
407-724-5861

Miami
Roots & Culture Fest
305-751-4222

Miami Area
Dade Heritage Days
305-358-9572

Navarre Beach
Annual Fun Festival
904-939-3267

Opa-Locka
Arabian Nights Festival
305-758-4166

Ormond Beach
Tomokafest
904-676-4050

Oviedo
Taste of Oviedo
407-365-6500

Ozello
Pioneer Day
352-795-1547

Pace
Scottish Festival
904-995-4553

Palatka
Blue Crab Festival
904-325-4406

Palm Bay
Palm Bay Days
407-951-9998

Panacea
Blue Crab Festival
904-984-5733

Panama City
Annual Festival of the
   Arts
904-271-9505

Pensacola
Annual Beach Lobster
  Fest
904-9343108

Pensacola
Crawfish/Creole
  Festival
904-433-6512

Pensacola
Fiesta of Five Flags
904-433-6512

Pensacola
Jammin'
  Jumbalaya
  Festival
904-968-
  2601

Pensacola
Springfest
904-469-
  1069

Pensacola Beach
Cinco de Mayo
800-635-4803

Plant City
Pioneer Days
813-757-9236

Punta Gorda
Florida Frontier Days
941-639-3777

St. Augustine
Centuries of
  Celebration
800-OLD-CITY

St. Augustine
Day in the Park
904-824-1761

St. Augustine
Drake's Raid
904-824-9823

St. Augustine
Nautical Festival
904-824-9111

St. Augustine Beach
Beach Bash
904-461-2000

St. Augustine Beach
Gamble Rogers Folk
  Festival
904-794-0222

St. Augustine Beach
Lighthouse Victorian
  Fair
904-829-0745

Sarasota
Sarasota Music Festival
800-287-9634

Siesta Key
Sand Sculpture
  Contest
941-316-1268

Tallahassee
Emancipation
  Celebration
904-891-3970

Tallahassee
Florida History Fair
904-487-1902

Tallahassee
Southern Shakespeare
  Festival
904-216-6109

Tarpon Springs
  Sponge Docks
  Festival
  954-472-3755

Webster
  Pepper Festival
  352-793-7541

Wellborn
  Blueberry
  Festival
904-208-1733

West Palm Beach
Pioneer Days
561-793-3333

White Springs
Florida Folk Festival
904-397-2733

Ybor City/Tampa
Tropical Heatwave
  Festival
813-238-8001

Zellwood
Sweet Corn Festival
407-886-0014

WHAT'S GOING ON AROUND FLORIDA IN JUNE

Chiefland
Annual Watermelon
  Festival
352-493-2210

Chipley
Panhandle
  Watermelon Festival
904-638-6180

Clermont
Harvest Festival
800-768-WINE

Fort Myers
Juneteenth
941-334-2797

Jacksonville
Jacksonville Landing
  Celebration
904-353-1188

Jacksonville
Juneteenth
904-396-0250

Jacksonville Beach
Fiesta Playera Dia de
  San Juan
904-249-3972

La Crosse
Blues and Blueberry
  Festival
904-462-7965

Live Oak
Suwannee River
  Jubilee
904-364-1683

Monticello
Watermelon Festival
904-997-5745

Newberry
Watermelon Festival
352-472-5864

New Smyrna Beach
Seaside Fiesta
904-427-2773

Orlando
Annual Florida Film
  Festival
407-629-1088

Palm Coast
Juneteenth Day
904-446-5078

St. Augustine
Datil Pepper Festival
904-825-1010

St. Augustine
Greek Landing Day
904-829-8205

St. Augustine
Spanish Fiesta
904-824-7740

St. Augustine
Spanish Night Watch
904-824-9550

St. Augustine
Torchlight Parade
904-824-9550

St. Augustine
Voices of the Past
904-824-9550

St. Petersburg
Juneteenth
813-821-3833

Tampa
Florida Dance Festival
800-252-0808

Treasure Island
Pirate Days
813-547-4575

West Palm Beach
Tropical Fruit Festival
561-233-1759

WHAT'S GOING ON AROUND FLORIDA IN JULY

Arcadia
All Florida
  Championship
  Rodeo
800-749-7633

Big Pine Key
Underwater Music
  Festival
800-872-3722

Boca Raton
Boca Festival Days
561-395-4433

Bradenton
Birthday Party and
  Wildlife Festival
941-746-4131

Fort Pierce
Chili Cookoff
561-465-6011

Havana
Pepper Festival
904-539-8020

Homestead
Tropical
  Agricultural
  Festival
305-247-5727

Lake Worth
Tropic Fest
561-533-7359

Miami
Everglades Music and
  Craft Festival
305-223-8380

Miami Beach
Carnabeach-Brazilian
  Festival
305-534-2090

Pensacola
American Street Party
904-434-6211

Pensacola
Crabfest
904-434-6211

Pompano Beach
Rainbow Festival
954-974-7394

St. Petersburg
Caribbean Calypso
  Carnival
813-866-0759

Sanibel Island
International
  Hemingway Festival
941-338-3500

Sarasota
Offshore Grand Prix
941-342-6200

Tallahassee
Summer Swamp
  Stomp
904-576-1636

WHAT'S GOING ON AROUND FLORIDA IN AUGUST

Big Pine Key
Seacraft Race and
  Festival
305-872-2217

Boca Raton
Boca Days
561-495-0233

Bushnell
Southwest Festival
352-659-1127

Caryville
Worm Fiddlin'
904-548-5116

Clermont
August Stomp
352-394-8627

Cocoa Beach
All-Star Jazz
  Festival
407-783-2271

Cocoa Beach
End of Summer Bash
407-452-5352

Cocoa Beach
Surfing Festival
407-783-1047

Crystal River
Ramblin' River Raft
  Race
352-795-9595

Daytona Beach
Back to School
  Jamboree
904-353-3330

Daytona Beach
Day in Florida History
904-985-4212

Daytona Beach
Sunrise Park Jam
904-677-8175

DeLand
Old Fashioned
  Neighbor Day
904-749-2959

DeLand
Open Championship
  Rodeo
407-330-5150

Delray Beach
Bon Festival
561-495-0233

Englewood
Pioneer Days
941-475-2380

Fernandina Beach
Civil War Garrison
904-277-7274

Fort Myers
Bluegrass for a Blue
  Planet
941-432-2004

Fort Walton
Beach
Thistle National
Championship
904-582-3317

High Springs
Ginnie Springs
Festival
904-454-2202

Keystone
Heights Festival
of the Lakes
904-473-8000

Kissimmee
Celebration in the Sun
407-344-0937

Miami
Reggae Festival
305-891-2944

Mount Dora
Caribbean Festival
352-383-6994

Ocala
Ocalifest
352-629-8358

Ocala
Shrine Rodeo
352-694-1515

Okeechobee
Festival and Rodeo
941-763-6464

Orlando
New Chinese Cinema
  Series
407-629-1088

Pensacola
Bushwacker Festival
904-934-3108

St. George Island
Hermit Crab Races
904-927-2600

Sanford
Caribbean Parade and
  Festival
407-260-1751

Sarasota
Child Day at Selby
941-366-5731

Sarasota
Quay Craft Festival
941-962-0388

Stuart
Dancing in the Streets
407-286-2848

Tallahassee
Caribbean Festival
904-878-2198

Tampa
Ybor Blues Festival
813-273-6364

Treasure Island
Street Festival
813-367-4529

Venice
Sharktooth and
  Seafood
941-488-2236

Vero Beach
Summerfest
407-567-3491

Wausau
Possum Festival
904-638-7888

WHAT'S GOING ON AROUND FLORIDA IN SEPTEMBER

Altamonte Springs
Concours D'elegance
407-831-2705

Amelia Island
Fort Clinch Programs
904-277-7274

Belleair
Family Festival
813-584-8634

Branford
Suwannee River Riding
  Club Rodeo
904-758-1300

Bushnell
Country Pioneer
  Weekend
904-659-1127

Casselberry
Annual Oktoberfest
407-263-7180

Clearwater
Autumn Gathering
813-787-6027

Clearwater
Little Munich
  Oktoberfest
813-725-5447

Clermont
Labor Day on the Lake
352-394-4191

Cocoa Beach
End of Summer Bash
407-452-5352

Cocoa Beach
Surfing Festival
800-927-9659

Dade City
Pioneer Florida Day
904-567-0262

Daytona
Beach
Kite and Sandcastlefest
904-255-7407

Defuniak Springs
Chautauqua Harvest
  Celebration
904-892-5887

DeLand
Annual Christmas in
  September
407-860-0092

DeLand
Annual River Raft
  Race
904-734-3499

Englewood
Annual Pioneer Days
941-475-2380

Fort Lauderdale
Annual Los Olas
Art Fair
305-472-3755

Fort Lauderdale
New River Festival
305-791-0202

Gulf Breeze
International Festival
904-932-7888

Islamorada
Seafood Fest
305-383-7266

Jacksonville
Labor Day at the
  Landing
904-355-1188

Jacksonville
Riverside Arts and
  Music Festival
904-389-2449

Jacksonville
Seafest
904-630-3520

Jacksonville Beach
Hot Summer Blues
  Fest
904-249-3972

Jupiter
A Dickinson of a Day
407-746-7111

Keystone Heights
Festival of the Lakes
352-473-7234

Kissimmee
Osceola Art Festival
407-931-1646

Lake City
Civil War Expo
904-374-8848

Lakeland
Fall Festival
941-680-2787

Lakeland
Family Day
941-680-2787

Lake Placid
Caladium Festival
941-297-6886

Live Oak
Old Tyme Labor Day
  Weekend
904-364-1683

Miami/Key West
Annual Motorcycle
  Run
305-296-9000

Miami Lakes
Taste of Jazz
305-817-4006

Ocala
Shriners Rodeo
352-694-1515

Okece
Hobee Festival and
  Rodeo
941-763-6464

Panama City
Bay County Fair
904-769-2645

Panama City Beach
Treasure Island King
  Mackerel Tourn-
  ament
904-234-6533

Pensacola
Annual Seafood
  Festival
904-433-6512

Port Canaveral
Annual Port Weekend
407-783-7831

Punta Gorda
Southwest Florida Boat
  Show and Seafood
  Festival
941-388-2355

St. Augustine
Founders
  Day/Menendez
  Landing
904-824-9823

St. Petersburg
Labor Day at the Pier
813-821-6164

St. Petersburg
Tampa Bay Raid
813-866-1686

Sanford
Caribbean Parade and
  Festival
407-260-1751

Sebring
Tour of Sebring
561-683-2851

Tallahassee
Native American
  Heritage Fest
904-575-8684

Tampa
Recreation
  International Fest
813-931-2106

Venice
Island Days
941-484-6722

West Melbourne
Crackerfest
407-952-4525

WHAT'S GOING ON AROUND FLORIDA IN OCTOBER

Bartow
Cracker Storytelling
  Festival
352-357-2251

Boca Raton
St. Jude's Fall Festival
407-451-4485

Bonifay
Greater Holmes
  County Fair
904-457-3394

Bonifay
Northwest Florida
  Championship
  Rodeo
904-547-4876

Bonifay
Pioneer Day
904-547-4682

Bradenton
Hunsader Farms
  Pumpkin Festival
941-727-7580

Bronson
Annual Fall Folk
  Festival
352-486-2354

Brooksville
Annual Pumpkin
  Festival
352-799-0129

Brooksville
Cattleman's Rodeo
352-683-3700

Callahan
Northeast Florida Fair
904-879-1029

Cape Coral
Munich in Cape Coral
941-945-1802

Cedar Key
Seafood and Arts and
  Crafts Festival
352-543-5596

Clearwater
Jazz Holiday
813-461-5200

Cocoa
Seminole Indian and
  Pioneer Festival
407-632-1111

Coral Springs
Ourtown Celebration
407-451-4485

Daytona Beach
Annual Halifax Art
  Festival
904-788-4718

Daytona Beach
Harley Davidson
  Seafood Fest
904-248-0580

Deerfield Beach
Broward County
  Pioneer Days
954-765-4671

DeFuniak Springs
Walton County Fair
904-892-5260

Delray Beach
Heritage Month
407-279-1384

Destin
Annual Seafood
  Festival
904-837-6241

Destin
Boggy Bayou Mullet
  Festival
904-678-1615

Destin
Fishing Rodeo
904-837-6734

Estero
Civil War Reenactment
941-992-2184

Estero
Koreshan Unity Solar
  Festival
941-992-2184

Fernandina Beach
Heritage Classic Car
  Celebration
800-226-3542

Flagler Beach
Annual Columbus Day
  Festival
904-439-1627

Fort Lauderdale
Annual Fleet Week
954-767-6289

Fort Myers
Calusa Nature Center
  Haunted Walk
941-275-3435

Fort Myers
Halloween Express
941-275-3000

Fort Myers
Hispanic Heritage
  Festival
941-334-3492

Fort Walton Beach
Fiesta Italiana
904-862-6734

Hernando Beach
Seafood Festival
352-683-3700

Jacksonville
Greater Jacksonville
  Agricultural Fair
904-353-0535

Jasper
Hamilton County Fair
904-792-1276

Jensen Beach
Leif Erikson Days
561-334-3444

Kissimmee
Horton Ranch
  Bluegrass Fest
407-847-0561

Kissimmee
Kissimmee/St. Cloud
  Senior Games
407-847-2388

Kissimmee
Octoberfest
407-344-0937

Lake Mary
Annual Festival of the
  Arts
407-333-1570

Largo
Annual Country
  Jubilee
813-582-2123

Laurel Hill
Annual Hobo Festival
904-652-4441

Live Oak
Bluegrass and
  Halloween Festival
904-364-1683

Live Oak
Suwannee River
  Gospel Jubilee
904-364-1683

Live Oak
Suwannee River Jam
904-364-1683

Live Oak
Youth Ranch Open
  House
352-842-5501

MacClenny
Baker County Fair
904-259-7314

Madeira Beach
John's Pass Seafood
  and Crafts Fest
813-397-1571

Marianna
Jackson County Fair
904-482-2290

Masaryktown
Czechoslovakian
  Independence Day
352-796-9260

Mayo
Annual Pioneer Day
904-294-2705

Mayport
Annual Seafood
  Festival
904-241-9591

Mcintosh
Heart of Country Fall
  Festival
352-591-1053

Mcintosh
Mcintosh 1890s
  Festival
352-591-1053

Melbourne
Harvest Days Family
  Fun Festival
407-242-9124

Merritt Island
Plane Fun Day
407-729-3485

Miami
Annual Hispanic
  Heritage Fest
305-541-5023

Middleburg
Annual Historic
  Festival
904-282-3150

Mount Dora
Bicycle Festival
352-383-2165

Naples
Swamp Buggy Races
914-774-2701

New Smyrna Beach
Oktoberfest Olympics
904-428-4621

Niceville
Boggy Bayou Mullet
  Festival
904-678-1615

Ocala
Marion County Fair
  and Florida Peanut
  Fest
352-694-2500

Orange City
Annual Fall Fest
904-775-2793

Orange Park
Fall Festival
904-264-2635

Orlando
Annual Pioneer Days
407-855-7461

Palatka
Fall River Fest Art
  Show
904-325-8750

Panama City
Bay County Fair
904-769-2645

Panama City Beach
Indian Summer
  Seafood Festival
904-234-3193

Pensacola
Pensacola Interstate
  Fair
904-944-4500

Pensacola
St. Anne's Roundup
904-456-5966

Perry
Florida Forest Festival
904-584-8733

Port Orange
Annual Family Days
904-756-4485

Port St. Joe
Annual Arts & Crafts
  Festival
904-227-1223

Punta Gorda
Waterfront Food, Arts,
  and Jazz Fest
941-639-3720

St. Augustine
Annual Colonial Folk
  Fest
904-824-2310

St. Augustine
Crackerday
800-653-2489

St. Augustine
Halloween Haunts
800-653-2489

St. Augustine
Lincolnville Festival
904-829-8379

St. Cloud
Antique Tractor Show
  and Recreation
407-847-5000

St. Petersburg
Fish Broil and Carnival
813-893-2630

St. Petersburg
Sail Expo
813-817-7245

Salt Springs
Annual Salt Springs
 Festival
352-546-2205

San Antonio
Annual Rattlesnake
 Festival
352-567-0262

Sanford
Pioneer Days/Ways
 Festival
407-321-2489

Sarasota
Oktoberfest
 Downtown Sarasota
941-962-0388

Sorrento
Pioneer Day Fall
 Festival
904-383-8801

Starke
Festival of the Arts
352-395-5355

Sun City Center
Oktoberfest
813-634-5111

Surfside
International Festival
305-864-0722

Tallahassee
North Florida Fair
904-878-3247

Tampa-Ybor City
Guavaween/Halloween
 Latin Style
813-621-7121

Titusville
Harvest Festival
407-269-7363

Titusville
Polish American
 Festival
407-267-4111

Venice
Annual Sun Fiesta
941-484-5884

Vero Beach
Autumn in the Park
407-567-3491

Waldo
Bluegrass and Gospel
 Reunion
352-468-2622

Williston
Peanut Festival
352-528-6169

Winter Haven
Cypress Gardens
 Gospel Sing
941-324-2111

Winter Park
Autumn Art Festival
407-644-6066

WHAT'S GOING ON AROUND FLORIDA IN NOVEMBER

Amelia Island
Fort Clinch State Park
  Festival
904-277-7274

Apalachicola
Annual Seafood
  Festival
904-653-9419

Arcadia
De Soto County
  Harvest Festival
941-494-4033

Barberville
Fall Country Jamboree
904-749-2959

Boca Raton
Family Frontier Days
407-994-1021

Boca Raton
St. Jude's Fall Festival
407-451-4485

Bradenton
Street Fair
941-741-7242

Brandon
Annual Art and Craft
  Festival
813-689-0491

Captiva Island
'Tween Waters Inn
  Oktoberfest
941-472-5161

Casselberry
Cultural Florida BBQ
  Fest
904-774-5055

Clearwater
Festival of the Trees
813-536-9427

Cocoa
Brevard County Fair
407-633-4028

Cocoa Beach
Annual Space Coast
  Art Festival
407-784-3322

Coconut Grove
Banyan Arts and Crafts
  Festival
305-558-1758

Coral Gables
International Festival
  of Fine Arts
305-445-9973

Cross Creek
Fall Festival
352-466-4065

Crystal River
Presentations under
  the Pines
352-795-1856

Dade City
Youth Ranch Bluegrass
  Festival
904-637-5381

Daytona Beach
Tails and Tots
904-253-3330

Deerfield Beach
Deerfest
305-427-1050

DeLand
Fall Country Jamboree
904-749-2959

DeLand
Volusia County Fair
  and Youth Show
904-734-9514

Delray Beach
Harvest Festival
561-279-1382

Dunedin
Annual Art Harvest
813-442-0223

Dunnellon
Withlacoochee River
  Bluegrass
904-489-8330

Eustis
Christmas in Eustis
352-483-0046

Floral City
Renaissance Festival
407-380-9151

Fort Walton Beach
Greater Okaloosa
    County Fair
904-862-0211

Gainesville
Alachua County Fair
352-372-1537

Green Acres
Hoffman's Holiday
    Wonderland
407-967-2213

Haines City
Fall Festival with Arts
    and Crafts
941-421-3773

Hallandale
Broward County Fair
954-963-3247

Hollywood
Jazz Festival
954-921-3404

Homosassa
Old Homosassa
    Seafood and Crafts
352-628-2666

Inglis/Yankeetown
Seafood Arts and
    Crafts Festival
352-447-0329

Jacksonville
Caribe Festival
888-633-8529

Jacksonville
Jacksonville Jamboree
904-630-4087

Jacksonville
Jazz Festival
904-358-6329

Jensen Beach
Pineapple Festival
561-334-3444

Lake Buena Vista
Jimmy Dean Country
    Showdown
407-397-6397

Lake City
Festival of the Lights
    Olustee Park
904-758-1555

Lake Wales
Bok Tower
    Thanksgiving
    Carillon Concert
941-676-6770

Lake Wales
Veterans Day Recital at
    Bok Tower
941-676-6770

Land O' Lakes
Fall Flapjack Festival
813-996-5522

Live Oak
New Star Rising
  Bluegrass Festival
904-758-1555

Live Oak
Old Tyme Farm Days
  and Thanksgiving
904-758-1555

Longwood
Arts and Crafts
407-332-0225

Melbourne
Harbor Festival
407-724-5400

Melbourne
Spanish Fiesta
407-724-0555

Miami
Harvest Festival
305-375-1492

Miami
White Party at Vizcaya
305-759-6181

Micanopy
Fall Festival
904-466-7026

Middleburg
Annual Ham Jam
  Festival
904-282-1537

Milton
Depot Days
904-623-8493

Naples
Native American
  Powwow
941-774-2701

New Smyrna Beach
Flamingo Follies
904-424-2175

North Miami
Winternational
  Festival
305-893-6511

Ocala
Florida Pioneer
  Weekend
352-236-5401

Orlando
American Indian
  Association Powwow
407-656-2170

Orlando
Fiesta in the Park
407-649-3152

Ormond Beach
Christmas Walk at the
  Casements
904-676-3257

Oviedo
Great Day in the
  Country
407-365-5779

Pahokee
Grassy Waters Festival
  and Car Show
561-924-5579

Panama City
Celebration of the Arts
  and Environment
904-769-4451

Polk City
Wings and Strings
  Music Festival
941-984-8445

Port Charlotte
Charlotte County Fair
941-629-4252

Port Charlotte
International Fall
  Festival
941-627-2568

Ruskin
Seafood and Art
  Festival
813-645-3808

St. Augustine
Lincolnville Festival
800-653-2489

St. Petersburg
Pioneer Jamboree and
  Engine Show
813-894-7519

Sanford
Holiday Arts, Crafts,
  and Antique Fest
407-322-2212

Sarasota
Cine-World Film
  Festival
941-364-8662

South Miami
Annual South Miami
  Art Festival
305-661-1621

Spring Hill
Chicken Pluckin'
904-683-1617

Stuart
River Dayz Festival
561-221-3981

Tallahassee
Merry Market
  Extravaganza
800-226-5305

Tallahassee
North Florida Fair
904-878-3247

Tampa
Bayfest
813-254-1414

Tampa
Greater Hillsborough
  County Fair
813-689-5161

Tavernier
Island Jubilee
305-451-1414

Titusville
Family Fun Festival
407-633-7250

West Palm Beach
Fiesta on Flagler
407-582-3514

West Palm Beach
Florida Heritage
  Festival
561-832-6397

Winter Haven
Mum Festival at
  Cypress Gardens
800-282-2123

Zephyrhills
Winter Fest and Air
  Show
813-782-1913

WHAT'S GOING ON AROUND FLORIDA IN DECEMBER

Alachua
Dickens Festival
352-334-2197

Amelia Island
Fort Clinch Confed-
erate Christmas
904-277-7274

Atlantic Beach
First Night New Year
Celebration
904-241-4339

Bushnell
Dade's Battle
352-793-4781

Bushnell
Spirit of Native
America
904-659-1127

Coconut Grove
King Mango Strut
305-445-1865

Dunedin
Happy Holly-Daze
813-738-1898

Fort Myers
Edison/Ford Homes
Holiday Tour
941-768-6261

Fort Myers
Holiday Express Tour
941-275-3000

Greenacres
Hoffman's Holiday
Wonderland
407-967-2213

Gulf Breeze
Holiday Lights at the
Zoo
904-932-2229

Holmes Beach
Annual Festival of the
Arts
941-778-2099

Kissimmee
Annual Holiday
Extravaganza
407-932-4050

Lake Wales
Christmas at Bok
Tower Gardens
407-932-4050

Longwood
Christmas in Old
Longwood
407-332-6920

Melbourne
Native American
Indian Festival
407-253-6149

Miami
Big Orange New Year's
Eve
305-447-1224

Miami
Kwanza Fest
305-638-6771

Miami
Orange Bowl Parade
305-371-4600

Miccosukee Village
Indian Arts Festival
305-223-8380

Mount Dora
Christmas Walk
352-735-0660

Orlando
A Storybook
   Christmas - Leu
   Gardens
407-246-2620

Palm Coast
Kwanza Celebration
904-446-5078

Polk County
City Tour and Cypress
   Gardens
941-534-4375

St. Augustine
Fall Arts and Crafts
   Fair
800-OLD-CITY

St. Augustine
Olde World Christmas
800-OLD-CITY

Sarasota
Christmas Boat Parade
   of Lights
941-329-7672

Tallahassee
Celebration of Lights
   Winter Festival
904-891-3866

White Springs
Stephen Foster
   Christmas Fest of
   Lights
904-397-4331

Contributors

T hanks to the following people, businesses, and organizations for their contributions to this almanac. Internet addresses are listed so you can explore further on your own.

Scott Ball (Florida Game and Fresh Water Fish Commission)
    http://fen.state.fl.us
Tom Baurley (Florida Division of Historical Resources)
    http://www.dos.state.fl.us/flafacts/seminole.html
James Bell
Kathryn Bender (U.S. Fish and Wildlife Service)
    http://www.fws.gov/hotlist.html
Barbara Bose (Absolute Florida)
Robbie Bouplon (Florida Corrections Commission)
    http://www.dc.state.fl.us/
Debbie Buchanan (Florida Department of Corrections)
    http://www.dos.state.fl.us/corrections
Debra Burleson (Nova Scotia Museum of Natural History)
    http://www.ednet.ns.ca/educ/museum/summer.html
Robin Burr (Quantum Leap)
Lucy Carter (Florida Department of Agriculture and Consumer
    Services) http://www.doacs.state.fl.us
Joe Clark (Supernet) http://www.supernet.net/
Crash Craddock (Tennessee Net) http://www.grits.com/web-
    wvrml.html
Lynda DeTray (DeTray Associates) http://www.detray.com
Michael Dodson (Joint Legislative Management Committee)
    http://www.leg.state.fl.us/
Dom (Atlantic Coast Kayak Company)

Don Phillips (The Tropical Angler)
Chris Donald (Atlantic Dialog) http://www.keywest.com
Damien duToit (Geocities) http://www.geocities.com/colosse-um/4569
David Exley (Florida Parent-Educators Association) http://www.fpea/com
Jim Fitch (Museum of Florida Art and Culture) http://www.aarf.com/mofac
Marty Fleischmann (Florida Gaming Corporation)
Steven Fletcher (Fletcher's Pet Pals) http://www.petpals.com
Warren Gash (Environment Canada) http://www.ns.ec.gc.ca/
Sierra Godfrey and Jason Roberts (Learn2) http://www.learn2.com
Michael Godwin (MagicNet)
Michael Gooch (Grandpa's Workshop)
Kelly Grass (Florida Tourism Industry Marketing Corporation)
Alan Greilsamer
Heidi (Florida Scuba News) http://www.scubanews.com
Bob Heussler (Milford Jai-Alai) http://www.jaialai.com
Jay Hudson (BigBirds)
Lawrence Kestenbaum (The Political Graveyard) http://www.poti-fos.com/tpg/
Kitty (World Wide Travel Exchange) http://wwte.com
Margaret Koogle (Lilypons Water Gardens)
Joyce LaFray (Famous Florida) http://www.famousflorida.com
Lazaro (Miami Jai-Alai)
M. C. Bob Leonard (Hillsboro Community College-Ybor City College) http://www.hcc.cc.fl.us/
David McRee http://www.cyberisle.com/tropical/angler.htm
Seth Morabito http://www.loomcom.com/raccoons/
Doug Moss (*E/Environmental Magazine)* http://www.emagazine.com
Dixie Nims (media librarian)
Allen Parsons (Florida Department of Environmental Protection) http://www.dep.state.fl.us/law
Vic Ramey (Center for Aquatic Plants, University of Florida) http://www.aquat1.ifas.ufl.edu/
Dennis Raines http://www.polaris.net/~fishboat
Richard Roberts (Florida State Archives)
Jerry Rockwell (Eurekanet) http://www.eurekanet.com/
Dr. Gary Rosenberg (Academy of Natural Sciences) http://www.acnatsci.org
Morris Rozen (The Houseboat Page) http://www.houseboat.net/
H. Russo (Daytona Community College)
Jerry Swartz (Florida Explorer)

Greg Salyer (Florida Weather Bureau) http://www.florida-weather.com

Sandee (Everglades Adventures) http://www.ivyhouse.com

Paulo Santos http://www.airnav.com

Stacy Schulte (Frontier Herbs) http://www.frontierherb.com

Debra Sears (Florida Government Information Service) http://www.dos.state.fl.us/fpc/

Silva (Real Beer) http://www.realbeer.com

Alice Skidmore

Floyd Stayner (South Carolina Department of Natural Resources) http://www.dnr.state.sc.us/

Chet Townsend (Florida Citrus Commission)

Gavin Trot (Australian Wine Center) http://www.auswine.com.au

Sam Trumbore

V (The Electric Chair Company) http://www.theelectricchair.com

Steve Warrington (Ostriches OnLine) http://www.ostrichesonline.com

Chris Wilkes (Florida State University)

Christopher Wolfe (Dragonfly) http://www.miav1.muohio.edu/

Rick Williams (ScubaCentral)

Academy of Natural Sciences
AirNav
Area Development Corporation
Atlantic Coast Kayak Company
Audubon Society
Australian Wine Center
Born Free Foundation
Center for Aquatic Plants, University of Florida
Computer Applications, University of Florida
Daytona Community College
Defenders of Wildlife
Department of Citrus
DeTray Associates
The Electric Chair Company
Environment Canada
E/Environmental Magazine
Everglades Adventures
Fletcher's Pet Pals
Florida Corrections Commission
Florida Department of Agriculture and Consumer Services
Florida Department of Environmental Protection
Florida Department of State
Florida Explorer

Florida Game and Fresh Water Fish Commission
Florida Gaming Corporation
Florida Juggling Clubs
Florida Legislature
Florida Lottery
Florida Museum of Natural History
Florida Parent-Educators Association
Florida Scuba News
Florida State Archives
Florida State University
Florida Tourism Industry Marketing Corporation
Florida Trend
Florida Weather Bureau
Florida Wildlife Society
Frontier Herbs
The Gator Hole
Grandpa's Workshop
Harvard Medical School
Hillsboro Community College
Learn2
Legislative Information Division/Florida
Miami Jai-Alai
Milford Jai-Alai
Museum of Florida Art and Culture
National Park Service
National Wildflower Research Center
Nova Scotia Museum of Natural History
Ostriches OnLine
Players SportsWare
The Political Graveyard
Real Beer
South Carolina Department of Natural Resources
State Library of Florida
Tennessee Net
The Tropical Angler
U.K. OnLine
University of South Florida
U.S. Fish and Wildlife Service
World Wide Travel Exchange

*I*f you enjoyed reading this book, here are some other Pineapple Press titles you might enjoy as well. To request our complete catalog or to place an order, write to Pineapple Press, P.O. Box 3899, Sarasota, Florida 34230, or call 1-800-PINEAPL (746-3275).

Art Lover's Guide to Florida by Anne Jeffrey and Aletta Dreller. Tour 86 of the most dynamic and exciting art groupings in Florida, and learn about the distinctive and eccentric personalities connected with the world of art. ISBN 1-56164-144-8 (pb)

Book Lover's Guide to Florida edited by Kevin M. McCarthy. Exhaustive survey of writers, books, and literary sites. A reference, guide for reading, and literary tour guide. ISBN 1-56164-012-3 (hb); 1-56164-021-2 (pb)

Cheap Thrills, Florida: The Bottom Half by Frank Zoretich. Humorous and informative sketches about excursions, attractions, and points of interest in Florida that can be enjoyed for less than $10 per person. ISBN 1-56164-058-1 (pb)

The Florida Chronicles by Stuart B. McIver. A series offering true-life sagas of the notable and notorious characters throughout history who have given Florida its distinctive flavor. Volume 1: Dreamers, Schemers and Scalawags ISBN 1-56164-155-3 (pb). Volume 2: Murder in the Tropics ISBN 1-56164-079-4 (hb)

Florida Fun Facts by Eliot Kleinberg. At last—a collection of every fact, large and small, that you need to know about Florida. Answers to questions like these: What's bigger, Lake Okeechobee or Rhode Island? What's wrong with Citrus County's name? And hundreds more! ISBN 1-56164-068-9 (pb)

Florida Island Hopping: The West Coast by Chelle Koster Walton. The first tour guide to Florida's Gulf Coast barrier islands, including a discussion of their histories, unique characters, and complete information on natural attractions, shopping, tours, and other diversions. ISBN 1-56164-081-6 (pb)

Florida Place Names by Allen Morris. This book paints a rich historical portrait of the state and reveals the dreams, memories, and sense of humor of the people who have called Florida home over the years. ISBN 1-56164-084-0 (hb)

Florida Portrait: A Pictorial History of Florida by Jerrell Shofner. An in-depth reference—packed with hundreds of rare photographs—that chronicles Florida's history from the earliest Spanish explorers and Native American cultures to the space age and rampant population growth in the late twentieth century. ISBN 1-56164-121-9 (pb)

Florida's Past, Volumes 1, 2, and 3 by Gene Burnett. Collected essays from Burnett's "Florida's Past" columns in *Florida Trend* magazine, plus some original writings not found elsewhere. Burnett's easygoing style and his sometimes surprising choice of topics make history good reading. ISBN **Vol. 1** 0-910923-27-2 (hb); 1-56164-115-4 (pb). **Vol. 2** 0-910923-59-0 (hb); 1-56164-139-1 (pb). **Vol. 3** 0-910923-84-1 (hb); 1-56164-117-0 (pb)

Guide to Florida Historical Walking Tours by Roberta Sandler. Put on your walking shoes and experience the heart of Florida's people, history, and architecture as you take a healthful, entertaining stroll through 32 historic neighborhoods. ISBN 1-56164-105-7 (pb)

Guide to the University of Florida and Gainesville by Kevin McCarthy and Murray Laurie. Each significant building on campus and in town is described here, with information on its history, architecture, and current use. Fifteen maps and over 100 black-and-white photographs complete this thorough tour. ISBN 1-56164-134-0 (pb)

Haunt Hunter's Guide to Florida by Joyce Moore. Whether you believe in ghosts or not, visit 37 of the most bone-chilling places in the Sunshine State! Includes information on each site's history and character, its "haunt history," and nearby attractions. ISBN 1-56164-150-2 (pb)

Historical Traveler's Guide to Florida by Eliot Kleinberg. Investigate more than 60 travel destinations in Florida of great (and not-so-great) historical significance, all in the spirit of fun and exploration. ISBN 1-56164-122-7 (pb)

Visiting Small-Town Florida by Bruce Hunt. From Carrabelle to Bokeelia, these out-of-the-way but fascinating destinations are well worth a side trip or weekend excursion. ISBN 1-56164-128-6 (pb)